Gene Kilgore's

RANCH VACATIONS

The Leading Guide to Guest and Resort, Fly-Fishing, and Cross-Country Skiing Ranches in the United States and Canada

Sixth Edition

AVALON
TRAVEL

RANCHES IN THE UNITED STATES AND CANADA

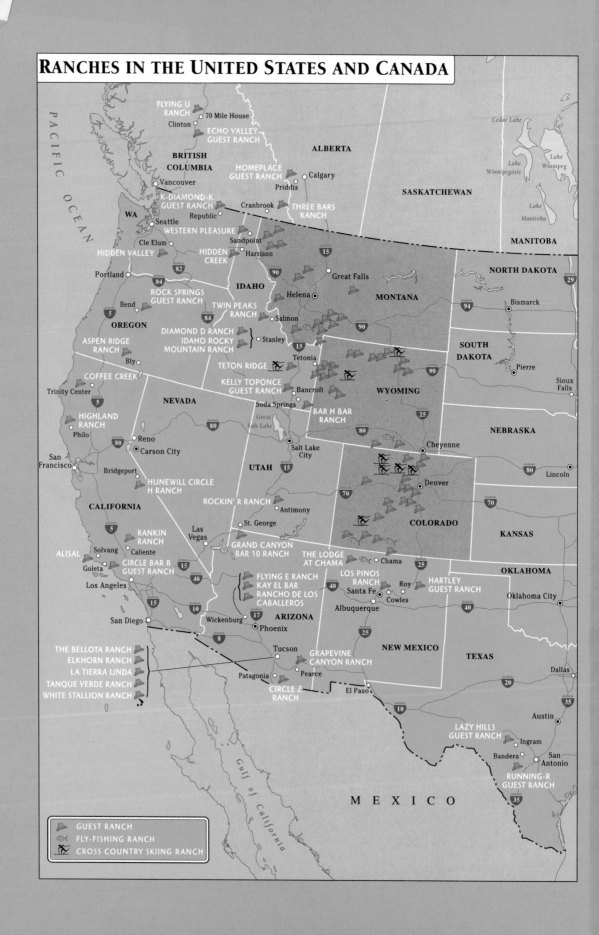

PACIFIC OCEAN

Cedar Lake

Lake Winnepegosis

Lake Winnipeg

Lake Manitoba

FLYING U RANCH
70 Mile House
Clinton
ECHO VALLEY GUEST RANCH

ALBERTA

BRITISH COLUMBIA

HOMEPLACE GUEST RANCH
Calgary
Priddis

SASKATCHEWAN

K-DIAMOND-K GUEST RANCH
Cranbrook
THREE BARS RANCH

MANITOBA

WA
Republic
Seattle
WESTERN PLEASURE
Sandpoint
Cle Elum
HIDDEN VALLEY
HIDDEN CREEK
Harrison

15

NORTH DAKOTA
29

Portland
82

ROCK SPRINGS GUEST RANCH
84

Bend

IDAHO
Helena
Great Falls

MONTANA

90

Bismarck
94

OREGON

TWIN PEAKS RANCH
84
Salmon

90

SOUTH DAKOTA

ASPEN RIDGE RANCH

DIAMOND D RANCH
IDAHO ROCKY MOUNTAIN RANCH
Stanley

Bly
5

COFFEE CREEK

TETON RIDGE
Tetonia

15

Pierre

Trinity Center

NEVADA

KELLY TOPONCE GUEST RANCH
Bancroft

WYOMING

90

Sioux Falls

HIGHLAND RANCH
Philo

Soda Springs

Great Salt Lake

BAR H BAR RANCH

25

NEBRASKA

Reno
80
Carson City

San Francisco

Bridgeport

80

Salt Lake City

80

Cheyenne

Lincoln
80

HUNEWILL CIRCLE H RANCH

UTAH
625

Denver

CALIFORNIA
5

ROCKIN' R RANCH
Antimony

70

70

COLORADO

KANSAS

RANKIN RANCH

Las Vegas

St. George

ALISAL
Solvang
Caliente

CIRCLE BAR B GUEST RANCH
15

GRAND CANYON BAR 10 RANCH

THE LODGE AT CHAMA
Chama

25

OKLAHOMA

Goleta

40

FLYING E RANCH
KAY EL BAR
RANCHO DE LOS CABALLEROS

LOS PINOS RANCH
Santa Fe
Roy
Cowles

HARTLEY GUEST RANCH

Oklahoma City

Los Angeles
15

10

Albuquerque
40

San Diego
Wickenburg
17
Phoenix

ARIZONA

25

8

THE BELLOTA RANCH
ELKHORN RANCH
LA TIERRA LINDA
TANQUE VERDE RANCH
WHITE STALLION RANCH

Tucson

GRAPEVINE CANYON RANCH

NEW MEXICO

TEXAS

Dallas

Patagonia
Pearce

20

CIRCLE Z RANCH
El Paso

10

Austin
35

LAZY HILLS GUEST RANCH
Ingram

Bandera
San Antonio

RUNNING-R GUEST RANCH

35

M E X I C O

Gulf of California

Legend

GUEST RANCH
FLY-FISHING RANCH
CROSS COUNTRY SKIING RANCH

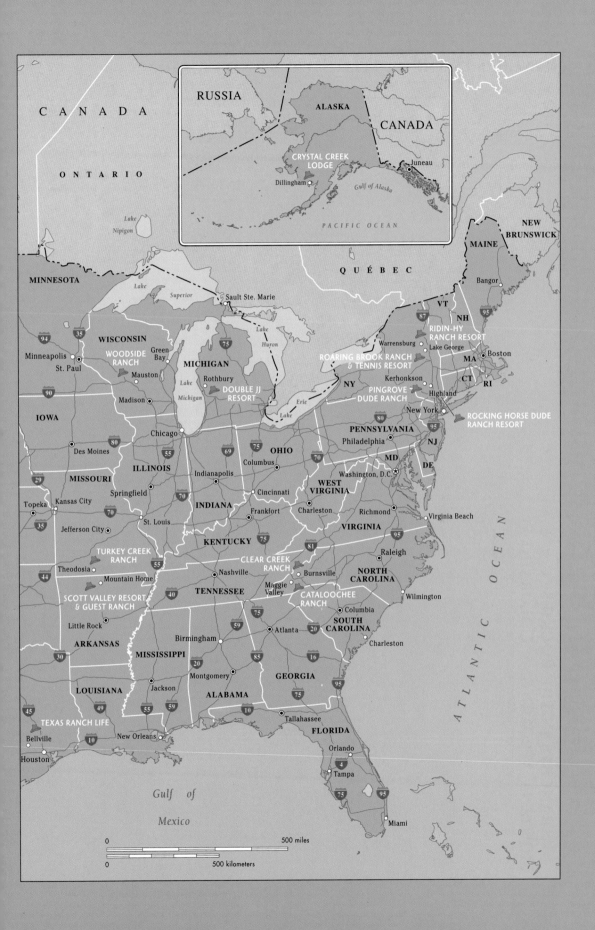

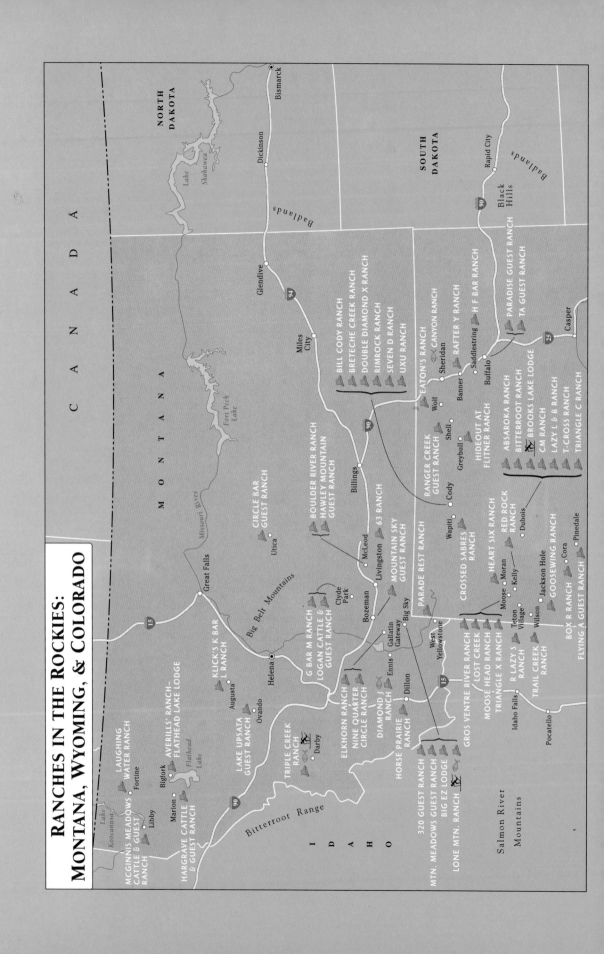

RANCHES IN THE ROCKIES: MONTANA, WYOMING, & COLORADO

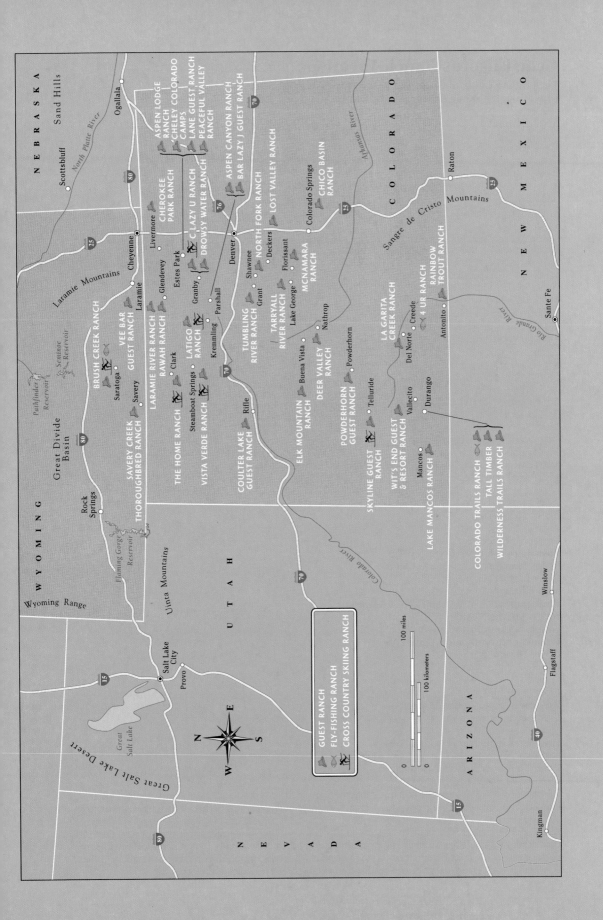

Gene Kilgore's Ranch Vacations

The Leading Guide to Guest and Resort, Fly-Fishing, and
Cross-Country Skiing Ranches in the United States and Canada

Sixth Edition

Gene Kilgore

Published by
Avalon Travel Publishing
5855 Beaudry St.
Emeryville, CA 94608, USA

Please send all comments, corrections, additions, amendments, and critiques to:

RANCH VACATIONS Sixth Edition
AVALON TRAVEL PUBLISHING
5855 BEAUDRY ST.
EMERYVILLE, CA 94608, USA
email: atpfeedback@avalonpub.com
website: www.travelmatters.com

Printing History
1st edition—1989
6th edition—November 2001
5 4 3 2 1

Text © 2001 by Eugene Kilgore.
   All rights reserved.
Maps and illustrations © 2001 by Avalon Travel Publishing, Inc.
   All rights reserved.

ISBN: 1-56691-318-7
ISSN: 1535-3788

Editor: Angelique S. Clarke
Assisting Editor: Marybeth Griffin
Series Manager: Angelique S. Clarke
Copy Editor: Marybeth Griffin
Map Editor: Naomi Dancis
Cartography: Mike Morgenfeld, Kat Kalamaras
Index: Marybeth Griffin
Graphics Coordinator: Susan Mira Snyder
Production Coordinator: Darren Alessi
Cover Design: Darren Alessi

Front cover photo: 63 Ranch, Montana
Back cover photo: Robert Holmgren
Illustrations on pages viii, 1, 359, 371, 391, and 415: Barrett Cox

Distributed by Publishers Group West

Printed in China through Colorcraft Ltd., Hong Kong

This New Millennium Edition Is Dedicated—

To the women and men who share their ranches with all of us;
To the children of the world—may we always think of them first in
all that we do here on earth;

To my son, William Francisco, age six, who is my inspiration and
just happens to be my favorite little cowboy;

To my wife, Regina, who is my guiding light;

To my father who shared his love and has taught me so many important
lessons throughout my life, who raised me in the country and took me to
my first rodeo when I was five, to my first dude ranch when I was nine, and
thus helped to plant the seeds of my passion.

To my Uncle Harry Snyder whose devotion to animals, his special way with
people, and his affection all these years, has hopefully guided me to
being a better person;

To Sharon Peterson, whose ongoing love of horses, the West, and the "cowboys and Indians" of her childhood, and her incredible work ethic has made
it possible to get all six editions to the publisher on time;

To Jeff Winslow, Chris Heffelfinger, and Kevin O'Donnell who are three of
the greatest friends a man could ever hope for;

To Jim Nassikas, Albert and Barbara Simms, Barnaby Conrad, Peter Hillman,
Harold Wagstall, Stan Galli, John Bergman, William Matthews, and William
Close for their continued inspiration and friendship; and

To Bill Westheimer, who never gave up on me and convinced me not to give
up on myself or my dream of this book.

It is with much love that I dedicate this book to my sister Bee and in loving
memory of my dear mother, Mimi, and my Aunt Elinor.

Finally, to God, for showing me His way.

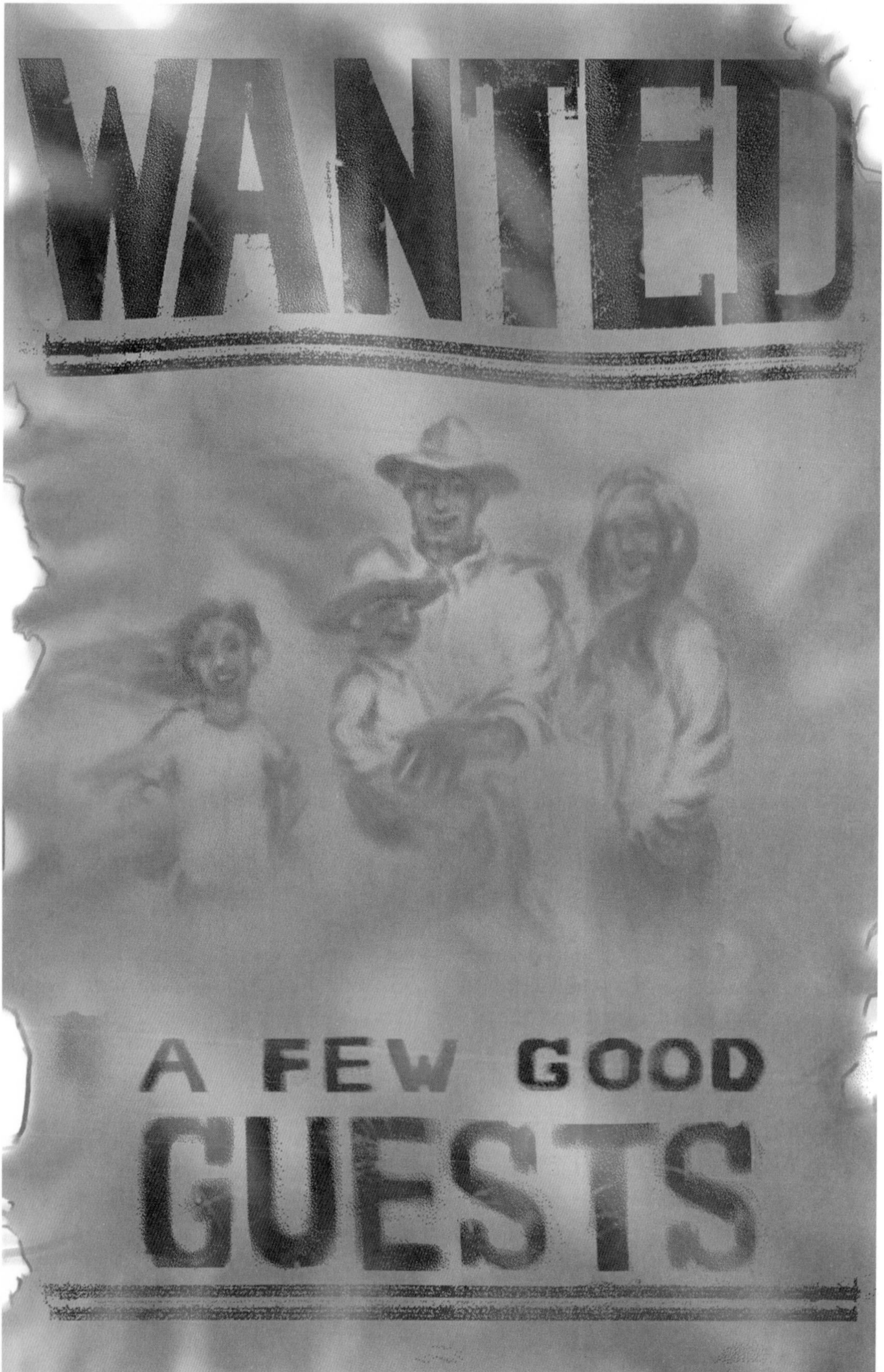
WANTED
A FEW GOOD
GUESTS

You're about to begin one of your most exciting adventures: selecting the right ranch or lodge for you, your family, your friends, your company, or your clients. So, sit back and relax, maybe prop your feet up on your desk or settle into your favorite chair in front of a blazing fire. Our goal is to help you by connecting you with a wide variety of properties across the United States and Canada. After you've looked at the beautiful photos, and read about the ranches and lodges, contact those that interest you. Unlike any other holiday experience that I know of, the secret to this one is chemistry. And just like a marriage, if the chemistry is good, the marriage is golden. If not, as an old cowboy once told me, "Better saddle up and ride on."

So mosey through this guide, enjoy the photos, make some calls, ask questions, and—**this is very important**—ask for references (former guests who have enjoyed the ranch or lodge and whom you may call). We also invite you to visit the Worldwide Ranch Headquarters on the Internet at **www.Ranchweb.com.** You may have to do a little work, but just like a horseback ride, once you get in the saddle, all kinds of exciting things can happen.

GENE KILGORE'S FAVORITE RANCH SAYING

We have gentle horses for gentle people,
Spirited horses for spirited people,
And for people who don't like to ride,
We have horses that don't like to be ridden.

—First Seen at Lake Mancos Ranch, Colorado

THE SPIRIT OF THE WEST

Out where the hand clasps a little stronger
Out where the smile dwells a little longer
That's where the West begins;

Where there's more of singing and less of sighing;
Where there's more of giving and less of buying,
And a man makes friends without half trying—
—Arthur Chapman (1915)

WHAT RANCH GUESTS ARE SAYING:

"We are still filled with warmth, smiles, a few extra pounds, and all the wonderful and unforgettable memories of your ranch. We reminisce among ourselves and our friends about our cozy cabin, the yellow and orange marshmallow-eating rainbow trout, and the beautiful lake they lived in, rowboating, the lodge—never without a crackling fire on chilly days and nights—the sing-alongs, square dancing, food, rodeos, prizes, guests, and all you great people who created such a relaxing and 'truly Western' experience for us."

—W.C.

"I count myself as one of the very fortunate to be among your pampered guests. You all contributed in a very real way to our experience. The ways you made every effort to help us feel like family were the most satisfying. We love the way your kids' program not only entertains but educates about nature and the environment. The whole experience provides a great foundation for kids to help preserve what is most vulnerable in this age of high technology."

—N.G.

"In today's age, where 'service' businesses fall short of caring about their customers, yours puts the customers first—a simple concept that's rarely adopted. Today was my first day back at work and all I could think about was riding and the pure serenity at your ranch."

—J.R.

WHAT RANCHERS ARE SAYING ABOUT GENE KILGORE:

"We stand in awe! You're like having all the railroads rolled into one and then accomplishing even more. You have worked marvels. Your book is done with such care, such insight, and with the knack, it would seem, of leading potential guests to the ranch that will be right. You've managed to lift awareness of dude ranching in the midst of all sorts of other vacation opportunities right to the top. And once that awareness takes hold, your book leads each person in the right direction. It's as if a friend were advising each person as to the place that would suit him best."

—Elkhorn Ranch

"I can only try and explain the degree to which your involvement and dedication to the Ways of the West and to those of us who share our hospitality has furthered our commitment to our purpose. Thank you."

—Lost Creek

"Gene Kilgore's, Ranch Vacations *is the Bible for ranch vacations. Thank you so much."*

—Wit's End Resort Ranch

"I want to express my overwhelming appreciation for all your efforts to compile, write, publish and promote your book, Ranch Vacations. *Keep up the good work. You are the authority in this field."*

—The Home Ranch

"No one has ever done more for the dude ranch industry than you."

—Flying E Ranch

"I think the dude ranch is a wonderful thing for America and the world. You have surely done more than anyone to foster the idea."

—Bitterroot Ranch

"I can't say enough about Gene Kilgore's, Ranch Vacations.*"*

—Klick's K Bar L Ranch

"Every week some of our guests have come to us through your book. Thanks for all of your work in making this book such a success."

—Gros Ventre River Ranch

Contents

Foreword

For almost 24 years, my wife, our six children, and I lived successively in three European countries with different cultures and languages. The children pointed out recently that one word common to all was "Bam Paw," our youngest son's name for police cars and ambulances, derived from the distinctive and reassuring sound of their warning signals. To me, the sound is also symbolic of city living with all its noises and hustle in any part of the world.

Now the children are all educated, working, and/or parenting . . . in cities, of course. But I no longer spend much time in cities. No lawyering, no managing, no financing for me. You see, I am FREE. I am FREE AT LAST! I own a guest ranch in California where I get up with the sun, then sweat over horses, fences, trail clearing, and related matters. I am also in charge of marketing, accounting, housekeeping, food and beverage planning and preparations, human resources (people), and quality control. And I get to eat, drink, and play with some of the most attractive people in the world— our guests. The result of all this is profound contentment for me. I love the work. No committee meetings, no quarterly P/E concerns, no shareholder suits, no board meetings. I AM FREE!

Now I am truly in touch with the world in which I want to live. I touch it literally when I plant a new fruit tree; when I dig worms for a child's fishhook; when I dig a fence posthole. And I am touched in turn by it when my tree blossoms; when I see the unmistakable first-fish smile on a child's face; and when I help the newly born foal stand in a safe pasture to discover and share my world.

Because of Gene Kilgore and past editions of *Ranch Vacations,* I have met hundreds of guests who are now my good friends. And I have gotten to know other ranch owners who welcome paying guests. Some own enormous spreads with large herds of cattle, while some (like us) are relatively small with no cattle. Some are in mountains, others in valleys. Some are seasonal and others are open year-round. Whatever the differences, we owners share two strong traits—we like people and we are doing what we do because we want to do it. And this so obviously relates to Gene and this unique book. He shares our feeling about ranches and people and connects us with new friends. He is the "Bam Paw," the authority, we all know and respect as a distinctive and reassuring voice in the life we all love freely.

—George Gaines
Highland Ranch, California

It was the summer of 1930 when my family first began welcoming guests to the 63 Ranch near Livingston, Montana. Today, nearly 71 years later, we're among some of the oldest dude ranches in America still owned and operated by the founding family

As I reflect back on growing up in this way of life, I'm continuously reminded of why it is that my heart is into continuing on with the family tradition, just as my predecessors have done. Never mind the chills that run down my spine every time I take an overnight pack trip over the 8,500-foot mountain pass en route to our Bear Wallow campsite in the Absaroka Beartooth Wilderness. Memories like this are so vivid that at any point in time I can envision the look of disbelief and utter amazement displayed among the riders' faces as if they've never seen country so breathtakingly beautiful. Nothing but snowcapped peaks and endless sky for as far as one can see. The fact is, every time I crest the pass on one of these trips, I'm still awed at how pristine and "real" this experience really is. In fact, it's numbingly so, as evidenced by my guests' ooohhhs and aaahhhs, with a sigh or two in between.

It's through sharing experiences like this, with people from all over the world, that allows me to fully appreciate dude ranching. I realize now that the experience we share is something so separately needed by those who, through their own personal sacrifices, have contributed significantly to our ever-increasing standard of living that most of us enjoy today. Unfortunately, our prosperity has not come without a price in terms of the insurmountable tolls on the individuals themselves, not to mention their respective families. It becomes clearer every summer as I continue to observe the dramatic and positive changes in the emotional well-being of these people in seven short days. I see it in their facial expressions and body language. I sense it in their deep conversations about life in general.

The ranch vacation experience is an opportunity to rediscover the simplest of pleasures like learning to distinguish the difference between a sorrel horse and a bay horse, a bull and a cow (whether they have horns or not!), a wild choke cherry and a service berry, or a "bucking" horse from a "stumbling" horse. It's difficult to fully appreciate the degree of happiness and self-accomplishment displayed by someone who has experienced their first lope across a meadow, their first time gathering and trailing a bunch of cows, or their first real-life experience observing a black bear teaching her two cubs how to dig insects out of a decaying log. Who cannot notice the shrieks of laughter among children as they learn to trot their horse for the first time? How about the look in a parent's eyes as they observe their child master the art of horseback riding as if they were born to do it? I can only refer to these moments as "precious" since they're far beyond words of adequate description.

Here's the clincher for me; the avalanche of personal cards and letters we get every year from guests who share comments like " . . . you made us feel so welcome," and " . . . it was the best vacation we have ever had!" After hearing from so many guests this past winter who had recently received word of my grandmother's passing in May of 2000, I am convinced that my degree of success in life will be measured by the number of people whose lives I have touched and not by the amount of money I have made. "Touched" comes closest to describing the emotional impact of each person's remembrance of a true matriarch and the legacy she has left behind in our care.

I remain confident in suggesting to the rest of my generation and the generations that follow, that even though many of us choose to pursue a faster pace in life, one where things "are happening!" (As someone once informed me), there will come a day when we will come wanting, quite possibly needing, somewhat of a simpler experience. Few opportunities exist today that enable us to compliment memorandum experiences with an added opportunity to "reconnect" with ourselves, each other, as well as with the land. Gene recognized this notion more than 20 years ago and has since traveled extensively sharing his personal, heartfelt compassion for guest ranching. Since his first unforgettable dude ranch experience as a nine-year-old, he's dreamed about it, researched it, preached it, breathed it, and continues to "live it" even to this day. No one, to my knowledge has ever committed themselves to "spreading the word" about ranch vacations quite like Gene. Through his own personal commitment and determination, he has made "Ranch Vacations" a familiar phrase within the travel industry. His Sixth Edition of *Ranch Vacations* will, without a doubt, further secure his leadership role in providing his readers with the most comprehensive, objective, and credible list of ranches and lodges available today.

—Jeff Cahill
63 Ranch, Montana

Preface

Welcome, new friends and old, to the Sixth Edition; it is, indeed, better than ever. We now have over 130,000 copies of *Ranch Vacations* in print. It is, thanks to you, our readers from around the world, and all of our ranchers, a best-seller. The new all-photo Sixth Edition will open your eyes to a world of unforgettable pleasure, natural beauty, and wholesome fun. It will put you in touch with ranches and lodges throughout the United States and Canada, as well as top Western museums and annual Western events in North America.

Ranch vacations today offer much more than horseback riding. In fact, you don't even have to like horses or horseback riding to enjoy the properties described in this guide. Some ranches today offer fly-fishing, gourmet dining, tennis, swimming, white-water rafting, natural-history guides, massage, and more. Quite simply, what makes these vacations so special is their wholesome and unforgettable adventures in nature. Everyone—grandparents, children, singles, and families—can find a ranch vacation to suit them. Ranches offer facilities to professional groups, corporations, schools, and churches for seminars, retreats, and workshops. They also offer wonderful opportunities for family reunions, weddings, and honeymoons.

I began researching the first edition of this guidebook in 1979 while I was working as a cowboy for one of the largest cattle operations in the country, Miller Land and Livestock, about 75 miles south of Jackson Hole, Wyoming, and later as a dude wrangler for the one-and-only Frank Galey at his famous White Grass Ranch at the foot of the Tetons. I undertook this exciting project to share with people around the world a truly magnificent way of life.

Today, more than ever, people are seeking relief from the ever-increasing stresses of our fast-paced world. There is no better way for families and individuals to unwind, recharge batteries, gain perspective, reconfirm values, spend time with family members, meet interesting people from around the world, and, most of all, experience the natural beauty and tranquility of the outdoors than on a ranch vacation. As we go faster and faster in our everyday personal and business lives, I believe there will continue to be a reawakening and interest in our great North American wilderness heritage.

The more advanced we become technologically, the more we will crave the simpler pleasures of life. Nature, home-cooked meals, kindness, and sincere hospitality. This guide will put you in touch with a wonderful, unique group of ranches and people who offer an incredible life-enhancing experience. A way of life. A vacation to be enjoyed by both the young and the young at heart.

Ranch vacations offer one of the greatest year-round vacation opportunities in the world today. Welcome to Gene Kilgore's Ranch Country.

Sixth Edition Thoughts

We are proud to present you with our best ever, all-photo Sixth Edition, bringing you the latest and greatest of ranch country from across North America.

In 1979 I began researching *Ranch Vacations* in Wyoming. I was convinced that ranch country—the wide-open spaces, nature's beauty, wildlife, and old-fashioned hospitality—was, next to the air we breathe and water we drink, the absolute greatest. Now, 23 years later, I am convinced more than ever that it is.

Today we have more than 130,000 copies of our guide in print, and I am proud that we have been able to help so many people experience this magnificent way of life. We are also bringing travelers to ranch country through Worldwide Ranch Headquarters on the Internet at www.Ranch web.com.

It always amazes me how much change takes place over the course of three years-new ranches being created, new programs being developed, and ranches being sold. Probably the biggest change over the past two years has been the explosion of information available on the Internet. You will note that most every property in this book has e-mail and Internet addresses.

In this edition you will find many new ranches and completely updated information on each ranch or lodge that we feature. We've uncovered some exciting properties for you and know that you'll enjoy discovering them as you mosey through.

As the world turns, the explosive growth of technology has brought about tremendous changes in the way we do business, and where we can work and play. Wherever I go, traveling men and women light up about the possibility of visiting one of the properties in our book. Those who have already done so go on and on about the unforgettable experiences they had.

There were many highlights over the past several years. My young son has already turned six and graduated from kindergarten to first grade. That little boy—my favorite cowboy—has traveled to more ranches than any little fellow I know. It is so special to see the wonder and joy in his eyes over his experiences and discoveries, and I am grateful to be able to share the best of ranch country with him. It is my hope that the Sixth Edition will bring ranch country to more children than ever before.

I am proud of what we have been able to accomplish and grateful to my wife, Regina, and son, William Francisco, for their inspiration, to my father and sister, and to the talented team that helps me.

Most of all I would like to thank all of the ranch and lodge owners who have shared their homes and way of life with me and my family, and have made this book possible.

And last, and possibly most importantly of all, to you readers who have helped make *Ranch Vacations* the success it is—thank you! Ride on partner!

Acknowledgments

There are so many special people who have helped make this book such a success all these years—over 130,000 copies in print now, and the Sixth "Millennium" Edition! Wow.

To all of you, family, friends, ranch and lodge owners, television and radio producers, newspaper and magazine writers, state and government agencies, all our readers along with all my associates, I say thank you!

I am especially grateful to my friend and colleague, Sharon Peterson, who has typed all six manuscripts and has been with me since 1988—an incredible spirit, typist, and horsewoman in her own right.

My sincere thanks to Kim Savoie and Barbara Bazett, my assistants in Sonoma.

To ranchers George Gaines and Jeff Cahill who shared their thoughts and stories in the Forewords—my special thanks!

Finally, to my editor and everyone at Avalon Travel Publishing. I truly believe we are making a difference in the lives of people who experience a ranch vacation. Thanks for helping to make this our best ever. Here's to more happy trails!

The Kilgore Ranch Network— Real Estate Marketing Division

The Kilgore Ranch Network-Real Estate Marketing Division is the leader in dude, guest, resort, fly-fishing, wing shooting, and recreational cattle ranch properties.

Why Buyers and Sellers Use the Network
1. #1 in knowledge and experience.
2. #1 and powerful central source of ranch information.
3. Worldwide visibility in the marketplace.

If you're interested in buying or selling a . . .
- Dude/Guest Ranch
- Resort Ranch
- Wing Shooting Lodge
- Trophy Ranch
- Cross-Country Ski Ranch
- Fly-Fishing Lodge
- Working Cattle Ranch
- Luxury Ranch

Call or Write:
Kilgore Ranch Network—Real Estate Marketing Division
Worldwide Ranch Headquarters
809 Broadway, Suite 1
Sonoma, California 95476, USA
Phone: 707/939-3801
Fax: 707/939-3795

"The world's leading authority."
      —American Express

The Kilgore Ranch Network— Internet Division— www.Ranchweb.com

Welcome to Ranchweb.com, the #1 Internet site for ranch vacations. Here you will find the best of the best of ranch country online, including:

- Ranch Travel
- Ranch Adventure Categories
- Guest Reviews
- Chat Room
- Children's Programs
- Dude Ranch Jobs
- and so much more.

Come visit www.Ranchweb.com—the #1 Internet site for ranch vacations
Call or Write:

Kilgore Ranch Network—Internet Division
Worldwide Ranch Headquarters
809 Broadway, Suite 1
Sonoma, CA 95476, USA
Phone: 707/939-3801
Fax: 707/939-3795
www.Ranchweb.com

Introduction

How does a fellow born in New York City, raised in the country in Northern California, schooled in California, Canada, Pennsylvania, New York, and Montana, and started out to be a doctor, get ranch fever?

Well, I'll tell you. Cowboys, Indians, horses, cattle, and ranches have been in my blood since I remember going to my first rodeo, and seeing my first TV Western when I was five years old. The cowboy's rugged independence, his lifestyle, together with the wide-open spaces, still captures our imaginations and conjures up images that hold a special place in my heart. More than ever ranches are in. Every year, Americans, Canadians, Europeans, and visitors from around the world trade in their city shoes for cowboy boots to dream about and experience this unique way of life.

One of the most remarkable things about a ranch vacation is the lasting impression it makes, especially on children. One of my most famous sayings goes like this: "Take your children to the beach for a week. Ten years later ask them the name of it; they will have forgotten. Take them to a ranch, and for the rest of their lives they will remember the name of the ranch, the name of their horse, and maybe even the name of their wrangler." And that's really true!

The history of ranch vacations can be traced to the days of Theodore Roosevelt's Rough Riders in the late nineteenth century. As the story goes, the Eaton Brothers—Howard, Willis, and Alden—established a hay- and horse-ranch near Medora, North Dakota, in 1879. Soon, friends from the East headed west by train to be a part of the Eatons' new and exciting life. Before they knew it, the Eatons were baby-sitting these big-city dudes, taking them out to help with the chores and cattle. The more the dudes did and the dirtier they became, the happier they were.

Word spread, and soon more of these early-day city slickers came out and fell in love with the rugged simplicity of the West and all it gave them. In those days visitors came by train, not for a week but for months at a time. One guest was so at home on the range that he asked Howard Eaton if he could pay room and board in order to stay on. This exchange of money gave birth to an industry.

The Eaton brothers realized the potential in dude ranching and hosting visitors with varying backgrounds and interests. In 1904, they moved their operation from the flatlands of North Dakota to the mountains of Wolf, Wyoming. Today, the Eaton Ranch is run by the third and fourth generations of the family.

Other ranchers soon got into the act. In 1926, The Dude Ranchers' Association held its first meeting. This association is more active today than ever. In 1934 a group of Colorado ranchers formed their own Colorado Dude and Guest Ranch Association. In 1989 ranchers in British Columbia, Canada, started the British Columbia Guest Ranchers' Association. Since then, many other associations have formed. All of these groups (not to mention all the first-rate fly-fishing, cross-country skiing, hunting, and outfitting organizations) are dedicated to preserving and maintaining high standards in their respective industries.

In general, the underlying theme of today's ranch vacation is the horse. Most of the properties included in this guide provide a variety of riding opportunities—for beginner, intermediate, and advanced riders. Every ranch is different, expressing the personality of the terrain as well as that of the host or owner.

Today, while most of the properties are preserving the Old West, many are keeping up with the present by offering modern amenities and services. Besides horseback-riding programs, many offer swimming, mountain biking, fishing, hiking, rodeos, tennis, skeet shooting, hayrides, and even ballooning. Many have incorporated naturalist talks, art, and photography workshops.

A ranch vacation also enables parents to vacation with their children, where both learn an appreciation for animals and nature. In addition, on a ranch vacation people of all ages and from all walks of life can interact socially, intellectually, and artistically in a marvelously wholesome, intimate, and unique atmosphere.

Accommodations range from very rustic cabins (even sleeping under the stars) to luxury suites. Some have natural hot-spring pools, golf, and tennis; others feature whirlpool spas, saunas, exercise equipment, and even massage.

Ranches that take guests include guest ranches, resort ranches, working cattle ranches, fly-fishing ranches, hunting ranches, and cross-country skiing ranches. They can be found throughout the United States and Canada. Most are in the western United States (Colorado, Wyoming, Montana, Idaho, California, and Oregon), the Southwest (Arizona and New Mexico), the Southeast (North Carolina), Texas, and New York State. In Canada, the majority are in the provinces of British Columbia and Alberta.

Ranches in the Southwest and Southeast will have different weather and landscapes from those in the Northwest. Native ranch customs, architecture, equipment, and clothing will vary, too. If you want to see adobe buildings and mesquite and enjoy arid, warm temperatures, there is a property in this guide for you. If the saw-toothed Rocky Mountains are more to your liking, you can experience that, too. Each region offers different attractions and activities. While the location and climate vary, one thing usually remains the same—down-home hospitality.

On Being a Good "Dude"

The term "dude" goes way back. Lawrence B. Smith, in his book, *Dude Ranches and Ponies,* wrote, "'Dude' was applied to an outsider, city person, or tenderfoot; one who came from another element of society and locality; in short, a stranger as far as the West and its ways were concerned. As dude was applied to a male, so the word 'dudeen' later was made to fit the female, and the business of catering to them was called 'dude ranching.'"

If you feel uncomfortable being referred to as a "dude," you might like to know that President Theodore Roosevelt was one of the first men to receive this name. It could be said that everyone is a dude when traveling in unfamiliar territory. Most ranchers and guests would agree that the key ingredients to being a great dude are a love and respect for nature, a willingness to listen and learn, patience, and understanding. One rancher summed it up by saying, "The perfect dude is one who sees beauty, savors nature's peace and quiet, has compassion for his or her fellow man, and has an understanding for what the ranch host must contend with each day to make the ranch holiday seem effortless."

The perfect dude takes it easy the first two days at the ranch and works into the program slowly. "Relax, unwind, don't push too hard too fast," said one rancher to a young Wall Street broker. He added, "Remember, you'll be able to come back year after year for the rest of your life." Most of all, the ability to relax and have fun is essential to being the perfect dude.

Selecting a Ranch

The ranches included in this guide offer a wide range of choices. The most challenging part of your vacation will be selecting where you want to go. As rates are in constant fluctuation, we have chosen to use the following daily rate code:

$$\$ = \$0–\$100 \text{ per person per day}$$
$$\$\$ = \$100–\$150$$
$$\$\$\$ = \$150–\$250$$
$$\$\$\$\$ = \$250–\$300$$
$$\$\$\$\$\$ = \$300–\$400$$
$$\$\$\$\$\$\$ = \$400 \text{ up}$$

For the most part, rates listed are American Plan with meals, lodging, and activities included. Ranches that offer Modified American Plan and European Plan rates have been noted. When you're confirming your reservation, we recommend you verify the rates and exactly what they include. The symbol • preceding the rate code indicates that the ranch offers travel-agent commissions.

To find ranches that offer your special interests, turn to the Special Ranch Features section. Then write, telephone, or e-mail the ranches that interest you. I suggest you telephone and speak personally with the owners or managers; you can get a pretty good feel for things by phone. Ask for a brochure and for the names of several past guests you might contact. Call them and ask what sort of time they had, if they have children, too, and if they have any special considerations like yours. Perhaps the most important thing of all in ranch travel is chemistry between owner/manager/staff and you, their guest.

Here are some questions you might like to look over before you call a ranch or lodge. Also, you might wish to visit www.Ranchweb.com to look at guest reviews and more.

Questions to Ask

Rates
• What are your rates?
• What is the tipping/gratuity policy?

- Are there special rates for families, children, seniors, and corporations?
- Do you have a nonriding rate?
- Are there off-season rates?
- Is there a minimum length of stay?
- Besides state and local taxes, what do your rates not include? What is the tipping policy? (Rates don't always include gratuities or all activities.)

Vacationing with Children
(See Special Ranch Features "Children's Programs")
- What does the ranch's children's program include?
- What age must children be to ride? (Today's insurance regulations may not allow very young children to ride.)
- Is child care provided and to what extent?
- Is this a child-oriented ranch?
- Can children ride with parents?
- Are parents welcome in children's activities?
- Can parents ride with children?
- Do children eat separately?
- Can children eat together?
- What are the qualifications of the childcare providers?
- Is baby-sitting available?

Horses and Riding
- Are riding lessons available?
- What kind of riding program does the ranch have?
- What kind of rides are there—morning, afternoon, all-day, side-by-side, slow to fast?
- What style of horsemanship do you use or teach?
- Is it open-meadow riding, or head-to-tail mountain-trail riding?
- Is the program best suited for beginners or are there opportunities for intermediate and advanced riders, too?
- Are riding helmets required?
- Are riding helmets provided?
- Can I bring my own helmet?

- Are there nonriding days?
- Do I need my own cowboy boots or is there a boot rental program?
- Do I get the same horse all week?
- Can I brush and saddle my own horse?
- Do the owners/managers take part in the riding program?
- How long are typical rides?
- If I'm an intermediate or advanced rider can I jog or lope?
- How many wranglers and guests go out on rides at a time?
- Can I bring my own saddle?
- Can I bring my own horse?
- Do I ride all days of the week?
- Will I need to sign an assumption of risk or waiver form before riding?

Cattle Work

- How many cattle do you run?
- Do guests participate in all cattle activities?
- Can guests brand with the cowboys?
- Do you teach roping?
- Do you teach cattle or team penning?

Miscellaneous

- Is there a staff naturalist?
- Are the activities of the ranch or lodge sufficient for nonriding or nonfishing members of a family?
- Will the ranch cater to special diets? (Some have vegetarian, low-salt, and low-cholesterol menus.)
- Will the ranch provide guest references?
- Are there special clothing requirements?
- Will the ranch provide a clothing/equipment list? (Usually standard procedure.)
- What equipment does the ranch provide? (Fishing rods, tennis rackets, etc.)
- Do I need a license to fish? Should I buy one before I arrive?
- What will the weather be like?
- Can we buy sundry items at the ranch? (Not all ranches have stores on the premises.)
- Do you provide airport, train, or bus pickup? (Many ranches are happy to pick you up. There is often a nominal charge.)
- Do you recommend rental cars? (In most instances, once you arrive you'll not want to leave the ranch. However, you may opt for flexibility and independence.)
- Are laundry facilities available? (Many ranches have laundry facilities; some will even do your laundry.)
- What is your liquor policy? (Many ranches ask that you bring your own wine or liquor. If desired, you can pick these up on your way or the ranch will get them for you with advance notice. Some ranches offer wine and beer and a number have fully licensed bars and extensive wine lists.)
- Are any foreign languages spoken?
- Are pets allowed?
- What is the elevation of the ranch?
- Are there wheelchair facilities?
- What is your smoking policy?
- Are there nonsmoking rooms?
- Do you provide e-mail access?
- Do you allow cellular telephones?

Getting There

Whatever method of transportation you choose, it's a good idea to check with the ranch or lodge before you make travel plans. Your hosts will advise you about roads, major commercial airports, and private airstrips. Should you fly or take the train? They'll also tell you whether they will pick you up.

What to Wear

Clothing is an essential part of the ranch-vacation experience. It's important to pack correctly and bring clothes that will enable you to enjoy your Western experience—a pair of boots, several pairs of jeans, a good cowboy belt with buckle, a cowboy hat, several shirts, and a warm jacket are about all you'll really need. Over the years, after hundreds of miles on horseback and thousands of miles in automobiles and airplanes, I know quality clothing is better than quantity. (Well, I guess that goes for most everything in life.)

Here are a few Gene Kilgore clothing tips. Along with quality, think comfort. Invest in a good pair of boots and a cowboy hat. Make sure your boots are well-worn before you arrive—you don't want blisters. Buy at least three pairs of jeans and wash them at least four times, using softener. They'll be much more comfortable and will have faded a bit so you don't look quite so "green." Take along a warm jacket, a sweater, and even a vest. Early mornings and evenings can be cool.

Finally, when making your reservation, ask the ranch or lodge to send you a clothing list to help with your packing. And pardner, one last thing, don't forget a flashlight, some lip protection, mosquito repellent, and sunblock. The ranch or lodge you've selected will be more than happy to give you all the advice you require.

Definitions

ADRA (Arizona Dude Ranch Association): An association of Arizona dude ranches.

BCGRA (British Columbia Guest Ranchers' Association): An association of Canadian ranches in the province of British Columbia, formed in 1989 to market ranch vacations throughout Canada and the United States.

CDGRA (Colorado Dude and Guest Ranch Association): An association founded in 1934, made up solely of Colorado ranch and ranch resort properties dedicated to marketing and maintaining excellence in the Colorado guest-ranch industry. Members meet annually.

Cross-Country Skiing Ranch: A ranch that offers cross-country skiing opportunities. Trails are normally groomed with specialized, professional equipment. Instruction, guide service, and equipment are usually available.

Day Ranch: A ranch or ranch setting (maybe even a Western town) that offers travelers the opportunity to visit and enjoy the spirit of the Old West without providing overnight accommodations. Often horseback rides and full-meal service are available.

Dude: Any individual who is not in his or her natural environment. A business or pleasure traveler who is in another state or even a foreign country. Basically, a dude is you and me—we're all dudes in one way or another!

Dude/Guest Ranch: Usually a family-owned and -operated ranch with the primary objective of offering its guests a Western experience. Horseback riding is usually the main activity; hiking, fishing, and swimming are often included.

DRA (The Dude Ranchers' Association): An association of Western dude ranches, founded in 1926, dedicated to maintaining the quality and high standards of Western hospitality established by early ranches.

Fly-Fishing Ranch: A facility offering an extensive fly-fishing program with instruction and guides. Some ranches/lodges have on-premises tackle shops.

Hideaway Report: A privately published newsletter dedicated to the discovery of peaceful vacations and executive retreats for the sophisticated traveler. Author's Note: This monthly newsletter is highly esteemed by experts in the travel industry. All properties that have been featured in the *Hideaway Report* are so noted under "Awards."

Gymkhana: A series of games or events on horseback.

Hunting Lodge: A facility that specializes in seasonal big-game or bird-hunting. Many of these lodges offer activities for nonhunting family members. Some provide full-service hunting and support facilities. Many have father-son programs.

Kilgore Luxury Group (KLG): Exclusive ranches with luxury features noted under "Awards". Visit www.ranchweb.com and see Luxury Group.

MDRA (Montana Dude Ranch Association): An association of Montana dude ranches.

Naturalist: One who is trained in the appreciation and understanding of nature and the outdoor world.

Orvis-Endorsed: Orvis, the respected fly-fishing company, realized there was a need to check out and endorse top-notch fishing lodges with first-rate guides. Today, Orvis personnel monitor Orvis-endorsed lodges. These lodges provide complete fly-fishing guide services. Each has its own fly-fishing tackle shop. Orvis-endorsed lodges in this book are designated as such.

Pack Trip: An overnight, multiple-day, weeklong, or monthlong trip on horseback. All supplies, including food, tents, and equipment, are carried by horses, mules, or sometimes even llamas. Usually a magnificent wilderness experience.

PRCA (Professional Rodeo Cowboys Association): An association dedicated to promoting and setting the standards of the professional rodeo industry.

Resort Ranch: A facility that may or may not have a Western theme but does offer horseback riding. Usually the amenities are upscale, with a range of resort activities offered. Note: Some properties use "resort" in their names but may not offer resort amenities.

Rodeo: A cowboys' tournament or competition in which men and women compete in an arena; involves livestock (horses, steers, bulls) and barrel racing.

TGRA (Texas Guest Ranch Association): An association of Texas dude ranches.

Wilderness Lodge: In the heart of wilderness areas, these facilities offer a retreat from civilization. Generally, all supplies arrive by plane, boat, horse, or sometimes four-wheel-drive vehicle.

Wrangler: Originally, a cowboy who was hired on at a guest ranch to "wrangle" (herd and care for) horses and take dudes out on day and overnight rides. Today, a wrangler may be male or female, a college student or a cowboy. There is no telling what a wrangler's background might be. The important ingredient is that the wrangler is experienced with horses, and patient, understanding, and friendly with dudes.

WDRA (Wyoming Dude Rancher's Association): An association of Wyoming dude ranches.

Guest and Resort Ranches
in the United States

Crystal Creek Lodge
Dillingham, Alaska

You've probably dreamed about Alaska—and with good reason. It's big, fresh, wild, free, and filled with adventure. This is a land of mountains, tundra, glaciers, and lakes, where the scenery is overwhelming and the wildlife abundant and untamed. Located amid all this is Crystal Creek Lodge. Owners Dan and Lori Michels and their fine staff offer guests an Alaskan adventure experience second to none. At Crystal Creek Lodge you'll be welcomed as friends and given the opportunity to fish and to extensively see and explore some of Alaska's most beautiful areas. The lodge, located on the peaceful and remote shores of Lake Nunavaugaluk, is surrounded by the millions of acres that make up the Wood-Tikchik State Park and Togiak National Wildlife Refuge. Guests fly out daily by floatplane or helicopter with a guide to flyfish, view wildlife, hike, kayak, or explore the 10,000-square-mile Bristol Bay region.

Address: P.O. Box 872729, Wasilla, Alaska 99687
Telephone: 800/525-3153, 907/357-3153; fax: 907/357-1946
Email: info@crystalcreeklodge.com
Internet: www.crystalcreeklodge.com
Airport: Dillingham, 15 miles
Location: Bristol Bay area, southwest Alaska; 320 miles southwest of Anchorage, 15 miles northwest of Dillingham
Awards: Orvis-endorsed Lodge, Orvis-endorsed Expedition, Kilgore Luxury Group
Medical: Kanaknek Hospital in Dillingham, 10-minute helicopter flight from the lodge
Conference Capacity: 24
Guest Capacity: 24
Accommodations: The 10,200-square-foot main lodge is the center of the operation, with 14 double occupancy guest rooms, including four at lakeside, and 10 with mountain views. Each room is modern with full amenities, including queen-size beds, and full bathrooms with plenty of hot water. Daily maid service and midweek laundry services are included. A masseuse is on duty each evening.
Rates: • $$$$$$ American Plan. Sunday to Sunday with six full days of activities and seven nights lodging. Package includes everything except liquor, massages, gratuities, and round-trip airfare between your home and Dillingham.
Credit Cards: None. Personal and traveler's checks accepted.
Season: June through September
Activities: This area of Bristol Bay is known for its pristine wilderness, abundant wildlife, and world-class fishing. The lodge is famous for its fly-fishing and fall bird-hunting programs, and offers a Sky Trekking Program that includes many outdoor activities. Wildlife viewing includes Alaskan brown bear, Pacific walrus, and seabird rookeries at Cape Pierce. Innuit culture tours, kayaking in Silver Horn Fjord, and hiking on a glacial moraine. Sporting clays course at the lodge. Waterfowl and upland bird-hunting in September. All equipment for fishing, hunting, and trekking activities provided at no extra charge.
Children's Programs: Children and families are welcome and encouraged to participate together. Recommended for children age 10 and older.
Dining: Excellent cuisine, cooked to order. Three different dinner entrées are offered and change daily. Choose from beef, chicken, pork, salmon, halibut, or a hearty "home-style" entrée. Sack lunches for streamside picnics available, and occasional fresh-caught salmon prepared by your guide. Complimentary house wines are served with dinner. A fine wine list and extensive beer selection are also available.
Entertainment: After a full day of activities most guests are delightfully worn out. Outdoor spa, sauna, massage therapist, full-service bar, and miles of beaches to stroll. Practice fly casting in the fishing hole right outside the front door. The evening lighting is excellent for avid photographers. Ask about the Iditarod Trail Sled Dog Race slide show.
Summary: Kilgore's "Best of the Best." World-class adventure lodge offering incredible fly-in and fly-out Alaskan wilderness experiences. Superb wildlife viewing, fly-fishing, wing shooting, and breathtaking beauty for men, women, and children who appreciate excellence.

The Bellota Ranch
Tucson, Arizona

Following in the footsteps of its famous sister ranch, the Tanque Verde (see page 22), The Bellota (Bay-oh-tah) Ranch is a step back into a more romantic and historic time of the Southwest. Dating back to 1890, The Bellota Ranch is nestled in a valley between the Santa Catalina and Rincón Mountains, and provides a backdrop of mystique, majesty, and history for singles, couples, family reunions, or corporate groups. Though small and intimate, the ranch offers terrific hiking and horseback riding over 65,000 acres of the Coronado National Forest. Cattle drives and roundup programs offer the more accomplished rider outstanding opportunities to experience Western heritage up close and personal. Seeing this part of the country from the back of a good horse truly brings the feeling of the Old West to life, and it is easy to imagine the days when Apache attacks made settling and living in this part of the country uncertain. The white-washed walls of the original adobe house, chapel, and hacienda ranch house with its classic enclosed courtyard create the magic and charm of a step back in time to the days of señoritas and caballeros.

Address: 14301 East Speedway, Dept. K, Tucson, Arizona 85748
Telephone: 800/234-3833 (will answer Tanque Verde), 520/296-6275; fax: 520/721-9426
Email: dude@tvgr.com
Internet: www.bellotaranch.com
Airport: Tucson, 30 miles
Location: 30 miles east of Tucson in the Coronado National Forest
Medical: Tucson Medical Center, 15 miles
Conference Capacity: 16
Guest Capacity: 24
Accommodations: A large, renovated Mexican hacienda provides an historic Southwestern ambiance with a down-home feel. All eight rooms have private baths, five with fireplaces. A spacious great room beneath a vaulted 12-foot ceiling, and a traditional hacienda courtyard provide perfect settings for relaxing after long hours in the saddle. Share your adventures with newfound friends in front of the enormous copper fireplace, or spend a little quiet time in the nature nook. Game room, TV/VCR with cable. Surrounded by magnificent views, a swim in the unique pool that once was a cattle tank, or a soak in the hot tub is enjoyed by all.
Rates: • $$$–$$$$ American Plan. Rates vary with the season; cattle-drive packages available.
Credit Cards: VISA, MasterCard, Discover, American Express
Season: Year-round
Activities: Riding is the main activity and is best suited to more advanced and knowledgeable riders. A one-on-one experience is offered where you may catch, groom, and saddle your horse for a day of riding through the spectacular, rugged terrain that makes the Southwest so special. Five-day roundups and cattle drives during four two-week periods each year provide guests with an authentic Old West experience. Nonriding activities include hiking and mountain biking.
Children's Programs: Children must be at least 13 years old and participate in all the ranch activities with their parents. Custom programs can be developed for younger children if a family books the entire ranch.
Dining: A chef prepares fine meals with different themes daily, which are served in the country kitchen. Wine and liquor available.
Entertainment: Relaxing in the great room or hacienda-style courtyard, swimming in the cattle tank pool, soaking in the hot tub. A family atmosphere prevails and guests enjoy the camaraderie and spirit of this old hacienda. Weekly campfires and sing-alongs.
Summary: A wonderful, historic hacienda, built in 1933, that continues the traditions and history of the early Arizona frontier spirit. Today, this guest and working cattle ranch is owned and operated by its sister ranch, the Cote family's world-famous Tanque Verde Ranch, also featured in this book. Yearly cattle work and year-round riding and hiking. Personal attention for families, small business groups, couples, and singles. Ask about the chapel for weddings.

Circle Z Ranch
Patagonia, Arizona

The Circle Z Ranch, founded in 1926, nestled in a picturesque mountain valley at 4,000 feet surrounded by colorful hills and dramatic mountain backdrops. Unique to the ranch, and most unusual in southern Arizona, is a wonderful creek they call "Sonoita," which is bordered for miles by century-old cottonwood trees. This was Apache country, and relics of the Spanish conquistadors are still found. Hollywood has been here, filming *Broken Lance*, John Wayne's *Red River*, and television's *Gunsmoke*, to name a few. The Circle Z is romantic, with its adobe buildings reflecting the Spanish influence and early-West simplicity. Circle Z is run by delightful resident managers and has been owned since 1974 by Lucia Nash, who fell in love with it when brought here by her family as a child. Ranch-bred horses and a variety of trails coupled with delicious food and warm hospitality bring guests back year after year. Bird-watchers flock to the Circle Z to see some of the rarest species in the United States. You'll find all the easygoing pleasures of dude-ranch life at the Circle Z.

Address: P.O. Box 194, Patagonia, Arizona 85624
Telephone: 888/854-2525, 520/394-2525; fax: 520/394-2058
Email: info@circlez.com
Internet: www.circlez.com
Airport: Tucson; private planes at Nogales, eight miles away
Location: 60 miles south of Tucson, directly off Highway 82; 15 miles north of Mexican border
Memberships: The Dude Ranchers' Association, Arizona Dude Ranch Association, American Quarter Horse Association
Medical: Carondelet Holy Cross Hospital, 15 miles
Guest Capacity: 40
Accommodations: Charming, comfortable, and attractive. There are seven adobe cottages with 24 rooms with private baths and showers (many with Mexican tile), a variety of bed sizes, and colorful rugs on wooden floors. Electric blankets are available. All rooms, suites, and cottages have individually controlled heat and outside entrances onto porches or patios. Laundry facilities available.

Rates: • $$–$$$ American Plan. Weekend and off-peak rates available. Three-day minimum stay.
Credit Cards: None. Personal checks accepted.
Season: November to mid-May
Activities: Experienced wranglers lead twice-daily all-day scenic and picnic rides on a remarkable variety of trails across 6,000 acres of deeded ranch land and the contiguous Coronado National Forest. Rides are broken into small groups according to level of ability. You may keep the same horse throughout your stay. Ask about team penning and gymkhanas. The emphasis is on maintaining the atmosphere of an old-time family ranch: riding instruction, hiking, swimming in an outdoor heated pool, and an all-weather tennis court. Fishing in Lake Patagonia and an 18-hole championship golf course nearby.
Children's Programs: Although there is no planned children's program and child care is not provided, children are welcome. Table tennis, shuffleboard, horseshoes, basketball. Kids' cantina with foosball table and jukebox. Children begin riding at age five and older.
Dining: Meals are served in the dining room or on the patio of the main lodge offering a variety of fine-quality cuisine. Ranch specialties include mesquite-grilled steaks, mild Southwestern dishes, home-baked breads, and desserts. Adobe cantina for adults has piano, pool table, and large wooden deck for relaxing. BYOB. Children dine earlier in their own dining room and parents are welcome to join them.
Entertainment: Hayrides, surrey rides, bonfires, and occasional country-music entertainers; player piano with 100 tunes.
Summary: Old-time, easygoing spirit and charm prevail! Vast and varied riding and hiking are the main activities. Great for people who enjoy nature and won't miss TV and in-room telephones. Unstructured other than riding and meals. Bird-watcher's paradise at ranch and adjacent Nature Conservancy preserve. Nearby: Mining and ghost towns, an artisan village, Spanish mission, Mexican border-town shopping, and visits to Old West tourist towns of Tombstone and Bisbee. Spanish spoken.

Elkhorn Ranch
Tucson, Arizona

The Millers' Elkhorn Ranch is old-time dude ranching at its best! At 3,700 feet, the ranch sits in a secluded valley, surrounded by the picturesque Baboquivari Mountain Range, with canyons, rolling hills, mesquite, and open desert to the east. The ranch is small and informal, well out of the city, with activities centering on the outdoors. It's a lovely part of the Southwest. The Miller family has been operating this riding ranch since 1945; today it's run by the third generation—Charley and Mary Miller and their young children. The Elkhorn offers unexcelled riding and a relaxed way of life for 32 guests. The ranch spirit encourages family group fun but offers lots of time to be alone if you wish. The cabins and ranch buildings are designed in a Southwestern architectural style. With 10,000 acres and over 100 horses, unlimited riding and hiking are assured. The less adventurous can relax by the pool or outside each cabin. Bring your camera and binoculars—Arizona's birds are numerous.

Address: HC1 Box 97, Tucson, Arizona 85736
Telephone: 520/822-1040
Internet: www.guestranches.com/elkhorn
Airport: Tucson
Location: 50 miles southwest of Tucson, off Route 286 between Mileposts 25 and 26
Memberships: The Dude Ranchers' Association, Arizona Dude Ranch Association
Medical: St. Mary's Hospital in Tucson, 50 miles
Guest Capacity: 32
Accommodations: Guests enjoy Southwestern-style cabins that vary from one to two bedrooms, some with a sitting room and some with open fireplaces with mesquite firewood, all with private baths and electric heat. Cabins have tiled and cement floors with Mexican throw rugs, some original art, and all with bird feeders. Daily maid service and nightly bed turndown service.
Rates: • $$–$$$ American Plan. Special rates for stays of two or three weeks or longer. One-week minimum stay in high season tends to be Sunday to Sunday, four-night minimum stay in low season.
Credit Cards: None. Personal checks and traveler's checks accepted.
Season: Mid-November through April
Activities: Some of the best riding in the country.

Each morning at breakfast, Charley Miller meets with guests to discuss riding interests and options. As Charley says, "If someone really wants to ride, we sure try to accommodate them." And he does! With more than 100 horses, all levels of guided riding are provided on desert or mountain trails. Moonlight rides offered. Surfaced tennis court and kidney-shaped 50-foot heated swimming pool. Shuffleboard, table tennis, horseshoe pitching, and a pistol/rifle range (bring your own guns) are offered, as well as bird-watching and hiking.
Children's Programs: Children of all ages are welcome, but are the responsibility of their parents. Riding begins at age six. Nannies are welcome.
Dining: Delicious home-cooked meals served buffet-style in the longhouse or on the patio. Cookouts on the trail, picnics in the desert, and dinners cooked on the barbecue. BYOB in cabins only.
Entertainment: Rest and relaxation. Stargazing, puzzles, evening strolls, or enjoy the ranch's extensive library—you're pretty much on your own.
Summary: One of the old time greats and one of the nicest families in the business. Many repeat families, couples, and singles. Newcomers always feel a part of the family. Superb desert and mountain riding. Excellent ranch-raised horses and one of the best ranch riding programs in the country for all levels of horsemanship. Beginners can learn here, and advanced riders can be challenged. Great birding. Nearby: Arizona-Sonora Living Desert Museum, Kitt Peak Observatory, the Tohono O'odham Reservation, and old Spanish missions of San Xavier and Tumacacori.

Flying E Ranch
Wickenburg, Arizona

Flying E Ranch, the "riding ranch," is four miles west of Wickenburg. Since 1960, owner Vi Wellik and her caring staff have been hosting families, couples, and singles that come to savor the ranch's wonderful spirit and friendly hospitality. As Vi says, "We've been hosting guests for 40 years and serving up our own brand of dude-ranch hospitality." Located in the Hassayampa Valley on the north edge of the Sonoran Desert, the Flying E rests on a 2,400-foot mesa at the foot of historic Vulture Peak. Warm days, starlit nights, beautiful desert scenery, relaxed ambiance, family camaraderie, and privacy keep guests returning year after year to ride, swim, play tennis, relax, or stroll the scenic walking paths. Flying E is one of the most immaculately kept ranches I've ever seen. Vi, her manager Bobbie Rottmayer, her dedicated staff, and her famous dude ranch are very special and will receive you with open arms!

Address: 2801 W. Wickenburg Way, Dept. K, Wickenburg, Arizona 85390-1087
Telephone: 888/684-2650, 520/684-2690; fax: 520/684-5304
Email: vacation@flyingeranch.com
Internet: www.flyingeranch.com
Airport: Phoenix Sky Harbor. Private planes and executive jets land at Wickenburg Municipal Airport (Wellik Field), across from the ranch.
Location: On Highway 60, approximately 65 miles northwest of Phoenix Skyharbor Airport; four miles west of Wickenburg's town center
Memberships: The Dude Ranchers' Association, The Arizona Dude Ranch Association
Medical: Wickenburg Regional Hospital, five miles
Guest Capacity: 34-plus
Accommodations: Rooms are "squeaky clean," comfortable, electrically heated and air-conditioned, with delightful Western decor. All rooms have TVs, private baths, air-conditioning, electric blankets, refrigerators, and wet bars.
Rates: • $$$ American Plan. Children's rates available when occupying same room as parents. Horseback riding extra. Two-night minimum (November and December), three-night minimum (January to May), four-night minimum (all holiday periods).
Credit Cards: None. Personal and traveler's checks, and cash accepted.
Season: November 1 to May 1
Activities: Do as much or as little as you wish. You won't be programmed every minute. Two-hour morning and afternoon horseback rides to places like Mt. Everett, Robbers Roost, and Yucca Flats. Beginner, intermediate, and advanced rides. Instruction available. Breakfast cookouts, lunch rides, chuck wagon feeds, and occasional hayrides. Beautiful heated pool, hot spa, exercise room, sauna, shuffleboard, basketball, volleyball, horseshoe-pitching, rock-hounding, and lighted tennis court. While many come to horseback ride, some prefer to experience the desert by foot on the many walking trails. Eighteen-hole championship golf course at nearby Los Caballeros Golf Club; guests may play on ranch membership. Town offers outstanding Desert Caballeros Museum, art galleries, and fine Western stores.
Children's Programs: The ranch loves "well-behaved" kids of all ages. Children are parents' responsibility and participate right along with all the guests.
Dining: Hearty and genuinely good food served family-style in private dining room. Social hour with hors d'oeuvres each evening. BYOB. No bar.
Entertainment: Occasional "inter-ranch" square and line dancing in barn loft, and "dudeos" (games on horseback for guests) in ranch arena. A cozy living room with fireplace, entertainment center, grand piano, and lots of card games.
Summary: Vi says, "Flying E is a spirit," and so it is. The ranch staff is dedicated to sincere, friendly service. Because of this, many of the families, couples, and singles that come are repeat guests or friends of guests. For many, the ranch is their "Camelot of the Old West."

Grand Canyon Bar 10 Ranch
in Arizona near St. George, Utah

The lodge at the Bar 10 Ranch is located about nine miles from the north rim of the Grand Canyon. From this sandstone-brick lodge, you can see the distant grandeur of these canyon cliffs. For years, the Bar 10 Ranch has been a starting and ending point for guests on Colorado River rafting trips. The history and excitement of the Grand Canyon and the Colorado River are yours at the Bar 10, a working cattle ranch that boasts 60,000 acres and 400 head of cattle. There are no telephone lines or oiled roads within an 80-mile radius! Satellite phone or two-way radio deliver urgent messages. The Heaton family hosts guests who come to experience Colorado River rafting trips and ranch tour packages. The Bar 10 offers a unique blend of remoteness and modern comforts. One guest wrote, "You have created an experience that enriches the lives of your guests! The Bar 10 Ranch is an unforgettable experience!" Hearty country meals, varied ranch activities, and genuine Western hospitality provide guests with a lasting Grand Canyon ranch experience! The Bar 10 office can be your one-stop shopping site for ranch tours and/or reservations with any of the numerous Grand Canyon river-rafting companies.

Address: P.O. Box 910088 K, St. George, Utah 84791
Telephone: 800/582-4139, 435/628-4010; fax: 435/628-5124
Email: reservations@bar10.com
Internet: www.bar10.com
Airport: McCarren International, Las Vegas, Nevada; St. George Airport, Utah; direct charter flights from Las Vegas and St. George available; 4,280-foot by 40-foot runway at the ranch (radio frequency 122.9)
Location: 80 miles south of St. George, Utah (two-hour drive on dirt road, 30-minute flight); 200 miles east of Las Vegas (four-hour drive, 50-minute flight); most guests fly in.
Medical: Dixie Medical Center, St. George, Utah; University Medical Center of Southern Nevada, Las Vegas; helicopter available for emergencies during rafting season.
Conference Capacity: Great for business/incentive groups and seminars

Guest Capacity: 50 overnight, more for day groups
Accommodations: For the adventurous, there are covered wagons for private sleeping on the hillside behind the main lodge—great for couples. Surrounded by lawns and desert landscape, the two-story Bar 10 lodge has comfortable dormitory-style rooms with bunk beds and common bathrooms. The main floor of the lodge is home to the Bar 10 Trading Post, which sells supplies, books, gifts, snacks, T-shirts, and other unique souvenirs.
Rates: • $$ American Plan. Call for custom and package rates. Airfare, ATV tours, and helicopter rides extra.
Credit Cards: VISA, MasterCard, Discover
Season: May through September. Off-season dates available.
Activities: The Bar 10 Ranch offers a variety of activities and tour packages, including Colorado River rafting trips, overnight packages consisting of one or more days at the ranch, wagon train, ATV tours, horseback pack trips, and scenic flights combined with part- or full-day ranch adventures. Ranch activities may include horseback riding, horseshoes, ranch demonstrations, trapshooting, hiking, billiards, volleyball, line dancing, and other group activities. Scenic helicopter rides available most days during the peak season (extra).
Children's Programs: No specific programs. Youth groups welcome; call ranch for details.
Dining: Cowboy breakfast, sandwich-bar lunch, Dutch-oven dinners. BYOB.
Entertainment: The Bar 10 crew puts on a terrific evening show with singing, clogging, cowboy poetry, fiddle-playing, and a slide show depicting the evolution of the Bar 10. The show usually ends with watermelon and mingling.
Summary: Remote ranch located about nine miles from the north rim of the Grand Canyon, specializing in ranch tours and spectacular river-rafting packages. Many families, couples, business/incentive groups, and youth groups come for the day, some for overnight, and others stay longer for various adventure programs. Most guests arrive by helicopter or airplane.

Grapevine Canyon Ranch
Pearce, Arizona

THE DUDE RANCHERS'
ASSOCIATION

ARIZONA
DUDE RANCH ASSOCIATION

Grapevine Canyon Ranch, a working cattle ranch as well as a guest ranch, lies in the heart of Apache country at a 5,000-foot elevation. The ranch buildings, nestled in groves of Arizona oak, manzanita, and mesquite trees, are almost invisible in this wooded canyon, with mountains forming a three-sided backdrop. The ranch is owned and operated by Eve and Gerry Searle, whose philosophy can be summed up in two words: personal attention. Gerry, a longtime rancher, also spent many years in the movie industry, doubling for stars in stunt riding, including every episode of *High Chaparral*. Eve came to the United States from Melbourne, Australia, where she worked as a flight instructor. She has a cosmopolitan background, having lived in Europe, India, Australia, and Mexico, before settling in Arizona. Grapevine is famous for its program of trail rides, seasonal cattle work, horsemanship seminars, horseback games, all-day rides, and lessons, as well as history rides to abandoned ghost towns, Fort Bowie, and Chiricahua National Monument. One European couple summed up the ranch best: "As children we dreamed it, as adults we have lived it at Grapevine Canyon Ranch."

Address: P.O. Box 302 K, Pearce, Arizona 85625
Telephone: 800/245-9202, 520/826-3185; fax: 520/826-3636
Email: gcranch@vtc.net
Internet: www.ArizonaGuestRanch.com
Airport: Tucson
Location: 85 miles southeast of Tucson, off Interstate 10
Memberships: The Dude Ranchers' Association, Arizona Dude Ranch Association
Medical: Willcox Hospital, 40 miles
Conference Capacity: 25
Guest Capacity: 30
Accommodations: Two-room *casitas* or pleasant single-room cabins. Each is air-cooled; all are quiet and individually decorated in a delightful country style with a Southwestern touch. Most are secluded in groves of Arizona oak. All are fully carpeted and equipped with full or three-quarter baths, coffeepots, stocked refrigerator, sun deck, and porch.
Rates: • $$$–$$$$ Stocked refrigerator, sun deck, and porch. Three-night minimum stay.
Credit Cards: VISA, MasterCard, Discover, American Express. Personal checks accepted.
Season: Year-round; including Christmas, Thanksgiving, and Easter; closed December 1–8 .
Activities: Grapevine specializes in horsemanship and the most popular activity is horseback riding. Practical horsemanship and riding clinics offer everything connected with horse ownership—conformation, basic veterinary and farrier knowledge, safe trailering, saddling, selection and care of tack, and lots more (extra charge). Each student is taught at his or her level of knowledge and private one-on-one lessons are available. Long and short rides, catering both to novice and experienced riders, are on the program, and guests may unsaddle and brush their horses at the end of the day. For safety, a checkout ride is required before you can join the advanced rides. Range rides with a cowboy to check cattle are offered twice a week, and guests can participate in the cattle roundups done several times a year. Swimming in the heated pool (April–October), and hot tub. Sight-seeing in Mexico and to legendary Tombstone. Hiking trails, bird viewing, and fishing in a lake stocked with bass and catfish. Golf nearby (seven miles).
Children's Programs: No children under age 12.
Dining: Hearty ranch breakfasts cooked to individual order. Lunch and dinner are served buffet-style. Roasted Cornish game hens, chimichangas, barbecued pork and beef ribs, steak and roast beef, rich homemade desserts, and ice cream. Beer and wine available.
Entertainment: Video/TV room with film library, books, and magazines, weekly live country music. Ask about the Grapevine Band CD. Dummy steer-roping, darts, recreation room with pool table and table tennis.
Summary: Kilgore's "Best of the Best"–Horsemanship. Intimate guest ranch with extensive riding for the novice to the professional rider. International clientele. Emphasis is on personalized, friendly service and excellent horseback riding. Relaxation, seasonal cattle work in the beautiful Arizona high country. Group and corporate programs available.

Kay El Bar Ranch
Wickenburg, Arizona

The Kay El Bar has incredible charm! Established in 1926, this lovely old guest ranch is listed on the National Register of Historic Places. What attracted owners John and Nancy Loftis to the ranch was "the history, beautiful handmade adobe bricks, towering eucalyptus trees, the small size, and most of all the charm!" The ranch offers a desert oasis with friendly hospitality where guests quickly feel like part of the family. Guests enjoy beautiful, varied riding terrain and a relaxed atmosphere with folks from around the world who share a love of the West, horses, and camaraderie! Welcome to the Kay El Bar Ranch.

Address: P.O. Box 2480 K, Wickenburg, Arizona 85358
Telephone: 800/684-7583, 520/684-7593; fax: 520/684-4497
Email: kelbar@w3az.net
Internet: www.kayelbar.com
Airport: Phoenix Sky Harbor, 60 miles; private planes use Wickenburg Airport with a 5,000-foot airstrip, five miles
Location: 60 miles northwest of Phoenix off Route 89, five miles north of Wickenburg
Memberships: The Dude Ranchers' Association, Arizona Dude Ranch Association
Awards: National Register of Historic Places
Medical: Wickenburg Community Hospital, five minutes away
Guest Capacity: 24
Accommodations: The historic main lodge consists of eight rooms with private baths, a spacious living room with 13-foot ceilings, lots of books, and a big stone fireplace. There is also Homestead House, a two-bedroom, two-bath cottage with living room and fireplace, and a separate *casita* with two bedrooms, Casa Grande with sitting area and fireplace, and Casa Monterey with twin beds. Both have private baths and walk-in showers.
Rates: • $$–$$$ American Plan. Children's and special group rates available. Two-day minimum stay mid-October until mid-February. Four-day minimum stay mid-February to first of May and all holidays.
Credit Cards: VISA, MasterCard. Personal checks preferred.
Season: Mid-October to May 1

Activities: Very flexible riding program individualized to guests' abilities and interests. The Sonoran Desert terrain, with sandy washes, canyons, or rocky ridges, offers riding variety and beauty. There are magnificent saguaro cactus and views to the distant mountain ranges. Two rides daily, except Sundays and holidays with morning rides only. All-day rides available and riding instruction included. The hiking trail climbs to a lookout with panoramic views and beautiful sunsets. The hot tub and heated swimming pool get lots of use. Some guests enjoy hiking, and birdwatching and may get to see roadrunners, deer, javelina, coyotes, and big jackrabbits. Horseshoes, table tennis, and other outdoor games. Tennis and golf at two fine golf courses available in Wickenburg.
Children's Programs: Children join parents for ranch activities. Children must be age seven in order to ride.
Dining: Announced by the bell and served in the beautiful mission-like dining room. Wonderful home-cooked food including mesquite-grilled beef, pork chops, John's famous smoked ham, Southwestern dishes, and a full roasted turkey dinner with all the trimmings. Fresh vegetables, fruit, and dessert specials. Sunday brunch in the desert. Weekly cookouts on the banks of the Hassayampa River. Licensed bar.
Entertainment: Informal program of cowboy singing, poetry, and storytelling in front of the crackling lodge fireplace or around a roaring bonfire and under the Arizona stars. Large library.
Summary: Wonderful historic dude ranch with authentic Southwestern charm. On the National Register of Historic Places. Very cozy atmosphere in a lush desert environment. Singles, couples, and families will feel at home. Very casual. Only scheduled activities are meals and riding. Nearby: Desert Caballeros Museum, four hours from the Grand Canyon, two hours from Sedona, and only one hour and 15 minutes from the Phoenix airport. Cowboy poetry gathering in December.

La Tierra Linda Guest Ranch Resort
Tucson, Arizona

La Tierra Linda Guest Ranch Resort is one of Tucson's shining new stars. This family-run ranch was one of Tucson's original dude ranches that has hosted legends such as John Wayne during filming at Old Tucson Studios. Located in the foothills of the Tucson Mountains, this 30-acre ranch is surrounded by desert vegetation, wildflowers, and centuries-old saguaro cacti. Built back in the 1930s, the ranch today is owned by Mark Wolfe, a successful photographer, his wife Francie, and their young son Justin. In 1998, after extensive renovation, including the creation of the rustic Old West Town, the Wolfe family opened their doors to families, couples, weddings, and business groups, and today is proud of their reputation for returning guests. As Francie says, "La Tierra Linda offers a warm friendly atmosphere in a beautiful desert setting. Here we still have visiting wildlife including javelina and bobcats that reflect the true sense of the Arizona Sonoran Desert. Our young son Justin, who thinks of himself as a true cowboy, is a big part of the magic here and when he says come back and see us, he means it." Here you'll step back in time and experience Western hospitality and atmosphere at this family-run ranch resort.

Address: 7501 N. Wade Road, Tucson, Arizona 85743
Telephone: 888/872-6241, 520/744-7700; fax: 520/579-9742
Email: ranch@latierralinda.com
Internet: www.latierralinda.com
Airport: Tucson International
Location: 15 miles northwest of downtown Tucson off Ina Road. Call ranch for directions.
Memberships: Arizona Hotel & Motel Association, MTCVB, SALARA
Awards: AAA 3 Diamond
Medical: Northwest Medical Center, 10 miles
Conference Capacity: 450; 10,500-square-foot outdoor waterfall, patio, and adjoining Ramada area, 1,600-square-foot conference room, 800-square-foot conference room.
Guest Capacity: 50
Accommodations: 14 suites with Southwestern decor, offer one-, two-, three-, and four-bedroom suites, all equipped with king-, queen-, or twin-size beds. Larger suites have spacious living room areas, all have individually controlled heat and air-conditioning, outdoor patios, telephones, cable TV, mini-refrigerators, in-room coffee service, private bathrooms with tub/shower combinations, daily maid service, laundry facilities and room service available.
Rates: • $$$ Full American Plan and Modified American Plan. Includes two two-hour horseback rides per day. Children's rates available. Rates vary depending on season.
Credit Cards: VISA, MasterCard, Discover, American Express, Diner's Club
Season: Year-round
Activities: Early morning and late afternoon horseback rides wind through the Saguaro National Park. Heated swimming pool, hot tub, tennis court, volleyball court, horseshoes, baseball diamond, hiking trails, bird-watching, mountain biking, game room, and exercise room. Five minutes from world-class golf courses.
Children's Programs: Kids are the responsibility of parents. Ages 2–4 may ride with an adult. Trail riding begins at age five. Petting zoo with miniature donkeys, miniature horses, sheep, and goats, outdoor play area, and game room for the kids.
Dining: Ranch House Grill restaurant serves three meals daily, with lunch and dinner open to the public. The Grill offers a variety of Southwestern cuisine. Indoor and outdoor dining with spectacular mountain views. Full-service bar. Voted "Best of the West Dining" by *Tucson Weekly*.
Entertainment: Weekly scheduled barbecues in Old West Town, hayrides with Western music, and seasonal bonfires.
Summary: With a backdrop of the Tucson Mountains and the 24,000-acre Saguaro National Park, La Tierra Linda offers spectacular desert views in a resort setting. La Tierra Linda's dude-ranching heritage provides a special ambiance for families, couples, groups, wedding parties, and corporate retreats, and its Old West Town gives guests a true Old West experience. Nearby: Saguaro National Park, Arizona Sonoran Desert Museum, and Old Tucson Studios.

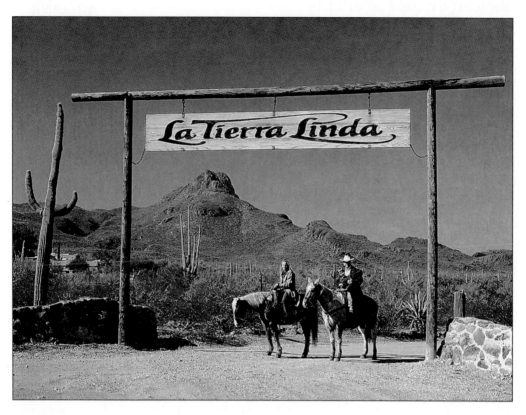

Rancho de los Caballeros
Wickenburg, Arizona

Rancho de los Caballeros is one of the premier resort ranches in North America and is celebrating its 54th season. Set amid 20,000 acres of beautiful desert scenery, the ranch has maintained a long tradition of excellence and continues to attract families, individuals, and groups, who enjoy a host of recreational activities and first-rate personal service and comfort. Los Caballeros is well known for its 18-hole championship golf course, consistently ranked in the top five in Arizona. Many guests come just to play golf, others to play tennis, ride horseback in the open desert, sit by the pool, or just enjoy the relaxing atmosphere. The ranch offers superb conference facilities in the Palo Verde Conference Center, ideal for small and large groups up to 250 people. Rancho de los Caballeros means, "Ranch of the Gentlemen on Horseback." Perhaps what it should really stand for is "excellence": great people, great resort amenities, great golf, and great riding.

Address: 1551 S. Vulture Mine Road, Wickenburg, Arizona 85390
Telephone: 800/684-5030, 520/684-5484; fax: 520/684-2267
Email: info@sunc.com
Internet: www.SunC.com
Airport: Phoenix Sky Harbor; private planes at Wickenburg Municipal Airport on a 5,000-foot paved runway, fuel available. Call ranch for details.
Location: Four miles southwest of Wickenburg, 56 miles northwest of Phoenix on Highway 60
Memberships: Arizona Dude Ranch Association
Medical: Wickenburg Community Hospital, four miles
Conference Capacity: 150; excellent 4,500-square-foot conference center, data ports available. Ask for conference brochure.
Guest Capacity: 150; 79 *casitas*
Accommodations: A variety of *casitas* with sun patios and separate entrances are available. Each room is tastefully decorated in Southwestern style, including handcrafted furnishings from Mexico and Santa Fe. TVs and telephones with data ports and voice mail in all rooms.
Rates: • $$$–$$$$$ American Plan. Children's

(under age five free) and group rates. Golf and riding packages available. Rates vary depending on season and type of accommodations.
Credit Cards: None. Personal checks accepted.
Season: October through May
Activities: The ranch offers scenic beginner, intermediate, and loping rides. Riding instruction available. Breakfast, lunch, and dinner cookout rides. Ask about the naturalist-led riding. Four tennis courts with resident tennis pro, heated swimming pool, and guided nature walks with information on flora and fauna. Trap and skeet shooting extra; guns and instruction provided. Hot-air ballooning on-site, mountain biking, and Jeep tours. Los Caballeros Golf Club's 18-hole course includes a head pro and several assistants, driving range, pro shop, locker rooms, golf carts, and rental equipment. Ask about the Turner Golf School. Food and beverages available at club grill. In-room massage available.
Children's Programs: Excellent morning and evening programs for kids ages 5–12. Riding, swimming, and hiking during the day, and games, and arts and crafts in the evening. Baby-sitting available for younger children (extra). Thanksgiving, Christmas, and holiday programs are popular.
Dining: Reserved individual tables. Menu features a four-course meal with five daily specials. Breakfast and luncheon buffets, as well as lunch at the golf club. Full-service bar. Children may eat together or with their parents.
Entertainment: Cookouts twice a week, card and table games, billiards, line dancing, and movies. Nature walks, putting tournaments, and gymkhanas. Occasional cowboy poetry, sing-alongs, and musical entertainment Wednesday, Friday, and Saturday evenings. Stargazing with local astronomer.
Summary: One of Kilgore's "Best of the Best"–Resort Ranch. This historic guest ranch and golf club offers championship 18-hole golf at one of the top five courses in Arizona. Golf and tennis pros on staff. Daily horseback riding. Excellent conference facilities. Nearby: Wickenburg

Tanque Verde Ranch
Tucson, Arizona

The Tanque Verde Ranch is a historic ranch dating to 1868 when the Carrillo family settled here and ran cattle up into the Rincón Mountains east of Tucson. Today, situated on 640 acres and bordered by the Coronado National Forest and the Saguaro National Park, the ranch now operates its cattle operation from its Bellota Ranch headquarters and continues to work 700 head of cattle on a 60,000-acre Forest Service lease. Tanque Verde has evolved into one of the premier ranch/resorts in the country, welcoming guests from around the world to a diverse program of riding, hiking, tennis, or just relaxing within a Sonoran-style architectural setting. Bob and Rita Cote and their dedicated staff provide guests with true Western hospitality every day of the year! The ranch continues to attract prestigious travel writers from around the world and is seen regularly in countless magazines and newspapers. Guests explore the fascinating Sonoran Desert through a comprehensive naturalist adventure program that is offered daily. A beautiful new nature museum highlights the flora and fauna of the Sonoran Desert, complete with live-animal exhibits. The Cote family's philosophy is simple: provide the very best in friendly, professional service in an exciting and stimulating environment for the entire family. Tanque Verde Ranch is truly an oasis in the desert and without question one of the country's finest resort ranches.

Address: 14301 E. Speedway, Dept. K, Tucson, Arizona 85748
Telephone: 800/234-DUDE (3833), 520/296-6275; fax: 520/721-9426
Email: dude@tvgr.com
Internet: www.tvgr.com
Airport: Tucson, 35 minutes
Location: 15 miles east of Tucson at the end of East Speedway. In the foothills of the Rincón Mountains.
Memberships: Arizona Dude Ranch Association
Awards: Mobil 4 Star
Medical: Tucson Medical Center, 15 miles
Conference Capacity: 150; conference facility, state-of-the-art multimedia, T-1 lines and data ports, 4,800 square feet of meeting space. Conference director on-site. Sales packets available.

Guest Capacity: 225
Accommodations: 74 *casita*-style rooms, from historic Ramada rooms to spacious deluxe suites with whirlpool tubs and Southwestern decor. Most with adobe-style fireplaces, private patios, and large picture windows. All with telephones and data ports. Laundry facilities available.
Rates: • $$$$-plus American Plan. Rates vary with season. All activities/facilities are included in room rates.
Credit Cards: VISA, MasterCard, Discover, American Express
Season: Year-round; including all holidays.
Activities: Over 130 horses with daily guided rides. Adults may ride with children in the children's program. Daily basic and intermediate horsemanship lessons. Slow scenic rides and some loping for the advanced rider. Breakfast, all-day, and picnic rides. Fun-khanas in winter season. All riding and instruction included. Overnight pack trips during summer months (extra). Five professional tennis courts (one Omni court), outdoor heated pool, indoor health spa with pool, saunas, whirlpool, and exercise room. Fishing, hiking, mountain biking, and bird walks. Over 175 species of birds seen at ranch. Golf at nearby courses.
Children's Programs: One of the most comprehensive, all-day and evening, counselor-supervised, children's programs for Buckaroos ages 4–6, and Wranglers ages 7–11. Special summer camp sessions.
Dining: The Doghouse Saloon for happy hour. Family-style seating in beautiful Southwestern dining room. Continental and American cuisine. Enormous lunch salad bar and 20-foot-long pastry and dessert table. Weekly barbecue cookouts in Cottonwood Grove. Wine and beer available at all meals (extra).
Entertainment: Nightly lectures by historians/naturalists, stargazing with astronomer, country-Western dancing, bingo night.
Summary: Kilgore's "Best of the Best." Internationally renowned ranch resort famous for its extensive programs including its superb children's program. One of the largest riding stables. Lots of Southwestern historical charm. Naturalists and nature museum. Ask about its Bellota Cattle and Guest Ranch.

White Stallion Ranch
Tucson, Arizona

Just 17 miles from downtown Tucson, surrounded by rugged desert mountains, is White Stallion Ranch. In the 1960s, the True family bought this quiet, peaceful, 3,000-acre ranch, which looks out to Safford and Panther Peaks and the Tucson Mountain Range. "The only sounds you'll hear are those of the desert and the ranch," says Russell True, who along with his brother Michael and their families, oversee this lovely high-desert ranch. Guests are impressed with the warmth and beauty of the land and the Trues' famous hospitality. The ranch features a herd of purebred Texas longhorn cattle and a rodeo each week with team roping, steer-wrestling, and barrel racing. Many scenes from the television series *High Chaparral* were filmed here.

Address: 9251 W. Twin Peaks Road, Dept. K, Tucson, Arizona 85743
Telephone: 888/WSRANCH (888/977-2624), 520/297-0252; fax: 520/744-2786
Email: info@wsranch.com
Internet: www.wsranch.com
Airport: Tucson
Location: 17 miles northwest of Tucson
Memberships: The Dude Ranchers' Association, Arizona Dude Ranch Association
Awards: Mobil 3 Star
Medical: Northwest Hospital, 11 miles
Conference Capacity: 30–75; 1,200 square feet
Guest Capacity: 50–75
Accommodations: White Spanish-style bungalows with adobe exteriors hold single rooms, suites, and deluxe suites and cabins. Each has a private bath, air-conditioning, and private patio with views through the cactus garden to the mountains and Saguaro National Park. There are no TVs or telephones. Ten deluxe suites have high ceilings with exposed beams, antique Mexican furniture, whirlpool tubs, and fireplaces. Laundry facilities. Daily maid service. Guest business center with telephone, computer, and Internet access.
Rates: • $$–$$$ American Plan. Nightly, off-season, weekly, and children's rates available.
Credit Cards: None. Personal or traveler's checks accepted.
Season: September through May; open

Thanksgiving, Christmas, and Easter.
Activities: Russell takes great pride in matching horses with riders. Children and adults may, if they wish, brush and saddle their own horses. Except on Sundays, there are four rides a day, usually two fast and two slow, and all-day rides into Saguaro National Park. If you think you're a fast rider, the ranch has a riding test for you. Breakfast and mountain rides. Team-cattle penning in arena is extremely popular with guests. Guided nature walks with trained naturalists along foothills of the Tucson Mountain Range, guided hiking program. Swimming in key-shaped heated pool, shuffleboard, volleyball, basketball, two professional tennis courts, and indoor redwood hot tub. Golf nearby.
Children's Programs: Children of all ages are very much a part of the ranch programs and participate fully; they'll enjoy all the animals in the petting zoo. Children are parents' responsibility. Children under age five ride with parents. Kids may eat together if they wish.
Dining: Breakfast menu-style, lunch buffet, dinner family-style or buffet. Wednesday hayrides, cookouts, and White Stallion's famous outdoor Native American oven dinner cooked in the decades-old style. Lunch and dinner menus posted daily. Vegetarian and special diets provided with advance notice. Happy hour with hors d'oeuvres precedes dinner, when Russell announces the ride schedule. No smoking in dining room.
Entertainment: Bonfire with cowboy singer, country line dancing and lessons, stargazing, and wonderful naturalist talks. Ask about astronomy and speaker programs.
Summary: The Trues' brand of hospitality and warmth is second to none! Excellent staff, immaculate grounds, delicious food, wonderful, private desert setting, and great value make White Stallion tops! Lovely Spanish-style ranch close to Tucson but isolated and private. Part of 100,000-acre game preserve adjacent to Saguaro National Park. Singles and families welcome.

Scott Valley Resort and Guest Ranch
Mountain Home, Arkansas

THE DUDE RANCHERS'
ASSOCIATION

In the serenity of the Ozarks, amid 625 acres of beautiful meadows, woodlands, rocky cliffs, and spring-fed streams, is the Coopers' Scott Valley Resort and Guest Ranch, which began operation in 1953. Kathleen Cooper has shared the joys of her ranch and her down-home hospitality with people from around the country since 1985. Rated as one of the most popular vacation spots in the Ozarks, Scott Valley offers a variety of activities for its guests, including riding for beginning, intermediate, and experienced riders. Anglers will enjoy world-class trout fishing on the famous White and Northfork Rivers. You'll feel the warm and friendly hospitality that is the secret of Kathleen's and son Tobin's success. Children, too, will experience all the treasures of the great outdoors.

Address: Box 1447 K, Mountain Home, Arkansas 72654
Telephone: 888/855-7747 (reservations), 870/425-5136; fax: 870/424-5800
Email: svr@centurytel.net
Internet: www.scottvalley.com
Airport: Springfield, Little Rock, Memphis, Mountain Home (via St. Louis, Missouri, or Dallas, Texas)
Location: Six miles south of Mountain Home off Highway 5, 156 miles north of Little Rock, 98 miles south of Springfield, Missouri
Memberships: The Dude Ranchers' Association
Awards: *Family Circle* magazine "Family Resort of the Year" for three consecutive years
Medical: Baxter County Regional Hospital, six miles
Conference Capacity: 65; up to 90 for family reunions
Guest Capacity: 65
Accommodations: Each of the 28 one- or two-bedroom, motel-type guest rooms has a full bathroom with tub and shower, air-conditioning, electric heat, and daily maid service. Ask about the five-bedroom, four-bath Hilltop Hideaway with a 360-degree view and its own pool.
Rates: • $$–$$$$ American Plan. Children under age two free. Prefer one-week stay. Weekly family, group, senior, law enforcement, fire fighter, and military rates. Rates include horseback riding

(canoes and boats on stays of three nights or more).
Credit Cards: VISA, MasterCard. Traveler's checks or personal checks accepted.
Season: March through November, including Thanksgiving and Easter. Hilltop Hideaway year-round.
Activities: Scheduled horseback rides. Experienced riders should inquire about the spring and fall rides. The Coopers specialize in the smooth-gaited Missouri fox-trotters. Hiking, swimming in pool or nearby lakes and streams. Mountain biking, table tennis, badminton, tennis, volleyball, and shuffleboard. Ten minutes from world-class fishing on the White and Northfork Rivers, as well as boating and canoeing. Jet-skiing, sailing, and scuba diving available at nearby Lake Norfork at an extra charge. Two 18-hole golf courses nearby.
Children's Programs: Fully equipped playground and petting zoo with lots of animals. Ranch encourages families to interact with their children. Pony rides for children under age seven. Baby-sitting available.
Dining: Down-home, good cooking including biscuits and gravy, ham, great Mexican fare, cornbread, and chicken and dumplings. Meals for lighter appetites too. Weekly dinner cruise on Lake Norfolk during summer season.
Entertainment: Some type of scheduled activity every evening during summer months. Be sure to ask Kathleen about the famous Western entertainment in Branson, Missouri, and Mountain View, Arkansas.
Summary: A haven for families to spend time together in a low-key, relaxing atmosphere. Gaited horses and Blue Ribbon trout fishing nearby. Spring and fall months best for adults, singles, couples, and experienced riders. Ask about the Hilltop Hideaway. Arkansas is one of the best values you can find for your vacation dollar and is one of the United States' great hidden treasures. Seen on *Live with Regis & Kathie Lee* and featured in *Western Horseman* magazine.

Alisal Guest Ranch
Solvang, California

The Alisal is one of the great resort ranches in North America. Opened in 1946, this 10,000-acre paradise really has it all: 50 miles of riding trails, two 18-hole championship golf courses, a private 96-acre lake, and seven tennis courts. In addition to first-class recreational amenities and lodging facilities, the ranch also has 2,000 head of cattle run separately from the guest operations. What also sets the Alisal apart is the level of personal service. General manager David Lautensack continues to maintain a terrific spirit of hospitality and personally gets out daily with his staff to meet and get to know his guests, in the true spirit of great ranching. The Alisal—a tradition of excellence.

Address: 1054 Alisal Road, Solvang, California 93463
Telephone: 800/425-4725 (reservations), 805/688-6411; fax: 805/688-2510
Email: info@alisal.com
Internet: www.alisal.com
Airport: Los Angeles, 2.5 hours; Santa Barbara with commercial jet service, 35 miles; Santa Ynez for private planes, five miles
Location: 40 miles northwest of Santa Barbara
Awards: *Hideaway Report* 1996, 1999; *Family Circle* magazine "Resort of the Year"
Medical: Santa Ynez Hospital, three miles
Conference Capacity: 150; 6,000 square feet of meeting space; full telecommunication services available
Guest Capacity: Up to 225
Accommodations: 73 cottages and garden rooms scattered around the grounds, which feature century-old sycamores, range from one-room studios to executive suites with nightly turndown service. All are modern with high ceilings, wood-burning fireplaces, and refrigerators. No TVs or telephones in the rooms, but TVs and pay phones are available in public areas. Laundry facility available.
Rates: • $$$–$$$$ Modified American Plan; includes breakfast and dinner. A wide variety of seasonal activity packages is available. Ask about the Roundup Vacation Package. Two-night minimum stay.
Credit Cards: VISA, MasterCard, American Express

Season: Year-round; including all holidays.
Activities: Two-hour trail rides go out twice each day, separated into walking, trotting, or loping over 50 miles of trails. Private rides and riding instruction available. Semiweekly breakfast rides, weekly guest rodeo (summer). Lake activities on 96-acre private Alisal Lake include fishing, boating, and sailing. The Ranch Golf Course (designed by Bill Bell), is a par-72 California classic that winds past stately oak, sycamore, and eucalyptus trees. The par-72 River Course follows the meandering of the Santa Ynez River and provides a panoramic view of the foothills. Seven tennis courts. Pro shops for both tennis and golf with professional instruction. Heated pool and whirlpool. Volleyball, shuffleboard, croquet, and horseshoes, and game room with table tennis and billiards.
Children's Programs: Summer: Lil' Wranglers Club with all-day supervised children's programs. Daily arts and crafts program. Extensive summertime and holiday programs and a year-round petting zoo. Evenings are busy with bingo, storytelling, and talent shows. Special events include the Giant Easter Bunny and egg hunt at Easter, the Fourth of July pageant, and Santa's visit with caroling and gifts at Christmas.
Dining: Dinner attire required. Served in the Ranch Room, the menu varies daily and features contemporary regional cuisine created by acclaimed chefs. Excellent wine selection. Summer lunches served poolside. Winter: lunches served in the main dining room or at the golf clubhouses.
Entertainment: The Southwestern-decorated Oak Room, with a large stone fireplace and cathedral ceiling, provides nightly dancing, cocktails, and relaxation with live music. The large, adults-only library is for quiet reading and email access. Large-screen TVs available in public areas.
Summary: Kilgore's "Best of the Best"–Resort Ranch. Excellent summer children's program, with fabulous petting zoo, horseback riding, shopping, and a renowned outdoor theater. Ideal for families. Video and CD-ROM available upon request.

Circle Bar B Guest Ranch
Goleta, California

About 20 miles north of Santa Barbara, hidden in Refugio Canyon in the foothills of the Santa Ynez Mountains, is the Brown family's Circle Bar B Guest Ranch. Cooled by ocean breezes from Refugio State Beach, three miles away, this nearly 1,000-acre ranch has played host to guests since 1939. Families, couples, and small corporate/business groups come for the friendly, casual atmosphere, and proximity to the ocean, Santa Barbara, and Los Angeles. The scenic trail rides head out the back gate and up through Indian Canyon where they cross streams, pass by seasonal waterfalls, and meander through the lush ferns, sycamore trees, and vegetation at the bottom of the canyon. After a short rest at Sweetwater, the trail climbs out of the canyon and over a ridge where guests can take in magnificent views of the Santa Ynez coastal mountains, the Pacific Ocean, and Santa Barbara's Channel Islands. The ranch borders former President Ronald Reagan's ranch, and has hosted guests from as far away as Australia, Europe, and Asia. At the Circle Bar B you'll find a relaxed and friendly atmosphere and wonderful accommodations.

Address: 1800 Refugio Canyon Road, Dept. K, Goleta, California 93117
Telephone: 805/968-1113; fax: 805/571-3618
Email: circleb@silcom.com
Internet: www.circlebarb.com
Airport: Santa Barbara Airport in Goleta; Los Angeles International
Location: 22 miles north of Santa Barbara at the Refugio State Beach Exit off Highway 101; 110 miles northwest of Los Angeles
Medical: Goleta Hospital, 18 miles
Conference Capacity: 40, excellent boardroom and full Internet access
Guest Capacity: 45
Accommodations: Guests are housed in eight delightful, private, beautifully appointed and decorated cabins. Each has a fireplace, porch, and comforters; some have small sleeping lofts. There are also five spacious rooms up the hill from the main lodge with king-size beds, private baths, wet bars, sitting areas, and one long, covered, connecting porch. Ask about the luxurious "Honeymoon Suite."

Rates: • $$–$$$ American Plan. Children's rates available. Riding extra. Call for theater rates. Two-night minimum on weekends. Three-night minimum on holiday weekends.
Credit Cards: VISA, MasterCard. Personal or traveler's checks accepted.
Season: Year-round; closed Christmas day.
Activities: Trail rides take you over the 1,000 acres surrounding the ranch, offering views of the ocean as well as the Channel Islands. Mountain horseback trail rides are a minimum 1.5 hours, with 2.5-hour rides, and half-day picnic rides offered as well. Fall, winter, and spring all-day rides on request. Enjoy hiking, ocean fishing, swimming pool, and hot tub. Nearby activities include golf and wine tasting in the Santa Ynez Valley.
Children's Programs: Children are welcome, have a great time, and make their own fun. Fritz, the miniature horse, and Daisy, the sheep, are big hits with the kids.
Dining: Hearty ranch cooking served buffet-style. Tri-tip beef barbecues, chicken, fish, and Mexican buffets. Special diets catered to with advance notice. Incredible avocados. Wine and beer served.
Entertainment: Dinner Theater (open to the public) on Friday and Saturday nights, April through November. Ask about the game room.
Summary: A great family-owned and operated year-round guest ranch with horseback riding to high California scenic bluffs overlooking the Pacific Ocean. Only two hours from Los Angeles. The ranch is very accommodating to families, children, and couples. Excellent for groups, corporate retreats, and family reunions. Beautifully appointed accommodations, ranch-style home cooking, and a family atmosphere that's informal, friendly, and sincere. Ask about the Dinner Theater and the incredible avocados. Nearby: Santa Barbara and the Santa Ynez wineries.

Coffee Creek Ranch
Trinity Center, California

THE DUDE RANCHERS'
ASSOCIATION

In the mid-1970s, Ruth and Mark Hartman sold their house in the San Francisco Bay area and bought this riverside ranch in northern California. Today, daughter Alicia and her husband Shane, carry on the ranch traditions in this beautiful part of Northern California. Coffee Creek Ranch, named after the creek that flows through the property, covers 127 acres at the base of the majestic Trinity Alps Wilderness Area. At 3,100 feet, Coffee Creek is in a river canyon, surrounded by a mountain wilderness area. The ranch is not far from Trinity Lake and 13 miles from the Trinity Center Airport.

Address: HC2 Box 4940 Coffee Creek Road, Trinity Center, California 96091
Telephone: 800/624-4480, 530/266-3343; fax: 530/266-3597
Email: ccranch@tds.net
Internet: www.coffeecreekranch.com
Airport: Redding or Trinity Center (3,000-foot runway), for small planes only
Train: Amtrak to Redding. Contact ranch concerning Greyhound bus.
Location: 278 miles north of San Francisco, 72 miles northwest of Redding, 45 miles north of Weaverville off Highway 3
Memberships: The Dude Ranchers' Association, California Hotel & Motel Association
Medical: Weaverville Hospital, 45 miles
Conference Capacity: 50; conference folder available
Guest Capacity: 50
Awards: AAA 3-Diamonds
Accommodations: All 15 cabins have porches. Most two-bedroom cabins have one or two baths and wood-burning stoves. The one-bedroom, one-bath cabins have potbellied stoves to keep you warm and cozy. All cabins have bathtub/shower combinations. Handicapped-accessible cabin or ranch-house room with front porch is also available. Daily maid service and laundry facilities on premises.
Rates: • $$$ American Plan. Summer horseback riding extra by the ride or weekly. Special rates for spring and fall include riding. Children's, teen, and senior rates available. One-week minimum stay during summer, Saturday to Friday. Two-day minimum stay spring and fall.
Credit Cards: VISA, MasterCard, Discover, American Express. Personal checks, cash, or traveler's checks accepted.
Season: Mid-March to December
Activities: Coffee Creek offers scheduled riding in the summer, including breakfast and twilight rides. Horsemanship clinics in the spring and fall. Picnic, all-day, and overnight rides including pack trips to mountain lakes. Guided hiking; fishing in stocked pond, Coffee Creek, Trinity Lake, and Alpine lakes. Archery, badminton, shuffleboard, volleyball, trapshooting, and rifle range (guns provided). Swimming in heated pool or in Coffee Creek and paddle boats on the pond. Health club with exercise room and river rock hot tub with waterfall.
Children's Program: Excellent youth program for ages 3–17. Specialized activities for various age groups. Wonderful international counselors. Baby-sitting during rides for children under age three. Petting zoo.
Dining: All you can eat, family-style; fresh fruit, vegetables, and family recipes. Barbecues and steak fries. Ask about the "crazy cake." Beer and wine available. BYOB, but it must be kept in the cabins.
Entertainment: Horse-drawn hayrides, bonfires, bingo, talent shows, gymkhanas, live music several times a week by the Coffee Creek band (The Rattlesnakes), square and line dancing. Rec room, pool table, table tennis, horseshoes, and basketball. Satellite TV.
Summary: One of Northern California's most famous guest ranches. Family-owned and operated with strong emphasis on families. Excellent youth program. Serious riders should consider early summer and fall. June through September (with fall colors) have the best weather and lots of wildflowers. National Scenic Byway. You may bring your own horse. Fly-fishing instruction available. Conference room seats 50. Spanish, Dutch, German spoken. Handicapped facilities. Nearby: Trinity Center Western Museum, historical town of Weaverville, and Chinese "Joss House" temple.

Highland Ranch
Philo, California

Highland Ranch is located in the beautiful wine and redwood country of northern California. Secluded and very private, the ranch sits above the Anderson Valley, known for fine wines and friendly vineyards. Highland Ranch is owned by George Gaines, who is, without question, one of the warmest and most gracious hosts I know. Following a successful international legal and business career, he bought Highland Ranch in the late 1980s and transformed it into a pastoral paradise. Here you'll find deer and other local wildlife, tall redwoods, fruit trees, wildflowers, and meadows divided by split-rail fences. The charming old yellow-and-white ranch house is the central gathering place, where guests relax by a crackling fire and savor subtle aromas from the kitchen. With its proximity to San Francisco, the Mendocino Coast, and some of California's finest wineries and towering redwoods, Highland Ranch is a slice of heaven and a piece of paradise.

Address: P.O. Box 150 K, Philo, California 95466
Telephone: 707/895-3600; fax: 707/895-3702
Email: george@highlandranch.com
Internet: www.highlandranch.com
Airport: San Francisco, Oakland, and Santa Rosa for commercial flights; Ukiah for private jets and small planes; Boonville for small planes only. Helicopter landing at ranch.
Location: Six miles northwest of Philo off Highway 128, 2.5 hours north of San Francisco
Medical: Ukiah Community Hospital, 24 miles
Conference Capacity: 12–20; 250-square-foot conference room
Guest Capacity: 22
Accommodations: Individual cabins and duplexes with various sleeping arrangements. Most have fireplaces and sitting areas; all have telephones, private baths, and electric blankets. Covered porches with rocking chairs.
Rates: • $$$$ American Plan. Two-day minimum stay; three-day minimum stay during major holidays.
Credit Cards: VISA, MasterCard, American Express. Personal and traveler's checks accepted.
Season: Year-round
Activities: Do as much or as little as you wish, from wine tasting or bird-watching to reading your favorite book. Very individualized program. If you are looking for set schedules and planned activities, this is not the place for you. Wonderful riding on over 100 miles of trails through the towering redwoods or open meadows, along the ridges overlooking the Anderson Valley, or along the Navarro River. Rides are tailored to experience levels and English saddles are available. Tennis on two surfaced courts, swimming in pool or three-acre pond, fishing, hiking, clay-pigeon shooting, or simply relaxing in four hammocks just outside the ranch house.
Children's Programs: Children are welcome, especially with family reunions, but there are no formal programs.
Dining: Exceptional food, featuring local produce and fresh fish, is served family-style in the charming Old World dining room. Fabulous country breakfasts and lunches. Each evening George pours complimentary cocktails and Anderson Valley and international wines with dinner. Special menus upon request. The food is outstanding and so is the ambiance.
Entertainment: Many enjoy relaxing in hammock heaven while reading their favorite book. Others enjoy the extensive music collection and library. Some tune into the ranch's satellite TV. Great local Anderson Valley entertainment available.
Summary: One of the finest hosts I've met in all my travels! A very, very special paradise! Wonderful, small, very private ranch in Northern California. Superb food, fine wine, great conversation, and hospitality second to none. Excellent for individuals, couples, honeymoons, family gatherings, reunions, and small corporate groups. French and Italian spoken. Video available. Well-behaved dogs are welcome. Nearby: Anderson Valley wineries and Mendocino Coast. Local vineyards include Lazy Creek, Pepperwood Springs, Roederer, Husch, Navarro, Greenwood Ridge, and Pacific Echo. Be sure to stop by the Apple Farm for fresh apple cider.

Hunewill Circle H Ranch
Bridgeport, California

THE DUDE RANCHERS'
ASSOCIATION

On the northeast side of Yosemite National Park, one of California's greats, the Hunewill Ranch is an old-time family ranch that has been attracting guests since 1930. The ranch is situated in the lovely, green, wide-open, cattle-ranching, Bridgeport Valley, highlighted by the spectacular Sawtooth Ridge. It was founded by the great-great-grandparents of the present owners, the Hunewill family. The ranch runs about 2,000 head of cattle over 5,000 acres. While horseback riding is the main activity, hikers will find miles of trails, and anglers can enjoy nearby streams, lakes, and the awesome 4.5-acre, spring-fed pond filled with rainbow trout. The Hunewills say, "We love this ranch and enjoy sharing it with others." The ranch offers many wonderful things including a beautiful setting, great hosts, and a relaxed Western atmosphere.

Address: P.O. Box 368 K, Bridgeport, California 93517 (summer); 200 Hunewill Lane, Wellington, Nevada 89444 (winter)
Telephone: 760/932-7710 (summer), 775/465-2201 (winter)
Email: hunewillranch@tele-net.net
Internet: www.hunewillranch.com
Airport: Reno International, Bridgeport for small private airplanes
Location: 115 miles south of Reno, Nevada on Highway 395, 50 miles north of Mammoth, California, five miles southwest of Bridgeport on Twin Lakes Road
Memberships: The Dude Ranchers' Association
Medical: Mono Medical Clinic, five miles
Guest Capacity: 45
Accommodations: Bridgeport was one of the early gold-mining areas, so the ranch buildings have a Victorian flavor. There are 12 cottages (24 rooms), each with private bath and porch, as well as the cozy Ranch House Suite. Guests dine in the ranch house, a lovely two-story Victorian, built in 1880 and surrounded by tall poplars. Laundry facilities available.
Rates: • $$ American Plan. Rates vary depending on accommodation and month. Children's rates. One-week minimum stay encouraged. Saturday to Saturday. Ask about three- and five-day packages.

Credit Cards: None. Personal and traveler's checks accepted.
Season: May to early October
Activities: Riding is the main attraction. Miles of open meadowland give riders the opportunity to really learn how to ride. Three rides go out mornings and afternoons for beginning, intermediate, and advanced riders. Well-cared for horses and great wranglers take guests on exhilarating lopes, splash rides, cattle moves, and to places like Eagle Peak, Buckeye Canyon, or Tamarack Lake. Beginners (both children and adults) appreciate special rides designed to build confidence and skills. Riding helmets provided for those who wish. Breakfast and lunch rides. Beautiful evening walks, volleyball, and horseshoes. Catch-and-release fly-fishing in spring-fed 4.5-acre lake (additional charge, by reservation only, bring your own gear).
Children's Programs: A kid's paradise! Though children are their parents' responsibility, they are included in all ranch activities. During adult riding times, youngsters under age six are watched over by a Buckaroo Counselor and may be led on a gentle horse. Kids age six and older have great fun riding out with wranglers on horses suited to their ability.
Dining: Ranch-style—everyone eats together. Two dinner barbecues and a breakfast ride each week. Ask about Hunewill's famous mountain-spring well water. BYOB.
Entertainment: Square dancing, talent night, bingo, roping practice, hayride, campfire, sing-alongs, marshmallow roasts, and a gymkhana.
Summary: Ranching since 1861 and accommodating guests since 1931, this is one of California's most renowned ranches. Wide-open country surrounded by spectacular mountains. Riding is the main attraction. Ask about the colt gentling. Buckeye Canyon cattle roundup. Cattle work weeks. Bridgeport rodeo in July. Fall color ride and five-day November cattle drive. Massage available. Nearby: Ghost town of Bodie and Buckeye Hot Springs.

Rankin Ranch
Caliente, California

The Rankin Ranch is one of California's old ranching traditions. It is here in a secluded valley in southern California that Bill and Glenda, along with Bill's mother, ranch matriarch Helen Rankin, share their love for people and the West. The Rankin family has been in the cattle business since 1863. On 30,000 acres in northern Kern County, things are pretty much as they always have been—slow and easy is the pace, warm and friendly are the folks. Over the years lots of people have driven up over the winding, slow-going road and down into this beautiful grassy valley to spend time at the ranch. Those who return yearly have a real appreciation for country living and are able to leave their businesses and professions behind. Here it's quality family time.

Address: P.O. Box 36 K, Caliente, California 93518
Telephone: 661/867-2511; fax: 661/867-0105
Internet: www.rankinranch.com
Airport: Bakersfield, free transportation available with one-week stay
Location: 42 miles northeast of Bakersfield off Highway 58 via Caliente-Bodfish Road
Memberships: National Cattlemen's and Cattlewomen's Associations, California Historical Society
Awards: California 100 Year Club
Medical: Lake Isabella Hospital, 25 miles
Conference Capacity: 24; 1,500-square-foot meeting/rec room
Guest Capacity: 40
Accommodations: 14 comfortable, wood-paneled duplex cabins are named after sites on the ranch, like Lightner Flat, Ruby Mine, and Rankin Hill. Each cottage has a bath, carpeting, and picture windows. Ask about the deluxe cabin. Daily maid service provided; cribs available on request.
Rates: • $$–$$$ American Plan. Children's rates. Rates vary depending on time of year. One-night minimum stay policy.
Credit Cards: VISA, MasterCard, Discover, American Express. Personal checks accepted.
Season: Late March through early October
Activities: Daily one-hour morning and afternoon guided horseback trail rides are included. This is scenic mountain country, so most riding is at a walk. In meadow areas, some loping can be done. When there are cattle to be moved in the meadow, guests are invited to help the cowboys. FYI: This is not a weekly activity. Julia Lake and Walker Basin Creek are stocked with rainbow trout (bring your own fishing pole). There's tennis, archery, and hiking. The ranch has a lovely, shaded, heated swimming pool and hot tub. Here guests enjoy swimming, reading, or just plain relaxing. Shuffleboard, table tennis, horseshoes, and volleyball are also available. Petting farm for kids.
Children's Programs: Fully supervised seasonal children's programs 9 A.M.–3:30 P.M. and 5:30–7 P.M. Excellent crafts program, talent shows, swim meets, picnics, and games. Ask about the kids' favorite afternoon-picnic Indian hike and bottle-feeding the baby calves. Baby-sitting available with advance notice.
Dining: Amid Rankin Ranch cowboy photos, guests enjoy three hearty ranch-style meals in the Garden Room. Breakfast is served from 7:30–9 A.M. BYOB for adult patio party at 5:30 P.M. daily featuring the Rankin Ranch's famous guacamole dip and chips. Vegetarians accommodated. One fun evening includes a hay-wagon ride, meadow barbecue, and horseshoe tournament. Ask about the Rankin Ranch Family Cookbook.
Entertainment: Something is planned each evening: square dancing, pool tournaments, hayrides, talent show, and indoor horse races. Rec room for all ages.
Summary: One of California's most famous cattle-ranching families running an old-time, working cattle ranch. Enjoy wonderful easygoing Western hospitality and kindness. Lots of space, peace, and quiet. Excellent for celebrating special birthdays, anniversaries, and family reunions. Featured in *Better Homes and Gardens* and *Sunset* magazine. Spanish spoken. Nearby: Gold rush town of Havilah, white-water rafting on the Kern River, famous Tehachapi Loop, and Morning Cloak Botanical Gardens.

Aspen Canyon Ranch
Parshall, Colorado

Built in 1987, the ranch is bordered on three sides by Forest Service lands and overlooks the Williams Fork River. Owned and operated by Steve and Debbie Roderick, along with their four children, it is a base camp for outdoor adventure. A wonderful family spirit prevails here, offering those with and without children a place to ride, hike, fish, and relax. At Aspen Canyon Ranch the schedule is flexible, personal, and tailored to its guests. And that's just the way it is!

Address: 13206 County Road 3, Parshall, Colorado 80468
Telephone: 800/321-1357, 970/725-3600; fax: 970/725-0044
Email: acr@rkymtnhi.com
Internet: www.aspencanyon.com
Airport: Denver; private aircraft to Kremmling
Train: Amtrak to Granby
Location: 25 miles north of Silverthorne, 90 miles west of Denver. Ranch will send you a detailed map.
Memberships: Colorado Dude and Guest Ranch Association, Colorado Guides and Outfitters
Medical: Kremmling Hospital, 26 miles
Conference Capacity: 40
Guest Capacity: 40
Accommodations: Guests stay in suites and fourplex log cabins named Deer Lodge, Elk Lodge, and Trout Lodge, each on the banks of the Williams Fork River. All have comfortable accommodations, natural-gas fireplaces, quilts, carpeting, refrigerators, coffeemakers, porches, and old-fashioned swings. You'll find a large jar of freshly baked cookies in your room each day. Ask about the three-bedroom Cliff House overlooking the Williams Fork River. The main lodge, with a wonderful porch, houses the dining and living rooms and two cozy fireplaces. Two riverside hot tubs and decks.
Rates: • $$$ American Plan. Children's, off-season, group, and winter rates available. Children under age three free. Part-time baby-sitting available. Cliff House bed-and-breakfast rates in winter.
Credit Cards: VISA, MasterCard, Discover
Season: Summer: June through early October. Winter: Snowmobiling mid-December to April.

Activities: Guests enjoy casting a line into the Williams Fork River for brook, brown, and rainbow trout. Three stocked ponds. Fishing gear and lessons included. Guides available on request. Breakfast and dinner rides. Scheduled easygoing mountain trail riding program. As Steve says, "We are flexible and try to meet our guests' expectations and abilities." Hiking (ask about the Lake Evelyn picnic hike), and half-day and all-day riding. Mountain bikes available. Golf and ballooning 30 miles away. Ranch gymkhana, calf-roping and barrel racing in rodeo arena, and skeet shooting. Rafting on the Colorado, Blue, Arkansas, and Clear Creek Rivers is available. Winter: ask about snowmobile program.
Children's Programs: Children's program for kids ages 3–12 while parents are riding, hiking, fishing, or rafting. Petting zoo and swimming hole.
Dining: Home-style ranch cooking. Everything is homemade! Special diets catered to. BYOB.
Entertainment: Cowboy music, sing-alongs, line and Western dancing, seasonal rodeos in town, and guest and staff gymkhanas.
Summary: Small, very friendly guest ranch for families who appreciate a wonderful family environment, river setting, and children's program. Terrific cabin amenities. Nearby: Breckenridge and Vail and Rocky Mountain National Park for day trips.

Aspen Lodge Ranch Resort
Estes Park, Colorado

Aspen Lodge shines bright, both as a ranch resort for families during the summer and as a corporate retreat/meeting conference center in the off-season. Situated at 9,000 feet, at the base of the Twin Sisters Mountains, the lodge and guest cabins look out to Longs Peak. Fresh air, spectacular views, and the surrounding Rocky Mountain National Park make for a tremendous vacation opportunity for everyone. The focal point of Aspen Lodge is the main lodge. Built of lodgepole pine, this magnificent 33,000-square-foot structure is one of the largest log buildings in North America. With access to more than 1,600 acres of wooded mountainside and Alpine lakes and meadows, Aspen Lodge Ranch Resort offers both summer and winter activities in proximity to one of Colorado's most famous national parks.

Address: 6120 Highway 7, Estes Park, Colorado 80517
Telephone: 800/332-6867 (nationwide), 970/586-8133; fax: 970/586-8133
Email: requests@aspenlodge.net
Internet: www.aspenlodge.net
Airport: Denver International
Location: 10 minutes south of Estes Park, 65 miles northwest of Denver off I-25
Awards: AAA 3 Diamond, Official Hotel Guide: Best Dude Ranch 1996, Delta Dream Vacation
Memberships: Colorado Hotel & Motel Association, Meeting Planners International
Medical: Estes Park Hospital, seven miles
Conference Capacity: 150; excellent conference center
Guest Capacity: 150
Accommodations: The lodge features several hospitality suites and 36 guest rooms. Separate from the main lodge are 23 multiroom cabins with porches and great views.
Rates: • $$–$$$ American Plan. Riding packages, children's, conference, and group rates available. Three-, four-, and seven-night packages in summer.
Credit Cards: VISA, MasterCard, Discover, American Express, Diner's Club
Season: Mid-May through October for families; meetings and conferences year-round.
Activities: Summer programs offer something for everyone. Trail-riding from the lodge into adjoining Rocky Mountain National Park. Instructional horse program available for kids and adults. Fishing in lake, hiking, climbing, kayaking, and heated outdoor pool with whirlpool. Two lighted tennis courts. The Sports Center has weights and exercise room, two racquetball courts, game room, and Finnish sauna. Guided fly-fishing, river rafting, and van tours can be arranged. Guided mountain bike tours, volleyball, and horseshoes. Par-70, 18-hole golf course nearby. Estes Park with shops and galleries is 10 minutes away.
Children's Programs: Summer only with extensive (flexible) children's program 9 A.M.–4 P.M. each day (except Sunday) that's fun as well as educational. Some riding (pony rides for kids under age eight), swimming, Indian lore, pioneer lifestyles, moviemaking, and nature exploration. Baby-sitting available.
Dining: Beautiful Longs Peak is framed through the dining room windows. The dining lodge offers "casual continental" to Colorado cuisine served family-style. Western bar and deck.
Entertainment: Hayrides, square dancing, barbecues, movies, two-stepping, weekend entertainers, and nature walks.
Summary: Ranch resort surrounded by the highest peaks of Rocky Mountain National Park. Abundant recreational activities with access to cultural opportunities of Estes Park 10 minutes away. À la carte and weeklong riding packages. Exciting children's program. A 33,000-square-foot lodge that is excellent for business and corporate groups, and family reunions. Year-round conference opportunities. Watch out for the elk! Indoor smoke-free policy.

Bar Lazy J Guest Ranch
Parshall, Colorado

The Bar Lazy J is the oldest continuously operating guest ranch in Colorado, and began entertaining guests in 1912, when it was known as the Buckhorn Lodge. It's situated right on the Colorado River at an elevation of 7,500 feet, about a half-mile from the little town of Parshall. In 1995, Jerry and Cheri Helmicki bought the ranch to share their love of the great outdoors with people from around the world. A unique feature of the ranch is the beautiful Gold Medal trout river, offering anglers the opportunity to fish right outside their cabin doors. Horseback riding and fishing are the featured activities. Each day riders have a choice of walking, trotting, or loping rides. Because of Cheri's extensive teaching background a strong emphasis is placed on children and families. Jerry and Cheri have put together a strong children's program with children's counselors and wranglers. At the Bar Lazy J you can ride, fish, or relax listening to the Colorado River sing its song right outside your cabin.

Address: P.O. Box N-K, Parshall, Colorado 80468
Telephone: 800/396-6279, 970/725-3437; fax: 970/725-0121
Email: barlazyj@rkymtnhi.com
Internet: www.barlazyj.com
Airport: Denver International, 100 miles
Location: 15 miles west of Granby, 100 miles northwest of Denver
Memberships: The Dude Ranchers' Association, Colorado Dude and Guest Ranch Association
Medical: Kremmling Hospital, 13 miles
Guest Capacity: 42
Accommodations: Guests stay in 12 cozy log cabins, named after wildflowers or fishing flies, which accommodate 2–8 people each. Most have wooden floors and enclosed covered porches overlooking the river and all have rockers, bathrooms, and thermostatically controlled heat. Ask about the family ranch house cabin that sleeps up to eight. Nightly turndown service and coffeemakers in each cabin.
Rates: • $$$ American Plan. Children's and off-season rates available. One-week minimum stay in June, July, and August; Sunday to Sunday. Adults only in September with three-day minimum stay.

Credit Cards: VISA, Discover, MasterCard. Personal and traveler's checks preferred.
Season: Late May through September
Activities: Most come here to fish, ride, and relax, and not necessarily in that order! Gold Medal fishing with weekly fishing clinic. Stocked fishing pond for kids and those who don't wish to fish the river. Horseback riding for many levels of experience. Breakfast, half-day, and all-day rides take guests through aspen groves of the Arapahoe National Forest, along the river, and over open fields that are dotted with sage and grazing cattle. Small groups (eight or fewer) go out on each ride. Scenic, moderate, and adventure rides. Other ranch activities include mountain biking, Jeep trips to the high country, hiking, swimming in the outdoor heated swimming pool, relaxing in the large Jacuzzi, shuffleboard, horseshoes, and volleyball. River rafting on the nearby Colorado River.
Children's Programs: Extensive program from 8:30 A.M.–5 P.M. each day. Ranch fun for kids ages 3–12 can be a full day of supervised activities. The program is flexible and optional. Children's playroom where all craft activities take place. Children eat with their parents but can eat with one another if they wish.
Dining: Meals are served family-style in the beautiful log dining room or on the porch overlooking the Colorado River. Traditional family-style meals. A variety of vegetarian meals and traditional Western favorites are always featured. BYOB.
Entertainment: Campfires, hayrides, volleyball, staff shows, and country dancing in the old barn.
Summary: The oldest continuously operating guest ranch in Colorado, located along the Colorado River. Lots of history. Buildings reflect wonderful old-time atmosphere. One of the top children's programs for ages 3–12. Great for families, couples, and singles who enjoy the outdoors without a highly structured program. All cabins overlook the river. Two-thirds of a mile of the Gold Medal trout river, the Colorado River, runs through the ranch property.

C Lazy U Ranch
Granby, Colorado

The C Lazy U Ranch story began back in 1919. In 1988, the Murray family, who had been guests each year since 1959, bought their favorite "home away from home." They have ensured that the C Lazy U experience continues to be one of the best in the business today. C Lazy U mixes rustic luxury with old-fashioned informality. The facilities and food are Western, comfortable, and of superb quality. The ranch continues to receive the prestigious Mobil 4-Star and AAA 5-Diamond ratings. This 8,500-acre ranch has it all, from designer soap to therapeutic massage that will soothe your tired muscles and help you unwind. Very family-oriented, the ranch has different programs for children and adults. Families eat breakfast together, then the kids go off to work—to work at having the most fun they've ever had.

Address: P.O. Box 379, Granby, Colorado 80446
Telephone: 970/887-3344; fax: 970/887-3917
Email: ranch@clazyu.com
Internet: www.clazyu.com
Airport: Denver International
Location: Six miles northwest of Granby off Highway 125, 95 miles west of Denver
Memberships: The Dude Ranchers' Association, Colorado Dude and Guest Ranch Association, Cross-Country Ski Association
Awards: Mobil 4 Star, AAA 5 Diamond, Kilgore Luxury Group
Medical: Granby Medical Center
Conference Capacity: 70; spring, winter, and fall
Guest Capacity: 110
Accommodations: The accommodations are comfortable and casual. Many cabins have fireplaces and vary from single rooms to family suites. Some have Jacuzzi bathtubs and stocked refrigerators. Full amenities include hair dryers, bathrobes, coffeemakers, humidifiers, nightly turndown service, a fruit basket that's replenished daily, and a fire that's reset daily.
Rates: • $$$$$ American Plan. Off-season and group rates available.
Credit Cards: None. Personal checks accepted.
Season: June through September. Mid-December through March. September is adults only.
Activities: Excellent progressive riding program:

fast, medium, and slow rides, depending on rider's ability; instructional rides for every level. Horsemanship and cattle-working clinics overseen by one of the nation's best horsemanship clinicians, Peter Campbell. Morning, afternoon, and weekly picnic rides. Some English riding. Horses are assigned for the week and matched to each rider's ability. Usually 6–8 to a ride. Adults and children ride separately, except on the weekly family ride. Indoor riding arena; two LayKold tennis courts, with tennis pro who gives complimentary instruction; spring-fed heated pool; indoor sauna and whirlpool; full fitness center and massage; trap and skeet range (extra); fishing in stocked pond or Willow Creek (guided fishing can be arranged on the Colorado River); white-water raft trips (30 minutes away, extra); and golf nearby. Winter: See chapter on Cross-Country Skiing.
Children's Programs: Kids and adults do their own thing. Parents and kids love it! Extensive children's program for ages 3–12; teen program 13–17. Children eat together at lunch and dinner, separate from adults. Families with children under age three must bring their own nanny/baby-sitter.
Dining: Guests enjoy happy hour before dinner in the cozy lodge bar, often accompanied by live grand-piano background music. Two entrées each evening. Prime rib, steaks, fresh vegetables, and homemade breads. Poolside cookouts twice weekly. Special meals on request. Full wine service with dinner.
Entertainment: Something is planned each evening. Square dancing, cookouts, campfires, and sing-alongs. Cowboy singer, staff shows, Western band, and weekly "Showdeo"—part show, part rodeo.
Summary: One of the top and most celebrated year-round destination guest ranches. Kilgore Luxury group. Premier children's programs for kids and teens. Superb for families and couples. September is adults-only month. October horsemanship clinic. Riding program both summer and winter.

C Lazy U Ranch, Colorado

Cheley Colorado Camps
Estes Park, Colorado

In 1921, Frank Cheley, the founder of Cheley Colorado Camps, had a dream to help boys and girls grow through the experiences of the great outdoors. He was convinced that youth learned most and best by first-hand experiences—"learning by doing." Today, on 1,600 acres high in the Colorado Rockies, Don and Carole Cheley continue the dream of Grandfather Frank by welcoming campers every summer from a dozen foreign countries and the U.S. Many first, second, third, and fourth generation campers attend each summer to take part in a series of experiences and adventures that greatly enrich their lives. The Cheleys have kept the activities rich and abundant with the kinds of experiences from which kids learn and grow. Here, young spirits and lifelong friendships come alive. As Frank Cheley said, "Great things happen when youth and mountains meet."

Address: P.O. Box 1170, Estes Park, Colorado 80517
Telephone: 800/226-7386, 970/586-4244; fax: 970/586-3020
Email: office@cheley.com
Internet: www.cheley.com
Airport: Denver International, 75 miles
Location: 75 miles northwest of Denver, four miles south of Estes Park off Fishcreek Road
Memberships: The American Camping Association, The Western Association of Independent Camps, Leave No Trace Partner
Awards: 1995 Eleanor Eels Award for Excellence in Programming
Medical: Estes Park Medical Center, four miles
Guest Capacity: 55–64 in each of the eight units-four camps for boys, four camps for girls; all divided by age and grade
Accommodations: Meticulously maintained cabins, dating back to the 1920s, are arranged in camp units and built in the same log and stone style as the lodges located with each unit. Each lodge has a piano, shuffleboard, fireplace, wood floors, and abounds with Old West artifacts. Trail's End ranches for ages 12–17 feature covered wagon-style accommodations that house four campers each. Central bathhouses serve each camp unit. Wooden bunk beds have monogrammed sheets and pillowcases and comfortable mattresses.

Rates: • $$$ for minimum 27-day camp. $$ for five-day family camp. Rates include everything except camp store charges and weekly personal laundry service.
Credit Cards: VISA, MasterCard
Season: Children's summer ranch camp for ages 9–17 mid-June through mid-August; Family Ranch Camp for ages four and older mid-August to September.
Activities: In-depth instruction for all levels of experience. Daily trail rides, three-day horse-packing trips, overnight rides, breakfast or dinner rides, colt training, gymkhanas. Extensive hiking to spectacular lakes and peaks, wilderness backpacking trips, river-rafting trips, rock-climbing, indoor climbing wall, and outdoor "challenge course." Mountain biking and overnight mountain bike trips, campouts in a tepee village, fishing, riflery, archery, arts and crafts, and astronomy. Cookouts, evening campfires, and sing-alongs. Family camp includes many of these activities for kids and parents.
Children's Programs: The summer programs are designed for youth development and wilderness adventures. Fun, friendship, laughter, and personal growth abound for boys and girls ages 9–17. Extensive supervision and instruction by college-age or older counselors and leaders for all activities. The Family Ranch Camp provides a special bonding and fun-filled time for parents and children.
Dining: Family-style dining with three hot and hearty meals a day. Manners are stressed, as is friendly conversation. Cheley has long been known for its home cooking that campers go home raving about.
Entertainment: Each day ends with an evening campfire program, songs under the stars, a group "goodnight," and Taps.
Summary: One of the top ranch camps in North America, offering a small group experience with lots of individual attention and instruction by superb collegiate and teaching staff. Recognized for its excellence by alumni, educators, parents, and campers. The Western flavor of Cheley is warm and accepting, making it a great place for kids to "learn by doing." Excellent riding, horsemanship, hiking, backpacking, and pack-trip programs.

Cherokee Park Ranch
Livermore, Colorado

Built in 1886, Cherokee Park is one of Colorado's oldest guest ranches. The lifeblood of dude ranching is the people, and so it is at Cherokee Park, with its Western comfort and big helping of Southern hospitality. It's the Prince family's personal touches that make a stay at their ranch so memorable. Previous guests will tell you that Christine and her staff make sure everything is "just right." This means building a special bond with your own horse for the entire week. It means sit-down family dining where all you have to do is show up with your hands scrubbed, ready to enjoy the varied and delicious fare. "Just right" means riding until you are ready for fishing, skeet shooting, hiking, or a trip to a local rodeo. For children, age-appropriate counselors make each child's stay memorable—from panning for gold to creating something unique each day. Older kids have the run of the place, including the heated pool, acres of climbable trees, and miles of mountain trails to explore. Cool Colorado nights and clear Columbine blue-sky days blend together in this perfect family ranch vacation.

Address: 436 Cherokee Hills Drive, Livermore, Colorado 80536
Telephone: 800/628-0949, 970/493-6522; fax: 970/493-5802
Email: cherokeeparkranc@aol.com
Internet: www.cherokeeparkranch.com
Airport: Denver International, 100 miles
Location: 100 miles northwest of Denver, 42 miles northwest of Fort Collins
Medical: Poudre Valley Hospital, Fort Collins
Conference Capacity: 25
Guest Capacity: 35
Accommodations: As you greet the day in the Sunrise Room in the main lodge, the morning sun streams through a sky-blue Columbine flower etched in stained glass. Each sleeping room in the historic lodge, and every guest cabin along the north fork of the Cache La Poudre River, contains an original stained-glass art piece made by the ranch owner, Christine Prince. Each guest room and every cabin has a history, and all have been remodeled with Christine's special Western touches—quilts and refurbished antique dressers and furniture—to create lots of authentic charm

and a cozy feel. All accommodations offer porches, wonderful relaxing swings, hummingbird feeders, and lots of bright flowers.
Rates: • $$–$$$ American Plan. Children's and off-season rates available. One-week minimum stay during regular season; Saturday to Saturday. Three-day minimum stay in low season.
Credit Cards: VISA, MasterCard. Personal and traveler's checks accepted.
Season: Mid-May through mid-September
Activities: Horseback riding is featured. There is also river rafting, swimming in heated pool, hot tub, fishing in the ranch's stocked trout pond or fly-fishing on the Cache La Poudre River, hiking, skeet shooting, and ranch-guided sight-seeing trips to Rocky Mountain National Park and historic Laramie, Wyoming. Evening activities include hayrides, Western dancing, campfires, cookouts, and sing-alongs. One overnight trip each week so you can rough it in comfort and style on the mountain and eat around a campfire.
Children's Program: One of the top children's programs in the country! Full-time counselors for ages 3–12. Older children can ride until the cows come home, while the younger set wrangles the rabbits, ducks, goats, and chickens. Each activity is hands-on from gold mining in the ranch's mica mine and building horseshoe sculptures, to pony rides and nature hikes.
Entertainment: Something special is planned for each evening. Cowboy poets, Western square dancing, guitar and fiddle music around the campfire, visits with local artists, and trips to the world-famous Cheyenne Frontier Days Rodeo in late July are just a few of the activities. You can also stroll along the river until you find that perfect spot for reading, and there is always the porch swing.
Summary: Kilgore's "Best of the Best"–Children's Program. Personal caring attention with an energetic Southern spirit. Great for families and single parents. Cherokee Park has it all and makes for a truly wonderful family experience.

Chico Basin Ranch
Colorado Springs, Colorado

Incredible views, 87,000 acres of wide-open country, 2,000 to 3,000 head of cattle, and freedom to ride. As one of the largest working cattle ranches in America, Chico Basin Ranch offers opportunities to learn and see firsthand what makes this way of life so special. Here at The Chico, your hosts Duke and Janet Phillips, their young family, crew, and friends offer a horseback and ranch adventure that you will remember for the rest of your life. As Duke says, "we would like every person who visits here to leave having learned about our incredible American heritage— how we make a living in the West, and about our holistic management practices and philosophy, and our land and wildlife that are so vital to who we are and where we are going. We have folks who have come from around the world—some just to view the wildlife and take in the open expanses, but most often to experience what it is really like on a big working cattle ranch." Duke was raised on a large ranch in Mexico and has spent his professional life ranching in the United States, Australia, and Mexico. Chico Basin Ranch is all about family, hospitality, education, and big-time cattle ranching.

Address: 22500 Peyton Highway South, Drawer K, Colorado Springs, Colorado 80928
Telephone: 719/683-7960 (tel./fax)
Email: info@chicobasinranch.com
Internet: www.chicobasinranch.com
Airport: Colorado Springs, 35 minutes; Denver International, two hours
Location: 35 minutes southeast of Colorado Springs, two hours south of Denver off I-25
Medical: Penrose & Memorial Hospitals, Colorado Springs
Conference Capacity: 12
Guest Capacity: 12
Accommodations: Two comfortable guesthouses (formerly the ranch manager's home), located near the Vega Pond. Both houses include private baths, kitchens, and sleep 6–8 people; one has a wood-burning stove. The "out of Africa-type" range camps feature tepees designed by Native Americans and wall tents. Both are comfortable with amenities you may not expect, including hot showers, beds off the ground, handmade furniture, and lighting.

Rates: • $$$ American Plan. Two-night minimum
Credit Cards: None; personal or traveler's checks
Season: April to mid-November
Activities: Early to bed and early to rise. Chico Basin Ranch offers intermediate and experienced riders a chance to ride side-by-side with real cowboys across miles of varying terrain. Guests can participate in the cattle work at whatever level they wish or ride and explore the natural world. Seasonal activities related to the cattle work include spring and summer branding, and gathering and herding up to 1,200 head in the fall. Also fishing, swimming, canoeing in the spring-fed lakes, skeet shooting, fossil hunting, and bird- and wildlife-watching. Special events include artist gatherings, photography, and fly-fishing.
Children's Programs: Best for older children interested in riding and the outdoors. Resident naturalist/artist leads children's program emphasizing nature walks in the wild and drawing.
Dining: Hearty ranch meals and regional specialties. These meals feature ranch-raised natural products such as grass-fed, dry-aged beef, seasonal organic vegetables and fruit, fish, and pasta. BYOB.
Entertainment: Emphasis is placed on privacy and personal enjoyment of the outdoors, quiet evenings watching wildlife, reading, and spending time together.
Summary: One of the great cowboy experiences in America! At the 87,000-acre Chico Basin Ranch, you'll take part in a traditional cowboy lifestyle that is part history, part romance, part discovery, and lots of time in the saddle in the great outdoors. Their programs are designed for those who want to see a ranch's day-to-day workings from inside the border fences. Early risers can get a glimpse of the remuda being run in for the day's horseback work, or watch the wagons departing slowly through the rising sun's first light. Ask about the exclusive spring and fall cattle roundup weeks. Spanish spoken.

Colorado Trails Ranch
Durango, Colorado

Over the years Colorado Trails Ranch has had one of the finest reputations in the guest-ranching business. It has always been famous for its outstanding riding, children's, and teen programs. Today, Jeanne Ross, along with her marvelous staff, continue to offer families a truly exceptional program. Colorado Trails Ranch is geared to family fun and children. Located in the beautiful San Juan Mountains at 7,500 feet, just outside the famous mining town of Durango, the ranch offers a comprehensive Western riding program with certified riding instructors. An extensive guided fly-fishing program has been developed with over four miles of private water on and near the ranch. At Colorado Trails you'll also enjoy the Western Town atmosphere, complete with Trading Post, that offers old-fashioned ice-cream treats. Colorado Trails Ranch is one of the best all-round family ranches.

Address: 12161 County Road 240, Durango, Colorado 81301
Telephone: 800/323-3833, 970/247-5055; fax: 970/385-7372
Email: info@coloradotrails.com
Internet: www.coloradotrails.com
Airport: La Plata, 18 miles from ranch
Location: 12 miles northeast of Durango on County Road 240; 200 miles north of Albuquerque, New Mexico; 350 miles southwest of Denver
Memberships: The Dude Ranchers' Association, Colorado Dude and Guest Ranch Association, American Quarter Horse Association, American Humane Association, American Riding Instructors Association, American Paint Horse Association
Medical: Mercy Medical Center, Durango
Conference Capacity: 30; 4,800 square feet; mid-May, late September, and October
Guest Capacity: 65 (33 rooms)
Accommodations: Guests can stay in four types of comfortably furnished cabins. All rooms have private bathrooms, carpeting, electric baseboard heat, and porches. Complimentary guest laundry is available.
Rates: • $$$$–$$$$$ American Plan; service charges included. Family, off-season, and nanny rates.

Credit Cards: VISA, MasterCard, Discover, American Express, Diner's Club
Season: Early June to October
Activities: One of the best riding programs in the country. Western riding instruction for beginners through intermediate riders. Extensive fly-fishing program (see chapter on Fly-Fishing). Ask about Mesa Verde trip. Heated swimming pool, whirlpool spa, and fishing. Archery, rifle shooting and trapshooting (guns provided), hiking, and water-skiing, and power-tubing on Lake Vallecito. Golf, adult float, and guided Mesa Verde trips extra.
Children's Programs: One of North America's best and most extensive programs for children ages 5–17. "Our program is designed to keep kids and teens active, learning, and sharing in exceptional camaraderie. Horseback riding, fishing, and float trips are just a few of the many activities." Kids eat together if they wish.
Dining: The dining room overlooks scenic Shearer Creek valley and Eagle Ridge. Hearty ranch food and plenty of it. Wonderful homemade breads and desserts. Drinking permitted in cabins only.
Entertainment: A program every evening, hayrides, cookouts, ice-cream socials, professional rodeos, and melodrama in Durango. End of week awards and Western steak barbecue.
Summary: One of the leading guest ranches in America. Outstanding ranch for families, children, and teens. Caring and personable staff. Full Western riding with certified instructors and fly-fishing programs. Ask about adults-only weeks, family reunions, and the exciting trip to Mesa Verde Indian Cliff Dwellings. Nearby: The famous Durango/Silverton narrow-gauge train.

Colorado Trails Ranch, Colorado

Coulter Lake Guest Ranch
Rifle, Colorado

Coulter Lake Guest Ranch is one of the few Western guest ranches that overlooks its own charming lake. The ranch is nestled in a small mountain valley on the western slope of the Rockies, deep in the White River National Forest at 8,100 feet. In operation since 1938, Coulter Lake retains that Old West flavor and is hosted today by Richard and Lisa Zimmerman, and owned by Don Hock. Coulter Lake Guest Ranch is surrounded by some of Colorado's most spectacular mountain country, stretching for miles in all directions, virtually unchanged since Indian times. Forests of quaking aspen and spruce overlook meadows of wildflowers. Coulter Lake Guest Ranch has been kept small, intimate, and rustic. Family members of all ages, as well as singles, will love and savor this extra-special mountain hideaway.

Address: 80 County Road 273, Rifle, Colorado 81650

Telephone: 800/858-3046, 970/625-1473; fax: 970/625-1473

Email: coulter@sopris.net

Internet: www.coulterlake.com; www.ranch-web.com/coulter

Airport: Grand Junction

Train: Amtrak to Glenwood Springs

Location: 21 miles northeast of Rifle beyond Highway 325

Memberships: The Dude Ranchers' Association, Colorado Dude and Guest Ranch Association, Colorado Snowmobile Association

Medical: Clagett Memorial Hospital, Rifle

Conference Capacity: 20 (spring and fall only)

Guest Capacity: 28

Accommodations: Seven cabins stand on the mountainside among the quaking aspen trees; Lakeside and Forest Haven are by the lake. They vary in size and can sleep from 3–10 people. Each has a private bath, some with fireplaces, most have porches. Ranch generates its own power (curling irons and hair dryers not recommended but can be used at the lodge).

Rates: • $$$ American Plan. Children's and family rates available. Off-season and group rates.

Credit Cards: VISA, MasterCard, Discover, American Express, and Novus accepted. Checks or cash preferred.

Season: Late May to October; mid-December to early April.

Activities: Riding includes short excursions to Little Box Canyon, Long Park, and Pot Holes. All-day rides go to Irish Point and Little Hill. Overnight pack trips with dinner and breakfast served atop a scenic overlook of the entire valley. Breakfast, lunch, and dinner rides during the week are fun for the whole family. Fishing for trophy rainbow trout in stocked lake or in Alpine streams and lakes (some equipment available). Hiking is great to Three Forks drainage, along east Rifle Creek, and to beautiful Rifle Falls. Horseshoes, occasional cattle drives, lake swimming, and volleyball are available. Eighteen-hole golf course just 12 miles from the ranch. Rafting and hot springs in nearby Glenwood Springs. Guided photographers safari on horseback—bring lots of film. Licensed outfitter (Reg. #73). Winter: Meals and lodging for snowmobilers and cross-country skiers. Guided snowmobile rentals and tours available at additional charge.

Children's Programs: Kids can be watched while parents are riding. Children seven and older ride with parents. Baby-sitters are available with advance notice. Supervised kiddie rides for children under seven. Lots for kids to do including swimming in the lake and canoeing.

Dining: Gourmet Southwestern meals prepared by the chef. A Friday night cookout across the lake features juicy steaks with all the trimmings. The wranglers cook breakfast on the mountain one day a week. Special diets are accommodated with advance notice. BYOB.

Entertainment: Fishing, lakeside strolls, and chats on the deck. Horseshoes, volleyball, and badminton.

Summary: Delightful, small, family ranch. Remote, beautiful lake side setting—no noise, no telephones. As Lisa says, "We are low-key. If you enjoy good people, riding, and nature, give us a call." Adults-only weeks in early summer and fall. Ask about three-day packages and pack trips. Featured in *National Geographic Traveler* magazine. Video available.

Deer Valley Ranch
Nathrop, Colorado

Deer Valley Ranch is bordered by 14,000-foot Mt. Princeton and Mt. Antero, with the Chalk Cliffs forming the backdrop. This Christian guest ranch has been in the same family since 1954. The DeWalt and Woolmington families are committed to creating a very special atmosphere for all ages. The ranch places a strong emphasis on the family and does not allow any alcoholic beverages. Their ranch resort program is extensive and offers a variety of rates for many budgets, with special activities planned from dawn to late evening.

Address: Box K, Nathrop, Colorado 81236
Telephone: 800/284-1708, 719/395-2353; fax: 719/395-2394
Email: fun@deervalleyranch.com
Internet: www.deervalleyranch.com
Airport: Colorado Springs or Denver; private planes to Buena Vista, 10 miles
Location: 12 miles southwest of Buena Vista, 100 miles directly west of Colorado Springs
Memberships: Colorado Dude and Guest Ranch Association
Medical: Buena Vista Medical Clinic, 10 miles; Salida Hospital, 25 miles
Conference Capacity: 125 can meet in the two-story, 1,500-square-foot, newly remodeled, Centennial Hall or in two other meeting areas (off-season only).
Guest Capacity: 125
Accommodations: The 10-bedroom guest lodge is attached to a Western living room with a large fireplace and ranch dining room that looks out on 14,269-foot Mt. Antero. The lodge also includes a spacious outdoor double deck for enjoying the mountain scenery. The 15 private family cabins, each with historical mining names, sit among the ponderosa and piñon pines. They are two-, three- and four-bedroom cottages with full kitchens, living areas, fireplaces, and decks.
Rates: $$–$$$ • American Plan in the lodge or Modified European Plan in the cottages. All cabin guests are asked to eat one meal a day in the lodge, but they have the option of eating in their cabins as well. Horseback riding is optional and conveniently charged on a per-ride basis with a weekly package. Children's rates for ages 3–5 and 6–12.

Credit Cards: None. Personal checks accepted.
Season: Year-round; open all holidays.
Activities: Complete à la carte horseback riding options including instruction; one-, two-, and three-hour rides; and all-day rides above timberline near the Continental Divide. Fully guided hiking program includes pre-breakfast hikes daily, mountain climbs, and trail hikes through the San Isabel National Forest. Tennis court, free golf at two local courses, two hot-spring pools (90-95_F), and indoor and outdoor hot tubs. Fly-fishing instruction in Chalk Creek and fishing trips to regional rivers and high lakes, as well as family fishing in stocked ranch lake. Snowsliding (June only), three-on-three basketball, nature hikes, family softball, gold panning. Unusually good white-water rafting on the nearby Arkansas River.
Children's Programs: All ranch programs are scheduled for families to be together. Children ages 4–11 have the option of 4–6 hours of their own programs each day. Two full-time children's directors plan hikes, crafts, swimming, and games. Special play area at the Western Town. Top-notch teen activities for ages 12–18 include overnight campout, bouldering, sand jumping, and river rafting.
Dining: Many cookouts and specialty meals. Special diets accommodated. Cottages include full kitchens.
Entertainment: Programs every night. Square dancing, history talks, hayrides with campfires, Western music, and cowboy poetry. Western staff show with guest participation. Satellite TV in Centennial Hall and lots of Western videos. Sunday morning worship service and evening hymn-sing is a highlight for many.
Summary: Christian family guest ranch for families, couples, single parents, and singles, with full program of ranch resort activities. You determine your own activities and even adjust your expenses by determining how many meals you want in the dining room and what riding you do. A complete family destination vacation. Be sure to ask about the Trading Post and the ranch cookbook.

Drowsy Water Ranch
Granby, Colorado

Drowsy Water Ranch is exactly what you imagine a classic mountain dude ranch would be. This 600-acre ranch is in the beautiful Rocky Mountains, bordered by thousands of acres of backcountry and the Arapahoe National Forest. Situated in a private valley at 8,200 feet and surrounded by shimmering aspen and scented pine, Drowsy Water is authentic and offers its guests genuine Colorado hospitality. The log cabins are situated along Drowsy Water Creek, which meanders through the ranch. The Foshas are hosts and owners. Ken, Randy Sue, and their sons, Justin and Ryan, offer a quality horse program for experienced to beginning riders, and a full program for children of all ages. There's old-fashioned goodness to this ranch. It brings to mind another century, when people were less hurried and really cared about treating each other right.

Address: P.O. Box 147 K, Granby, Colorado 80446
Telephone: 800/845-2292, 970/725-3456; fax: 970/725-3611
Email: whoadwr@aol.com
Internet: www.drowsywater.com
Airport: Denver
Train: Amtrak to Granby, six miles
Location: 90 miles west of Denver, six miles west of Granby off U.S. 40
Memberships: The Dude Ranchers' Association, Colorado Dude and Guest Ranch Association
Medical: Granby Clinic, six miles
Conference Capacity: 40
Guest Capacity: 60
Accommodations: Guests enjoy comfortable, clean log cabins that are sheltered in stands of aspen and pine overlooking Drowsy Water Creek and the ranch ponds. Cabins have covered porches. The largest sleeps nine and looks out over the children's fishing pond. The cabins accommodate 2–9 persons. The sleeping lodge has another eight rooms, all with private baths.
Rates: • $$$$ American Plan. Minimum one-week stay in high season, Sunday to Saturday. Family, children's, and off-season rates. Pack trips and river rafting extra.
Credit Cards: None. Personal and traveler's checks accepted.

Season: June to mid-September
Activities: One hundred fine horses provide all the riding you could possibly want. Ken and Randy Sue have raised many of their own horses and have a personal commitment to help each guest become a better rider. Faster loping and slow ambling trail rides go out mornings and afternoons, and all-day mountain rides travel to beautiful vistas at 10,500 feet. Weekly breakfast ride. Riding here will get you to some spectacular high country and views of the Continental Divide. Daily riding instruction available. River rafting on the Colorado River. Hayrides, fishing (equipment for beginners provided), heated pool, and whirlpool. Golf and tennis nearby. Two championship golf courses down the road and Alpine slide in Winter Park.
Children's Programs: This is one of the top children's ranch programs in the country. Parents may participate in kids' activities. Supervised children's program for ages 6–13 (Range Riders) with games and crafts. Children's riding program builds confident riders. Children under age five (Buckaroos) have a special program that includes horseback riding, games, crafts, and picnic hikes. Weekly kids' gymkhana.
Dining: Lots of home-cooked, hearty meals; salad bar. Special diets catered to. Families usually eat together. BYOB in cabins only.
Entertainment: Something different each night. Monday, dancing; Tuesday, hayride for kids with marshmallow-toasting and adults-only dinner; Wednesday, carnival night; Thursday, adults-only hayride; Friday, staff show.
Summary: An excellent children's program. Drowsy Water is one of the country's top family-owned and -operated ranches for parents with infants on up; also great for couples and singles. Lifelong friendships have formed here. Nearby: Rocky Mountain National Park.

Drowsy Water Ranch, Colorado

lk Mountain Ranch
Buena Vista, Colorado

THE DUDE RANCHERS'
ASSOCIATION

CDGRA

Elk Mountain Ranch is a cozy hideaway, 9,535 feet high in the Colorado Rockies, dedicated to families, wonderful sincere hospitality, and off-the-beaten-path charm. In operation since 1981, the lush aspen and evergreen forests of the beautiful San Isabel National Forest surround the ranch. Hosts Tom and Sue Murphy and their young kids, Hunter and Tyler, take great pride in pampering their guests. Elk Mountain is a family-oriented ranch (great for couples and singles, too, especially in the fall) with wonderful horseback rides and friendliness. One family remarked, "When we were blessed with three boys, I talked with them about one day going to a dude ranch, and my dream became theirs as well. We had planned for this vacation for five years, and everything you did and stood for made our vacation worth the wait. The focus on caring for the horses, on safety, on service with a smile, on great food, on a relaxed pace, on comfortable surroundings, on personalized attention, on upholding the traditions of the West with the cowboy poet and the hammered dulcimer, and the sheer natural beauty of the setting, all contributed to an extraordinary, memorable vacation."

Address: P.O. Box 910K, Buena Vista, Colorado 81211

Telephone: 800/432-8812, 719/539-4430 (tel./fax)

Email: info@elkmtn.com

Internet: www.elkmtn.com

Airport: Colorado Springs or Denver

Location: 120 miles southwest of Denver, 90 miles west of Colorado Springs, 20 miles southeast of Buena Vista; ranch will send you a detailed map.

Memberships: The Dude Ranchers' Association, Colorado Dude and Guest Ranch Association, America Outdoors

Medical: Buena Vista Medical Clinic, Salida Hospital

Conference Capacity: 25 (early June or late September for less than one week)

Guest Capacity: 32

Accommodations: The main lodge houses the dining room with fireplace, cowboy and mining artifacts, sitting room, library, sundeck, and the upstairs Elk guest suite. There are six one- and two-bedroom log cottages with private baths and queen- and king-size beds, and the Pioneer Lodge with three private rooms and baths, all tastefully furnished. Eight-person hot tub and large deck. A gift basket awaits your arrival. Sue loves flowers and has colorful arrays everywhere. The ranch generates its own electricity. Lights are out at 11 P.M.

Rates: • $$$ American Plan; includes overnight pack trip and white-water rafting. One-week minimum stay, Sunday to Sunday. Children's, off-season, and nonriding rates available.

Credit Cards: VISA, MasterCard. Personal and traveler's checks preferred.

Season: June through September

Activities: Horseback riding in small groups through a variety of terrain and unspoiled wilderness. Spectacular views of the distant Collegiate Peaks. Excellent horse-orientation program. Optional overnight wilderness pack trips to Cow Gulch, 12 miles away. Weekly brunch trail ride overlooking Brown's Canyon. Weekly white-water rafting on the Arkansas River. Auto trips to Aspen for the views and shopping. Rifle marksmanship and trapshooting (guns provided), trout fishing in two stocked ponds (some fishing gear is available), archery, horseshoes, and volleyball.

Children's Programs: Full children's program for ages 4–7. Riding for children eight years and older. Ranch encourages parents to interact with kids.

Dining: Great, hearty ranch food. Freshly baked breads, desserts, evening hors d'oeuvres. Weekly barbecues and Saturday candlelight dinners. BYOB.

Entertainment: Tractor-pulled hayrides with cowboy poet and fiddler, square dances, campfires, hammered dulcimer concert. Old Western and kids' movies, library, chess, backgammon.

Summary: Wonderful, remote, small, family-oriented ranch. Delightful, energetic hosts and excellent staff who love what they do—and it shows. Great for families, couples, and singles who enjoy an outdoor wilderness setting. Great Trading Post ranch store. Nearby: Buena Vista (the white-water capital of Colorado) and a large collection of mountains higher than 14,000 feet.

Forbes Trinchera Ranch
Fort Garland, Colorado

Malcolm Forbes was a man with a passion for business, people, and life. Forbes Trinchera Ranch was one of his hideaways where he would come to savor the tranquil wide-open spaces, to think, reflect, and entertain. Today, the ranch is owned by *Forbes Magazine*. It is located in the famous Sangre de Cristo Mountains and encompasses over 180,000 acres of spectacular mountain countryside. It has been developed into a facility for executive conferences. The main lodge and conference areas are situated in the Trinchera Valley, which is dominated by three 14,000-foot peaks on the ranch. The lodge itself is a virtual museum of art, seascapes, model ships, and bronzes that Malcolm collected over the years. With a warm family-like spirit, the Forbes Trinchera Ranch offers corporate and business groups beauty, privacy, and luxury. It is a place to think, create, recharge, and have fun. Malcolm Forbes wouldn't have wanted it any other way.

Address: P.O. Box 149, Fort Garland, Colorado 81133
Telephone: 719/379-3264; fax: 719/379-3266
Email: forbestrinchera@forbes.com
Internet: www.forbestrinchera.com
Airport: Alamosa Municipal Airport, 35 miles; Colorado Springs, 140 miles; Denver International, 200 miles
Location: Two miles east of Fort Garland, Colorado, on U.S. 160; 200 miles southwest of Denver
Awards: Kilgore Luxury Group
Medical: San Luis Valley Regional Medical Center
Conference Capacity: 46
Guest Capacity: 46
Accommodations: The lodge and accommodations have a Southwest flavor-adobe brown with white trim. The main lodge sleeps 30 with 16 luxurious bedrooms, most with two queen-size beds, several with king-size beds. Each has original art and cedar siding. The adobe house across the courtyard has six bedrooms, two with two queen-size beds, two with king-size beds, and two with one queen-size bed. The motif is country. The original log house next to the adobe house has two bedrooms with queen-size beds. All rooms have telephones, alarm clocks, and comforters.

Rates: • $$$$ American Plan. Six rooms, three-night minimum.
Credit Cards: American Express; personal checks and cash accepted.
Season: January through August
Activities: Activities are tailored to individual groups. Over the years, men and women alike have come to fish, hike, game spot, and horseback ride. Mountain bikes are available upon request. Fishing in Trinchera, Ute, and Indian Creeks for rainbow and brook trout. All small streams. All gear is provided. Horseback riding is limited to eight riders at a time, throughout the day. All riding is done at a walk. Skeet shooting with shotguns and ammunition provided. Eighteen-hole golf course nearby. Winter offers ice fishing in ponds, game spotting, guided snowmobile trips, skeet shooting, and cross-country skiing (equipment rental available in Alamosa).
Children's Programs: None. Children not advised unless entire ranch is booked for family reunion.
Dining: Malcolm Forbes always appreciated good food. The tradition continues. The resident CIA-trained chef will happily accommodate your culinary wishes.
Entertainment: You decide. The ranch's goal is to please you.
Summary: A world-class executive and group conference ranch/retreat. Kilgore Luxury Group. Great for family reunions too!

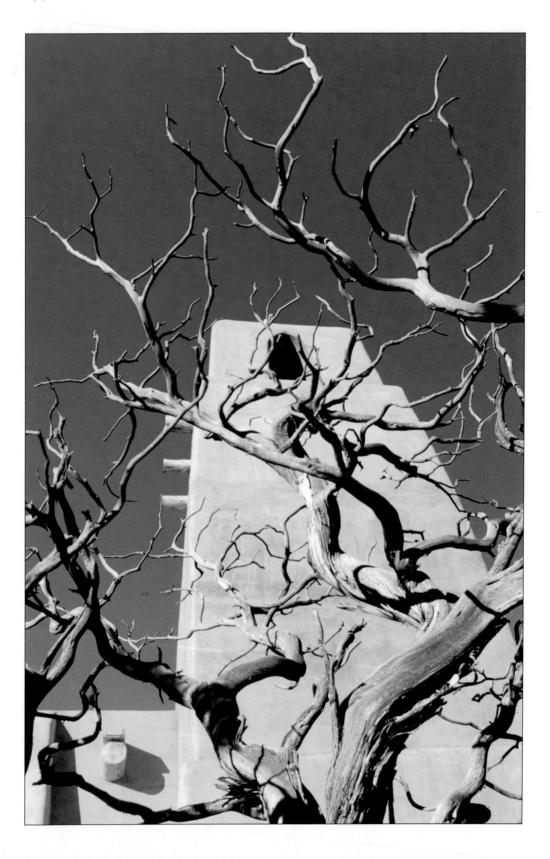

The Home Ranch
Clark, Colorado

THE DUDE RANCHERS' ASSOCIATION

As you drive up the gravel road to the ranch and see the hand-hewn log buildings set among shimmering aspens, two words come to mind: "paradise" and, maybe better yet, "heaven." The Home Ranch was the longtime dream of co-owner and builder Ken Jones. Ken grew up on horses and got most of his guest-ranch experience at the old Valley Ranch. While working there he met a guest who shared his enthusiasm. Ken and his partners, Steve and Ann Stranahan, have developed a leading equestrian learning center, and created a ranch so special that it boasts the highly coveted Relais & Chateaux membership, all in a magnificent and relaxed atmosphere. There's very little this ranch doesn't offer its guests. Best of all, it serves up plenty of Old West rustic elegance and hospitality. The *Los Angeles Times* captured the essence when it said, "Here, guests commune with a world as fresh as a Rocky Mountain raindrop."

Address: Box 822 K, Clark, Colorado 80428
Telephone: 970/879-1780; fax: 970/879-1795
Email: hrclark@cmn.net
Internet: www.homeranch.com
Airport: Steamboat Springs via Denver
Location: 18 miles north of Steamboat Springs off Highway 129
Awards: Kilgore Luxury Group
Memberships: The Dude Ranchers' Association, Relais & Chateaux
Medical: Steamboat Springs Hospital
Conference Capacity: 30
Guest Capacity: 45–50
Accommodations: Each beautiful log cabin is wonderfully furnished and set in a grove of aspen trees, ensuring privacy. Each has its own hot tub on a covered deck, great for total relaxation at the end of a day's ride. There are also rooms on both levels in the handsome main lodge. A wonderful 2,500-square-foot, two-floor, hand-hewn log cabin for large families is available as well. All rooms with nightly turndown service, flowers, and robes. Full laundry service available (extra).
Rates: • $$$$$ American Plan. Children's rates and packages for the Colorado Center for Equestrian Learning available.

Credit Cards: VISA, MasterCard, American Express. Personal checks accepted.
Season: Guest season is June through September, and mid-December through February. Colorado Center for Equestrian Learning clinics with leading horse experts are in May, early June, September, and October.
Activities: The ranch embraces the full Natural Horsemanship Program that creates a willing partnership between horse and rider and is the focus of the summer program. You're assigned your own horse for the duration of your stay. It's up to you how much you ride inside the adjoining one-million-acre Routt National Forest. Interested guests are taught how to saddle and bridle their horses. Rides go out in small groups each day accompanied by a wrangler. The ranch raises many of its own quarter horses; ask Ken about his quarter horse and warmblood-breeding program. Heated swimming pool, fishing and fly casting in the stocked pond or Elk River, and fly-fishing instruction. Extensive hiking program with two full-time nature guides. The hike to Gilpin Lake is a favorite. Tennis and golf can be arranged nearby. Winter: See Cross-Country Skiing section.
Children's Programs: Kiddie wrangler. Complete children's program for ages six and up. Kids are completely looked after, breakfast to sunset. Riding starts at age six. While the ranch is very flexible, there's a strict policy that absolutely no children under age six are allowed.
Dining: Excellent, mouth-watering gourmet meals. Children usually eat dinner before adults. BYO wine and liquor (ranch will pick up with advance notice).
Entertainment: The Home Ranch features its own Western band, which has recorded an album in Nashville. Ranch and Steamboat Springs rodeos, barrel racing. Top local entertainers.
Summary: Kilgore Luxury Group. A world-class guest ranch in a world-class setting! Focus on Natural Horsemanship. Excellent kids' program. Ranch-raised quarter horses. Full winter program. Ask about the Colorado Center for Equestrian Learning.

The Home Ranch, Colorado

arita Creek Ranch
Norte, Colorado

La Garita Creek Ranch, located at 8,100 feet, is located on the eastern slope of the San Juan Mountains and the Rio Grande National Forest in the high desert, "Indian Country," of southwestern Colorado. La Garita Creek Ranch offers family members of all ages, couples and singles as well, a wide variety of ranch activities, including hot-air ballooning, technical rock-climbing, cattle penning, and rafting the white waters of nearby rivers. Guests particularly enjoy the hands-on riding program in which guests actually care for their designated horse for the week, as well as the diverse activities and open beauty of southwestern Colorado.

Address: 38145 County Road E-39, Drawer K, Del Norte, Colorado 81132

Telephone: 888/838-3833, 719/754-2533; fax: 719/754-2666

Email: krv@lagarita.com

Internet: www.lagarita.com

Airport: Colorado Springs, Alamosa, Durango. Ranch has 2,500-foot dirt airstrip for private single-engine and twin-engine planes. Call for details.

Location: 200 miles southwest of Denver, 175 miles southwest of Colorado Springs, 125 miles east of Durango, 49 miles west of Alamosa

Medical: Rio Grande Hospital, 10 miles; Life Flight Helicopter service available.

Conference Capacity: 75 (off-season only)

Guest Capacity: 48

Accommodations: Seven guest rooms on the upper level of the Stone Mountain Lodge have private baths and Southwestern decor. Two duplex cabins with two rooms each accommodate a total of 18 guests; the Cliff Dwelling Family Cabin for eight, and the Blue Sky Family Cabin for nine. Some cabins have fireplaces, and decks out front for relaxing.

Rates: • $$–$$$ American Plan; includes all activities except hot-air balloon rides, llama treks, and fly-fishing instruction on the Rio Grande. Sunday to Saturday stays mid-May through September. Ask about adults-only weeks, and "Dirty Dudes" week (three days of working with the staff preparing for "the season," and three days of fun) for a 50 percent discount off the regular price. Children under age two are free; babysitting available (call for details).

Credit Cards: VISA, MasterCard, Discover, American Express. Personal and traveler's checks accepted.

Season: Summer: Early May through September

Activities: Scheduled and diverse weekly activities program. Very hands-on riding program. Guests care for their designated horse for the week. Activities include side-by-side and trail riding, fishing, skeet and target shooting, archery, hiking, mountain biking, swimming, and hayrides. A choice of white-water rafting, technical rock-climbing, golfing, riding the narrow gauge Cumbres & Toltec Scenic Railroad or visiting the Great Sand Dunes National Park and Alligator Farm is included. Winter activities include snowmobiling, snowshoeing, Alpine and cross-country skiing, and snowcat tours in the San Juan Mountains. Holiday activities and special weekly and weekend packages available.

Children's Programs: Excellent optional supervised children's program with counselors for ages 3–12, and teens. Nature hikes, picnics, fishing, exploring, swimming, treasure hunts, organized games, horseback riding, and crafts are just a few of the activities provided. One night a week children ages three and up head out for a supper campout, while the adults have a quiet candlelight dinner. Champagne breakfast the next morning.

Dining: Country cookin' with a gourmet flair served buffet-style or family-style. Cookouts, breakfast, and dinner rides. Special diets accommodated.

Entertainment: Sing-alongs, karaoke, Western movies (with popcorn), Western dance instruction, hayrides, local history talks, cattle penning, Showdeo, awards night, and boot branding.

Summary: La Garita Creek Ranch offers a very hands-on riding program where horse care is encouraged! Also a diverse activities program is offered, both on and off the ranch. A small, friendly ranch ideal for families, couples, and singles. Great kids' program. Perfect for family reunions. Friendly staff and children's counselors.

Lake Mancos Ranch
Mancos, Colorado

Lake Mancos Ranch, located at 8,000 feet looking out on the La Plata Mountain Range, has been owned and operated by the Sehnert family since the early 1950s. A favorite expression used by founder Lloyd Sehnert when initiating new staff was, "Every guest should be treated like a precious piece of gold." This philosophy is still present as Kathy, Todd, and Robin open their ranch and year-round home to their guests. Through personal service, Lake Mancos Ranch has established a tradition of providing wonderful, heartwarming vacations to first-time guests and generations of returning families. You'll find all the necessary elements that make a guest-ranch vacation so special: horses, spectacular scenery, outdoor activity, comfortable cabins, hearty meals, and fun activities for children. Judging from comments made by longtime guests, it's the Sehnerts' Western hospitality and family "quality time" that keep them coming back to Lake Mancos Ranch, their "home in the mountains."

Address: 42688 CR-N, Dept. K, Mancos, Colorado 81328
Telephone: 800/325-9462, 970/533-1190; fax: 970/533-7858
Email: ranchlml@fone.net
Internet: www.lakemancosranch.com
Airport: Durango via Denver, Phoenix, or Albuquerque
Location: Five miles north of Mancos, 35 miles west of Durango
Memberships: The Dude Ranchers' Association, Colorado Dude and Guest Ranch Association
Medical: Cortez Hospital, 25 miles
Conference Capacity: 40
Guest Capacity: 55
Accommodations: There are 17 bright red guest units with names like Spruce Mill, Golconda, and Bear Creek; cabins of various sizes; and four spacious units with private baths in the ranch house for couples and singles. All heated family cabins have comfortable living rooms and bedrooms, one or two bathrooms, private covered porches, king-size beds, refrigerators, and carpeting. Guest laundry available. Daily maid service.
Rates: • $$$ American Plan; Sunday to Saturday.

Nonriding, children's, and off-season rates. Three-day packages on a space available basis.
Credit Cards: VISA, MasterCard, Discover. Personal checks accepted.
Season: Early June to October. September is adults only.
Activities: Riding is the main activity at the ranch, with over 100 miles of scenic trails offering guests the opportunity to see some of Colorado's prettiest country. You'll explore shimmering aspen forests and lush mountain meadows. Children and adults usually ride separately. Family rides several times a week, along with team penning and arena activities. Guests are assigned their own horses for their stay and riding instruction is available. Hiking, mountain biking, pond and stream fishing (rods and introductory fly-fishing instruction provided). Heated pool and hot tub. Four-wheel-drive and wildflower trips. Many like to visit Mesa Verde National Park, raft in Durango, golf in Cortez, or ride the spectacular Durango-Silverton narrow-gauge train, which was started in 1882.
Children's Programs: Supervised Lil' Ropers, Cowpokes, Buckaroos, and Mavericks programs for children and teens ages four and up during all daily adult activities. Hiking, gold panning, arena activities, fishing pond, overnight campout, trail rides, lots to do. Children easily make friends here and initiate spontaneous activities!
Dining: Home-style cooking. Two entrées each night. Weekly steak-fry. Creek-side cookouts at Rendezvous Canyon. Bottomless cookie jar! Coffee and lemonade always plentiful. BYOB. Children may eat at children's table or with their parents.
Entertainment: Cowboy songs, hayrides, cookouts, skits, awards night, and fireside stories.
Summary: The Sehnert family is one of the oldest guest-ranching families in Colorado. Riding is the main activity. Many singles and couples enjoy the camaraderie of the family summer season. Lake Mancos is for down-to-earth families who enjoy vacationing together but appreciate some separate activities. Adults only in September. Nearby: Old Durango and Silverton Railroad, Mesa Verde National Park.

Lake Mancos Ranch, Colorado

...e Guest Ranch
...tes Park, Colorado

Lane Guest Ranch celebrated its 48th year of continuous operation in 2001. Host and owner Lloyd Lane has developed one of the most successful summer resort ranch experiences in North America. His secret is best described by guests, who write, "The staff was wonderful, the food excellent, and there were plenty of activities! Staff, food, scenery were all top-notch—we've never been to a more loving resort." Lloyd's success has come about because he offers a wide choice of activities (besides horseback riding), such as hiking, swimming, fishing, white-water rafting, overnight pack trips—along with all-day child care for infants and up, comfortable accommodations, and an excellent chef, all in one of the prettiest areas of Colorado—right next to Rocky Mountain National Park. Welcome to Lloyd Lane's famous "Colorado Vacation."

Address: P.O. Box 1766, Dept. K, Estes Park, Colorado 80517
Telephone: 303/747-2493; call for fax
Internet: www.ranchweb.com/laneranch
Airport: Denver International; shuttle available (extra)
Location: 67 miles northwest of Denver, 12 miles south of Estes Park off Highway 7
Memberships: American Hotel and Motel Association, Estes Park Chamber of Commerce
Medical: Estes Park Hospital, 11 miles
Guest Capacity: 80
Accommodations: Log-sided units accommodate from 2–6. Twenty-six units are comfortably furnished with queen-size beds, private baths, patios, hammocks, TV/VCR, complimentary stocked refrigerators, and radios. Most units have their own private hot tubs. Early morning wake-up coffee served to your room when you wish. Ask about the Doctor's House for family reunions. One-day laundry service offered.
Rates: • $$$$ American Plan; includes service charges. Children's, seniors', weekly, and honeymoon/anniversary packages available.
Credit Cards: VISA, MasterCard
Season: June to early September
Activities: Daily ranch activity sign-up sheet with lots of programs. Horseback riding (except Sunday) in Rocky Mountain National Park and Roosevelt National Forest. Wine-and-cheese rides for adults; two overnight pack trips. Guided hikes, scenic photography class, and morning fishing trips are very popular. Landscape drawing and silversmith classes. Heated outdoor pool, sauna, and hot tub. White-water rafting about two hours away. Eighteen-hole golf at country club in Estes Park. Massage available (masseuse on staff). Fitness center with complimentary trainer to assist guests. Gift shop featuring scenic photographs and paintings of the area.

Children's Programs: Extensive program with counselors; full child care available for infants and older children during the day. Kiddie wrangler. Baby-sitting available in the evening (extra). Playground and children's activities. Kids' horseback rides (parents may go).

Dining: Guests have a choice of a dozen dinner entrées. The menu includes charcoal-broiled steaks, seafood, broiled and poached chicken breasts and salmon, fresh trout, prime rib, pastas, excellent clam chowder, full salad bar, wonderful desserts, and homemade soups and rolls. California wines and mixed drinks (licensed bar), cappuccino and espresso, poolside café; special diets gladly accommodated.

Entertainment: Four nights of live entertainment including a magic and comedy show, and a jazz quartet that plays during and after dinner. Shuffleboard, volleyball, horseshoes, well-stocked library, chess, table tennis, TV, over 800 video movies, and karaoke; Estes Park rodeos (July).

Summary: Lloyd Lane has celebrated more than 48 years of operation and is proud of his better than 90 percent occupancy rate. The ranch is in one of the prettiest areas in Colorado, with high mountain peaks, natural splendor, and temperatures in the 70s. Come here to enjoy a wide variety of activities, food, and entertainment. If all you want to do is horseback ride, this is not the ranch for you. High staff-to-guest ratio (55 staff to 80 guests). One of the best children's programs for infants on up. Lots of families and couples. European-type concierge. Pets welcome. Advertised in the *Wall Street Journal* for over 45 years. Nearby: Estes Park and Boulder for shopping trips.

Lane Guest Ranch, Colorado

Laramie River Ranch
Glendevey, Colorado

The spirit of Bill and Krista Burleigh's Laramie River Ranch is captured by this recent guest quote: "Our family loves riding and fishing and we got to do plenty of both. Laramie River Ranch is blessed with exceptional scenery offering incredible horseback rides. With a mile and a half of river running through the property, there is plenty of opportunity for great fishing. The area is stunningly beautiful." The ranch is located in the Laramie River Valley of northern Colorado, not far from the Wyoming border. In 1995 Bill and Krista bought this historic ranch, which was homesteaded in the late 1800s and had entertained guests for over 50 years. Today, along with young son Christopher, they grow hay, graze cattle, and share their way of life in this remote valley. Here you will experience genuine Western hospitality, side-by-side horseback riding, private fishing, and a host of naturalist-led activities.

Address: The postal address is 25777 N. County Road 103, Drawer K, Jelm, Wyoming 82063
Telephone: 800/551-5731, 970/435-5716; fax: 970/435-5731
Email: vacationK@lrranch.com
Internet: www.lrranch.com/indexK.html
Airport: Laramie, Wyoming, and Denver, Colorado; free pickup from Laramie
Location: 42 miles southwest of Laramie; 150 miles northwest of Denver
Memberships: The Dude Ranchers' Association, Colorado Dude and Guest Ranch Association
Medical: Laramie Ivinson Memorial Hospital
Conference Capacity: 25
Guest Capacity: 25
Accommodations: The lodge was built in the 1880s and completely renovated in 1996. A living room with an old stone fireplace, two open porches with rocking chairs, and a large enclosed porch overlooking the Laramie River provide guests with lots of room to relax. Choose one of seven unique rooms in the historic lodge, or one of five cozy log cabins that sit along LaGarde Creek and the Laramie River. One guest wrote, "We loved being on the river listening to the sound of rushing water, windows wide open!" Homemade cookies and fresh flowers in your cabin are just a few of the nice, friendly touches here. Daily maid service. Down pillows available. Smoke-free policy.

Rates: • $$$ American Plan. Children's, group, and off-season rates. Seven nights, Sunday to Sunday. Some three- and four-night stays available.
Credit Cards: VISA, MasterCard. Personal and traveler's checks accepted.
Season: Early June through early October
Activities: Morning, afternoon, cookout, and all-day rides are available for riders of all abilities; usually in small groups. There is an abundance of open terrain suitable for loping. Guests are welcome to help groom and saddle their own horses. Riding instruction available. Overnight pack trips. Fishing for wild brown and rainbow trout. Fly-fishing instruction provided, with guides and gear available. Other activities include cattle penning, tubing down the river, birding, hunting for wildflowers, roping a steer dummy, exploring beaver dams, orienteering, volleyball, and horseshoes.
Children's Programs: Full-day program for children six and older includes horseback riding and naturalist activities. Supervised half-day program for children five and under. Activities are family-oriented so parents and children can explore the ranch together.
Dining: Hearty meals are served family-style with varied entrées, warm homemade breads, and provocative desserts. Vegetarian alternatives available. Breakfast and lunch cookout rides are favorites. BYOB.
Entertainment: Western music, bonfires, and dancing. Evening stargazing with a fascinating talk on the mythology of the constellations, steer-roping demonstrations, local rodeos in July.
Summary: Bill and Krista Burleigh have created one of the best family guest-ranch experiences in the Rockies. One family summed it up—"The amount of activities was perfect for us, not too much, not too little, and we really appreciated the optional aspect. We had time for hiking, riding, reading, visiting, and napping."

Laramie River Ranch, Colorado

Laramie River Ranch, Colorado

Latigo Ranch
Kremmling, Colorado

What a view! At 9,000 feet, looking out to the spectacular Continental Divide, the air is crisp and the hospitality sincere. Nature lovers will enjoy the breathtaking scenery and the abundance of wildflowers and wildlife on thousands of acres. Latigo Ranch runs a four-season program, from hayrides in summer to cross-country skiing in winter. Here you can ride, hike, swim, fish, and interact with Salvadore or Pepe, the ranch llamas. Whether you and your family are at the ranch for Fourth of July or Christmas, you can be sure of one thing—many special memories. If you want to have some stimulating conversations, just ask your hosts about their interesting educational backgrounds. The George and Yost families, who own and operate the Latigo Ranch, often engage in provocative discussions with their guests. Mostly, though, everyone takes in nature's beauty and serenity. As one guest wrote, "Between the depth of instruction in nature and riding, combined with the spirit of kindness that permeates the ranch, our experience was grand!"

Address: P.O. Box 237K, Kremmling, Colorado 80459
Telephone: 800/227-9655, 970/724-9008
Email: latigo@compuserve.com
Internet: www.latigotrails.com
Airport: Denver
Location: 130 miles northwest of Denver, 55 miles southeast of Steamboat Springs, 16 miles northwest of Kremmling
Memberships: The Dude Ranchers' Association, Colorado Dude and Guest Ranch Association
Medical: Kremmling Memorial Hospital
Conference Capacity: 38
Guest Capacity: 38
Accommodations: Guests stay in contemporary log duplexes nestled in the pine forest and one fourplex. Each is carpeted, with sitting room and fireplace or wood-burning stove. All have refrigerators and Latigo's famous homemade caramel corn. Daily maid service.
Rates: • $$$$ American Plan; all-inclusive, gratuities included, no extras. Children's rates available. Rates vary depending on the season. Three-to six-night minimum stay. Overnight pack trip and river rafting included in price.

Credit Cards: VISA, MasterCard
Season: Summer: Late May to October; Winter: Mid-December to April.
Activities: The main emphasis is on the horseback riding and the quality of the instruction for all levels on the trails, as well as in the arena. The ranch prides itself on a high wrangler-to-guest ratio so that ride groups are small and can be better tailored to fit guests' levels and interests. Rides include morning, afternoon, all-day, breakfast, sunset, and overnight pack trips to High Rock Creek. Riding at 9,000 feet with 360-degree views and serenity offers a genuine Rocky Mountain high. Heated swimming pool, fishing in streams and ranch pond. Jim Yost offers fly-fishing instruction and day fishing trips. Hot tub available for sore muscles. Lots of hiking and rafting included nearby. Be sure to ask about weekly team cattle penning and fall cattle roundup! Winter: See Cross-Country Skiing section.
Children's Programs: Optional fully supervised program for children ages 3–13, while adults are riding. Families may ride exclusively together. Arts and crafts center. Kids under age six do not ride on the trail. Baby-sitting available.
Dining: Excellent food both summer and winter. Ranch fare with variety and gourmet touches. Weekly breakfast, lunch, and dinner cookouts. BYOB.
Entertainment: The three-story Social Club is a log-sided entertainment building where guests enjoy relaxing, square/line dancing, cowboy singing, piano, pool table, library, and hot tub.
Summary: One of the best Summer and Winter guest ranches. Latigo Ranch is known for three things: its hospitality (high staff-to-guest ratio), scenery, and horse program. Open, expansive, high-mountain setting with excellent panoramic views. Jim's geology and wildlife lectures. Be sure to see Jim Yost's movie on Ecuador, *Nomads of the Rain Forest,* a beautiful show seen on *Nova.* Fall cattle roundup in late September. (Also see entry in Cross-Country Skiing section.)

Lost Valley Ranch
Deckers, Colorado

In the world of guest ranching, Lost Valley Ranch is right at the top. The qualities that make the Foster family's ranch so unique are their superb staff, excellent accommodations, and fabulous children's/teen program. Everyone at the ranch exudes a caring and enthusiastic spirit and guests quickly become friends. Lost Valley has been in the ranching business for more than 100 years and under the ownership of generations of Fosters since 1960. This year-round cattle and horse ranch is a private island in the middle of 40,000 acres of the Pike National Forest. At Lost Valley, adventure is combined with fun. If the number of returning guests is any indication, the Fosters are doing everything right. Walt Disney stayed here years ago and told the Fosters, "If I had this place, I would do all that I could not to change its character." The Fosters took his advice. This is one of the best family ranches in the business.

Address: 29555 Goose Creek Road, Box K, Sedalia, Colorado 80135-9000
Telephone: 303/647-2311; fax: 303/647-2315
Email: lostranch@aol.com
Internet: www.lostvalleyranch.com
Airport: Denver or Colorado Springs
Train: Amtrak to Denver
Location: Two hours southwest of Denver, 1.5 hours northwest of Colorado Springs, 12 miles southwest of Deckers
Memberships: The Dude Ranchers' Association, Colorado Dude and Guest Ranch Association
Awards: AAA 4 Diamond; Mobil 3 Star
Medical: Langstaff-Brown Medical Clinic, one hour
Conference Capacity: 60, fall and spring only; largest room 1,600 square feet
Guest Capacity: 95
Accommodations: The 24 cabin suites (one, two, and three bedrooms) are some of the finest in the business. All have living rooms, fireplaces, refrigerators, covered porches with swings, full private tub/shower baths, and amenities such as daily maid service, oversized towels, coffeemakers, and delightful cowboy-hat amenities baskets. To ensure peace and quiet the cabins are nicely spaced among the pines. No TVs or telephones.

Laundry facilities are available. Smoke-free policy in dining room and cabins.
Rates: • $$$$ American Plan; all-inclusive rates include gratuities. Children's, teen, and spring/fall rates available. During summer there is a seven-day minimum stay policy, Sunday arrival. Trapshooting and Orvis-endorsed fishing guides are available at additional cost.
Credit Cards: None. Personal checks accepted.
Season: March through November
Activities: All levels of Western riding. With 150 horses and 200 head of cattle, guests are encouraged to participate in ranch and cattle work. Quality fishing in Goose Creek, which runs through the property, or drive 20 minutes and wet your fly in the world-famous Cheasman Canyon on the South Platte River. Orvis-endorsed fishing guides are available (additional fee). Heated outdoor swimming pool, two whirlpool spas, two plexi-paved tennis courts, trapshooting (additional fee), and guided hiking. Ranch store. Seasonal cattle and horsemanship weeks.
Children's Programs: This is one of Lost Valley's strongest attractions. A superb collegiate staff supervises children. This program provides tremendous fun for children ages 3–12, yet gives parents peace of mind knowing their children are safe and happy. The teens operate within a framework of freedom, friendship, and fun provided by the collegiate staff.
Dining: Mother Marion's recipes are famous. Down-home ranch cooking served at a buffet and plate-style by friendly waitresses. Special diets accommodated. BYOB in cabins only.
Entertainment: Entertainment is second to none. Lost Valley's staff is talented. Enjoy musical entertainment, melodramas, square dancing, hayrides, campfires, and sing-alongs.
Summary: One of the top family guest ranches in North America. Excellent staff and superb children's and teens' programs. Year-round riding, cattle roundups, special horsemanship weeks. Great for family reunions and off-season conference groups. A true destination vacation.

McNamara Ranch
Florissant, Colorado

McNamara Ranch takes only four guests, offers unlimited riding opportunities, and attracts mostly women and couples who enjoy working with horses and like being in the saddle six hours a day. As owner Sheila says, "I feel a kinship with women and have developed my program for women and couples to come, relax, and ride this magnificent country with me." And when it comes to riding, the sky's the limit. Sheila is quite a horsewoman—she spent 25 years in Maryland foxhunting, and showing hunters and jumpers. In fact, she still prefers an English saddle. As she says, "I've been riding for over 40 years in Maryland, Virginia, Pennsylvania, and Wyoming, and to me this area of Colorado is the ultimate with so much diversity in such a small radius!" If lots of undivided attention, a riding program tailored to your riding abilities, and delicious barbecued lamb chops (lamb is her specialty) sound like what you're looking for, read no further! Give Sheila a call.

Address: 4620 County Road 100, Florissant, Colorado 80816
Telephone: 719/748-3466
Internet: www.mcnamararanch.com
Airport: Colorado Springs, 55 miles
Location: 55 miles west of Colorado Springs, 13 miles south of Florissant
Medical: St. Francis Hospital, Colorado Springs
Guest Capacity: four
Accommodations: Two bedrooms in the main house, one with a double bed and loft, the other with a double bed. Both share one bath.
Rates: • $$ American Plan. Side trips extra. No minimum stay (most guests stay about four days).
Credit Cards: None. Personal checks accepted; prefer traveler's checks or cash.
Season: June through October
Activities: Sheila gets up about 5:30 A.M. and hits the sack about 9 P.M. You're welcome to help tend the 13 head of horses. Sheila begins to think about riding after morning chores. No set riding schedules; if you wish to ride to 12,000 feet and put five hours in the saddle, you may. If you wish to ride bareback around the ranch, just ask Sheila. No nose-to-tail riding here. Just about the only thing you can't do here on horseback is ride on your own. Ask about the buggy rides. With Sheila's knowledge of horses and the country, and her friendly, caring spirit, guests appreciate her riding, camaraderie, and commentary. Other activities include hiking, river rafting on the Arkansas River two hours away, hot springs, sight-seeing, Pike's Peak, fossil beds, Garden of the Gods, and Eleven Mile Canyon.
Children's Program: None. Best for older ("horsey") kids who really like to ride and love horses.
Dining: Sheila admits that riding is really her forte. She's a meat-and-potatoes chef. Enjoy hearty ranch cooking. Lamb is one of her specialties—steaks, chops, and leg of lamb. Sheila will ask what your preferences are, including beverages and wine. BYOL.
Entertainment: By day's end and after a big dinner, everyone is usually pretty tuckered out. The hot tub has a view of Pike's Peak, which the guests enjoy looking at. Early to bed and early to rise is a good rule of thumb.
Summary: One of the best hands-on riding programs in the country. This is a small, intimate ranch for those who love horses and want personalized unlimited riding in the unspoiled wilderness of the Colorado high country, and can appreciate and enjoy unending, magnificent vistas. Excellent for women and couples who enjoy being in the saddle two to five hours a day. A very hands-on program of horsemanship, horse care, and all levels of riding. Sheila wants you to feel like you're visiting a friend in Colorado. Horses may sometimes be trailered out to take in other great rides. Sheila tailors a program for each guest. Ask about her lakeside tepee for overnight camping. Permit allows rides into Pike National Forest. Occasional cattle work on neighboring cattle ranch. Year-round riding, weather permitting.

North Fork Ranch
Shawnee, Colorado

North Fork Ranch is located on the North Fork of the South Platte River. Dean and Karen May and their children, Hayley and Tyler, are the hosts and owners of this delightful riverside ranch. Dean and Karen moved out West in the early 1980s. Today, North Fork offers families of all sizes a chance to ride, fish, hike, river raft, swim, play, and have wholesome fun together. President Dwight Eisenhower made this part of the country famous when he came to fish and relax in this valley. North Fork is a 520-acre, turn-of-the-century property. The original homestead cabin dates back to the 1890s. One of North Fork's unique features is the beautiful estate built out of native rock, which looks out over the river and the ranch. Dean has a background in forestry and Karen in nursing; together they share with their guests an understanding of the land and a compassion for all those who travel through their ranch gates. What makes North Fork unique is that the Mays encourage children and their parents to spend quality time together. North Fork Ranch is wonderful for young and older families who love the outdoors and being together.

Address: P.O. Box B-K, Shawnee, Colorado 80475
Telephone: 800/843-7895, 303/838-9873;   fax: 303/838-1549
Email: northforkranch@worldnet.att.net
Internet: www.northforkranch.com
Airport: Denver International or Colorado Springs
Location: 50 miles southwest of Denver, six miles west of Bailey, 120 miles northwest of Colorado Springs
Memberships: The Dude Ranchers' Association, Colorado Dude and Guest Ranch Association, Colorado Mule Riders
Medical: Conifer Mountain Medical Center, 20 miles. Karen May is a registered nurse.
Conference Capacity: 20, spring and fall
Guest Capacity: 43
Accommodations: The main lodge offers six rooms with private baths. The Homestead cabin offers accommodations for three families of four people; each unit has two bedrooms and a private bath. The Klondike cabin is a spacious duplex log

cabin for families of four or six. Stonehenge, the three-story estate, offers several sleeping arrangements. All accommodations are decorated in a unique style with antiques and Western art. Daily housekeeping service.
Rates: • $$$ American Plan. Children's, off-season, and group rates available. Minimum one-week stay, Saturday to Saturday. Shorter stays in off-season.
Credit Cards: None. Personal checks accepted.
Season: May through September
Activities: Weekly program. Families enjoy riding together. Experienced wranglers guide groups of 6–8 on half-day and all-day rides, champagne brunch rides, and overnight pack trips. Whitewater rafting on the Arkansas River with certified outfitters. Target and trapshooting (guns provided); fishing in the stocked pond or on the North Fork of the South Platte River that flows right through the ranch. Sunday fly-fishing instruction. Private guided off-ranch trips and fishing equipment available. Swimming in heated pool next to the river or relaxing in the spa at Stonehenge.
Children's Programs: Counselors and babysitters are available from 9 A.M.–4 P.M. for kids under age six (including infants), so parents are able to participate in ranch activities. Fun-filled days are planned with pony rides, hiking, fishing, swimming, lunches in the tepee, and even a special kids' campout.
Dining: Guests and staff dine together. Enjoy fresh breads, full turkey dinners, barbecues, and steak cookouts. Ask about Dean's special Rocky Mountain oysters. Friday farewell dinner features fresh trout or duck. Special diets catered to with advance notice. BYOB.
Entertainment: Square dancing, mountain man storyteller. Campfire sing-alongs and hayrides, as well as fishing, horseshoes, and volleyball.
Summary: One of the best small ranches that focuses on families who like to vacation with their children. Infants welcome. Located in a beautiful valley with a wonderful riverside setting, only 50 miles from Denver. Featured on *Fox Morning News*, *Good Morning America*, in *Good Housekeeping* magazine, and on Travelocity.

North Fork Ranch, Colorado

Peaceful Valley Ranch
Estes Park, Colorado

Peaceful Valley Ranch is a ranch resort offering a host of outdoor recreational opportunities. With a focus on families in the summer and business retreats and wellness spa activities, the year-round Peaceful Valley provides its guests with unparalleled hospitality and personal attention in a Rocky Mountain setting. Near Rocky Mountain National Park and in the St. Vrain Canyon, Peaceful Valley offers wholesome family activities and fun for all. During summer, enjoy riding on scenic mountain trails. Hiking, breakfast on the mountain, riverside picnics, and backcountry tours of ghost towns and gold mines display Colorado's beauty. Summer months focus on families, with lots to do. The spirit of the ranch is one of camaraderie, friendship, and diverse activities. Winter comes alive with weekend getaways, beautiful weddings, and group and corporate meetings.

Address: 475 Peaceful Valley Road, Lyons, Colorado 80540-8951
Telephone: 800/955-6343, 303/747-2881; fax: 303/747-2167
Email: howdy@peacefulvalley.com
Internet: www.peacefulvalley.com
Airport: Denver
Location: 65 miles northwest of Denver
Memberships: Colorado Dude and Guest Ranch Association
Awards: AAA 3 Diamond; Mobil 3 Star
Medical: Longmont Community Hospital, 28 miles
Conference Capacity: Groups of eight to 100. Brochure available.
Guest Capacity: 100
Accommodations: 10 cabins and 42 lodge rooms. Units are cozy and comfortable, most with queen beds and sitting areas, some are adjoining. Superb, roomy accommodations with full tub/shower bathrooms and sitting areas with views. The best rooms are appointed with whirlpool baths, private balconies, desks, and refrigerators. All cabins have living rooms with stone fireplaces, full-size private hot tubs, and refrigerators. Daily maid service and coin-operated laundry. Most rooms have telephones.
Rates: • $$$–$$$$$ American Plan; all-inclusive including gratuities. Conference rates available.

Children under age three are free (baby-sitting extra). Two- three-, or six-day packages available. Three-day minimum in summer. Off-season nightly rates available.
Credit Cards: VISA, MasterCard, Discover, American Express, Diner's Club
Season: Open year-round. Riding mid-May through mid-October, Dude Ranch mid-June through August.
Activities: Extensive riding with indoor arena. Beginning lessons to all-day trail rides. A good cross-section of riding. Usually eight guests per wrangler. Ask about all-day trip to Continental Divide and the Jamestown ride. Adults-only rides available. Extensive hiking program with naturalist, indoor swimming pool, spa, sauna, mountain biking, and fly-fishing on St. Vrain River, which runs through the ranch. Golf and white-water rafting nearby. Winter: Cross-country skiing, snowshoeing, snowmobiling, and heated pool. Horse-drawn sleigh rides.
Children's Programs: Extensive program for kids ages four through teens. Nursery and supervised children's program in summer. Strong teen program. Children's petting farm. Separate kids' dining area (optional).
Dining: Hearty ranch cuisine served family-style, special diets not a problem with advance notice. Beer, wine, and liquor available.
Entertainment: Line and square dancing, magic show, Western melodrama, gymkhana (guest rodeo), hayrides, campfire sing-alongs, cowboy entertainment, talent show, happy hour each evening before dinner.
Summary: Summer: Wonderful ranch resort with excellent children's programs, focusing on families and family reunions, emphasizing very personal service (two-to-one guest-to-staff ratio). Lots of activities for nonriders as well, including a guided hiking program for all ages and abilities. Excellent for weddings—beautiful Alpine chapel with views to the Continental Divide. Winter: Conferences, weddings, retreats, wellness spa weeks. Family reunions are a specialty here! Rocky Mountain National Park. Nearby: Elk, deer, and bighorn sheep sometimes seen.

Powderhorn Guest Ranch
Powderhorn, Colorado

Powderhorn Guest Ranch has a picture-perfect setting in a narrow mountain valley. Owners and hosts Greg and Shelly Williams are continuing the rich tradition of the ranch, making unbelievable vacation adventures come true. With almost a mile of scenic Cebolla (sa-VOY-a) Creek in southwestern Colorado, the Powderhorn Ranch, which used to be a fishing retreat and vacation resort, offers a peaceful, beautiful, and secluded hideaway for your adventures. Greg and Shelly are becoming famous for their hospitality and love of the Colorado highlands. Greg leads Jeep trips describing the rich history of the area and pointing out the abundant wildlife and wildflowers (nearby Crested Butte is the wildflower capital of North America). Shelly leads trail rides into primitive wilderness areas only accessible on horseback or on foot. Powderhorn attracts lots of families, couples, and singles. Greg and Shelly offer each visitor a unique, fun-filled adventure in some of Colorado's most beautiful and secluded high country.

Address: 1525 County Road 27, Powderhorn, Colorado 81243
Telephone: 800/786-1220, 970/641-0220; fax: 970/642-1399
Email: powguest@mindspring.com
Internet: www.powderhornguestranch.com
Airport: Gunnison via Denver; Colorado Springs, or Phoenix, Arizona; complimentary pickup at Gunnison
Location: 38 miles southwest of Gunnison, 36 miles northeast of Lake City
Memberships: The Dude Ranchers' Association, Colorado Dude and Guest Ranch Association, Lake City Chamber of Commerce, Gunnison Chamber of Commerce
Medical: Gunnison Valley Hospital
Conference Capacity: 40
Guest Capacity: 35
Accommodations: Thirteen individual, comfortable log cabins. All have refrigerators and coffeemakers with inviting front porches and chairs. All are carpeted and have private baths. Daily maid service is provided, with laundry facilities available.
Rates: • $–$$ American Plan. Children's and off-season rates. Six-day programs (Sunday to Saturday). Minimum stays apply.
Credit Cards: VISA, MasterCard, American Express. Personal checks and cash accepted.
Season: Mid-May to late October
Activities: Horseback riding with emphasis on safety and pleasure. Special attention given to novice riders. Scenic venue surrounded by 1.4 million acres of BLM (Bureau of Land Management) and national forests. Backs up to 64,000 acres of primitive wilderness. Secluded and remote. Weekly instruction in the arena. Weekly gymkhana, dinner ride, all-day rides. Guided Jeep tours and hikes. Excellent fishing on some of Colorado's best private waters, as well as two stocked ponds for beginners. Weekly fly-fishing clinics and guided fishing. Swimming in large heated pool or relax in the 12-person hot tub. River-raft trip with your choice of relaxing float trip or white-water adventure. Specialty weeks and off-season instructional seminars, gourmet week, adults-only weeks, and corporate retreats.
Children's Programs: Kids must be six years old to ride. No formal children's program.
Dining: Home-cooked meals are all you can eat and served family-style or buffet. Several cookouts during the week and dinner on the island. Guests and staff eat together. Special diets accommodated. BYOB in cabins only.
Entertainment: Nightly entertainment. Classic Western movies, square dancing, Western entertainers, campfire sing-alongs, and weekly gymkhana. Lodge has pool table, foosball, table tennis, board games, big-screen TV for movies, and an extensive library. Friday night's highlights include the "video of the week."
Summary: Small, friendly, and fun! For down-home friendly guests in a beautiful river-valley setting. Family-owned and operated. Remote and peaceful without a strictly regimented program. Ask about adults-only week in September, and family reunion and corporate retreat group rates.

Rainbow Trout Ranch
Antonito, Colorado

Rainbow Trout was built back in the 1920s and its 18,000-square-foot log lodge and cabins were used as an exclusive sportsman's retreat by anglers and their families—thus its name. Today Doug, Linda, David, and Jane Van Berkum carry on this great tradition. As in years gone by, Rainbow Trout is a haven for families who come to rejoice in natural beauty, horseback riding, fly-fishing, and being together. Rainbow Trout serves up plenty of warm and friendly hospitality. Guests can enjoy varied riding, fish the Conejos River, join in evening activities, and savor all the family fun. There is white-water rafting out of Taos, sight-seeing in Santa Fe, or riding the Cumbres & Toltec Scenic Railroad. At Rainbow Trout Ranch guests have the best of the Colorado Rockies with convenient proximity to New Mexico.

Address: 1484 FDR 250, Box 458 K, Antonito, Colorado 81120

Telephone: 800/633-3397, tel./fax: 719/376-5659

Email: rainbow2@amigo.net

Internet: www.rainbowtroutranch.com

Airport: Alamosa (available pickup extra); guests also fly into Colorado Springs, Denver, or Albuquerque, New Mexico

Location: Two miles off Highway 17 between Antonito, Colorado, 22 miles; and Chama, New Mexico, 29 miles; one hour southwest of Alamosa, Colorado; 2.5 hours north of Santa Fe, New Mexico

Memberships: The Dude Ranchers' Association, Colorado Dude and Guest Ranch Association

Medical: Regional hospital, La Jara; 45 minutes

Conference Capacity: 60; late May and September

Guest Capacity: 60

Accommodations: 15 old-time cabins with names like Deer, Birch, Cottonwood, and Cougar are situated above the main lodge and interspersed among the aspen and pines. They range in size from two bedrooms and one bath to three bedrooms and two baths. Larger cabins have living rooms and fireplaces. All have covered porches. Daily housekeeping. Laundry room.

Rates: • $$$ American Plan. Children's, off-season, and June rates. Sunday-to-Sunday stays June through August. Rafting, pack trips, and train rides extra.

Credit Cards: None. Personal and traveler's checks accepted.

Season: Late May through September

Activities: Horseback riding and fishing are the most popular ranch activities. You'll have your own horse for the week. Five to eight riders per ride, divided according to guests' wishes and abilities. Individual families can often ride together. Weekly overnight pack trip for teenagers and adults. The ranch's Conejos River and its tributaries are known for great fishing. Personal instruction and some gear available. Ask about the local professional guide service available for serious anglers. Heated swimming pool, hot tub, volleyball, basketball, hiking, and trapshooting. Ask about white-water rafting near Taos, New Mexico.

Children's Programs: Excellent supervised children's program for ages 3–5, 6–11, and teens. Kids ages 3–5 ride with a counselor; ages 6–11 have their own horse for the week and take trail rides. Crafts, hiking, swimming, and kids' cookouts also offered. Parents welcome to join in children's activities.

Dining: Hearty, home-cooked meals are served family-style in the lodge dining room. Lunch cookouts by the pool, chicken-and-steak barbecues at the picnic area, and candlelight dinner for adults are favorites. BYOB.

Entertainment: Something is planned most evenings. Weekly square dancing, Western dance, hayrides, sing-alongs, and watching the wranglers team rope. The lodge, with its huge wraparound porch, is a great place to relax with a good book.

Summary: At Rainbow Trout you'll find the best of Colorado and proximity to some of New Mexico's most famous towns. Great for families who want to be together but enjoy different activities for varied interests and ages. Magnificent, historic lodge with views of the valley. Varied horseback riding and superb fishing in the Conejos River. Kids especially enjoy riding in Doug's century-old wagon. Nearby: Santa Fe and Taos.

Rawah Ranch
Glendevey, Colorado

Rawah (ray-wah) is Ute for "abundance," a word that fits Rawah Ranch today more than ever. Secluded, relaxed Rawah, nestled in a stunning, wildlife-rich valley 60 miles from town, is owned and operated by the Kunz family, whose 25-plus years of dude ranch experience is evident in their hospitality. At 8,400 feet, Rawah borders a pristine 76,000-acre designated wilderness area of tumbling mountain streams, waterfalls, wildflower meadows, Alpine lakes, and snowcapped peaks. The Laramie River flows through the ranch, just steps away from the main lodge and cabins. Rawah appeals to couples, singles, and families with kids six and older. Its program of unlimited riding is its specialty, but you can also enjoy exceptional hiking, fishing, and whitewater rafting, pitching a few horseshoes, shooting a game of pool, or dozing in one of the rockers on the main lodge's front porch. Whatever you decide to do, you're in good hands at Rawah. It's one of the best.

Address: Glendevey, Colorado Route, Dept. K, 11447 North County Road 103, Jelm, Wyoming 82063 (summer); 1612 Adriel Circle, Dept. K, Fort Collins, Colorado 80524 (winter). (Rawah is in Colorado; the nearest post office is in Wyoming.)

Telephone: 800/820-3152 (year-round); 970/435-5715, fax: 970/435-5705 (summer); 970/484-8288, fax: 970/407-0818 (winter)

Email: ride@rawah.com

Internet: www.rawah.com

Airport: Denver, with commuter air service to Laramie, Wyoming; Laramie pick up available

Location: 60 miles southwest of Laramie, Wyoming; 75 miles northwest of Fort Collins, Colorado

Memberships: The Dude Ranchers' Association, Colorado Dude and Guest Ranch Association

Medical: Laramie Ivinson Memorial Hospital; staff EMT

Conference Capacity: 32

Guest Capacity: 32

Accommodations: The log lodge is the hub of activity, with stone fireplaces in the living and dining rooms and a wonderful rocking-chair porch looking out at Middle Mountain. Five rooms with baths are in the lodge, and nine single or duplex log cabins are scattered around the ranch. Cabins have sitting areas, fireplaces, electricity, and full baths. All rooms have choice of twin or king-size beds.

Rates: • $$$ American Plan; Sunday to Sunday, and includes all gratuities and service charges. Lower rates for kids ages 6–9. Off-season rates available.

Credit Cards: None. Personal checks, cash, and traveler's checks accepted.

Season: Mid-June through September. Adults-only all September.

Activities: Rawah goes out of its way to accommodate guests' riding preferences. Enjoy mountain trail, breakfast, and loping rides, plus arena riding and complimentary instruction. Thanks to an unusually high ratio of wranglers to guests, each day there are several half-day rides every morning and afternoon, or all-day rides. High, low, fast, slow, short, or long rides—it's your choice. Guests may saddle horses. Wild-trout fishing on the Laramie River, which runs through the ranch; the Poudre River nearby; more than 25 Alpine lakes and the ranch's stocked pond. Weekly afternoon fly-fishing clinic with professional instruction included. Great guided or on your own hiking. Rafting too.

Children's Programs: A more "grown-up" ranch that kids love too. Children ages six and older are welcome to ride with their families or each other. No formal children's program. Fishing pond, playground equipment, separate recreation building.

Dining: Guests actually complain that Rawah's food is too good. Sunrise coffee, tea, or cocoa delivered to guest cabins. Special diets with advance notice. BYOB. Sunday evening welcome reception.

Entertainment: Cowboy singers, square dancing, geology presentation, "roll-o-roper," rec room, numerous games in lodge.

Summary: Terrific combination of riding, fishing, hiking, and Western hospitality. It's one of the best! Here guests ride at their own pace in small groups. One guest wrote, "We came seeking wonderful family fun and found it 'in abundance' as befits Rawah! Great food, great fellow guests, great horses and trails, great staff, great evening entertainment."

Skyline Guest Ranch
Telluride, Colorado

Skyline is a celebration of spirit and nature. The Farnys—Dave and Sherry, and Mike and Sheila—describe their ranch this way: "Skyline Ranch is a magical place of unsurpassed beauty where adventures are shared and individuals are comfortably stretched. Experiences (many life-changing) give families and individuals a belief in themselves in a way that is uncommon in today's world. Our guests are rejuvenated, refreshed, challenged (by choice), and taken care of as if they are members of our family." And so it is. In the southwestern corner of the state, Skyline is nestled in the high rugged peaks of the San Juan Mountains. The crisp air and the crystal-clear mountain water, not to mention the snowcapped 14,000-foot peaks, make this ranch one of the most beautiful. Mike and Sheila Farny, and young sons Luke and Andrew, preserve their "mountain joy" tradition, a spirit on which guest ranching was founded—honest and friendly hospitality. With postcard views all around, this is one of the best guest ranches in the West.

Address: 7214 Highway 145, Telluride, Colorado 81435
Telephone: 888/754-1126, 970/728-3757; fax: 970/728-6728
Email: skyline-ranch@toski.com
Internet: www.ranchweb.com/skyline
Airport: Telluride
Location: 15 minutes from Telluride
Memberships: The Dude Ranchers' Association, Colorado Dude and Guest Ranch Association
Medical: Telluride Clinic, eight miles
Conference Capacity: 35; conference center
Guest Capacity: 35
Accommodations: Guests stay in 10 comfortable lodge rooms or six cabins. All lodgings have private baths, and beds with down comforters and sheepskin mattress covers. Awaken in the morning to sweet aromas from Skyline's kitchen; outdoor hot tub. Laundry facility available. No smoking in buildings.
Rates: • $$$$ American Plan. One-week minimum stay, Sunday to Sunday. Winter: See Cross-Country Skiing section.
Credit Cards: VISA, MasterCard, American Express. Personal and traveler's checks accepted.

Season: Summer: June to mid-October; Winter: Mid-December to April; open Christmas.
Activities: Summer brings a full horse program with Mike's extensive and inspiring "natural horsemanship" instruction for all levels. Guests may become as involved as they wish—grooming, saddling, and riding. Up to eight guests per ride. Beginning, intermediate, and advanced rides. Be sure to ask about the Dunton Meadow, Lizard Head, and Wilson Mesa rides. Also ask the Farnys about their magnificent overnight to High Camp. Trout fishing is superb in the ranch's three mountain lakes and nearby streams. Lake swimming for the brave. Guided mountain biking, hiking, and four-wheel-drive trips over Ophir Pass and to the abandoned gold- and silver-mining camps of Tomboy and Alta. For true adventurers, try the 14,000-foot peak climb. Tours of Mesa Verde National Park. Half-day and all-day whitewater trips (extra). Hot tub, massage available (extra). See Cross-Country Skiing section for winter activities.
Children's Programs: Really best for older children. No children's program, but kids can participate with parents. Kids under age six are offered walking rides led by horsemen on foot.
Dining: Skyline's cuisine is fresh and scrumptious. Vegetarian and special dietary requests are no problem. Breakfast rides and dinner cookouts are favorites. Complimentary beer and wine served with happy hour and dinner.
Entertainment: Dave plays a mean accordion. Sing-alongs, swing dancing. Terrific library and cozy main lodge.
Summary: Kilgore's "Best of the Best"–Horsemanship. Skyline celebrates nature and the spirit of adventure in a spectacular mountain setting. Excellent natural horsemanship program, hiking, fly-fishing, and mountain biking. Ask about the four-day pack trip and in winter the full Alpine skiing program. Best for older children, singles, couples and families. Ask about weekly video and conference center. Nearby: Telluride—filled with galleries, music festivals, shopping, and the breathtaking gondola ride—just 15 minutes away.

Tall Timber
Durango, Colorado

Throughout this guide I've exercised my "authorly" privilege of including a few extra-special properties that don't fit the exact mold of a ranch but do capture the spirit of adventure, wilderness, and luxury. This is one of them. Perched high in the splendor of the San Juan Mountains at 7,500 feet, Tall Timber is an exclusive hideaway. This Mobil 5-Star property is so secluded that guests arrive by the Durango-Silverton, one of the last narrow-gauge trains in the United States, or by helicopter. Dennis and Judy Beggrow discovered this remote spot in 1970 and today their son, Johnroy, oversees the operation. No roads and no telephones equal seclusion, beauty, and, maybe most of all, a marriage of luxury and nature.

Address: #1 Silverton Star, Durango, Colorado 81301
Telephone: 970/259-4813 (radiotelephone; be patient)
Internet: www.talltimberresort.com
Airport: Durango-La Plata; private planes to Animas Air Park with 5,000-foot paved runway; helicopters land at Tall Timber
Location: 26 miles north of Durango
Awards: Mobil 5 Star, Kilgore Luxury Group
Medical: Mercy Medical Center, Durango; emergency helicopter available
Conference Capacity: 24
Guest Capacity: 24
Accommodations: All 10 condominium-style units are private and surrounded by quaking aspen. There are eight one-bedroom and two two-bedroom suites, each with its own living room, wet bar, floor-to-ceiling stone fireplace, and balcony. Turndown service is provided each evening. Furnishings emphasize casual comfort. The main lodge is a massive three-story structure with wine cellar, wet bar, lounge, and dining room. Each year the Beggrows and staff plant more than 65,000 petunias, pansies, and snapdragons.
Rates: • $$$$$$ American Plan; includes transportation to and from Durango by train or helicopter (your choice) and gratuities. Two-, four-, and seven-day packages. Low season and children's rates. Ask about helicopter tours.
Credit Cards: VISA, MasterCard, Discover. Personal checks accepted.

Season: Summer: Mid-May through October; Winter: Mid-December through mid-January.
Activities: Most guests come in the summer to hike, flyfish, and take advantage of the incredible private helicopter excursions to mountaintops or even to Telluride for the day. Also available, heated pool (ask one of the staff to tell you how the pool arrived), three outdoor whirlpools (one overlooks the Animas River), sauna, putting green, driving range, nine-hole par-29 golf course, tennis court, and fly-fishing with instruction. All horse activities begin at a sister property a mile away. Guided horseback riding to high-mountain lakes, Silver Falls (a wonderful seasonal waterfall); morning, picnic, or afternoon rides; riding instruction available. Massage available. Winter: Christmas and New Year's include free daily helicopter service to Purgatory for downhill skiing.
Children's Programs: Tall Timber is great for families who enjoy the outdoors together. Kids are the responsibility of their parents.
Dining: Superb! Each table in the dining room has its own picture window. A culinary academy-trained chef prepares meals. Pre-selected menu features eggs Benedict, grilled salmon, beef Wellington, steak and trout, lots of fresh breads, and pastries. Many vegetables and herbs are fresh from the garden. (Ask about the extensive garden!) Dinners are candlelit with crystal and gold-rimmed china. Helicopter picnic lunch to Emerald Lake is a favorite. Stocked wine bar and extensive wines from around the world.
Entertainment: The evenings are all yours.
Summary: Kilgore Luxury Group. Exclusive wilderness hideaway. Arrive by the historic Durango-Silverton narrow-gauge train or by private Tall Timber helicopters. Most come to hike, relax, and savor the pristine beauty and privacy. Helicopters are always available for private use of guests (extra). Special privileges for returning guests.

Tarryall River Ranch
Lake George, Colorado

THE DUDE RANCHERS' ASSOCIATION

CDGRA

Once a cattle operation, Tarryall River Ranch developed into a dude ranch in the 1930s. Located at 8,600 feet in the central high-arid landscape of the Rockies and adjoining Lost Creek Wilderness (with Pike's Peak seen from the Monday orientation ride), the ranch is also near the famous gambling town of Cripple Creek. With tremendous Old West ambiance and under the direction of Jimmy and Jeannine Lahrman, Tarryall opened its gates once again in 1995. Together with their young family and an energetic staff, Jimmy and Jeannine bring a tremendous knowledge about the outdoors and education to their guests. In 1990 Jimmy, who is a world-class outdoorsman, hiked 2,200 miles of the Appalachian Trail over six months. He then went on to climb Mt. McKinley (20,320 feet). At Tarryall you'll have one great vacation plus the opportunity to better understand what the West is all about.

Address: 27001.5 County Road 77K, Lake George, Colorado 80827
Telephone: 800/408-8407, 719/748-1214; fax: 719/748-1319 (summer), 970/726-8553 (winter)
Email: tarryallRR@aol.com
Internet: www.tarryallranch.com
Airport: Colorado Springs, 65 miles; Denver, 125 miles
Location: 60 miles southwest of Colorado Springs, 125 miles southwest of Denver
Memberships: The Dude Ranchers' Association, Colorado Dude and Guest Ranch Association
Medical: Langstaff-Brown Medical Clinic, 35 miles
Conference Capacity: 36
Guest Capacity: 36
Accommodations: Two single-family cabins, one duplex cabin (shared living room with fireplace), and four two-bedroom suites, each with a private bath. Tastefully decorated with many antiques. All cabins and rooms reflect the Western atmosphere of years gone by. None are equipped with telephones or TVs and all cabins have covered porches. Daily housekeeping and guest laundry facilities provided.
Rates: • $$$ American Plan. Children's and group rates. Sunday-to-Sunday stays June through August. Rafting, pack trips, and off-ranch activities extra.
Credit Cards: None. Personal and traveler's checks accepted.
Season: Late May through September
Activities: The ranch offers a variety of organized activities along with a heated swimming pool and hot tub. Adults and kids may ride together or separately. Riding terrain varies from rocky cliffs to open meadows, providing walking, trotting, and cantering rides. Ask about the Lizard Rock and Hankins Pass rides. Weekly overnight pack trip to a secluded high mountain meadow paradise. Fly- and spin-fishers enjoy the Tarryall River on the ranch and Gold Medal fishing at Spinney and Eleven Mile Reservoirs, about 30 minutes away by car. Orvis instruction included and fishing trips available. A full day of white-water rafting on the Arkansas River is enjoyed by all. Hiking and scenic day trips. Weekly trapshooting. Hikers and climbers, ask Jimmy to tell about his 30-day Mt. McKinley expedition and his 14,000-foot Colorado scenic adventures.
Children's Programs: Full-time children's counselors for kids ages five and under. The ranch is small and intimate, so adults and children usually do things together. Kids ages six and older may trail ride. Informal nature lessons and hikes. Kids love the Wednesday evening music program, weekly hayride, birds-of-prey program, and petting zoo.
Dining: Family-style meals served in the lodge. All meals are home-cooked and waiters provide full service. BYOB. Occasional wine and beer served.
Entertainment: Weekly evening hayride after Jimmy's famous chicken-and-ribs cookout. Square dancing. Country-Western sing-alongs.
Summary: One of the best—owners Jimmy and Jeannie have a tremendous knowledge about the outdoors! Young staff with a friendly, small, and very happy atmosphere. The ranch has that John Wayne-Old West feel to it; rustic, but not too rustic, with lots of heart and soul. Be sure to ask Jeannine about their ride across America.

Tumbling River Ranch
Grant, Colorado

Tumbling River is one of the most famous family and children's ranches in America. Hosted by Jim and Mary Dale Gordon and their daughter Megan and her husband Scott Dugan, they serve up Southern hospitality high in the Colorado Rockies. At 9,200 feet, the ranch is in Indian country on the banks of Geneva Creek and in the middle of Pike National Forest. The property is divided into an upper ranch that was built as a mountain retreat in the 1920s (where most of the activities take place), and a lower ranch house, the Pueblo, featuring carved beams and adobe walls, which was built by Taos Indians for the daughter of Adolph Coors. One of the best features at Tumbling River is the extensive children's program with caring college counselors. Tumbling River Ranch, in one word, is terrific and brings out the very best in families and children.

Address: P.O. Box 30K, Grant, Colorado 80448
Telephone: 800/654-8770, 303/838-5981; fax: 303/838-5133
Email: info@tumblingriver.com
Internet: www.tumblingriver.com
Airport: Denver or Colorado Springs
Location: Four miles north of Grant, 62 miles southwest of Denver
Memberships: The Dude Ranchers' Association, Colorado Dude and Guest Ranch Association
Medical: Denver hospitals
Conference Capacity: 40; off-season only
Guest Capacity: 55
Accommodations: Accommodations are in two clusters: the upper lodge, and the Coors family Pueblo, about a quarter-mile apart. Eight cabins (one is bi-level) have names like Indian Hogan, the Frenchman's Cabin, Big Horn, and Tomahawk. Most have fireplaces, arched ceilings, and twin, queen-size, or bunk beds for kids. Some are real log, some log-sided; all porches have swings and hanging geranium planters, and many bird feeders are scattered about.
Rates: • $$$$ American Plan. Children's, off-season, and group rates available. One-week minimum stay, Sunday to Sunday.
Credit Cards: None. Personal and traveler's checks accepted.
Season: Mid-May through mid-October

Activities: A wide variety of activities: scenic high country riding with weekly riding clinic and instruction for all levels; half-day and all-day rides; family, kids, and overnight rides for adults and kids ages 12 and older. Hiking to breathtaking 14,000-foot vistas. Fly-fishing with instruction in stocked ponds, streams, and mountain lakes. The heated swimming pool has a full-length cabana with tables and an eight-person hot tub with nearby old-time steam sauna. Weekly river rafting on Arkansas River (extra).
Children's Programs: Tops! Excellent morning and afternoon supervised Western programs for children ages three through teens. Kiddie wrangler and programs for children three years old and up. Separate programs for children ages 3–5, 6–11, and teens. Limited baby-sitting available for kids under age three. Children ages 3–5 ride with supervision. Ask about tepee overnight.
Dining: Complimentary coffee delivered to your cabin each morning. Every day except Wednesday there's a cookout. Favorite menus include apple pancakes with apple-cider syrup, and fajita lunch cookouts with homemade soup. Weekly "Gordon's hamburgers" poolside. Two adult candlelight dinners. Entrées include pork tenderloin with fettuccini Alfredo, beef tenderloin, and weekly Thanksgiving dinner. Pecan pies, too. Wine served with dinner. BYOB.
Entertainment: Every night offers something different: hayrides, mountain campfires with hot chocolate, square dancing, ranch rodeos, talent shows. Old-fashioned farewell hootenanny.
Summary: One of Kilgore's "Best of the Best-Children's Programs." Excellent family ranch with outstanding children's program! Hosts and staff are tops! Wait until you see the marvelous old ranch trading post. Nearby: Historic narrow-gauge train and the towns of Georgetown and Fairplay.

Vista Verde Ranch
Steamboat Springs, Colorado

Set in a secluded valley with hay meadows and mountain vistas, Vista Verde is not just a riding ranch. It offers tremendous diversity for those who want to experience other adventures like river rafting, fly-fishing, rock-climbing, and hot-air ballooning. The Munns have kept their ranch small and charming—a hideaway to forget your worries and savor a piece of paradise that will be protected forever through the Nature Conservancy. In his business career, John Munn made a specialty of buying companies and making them better. When John and his wife, Suzanne, escaped the Midwest in 1991 to fulfill their dream, they took the same approach with Vista Verde. As John says, "The ranch was already a wonderful property. What we've done has simply made it better." And so they have. With a beautiful lodge, upgraded cabins, a talented chef, and lots of energy, Vista Verde is indeed better than ever and one of the best year-round guest ranches in North America.

Address: P.O. Box 465K, Steamboat Springs, Colorado 80477
Telephone: 800/526-7433, 970/879-3858; fax: 970/879-1413
Email: vistaverde@compuserve.com
Internet: www.vistaverde.com
Airport: The ranch is remote yet very accessible, with the Hayden Airport just 40 miles away. Ranch Suburbans meet you there.
Location: 25 miles north of Steamboat Springs, off Seed House Road
Memberships: The Dude Ranchers' Association, Colorado Dude and Guest Ranch Association
Awards: Mobil 4 Star; Kilgore Luxury Group
Medical: Yampa Valley Medical Center
Conference Capacity: 30
Guest Capacity: 40
Accommodations: Named after surrounding mountains, log cabins are nestled in aspens and pines. Handsomely furnished, they include woodstoves, full baths, and comfortable porches that overlook the meadows and forest. All have private outdoor hot tubs and master suites for Mom and Dad. Three spacious rooms with splendid views are upstairs in the lodge. Fresh flowers and baskets of snacks and a fridge full of bever-

ages welcome arriving guests.
Rates: • $$$$ American Plan. Children's, low-season, and winter rates available. Hot-air balloon rides, overnight pack trips, and massages (extra). One-week minimum, Sunday to Sunday.
Credit Cards: None. Personal or traveler's checks accepted.
Season: Summer: Late May to September. Winter: Christmas to mid-March. (See Cross-Country Skiing section.)
Activities: Riding program includes in-depth arena instruction for all levels of experience. Numerous daily trail rides (such as Hole-in-the-Wall Canyon, The Cliffs, and Indian Hill) through the adjoining National Forest. Rock-climbing with instruction provides a thrilling experience. Rafting on the Colorado, kayaking on the Yampa, professional and ranch rodeos, extensive hiking and nature program, mountain biking, guided fly-fishing and instruction, hot-air ballooning. Special adult weeks in June and September for cattle drives, and fly-fishing.
Children's Programs: Complete supervised program for youngsters 6–18 is structured to provide some activities with parents (riding, rock-climbing, rodeo, most meals) and apart (gold panning, fire-engine rides, Indian lore, animal feeding, and treasure hunts). Special adventures for teens. Ask about the Coyote Corral and one-of-a-kind fountain deck.
Dining: Award-winning chefs prepare gourmet meals with a touch of country. Homegrown vegetables; homemade, just-baked everything; hand-cranked ice cream. Special dietary needs accommodated. Fine wine and beer available.
Entertainment: Reception Sunday evenings hosted by the Munns. Something is planned each night: folk music, cowboy poetry, barn dancing, staff show, pro rodeo, and steer roping by local cowboys.
Summary: One of the top year-round ranches in North America. Lots of wilderness, lots of great food, and lots of good company. With so many on- and off-ranch adventures, this is more than just a riding ranch. Ask about winter when it's Vista "Blanca." Nearby: Famous ski town of Steamboat Springs.

Vista Verde Ranch, Colorado

Wilderness Trails Ranch
Durango, Colorado

THE DUDE RANCHERS' ASSOCIATION

CDGRA

A soaring eagle, the songs of coyotes, a deer bounding across the meadow, horses grazing in the pasture, and twinkling stars in the clear mountain skies—welcome to Wilderness Trails Ranch, "a blend of the past and present." The Roberts family has owned this lovely Colorado Rockies ranch since 1970 and offer one of the finest ranch vacation experiences in the country. Their family and staff are committed to providing their guests with an extraordinary vacation experience and invite you to share in their passion…"a legacy of Western living." Wilderness Trails is snuggled next to the Piedra Wilderness in the San Juan Mountains of southwestern Colorado. The charming log lodge looks out over the secluded, picturesque Pine River Valley, which flows into beautiful Vallecito Lake. Wilderness Trails Ranch is one of the great family ranches in America today.

Address: 1766K County Road 302, Durango, Colorado 81303
Telephone: 800/527-2624, 970/247-0722; fax: 970/247-1006
Email wtrk@wildernesstrails.com
Internet: www.wildernesstrails.com
Airport: La Plata Airport in Durango via Denver; Albuquerque, New Mexico; or Phoenix, Arizona
Location: 35 miles northeast of Durango in southwest Colorado, 190 miles northwest of Albuquerque, New Mexico
Memberships: The Dude Ranchers' Association, Colorado Dude and Guest Ranch Association
Awards: Mobil 3 Star, AAA 3 Diamond
Medical: Mercy Medical Center, Durango; 35 miles; local rescue service
Guest Capacity: 48
Accommodations: Comfortable, well-appointed, two-bedroom log cabins with porches, nestled among pines, spruce, and aspen. Lovely country furnishings; queen, king, or single beds; modern, private baths with shower/tub combinations; amenities packet; hair dryers; and refrigerators. Three-bedroom, three-bath "cabin suites" feature wood-burning stoves in living rooms, separate room with minibar, coffeemaker, refrigerator, and robes. Daily maid service. Laundry facilities available.
Rates: • $$$$–$$$$$ American Plan; including gratuities. Family rates. Discounts early June and

September. Six-night minimum stay, Sunday arrival.
Credit Cards: VISA, MasterCard, Discover
Season: June through August for families; September, adults-only (six-night minimum).
Activities: Riding is central with certified riding instructors and ranch-owned horses. Here you'll expand your riding abilities and learn to communicate with, and understand your horse through "natural horsemanship." Scheduled morning, afternoon, all-day, and weekly family rides into the San Juan Mountains. Ask about the Lake Lookout and Vista Grande rides. No more than eight to a ride and rides are separated into "Sidekicks," "Trailhands," or "Trailblazers," depending upon ability. Boot rental available. Seventy-two-foot heated pool. Massage available. Weekly Jeep trip to Middle Mountain, tour to Mesa Verde cliff dwellings, river rafting, water-skiing, hiking, fishing, and hot tub. Historic Durango-Silverton steam train a favorite.
Children's Programs: One of the top children's programs in the country for ages 3–5, 6–10, 11–12. Terrific teen program for ages 13–17. Special kids' and teen wranglers, water-skiing, riding instruction, trail rides, hayrides, youth rodeo (rock-climbing for teens), and a variety of other activities keep the kids happy and entertained all day. Ask about the new foals and Indian "wildcrafting." Parents may do as much as they wish with their children.
Dining: Great dining program for parents and kids! Families dine together for breakfast. Kids can eat lunch and/or dinner separately with their counselors or newfound friends. Weekly gourmet candlelight dinner with wine for adults. Hearty ranch cuisine plus vegetarian selections. BYOB.
Entertainment: A variety of fun each evening—country dancing, campfire sing-alongs, and weekly rodeo in town. Horse-drawn hayrides too.
Summary: One of Kilgore's "Best of the Best"—Children's and Teen Programs. Beautiful, remote setting! Great hosts and staff attracting 95 percent families. Wide variety of activities and weekly adventure trips. Featured on *Good Morning America* and PBS special "Going Places." Outstanding destination for adults, families, reunions, or singles. September is adults only and also features a cattle roundup and horse seminar.

Wit's End Guest and Resort Ranch
Vallecito Lake (near Durango), Colorado

Wit's End Guest and Resort Ranch is located in the beautiful Vallecito Lake Valley just off County Road 500. Set amid thousands of aspen and pines, it offers guests a host of activities, all in a setting of luxury, charm, and quality. Wait until you see the exquisite craftsmanship and decor of the beautifully restored, century-old main lodge. The ranch is surrounded by 12,000- to 14,000-foot mountains and looks out over its own Chain O'Lakes and meadows. At Wit's End you can do as much or as little as you wish. Unlike many guest ranches, Wit's End offers rustic elegance with all the freedoms that you might find at a resort. The theme is luxury at the edge of the wilderness. It's a wonderful haven for families, singles, couples, children of all ages, and groups.

Address: 254 CR 500, Vallecito Lake, Durango, Colorado 81122
Telephone: 800/236-9483, 970/884-4113; fax: 970/884-3261
Email: witsend@bwn.net
Internet: www.ranchweb.com/witsend
Airport: Durango
Location: 24 miles northeast of Durango, directly off County Road 500 and U.S. 160
Memberships: Orvis-endorsed Lodge
Awards: 4 Stars by Star Rating Service; *Country Inns* magazine "One of the 12 Best in America;" Kilgore Luxury Group
Medical: Mercy Medical, Durango
Conference Capacity: 300
Guest Capacity: 160 in 40 cabins
Accommodations: All of the one-, two-, three-, and four-bedroom log cabins are decorated for the most discriminating taste: knotty-pine interiors, native stone fireplaces, queen-size brass beds, down comforters, Berber carpets, balloon draperies, French doors, TVs, telephones, china dishes, attractive kitchens with separate dining areas, and swings and willow furniture on the porches.
Rates: • $$$–$$$$$ American Plan; includes all ranch activities May through October. Three- and seven-day minimums. Ask about new spa and hydrotherapy center plus Orvis-endorsed fly-fishing program, and optional extras.
Credit Cards: VISA, MasterCard, Discover,

American Express. Personal and traveler's checks accepted.
Season: Year-round; high-summer season June through September.
Activities: A host of outdoor activities for children, adults, and families. Lakeside and extensive mountain riding (one hour to all day), guided wilderness hikes, swimming in 50-foot heated pool or lake. Orvis-endorsed fly-fishing on lakes and streams. Weekly arena activities in regulation rodeo arena; riding program includes beginning, intermediate, and selective advanced riding. Tennis, biking, hot tubs, mountaintop motor tours, hayrides, water-skiing, and pontoon boat rides. Massage, trapshooting, and wilderness overnight trips. Optional extras include white-water rafting, cattle drive, Native American ruins, golf, rodeos, and Durango-Silverton train. Winter: Cross-country skiing with equipment included. Sleigh rides, guided mountain snow-mobiling, and pond skating. Downhill skiing at Purgatory included in Full American Plan winter rates.
Children's Programs: Extensive summer program with counselors for kids ages 4–12, and teens too. Kids and teens each have own activity center and overnight campouts.
Dining: Dine in the exquisite, century-old lodge. Scrumptious meals served table side, and wonderful desserts. Campfire cookouts and kids' meals. Room service, full bar, and extensive wine list.
Entertainment: Nightly seasonal live entertainment, cozy bar and lodge open before and after dinner. Dancing, campfire singing, skits, roping, barrel racing, and karaoke.
Summary: World-class luxury ranch resort at the edge of the wilderness in Vallecito Lake Valley. Orvis-endorsed lodge. Superb cuisine, wonderful accommodations, and kids' program. Excellent for special occasions. Spa and conference center. Resort spirit—do as much or as little as you please. Featured on "Great Country Inns" on PBS, the Learning Channel, and Home and Garden Television. Nearby: White-water rafting, cattle drive, and Durango-Silverton train.

Wit's End Guest and Resort Ranch, Colorado

Wit's End Guest and Resort Ranch, Colorado

Bar H Bar Ranch
Soda Springs, Idaho

The Bar H Bar Ranch, steeped in pioneer history, is one of the oldest ranches in southeastern Idaho and was homesteaded by the Mormon Church. Owned today by McGee and Janet Harris. The deep ruts of the Oregon Trail are visible as they follow the Bear River, which runs through the 9,000-acre ranch. Bar H Bar is located in the Bear River Range of the Wasatch Mountains and borders Caribou Cache National Forest. You'll see Idaho in all its beauty—hay meadows, a splendid variety of stately pine and shimmering aspen, cold streams, wildlife, and breathtaking panoramas of wildflowers in June and July. This is a real working cattle ranch that runs 2,000 head of beef cattle, pasturing most of them on private land. The Harris family, Janet and McGee, sons Wade, Todd, Kurt, and Mark, along with their wives and children, keep very active in running this large working ranch. Guests enjoy not only the spirit of the family, but also all of the activities that are associated with cattle ranching today.

Address: 1501 Eight Mile Creek Road, Drawer K, Soda Springs, Idaho 83276
Telephone: 800/743-9505, 208/547-3082; fax: 208/547-0203
Email: barhbar@aol.com
Internet: www.barhbar.com
Airport: Salt Lake, 184 miles; Idaho Falls, 120 miles; Pocatello, 60 miles; Jackson, 100 miles
Location: 60 miles east of Pocatello off Highway 30 to Soda Springs
Medical: Caribou Memorial Hospital, eight miles
Memberships: National Cattlemen's Association
Guest Capacity: 4–6
Accommodations: There are four rooms in an old-fashioned, rustic bunkhouse. Each room has a private entrance and is furnished with native lodgepole pine furniture with a sprinkling of antiques that reflect the early years of this pioneer ranch. From a full-length porch you'll enjoy relaxing in rocking chairs and finding pleasure in the sights and sounds of nature.
Rates: • $$–$$$ American Plan. Family rates are available. Five-day minimum stay, Sunday to Saturday.
Credit Cards: None. Personal, traveler's and cashier's checks accepted.

Season: Summer: May through September; Winter: December through March.
Activities: Real working ranch experience. Activities vary according to the season and include calving, branding, fence repair, and moving cattle to spring and summer ranges; also salting and doctoring cattle, irrigating and preparing cattle for market, and moving to winter range. Other activities include nature hikes (you may see a variety of wildlife), fishing on and off the ranch, and just relaxing. Winter: Snowmobiling December through March.
Children's Programs: Best for children over age 15.
Dining: You'll eat with the Harris family. Most meals are cooked and served family-style in the old ranch cookhouse. Three hearty meals a day in the tradition of the West, which may include homemade bread, pies, and other goodies, Dutch-oven cookouts, and steak-fries. The cookhouse is open to guests 24 hours a day for late-night snackers.
Entertainment: Everyone is usually pretty tired at the end of the day. Many go for an evening stroll, some retire early, others enjoy listening to the coyote serenades.
Summary: A great American ranching family. The Harrises have been in the cattle ranching business for four generations. In 1993, they opened the ranch gates to the world and have been sharing their special love of the West and their way of life ever since. If you're looking for a real hands-on working-ranch vacation with plenty of good food, savvy cow horses, and a wholesome time, give the Harrises a call. Because they take only four to six guests there is some flexibility for riding and other ranch activities. Featured in Guest Ranch Roundup in *National Geographic Traveler* magazine.

Diamond D Ranch
Stanley, Idaho

The Diamond D is located in one of Idaho's hidden valleys. Many guests come by car and savor the long and winding gravel road up and over Loon Creek Summit that eventually switches back down into the rugged Salmon River Mountain Valley. This slow but scenic drive is breathtaking and gives everyone a chance to slow down and unwind to the pace that they will enjoy for their week or two, or more, at the ranch. The Diamond D is remote. On all sides it's bounded by millions of acres of wilderness and plenty of wildlife. Arriving at the ranch, you feel the same exhilaration the early gold miners must have felt when they exclaimed, "Eureka! We have found it!" The Demorest family has been running this wonderful ranch since 1951. No telephones—nothing but pure Idaho wilderness and wonderful family hospitality. The Diamond D is one of Kilgore's diamonds in the rough!

Address: P.O. Box 35 K, Stanley, Idaho 83278 (summer); P.O. Box 1555K, Boise, Idaho 83701 (winter)
Telephone: 800/222-1269; Summer: Radio-telephone, 208/756-4713, for emergencies only (The voice answering will probably say "McCall Air Taxi."); Winter: 208/336-9772; fax: 208/336-9772
Email: DIADlld@aol.com
Internet: www.diamonddranch-Idaho.com
Airport: Boise, 45 minutes by charter plane, four hours by car. Air charter service available from Boise to the 2,600-foot dirt airstrip just four miles from the ranch.
Location: 75 miles north of Sun Valley off Highway 75. Ranch will send you a map.
Medical: Emergency helicopter service available
Conference Capacity: 35
Guest Capacity: 40
Accommodations: Three comfortable two-bedroom cabins a short walk from the main lodge and near Loon Creek. One large four-bedroom cabin that sleeps 10, one-bedroom suites including the honeymoon/anniversary suite. Several upstairs lodge rooms. All rooms and cabins have electricity and modern bathrooms. A hydroelectric generator powers ranch. Guest laundry.
Rates: • $$$ American Plan. Children's rates

available.
Credit Cards: None. Personal checks and cash.
Season: Mid-June to mid-October
Activities: Lots of activities are available each day. Evening and morning sign-up sheets for horseback riding, hiking, guided fishing, and gold panning. Ask about guided hikes to Mystery Lake, a 3,000-foot climb, and the ride to Rob's Hot Springs and Pinyon Peak (tremendous lookout point at 10,000 feet) rides. The Diamond D offers 3–7 day pack trips to hot springs, mountain lakes, and historic ranches. Swimming in modern pool with adjacent hot tub. Ranch has its own lake with rowboats and fishing. Volleyball, badminton, and horseshoes on the green lawn in front of the lodge. Each summer the ranch hosts numerous weddings and renewal of vows in the beautiful, hand-built rock chapel overlooking Loon Creek.
Children's Programs: Fully supervised programs for children under age six. Kids under age six don't trail ride. Kids over six participate fully with parents.
Dining: Western ranch cooking. Special diets catered to with advance notice. Birthdays, anniversaries, and weddings (ask about their wedding cakes), are always special. BYOB.
Entertainment: Campfire sing-alongs. Cards, games, video movies, and fireside conversation in the lodge.
Summary: Incredible setting! One of the great family-run ranches for families on the headwaters of Loon Creek, which is a tributary of the Middle Fork of the Salmon River. Lovely remote ranch in the heart of some of Idaho's most pristine wilderness with all the comforts of home and its own private lake. The area is full of Western lore, gold mines, and Indian stories. If you drive, you'll want to see the old mining town of Custer and the Yankee Fork gold dredge. Ask about the wonderful crafts program. Private pilots should call Tom or Linda for details.

Hidden Creek Ranch
Harrison, Idaho

THE DUDE RANCHERS'
ASSOCIATION

Idaho, "The Gem State," is a nature-lover's paradise. Hidden Creek Ranch is one of Idaho's treasures. It has been created with great care by a couple who believes in love, respect, and understanding for nature. John Muir and Iris Behr searched the Rockies for a ranch where they could share their philosophy. As Iris says, "When we arrived at Hidden Creek, we felt the magic right away." John and Iris bring to the world of guest ranching a unique respect for nature and the environment. With European attention to detail, first-class accommodations, and a beautiful Idaho landscape, Hidden Creek Ranch is one of the best in North America!

Address: 7600 East Blue Lake Road, Harrison, Idaho 83833
Telephone: 800/446-3833, 208/689-3209; fax: 208/689-9115
Email: hiddencreek@hiddencreek.com
Internet: www.hiddencreek.com
Airport: Spokane; private planes use Coeur d'Alene and St. Maries
Location: Five miles east of Harrison off Highway 97; 78 miles southeast of Spokane; 40 miles southeast of Coeur d'Alene
Memberships: The Dude Ranchers' Association, Idaho Guest & Dude Ranch Association, Audubon Society, Sierra Club, Windstar Foundation, Nature Conservancy
Medical: Kootenai Medical Center, Coeur d'Alene; 40 miles; members of Life Flight
Conference Capacity: 40; excellent for corporate retreats. Ropes course for team and awareness building.
Guest Capacity: 40
Accommodations: Authentic log cabins, comfortably appointed with private baths, overlooking the valley and timber-ridged mountains. The lodge is a spacious dining and meeting facility. Wheelchair accessible.
Rates: • $$$$–$$$$$ American Plan. Children's, off-season, and group rates. Six-day stay Sunday to Saturday.
Credit Cards: VISA, MasterCard, American Express. Personal checks preferred.
Season: Year-round
Activities: Daily horseback riding: scenic, fast, challenging, all-day, lunch, and dinner rides; hay wagon rides, Centered Riding® instruction, horse grooming, saddling and draft team lessons, cow herding games, barrel racing rodeo, fly-fishing, pond fishing, mountain hikes, nature walks, medicine-trail hike, mountain bikes, archery, trap-shooting, and boat tours. The Body, Mind & Spirit Well-Being Program includes fitness hikes, jogging, yoga classes, stretching, breathing and relaxation training, meditation and massage services. In addition, there is a ropes course and climbing tower. Winters offer cross-country skiing, snowshoeing, horseback riding, and snowmobile tours.

Children's Programs: Extensive program for children ages three to teens. Special activities include daily horseback riding, nature awareness, beading, and nature arts and crafts. Picnics, hiking and biking expeditions, campfires with Native American storytelling, a cookout followed by an overnight in Tepee Village, and more.

Dining: Iris and John believe that good food is one of the greater pleasures in life. Their chef offers an eclectic gourmet dining experience. Buffet lunches, four-course family-style dinners, and seven-course candlelight dinner. Cocktail hour with wine, beer, soft drinks, and liquor available (extra), and complimentary hors d'oeuvres.

Entertainment: Evening activities differ nightly and include a dinner ride, Western dance, campfire activities, roping lessons, Native American pipe and sweat-lodge ceremonies. Stay concludes with seven-course candlelight dinner, and quick-draw contest.

Summary: Kilgore's "Best of the Best"– Outstanding children's program. A huge variety of activities with unparalleled Centered Riding® and Native American awareness program. You will find impeccable service with exceptional European attention to detail and gourmet cuisine. At Hidden Creek Ranch the emphasis is on environmental stewardship; and body, mind, and spirit well-being achieved through a life in balance. Excellent video available! German spoken.

Idaho Rocky Mountain Ranch
Stanley, Idaho

Breathtaking mountain views, historic architecture, a natural hot springs swimming pool, fine food, and proximity to Sun Valley in an outdoor adventure wonderland where guests have the freedom to choose their own activities—welcome to the Idaho Rocky Mountain Ranch! One of Kilgore's "Best of the Best," the ranch is located in the Sawtooth and White Cloud Mountain Ranges of central Idaho, which is one of the most spectacular and least-traveled regions of the United States. Recreational opportunities ranging from sunset viewing in rocking chairs on the front porch, to vigorous hiking, biking, horseback riding, and water adventures provide guests with an abundant variety of activities. The ranch helps guests create their own self-styled adventure vacation. Nearby Sun Valley offers memorable cultural events and shopping. The ranch's charming lodge and cabins were handcrafted in 1930 from the surrounding forests. Today, under the guidance of Rozalys Bogert Smith, whose family has owned the ranch since 1951, the ranch staff continues to offer gracious hospitality in this magnificent setting. Here you'll savor the magic of natural beauty and the spirit of friendship.

Address: HC 64, Box 9934 K, Stanley, Idaho 83278
Telephone: 208/774-3544; fax: 208/774-3477
Email: idrocky@ruralnetwork.net
Internet: www.idahorocky.com
Airport: Boise, 130 miles; Sun Valley (Hailey), 65 miles; grass airstrip in Stanley, 10 miles
Location: 50 miles north of Sun Valley/Ketchum
Memberships: National Trust for Historic Preservation, Nature Conservancy, Sun Valley-Ketchum Chamber of Commerce
Awards: National Register of Historic Places
Medical: Medical clinic in Stanley, nine miles; St. Luke's Hospital in Sun Valley, 50 miles
Conference Capacity: 42; for exclusive occupancy only (call for details)
Guest Capacity: 42
Accommodations: Beautifully preserved, 7,400-square-foot hand-hewn-log main lodge houses a large sitting room, dining room, and four rooms with queen beds and private baths. The lodge porch provides spectacular vistas of the valley below and mountains beyond, and the cane and hickory rockers are well used throughout the summer. Eight duplex log cabins and honeymoon cabin offer handcrafted furniture, stone fireplaces, private baths, and either twin or queen beds.
Rates: • $$ Modified American Plan; includes breakfast and dinner. Most activities are à la carte. Minimum three-night stay.
Credit Cards: VISA, MasterCard, Discover
Season: Early June through September
Activities: On-site summer activities include a popular horseback-riding program; hot springs swimming pool; fishing in the Salmon River and the private, stocked, catch-and-release ranch pond; mountain bike rentals; hiking trails; horseshoes; sunset and wildlife viewing. Nearby activities include rafting on the Salmon and Payette Rivers, fishing in the Salmon River and numerous pristine mountain lakes, hiking, and mountain biking. Rock-climbing, photography, nature study, ghost town tours, and browsing in world-famous Sun Valley are other popular activities.
Children's Programs: Children are welcome and are the responsibility of parents.
Dining: Breakfast and dinner meals are included for guests. Breakfast features a continental buffet including homemade baked goods and a choice of hot breakfasts. Dinners include appetizer, soup, salad, choice of entrée, and dessert. This is Idaho-country cuisine at its best, featuring fresh Idaho trout, steaks, lamb, pastas, and chef's specials. Vegetarian options are available. There are three special dinner events each week: a horse-drawn wagon ride to a Dutch-oven cookout, Western barbecue, and Idaho Night served family-style. Fine wine and beer bar.
Entertainment: Many guests enjoy relaxing and sharing the day's events on the front porch while taking in the awe-inspiring views. Contemporary live Western music with local musicians. Library and games.
Summary: Kilgore's "Best of the Best"–Historic Architecture and spectacular views. Most activities are à la carte. Hot springs pool and cultural events in Sun Valley area.

Kelly Toponce Guest Ranch
Bancroft, Idaho

Kelly Toponce Guest Ranch is a working cattle, hay, and thoroughbred ranch that welcomes a few individuals, couples, or one family at a time. Here in southeastern Idaho, Eileen and Mike Chambers, and their 18-year-old son Klinton, offer a down-to-earth, back-to-nature experience for those who wish to fish, ride, hike, take in the beautiful hay fields, rolling mountaintops, and enormous cloud formations, or enjoy Eileen's summer vegetable garden. It is also for folks who want to simply get away and enjoy the peace and quiet. Here your time is indeed your own, and as Eileen says, "We have folks come to be a part of our family, share what we love and savor, and have the option to work with us on the ranch." For the real horse enthusiast, be sure to ask Eileen about their career in thoroughbred training.

Address: 705 E. Toponce Canyon Road, Bancroft, Idaho 83217
Telephone: 208/648-7347 (tel./fax)
Email: chmbrsmuc@aol.com
Internet: www.ranchweb.com/kellytoponce
Airport: Pocatello Airport, shuttle available (extra), one hour; Salt Lake City, Utah, shuttle available (extra), 2.5 hours.
Location: 17 miles east of Lava Hot Springs in the Chesterfield Reservoir area, 50 miles southeast of Pocatello, 2.5 hours north of Salt Lake City, Utah
Memberships: Idaho Cattleman Association, California Thoroughbred Trainers Association
Awards: Trainer of the Year 1985, numerous trainer awards through the years
Medical: Soda Springs Hospital, 40 miles
Guest Capacity: 6
Accommodations: Two large newly-built cabins each with two queen-size beds. Both have full baths with handicap access. Sitting areas have propane stoves and coffeemakers. A porch adjoins the two cabins with hot tub and barbecue. One large bunkhouse has a fully equipped kitchen, a sitting/eating area, separate bedroom with king-size bed, bathroom, and deck off bedroom. Laundry room for guests.
Rates: • $$ American Plan. Three-, five-, and seven-day packages.
Credit Cards: VISA, MasterCard. Personal and traveler's checks accepted.

Season: May to September; January to March.
Activities: Guests may and are encouraged to bring their own horses. Horseback riding program is geared to more experienced riders. Wide-open country offers tremendous views, side-by-side riding in the open meadows, and trail riding in the steeper country of the Caribou National Forest. Guests will see cattle, sheep, and some wildlife including deer, elk, and the occasional moose. Fly-fishing for rainbows on the ranch pond, in Toponce Creek and in Chesterfield Reservoir (three miles away). Twenty-Four Mile Reservoir offers trophy fishing. Guests should bring their own gear. Winter brings snowmobile enthusiasts and some cross-country skiers. Snowshoeing too. Ice fishing in the reservoir is incredible.
Children's Programs: Best for older and well-behaved children. Children are parents' responsibility.
Dining: Good, wholesome, ranch-style cooking. Everyone eats together. BYOB.
Entertainment: No organized entertainment; guests can pretty much do what they want at the end of the day.
Summary: Working cattle, hay, and thoroughbred ranch. Owners and hosts have had an exciting and extensive career in thoroughbred horse training and care. Awarded Trainer of the Year in Seattle. Guests may, and are encouraged to bring their own horses. More experienced riders preferred, side-by-side meadow and scenic trail riding into the national forest. Guests may, if they wish, help with ranch work like feeding horses, fencing, irrigating, and moving cattle when needed. Terrific fishing on nearby lakes and reservoirs. Best for adults and older children who love the outdoors and appreciate a slow and easygoing, unstructured experience. Nearby: Chesterfield Reservior and Twenty-Four Mile Reservior for fly-fishing and trophy fishing.

Teton Ridge Ranch
Tetonia, Idaho

On the not-so-well-known west side of the Tetons is a paradise they call Teton Ridge Ranch. This luxurious guest ranch with splendidly designed log architecture overlooks the distant mighty Grand Tetons, rising some 13,775 feet. The ranch has hosted people from around the world, serving up warm, friendly, Idaho hospitality amidst this 4,000-acre pastoral paradise. If you're looking for lots of scheduled activities, read no further—this is not the ranch for you. Here the pace is slow: you can do as much or as little as you choose. You decide. At Teton Ridge Ranch, you'll relax, unwind, and savor exactly what you came here for...away from it all, on the other side of the Tetons.

Address: 200 Valley View Road, Drawer K, Tetonia, Idaho 83452
Telephone: 208/456-2650; fax 208/456-2218
Email: info@tetonridge.com
Internet: www.ranchweb.com/teton
Airport: Jackson Hole, 45 miles; Idaho Falls, 69 miles; small planes to Driggs Airport, 11 miles (7,200-foot paved and lighted airstrip). Extra charge for airport pickup at Jackson and Idaho Falls.
Location: 38 miles west of Jackson, Wyoming; 11 miles northeast of Driggs, Idaho
Awards: *Hideaway Report, Travel & Leisure,* Kilgore Luxury Group
Medical: Teton Valley Hospital, 12 miles
Conference Capacity: 14 overnight, 32 for the day. Excellent for very small corporate retreats.
Guest Capacity: 14
Accommodations: The main 10,000-square-foot log lodge has a spacious living room; lower-level dining room; and five suites, each with balconies commanding views of the Tetons, woodstoves, and large bathrooms with hot tubs. All rooms have telephones, teleports, and on-site computers available for convenient e-mail access. Separate 2,000-square-foot cottage with two bedrooms, large living room with fireplace, kitchenette, and 2.5 baths. All accommodations have fine art and views of the Tetons.
Rates: • $$$$$–$$$$$$ American Plan. Winter rates. Special rate if you reserve entire ranch. One-week minimum stay July and August.

Credit Cards: VISA, MasterCard
Season: Summer: June through October; Winter: January through March.
Activities: Summer: No set program. Horseback riding, hiking, fly-fishing, and plenty of R&R. Pack trips, white-water rafting, soaring, guided fly-fishing, sporting-clay shooting (the ranch has its own 16-station course) and trapshooting are extra. Bird-hunting for Hungarian partridge, pheasant, and native grouse in the fall (guns, guides, and dogs provided). Ask about the Bechler River Hot Springs horseback ride in Yellowstone. Winter: see Cross-Country Skiing section. Many use the ranch as a home base to ski at Grand Targhee, about 45 minutes away. Cross-country skiing from lodge on 25 kilometers of groomed trails.
Children's Programs: None. Well-behaved children over age six preferred.
Dining: Good food is an epicure's delight at Teton Ridge Ranch. Innovative American cuisine served nightly in candlelit dining room complete with two fireplaces, a view of the Teton Mountains, and good wine. Dinner might include mixed gathered greens with creamy lemon vinaigrette, cumin-roasted rack of lamb, grilled vegetables, Napoleons, and chocolate crème brûlée for dessert. Fresh bread served each night along with fresh vegetables, herbs, and greens grown in ranch garden during the summer. Special diets always accommodated. Featured in February 2000 *Gourmet* magazine.
Entertainment: Fireside chats, otherwise you're on your own.
Summary: Kilgore's "Best of the Best"–Luxury. Small, luxurious family and corporate retreat for those who appreciate and expect the finer things in life! No planned activities. You design your own program. Guided trips to Yellowstone a favorite. Sporting-clay clinic and bird-hunting in September. Massage available. Well-behaved pets allowed, kennel on property. Summer soaring at Driggs Airport. Nearby: Shopping and art galleries in Jackson Hole.

Twin Peaks Ranch
Salmon, Idaho

THE DUDE RANCHERS'
ASSOCIATION

Little was left out when E. DuPont developed his own dude ranch from the Twin Peaks Ranch homestead of 1924. Its location near Salmon, Idaho, is where the Lewis & Clark Expedition of 1804 was turned back by their "river of no return." This several-thousand-acre working dude ranch is nestled high within the Rockies' massive towering peaks. The ranch's excellent location offers guests high panoramic trails, nearby Rockies' activities, and the Salmon River's rated rapids. Owners, Allen and Lenabelle Davis, have added staffed outposts—a North Basin tent camp for a two-day wilderness pack trip, Williams Lake Lodge for fly- and outboard fishing lively rainbows, and Ram's Head Lodge for overnight accommodations at river's edge between two days of rafting the Salmon. The Davis' several outpost excursions reveal the pioneering challenges of Western activities. These features make Twin Peaks Ranch one of the best in America.

Address: P.O. Box 774, Dept. K, Salmon, Idaho 83467
Telephone: 800/659-4899, 208/894-2290; fax: 208/894-2429
Email: tpranch@earthlink.net
Internet: www.twinpeaksranch.com
Airport: Idaho Falls, or Missoula, Montana. Complimentary shuttle on Sundays; three-hour scenic trip from either airport.
Location: 18 miles south of Salmon off "Scenic Byway" Highway 93, three hours south of Missoula
Memberships: The Dude Ranchers' Association, Idaho Outfitters and Guides Association
Medical: Steele Memorial Hospital, Salmon; 18 miles; emergency helicopter service to most locations
Conference Capacity: 55; off-season only (spring and fall)
Guest Capacity: 55
Accommodations: The original seven rustic cabins for 2–4 persons have their own three-quarter baths. Each deluxe cabin unit has two bedrooms with whirlpool tubs, and a "center room" that easily converts into a sitting room with game table; accommodates up to six guests. Roll-aways available. The ranch suite is popular for families of six

or more. Enjoy the sun deck with heated pool and hot tub.
Rates: • $$$–$$$$ American Plan. Children's, group, and off-season rates. June through mid-September seven-day minimum; three-day stays if space available.
Credit Cards: VISA, MasterCard. Personal and traveler's checks accepted
Season: June through September; mid-September through November for guest ranch off-season and hunting.
Activities: An overnight pack trip provides an authentic feeling of life on the trail and river camping. Horseback rides take in a variety of spectacular scenery and wildlife viewing. Two days of white-water rafting is a favorite highlight. Fish for game rainbows in the ranch's two stocked ponds. Each Saturday roundup and drive wily Corriente longhorns to a regulation-size arena for calf roping and team penning competition. Shoot game targets and trapshoot from the ranch range facilities. (All activities are optional.)
Children's Programs: Parents and children interact together throughout the week. Kids begin riding at age six and usually eat meals together with newfound friends.
Dining: Delicious Western cuisine is offered buffet-style with scrumptious desserts. The panoramic view from the dining room is magnificent. Weekly breakfast cookout and dinner steak-fry barbecue served chuck wagon-style. Wine and beer are available in the lodge. BYOB in cabins.
Entertainment: Line-dancing instruction and dancing to a country-western band. Guest rodeo exhibitions. Nightly campfires, sing-alongs, marshmallow-roasting and s'mores around the campfire.
Summary: One of the best. Twin Peaks Ranch provides an unsurpassed variety of exciting activities. Here the Rockies offers some of the best: horseback riding, scenic and white-water river rafting, cattle roundups, outboard and fly-fishing, and an overnight pack trip that includes viewing wild game. Ideal for a great family adventure! As a writer for *House and Garden* magazine once wrote, it was "the guest ranch of my imagination."

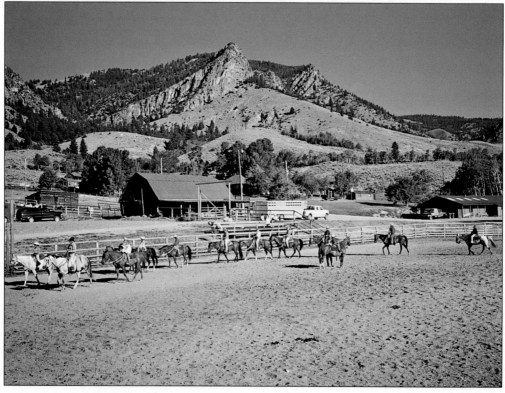

Western Pleasure Guest Ranch
Sandpoint, Idaho

On a winter day in 1939, Janice's grandpa packed up his family and left Colorado. Their destination was his beautiful dream ranch in northern Idaho. This ranch is now known as the Western Pleasure Guest Ranch. Since 1990, Roley and Janice Schoonover, and her parents, ranchers Jim and Virginia Wood, have transformed this third-generation family-owned and -operated cattle ranch into one of Idaho's quality guest ranches. Guests enjoy riding through the 960-acre cattle ranch or into the national forest. The ranch is located in northern Idaho's scenic Panhandle region famous for Lake Pend Oreille, one of the largest freshwater lakes in the United States, and Schweitzer Mountain, a premier skiing destination for the Northwest. Hosts Roley and Janice share their love for their family ranch along with the rich history, beauty, and traditions of the area. Western Pleasure is for folks who appreciate sincere, real country hospitality, while enjoying beautiful handcrafted log accommodations.

Address: 1413 Upper Gold Creek Road, Drawer K, Sandpoint, Idaho 83864
Telephone: 208/263-9066; fax: 208/265-0138
Email: stay@westernpleasureranch.com
Internet: www.westernpleasureranch.com
Airport: Spokane, Washington, 90 miles
Location: 90 miles northeast of Spokane, Washington; 60 miles north of Coeur d'Alene, Idaho; 16 miles northeast of Sandpoint, Idaho
Memberships: Idaho Outfitters and Guides Association, Appaloosa Horse Association
Medical: Bonner General Hospital, 16 miles
Conference Capacity: 34
Guest Capacity: 20
Accommodations: Three log cabins and six lodge rooms. The handcrafted log cabins are secluded among tall pines to assure privacy. Each cabin can accommodate up to six yet is cozy enough for two with one bedroom, loft, bathroom, and wood-stoves for cool evenings. In 1996, the 10,000-square-foot log lodge was completed. The lodge provides six comfortable guest rooms with private baths. A large great room where guests gather features a big river-rock fireplace. In the downstairs rec room, relax while playing a game of pool or while watching a favorite John Wayne movie.

Rates: • $$$ American Plan. June through September, three-day minimum stay. Off-season rates with shorter stays available.
Credit Cards: VISA, MasterCard
Season: Year-round
Activities: Horseback riding is the main activity, with varied terrain including ridges, forests, valleys, logging roads, and meadows. Slow, medium, and fast rides. Arena instruction. Ride mornings and afternoons for 2–2.5 hours, plus weekly all-day rides. Ask about the Big Hill panorama, Grouse Creek Falls, and Gold Ridge scenic rides. Group wagon and private buggy rides too. There is an 18-hole golf course less than 10 miles from ranch. Winter: Guests enjoy horse-drawn sleigh rides and cross-country skiing. Year-round hot tub.
Children's Programs: Roley and Janice have two children who welcome children of all ages. No formal children's program; kids and parents play together. The playground, with horseshoes, large log swing set, sandbox, tetherball, and volleyball, is a favorite.
Dining: Family-style meals served in the lodge. Home-cooking and plenty to eat. Steaks and prime rib are specialties, ranch-raised all natural beef. BYOB.
Entertainment: Nightly entertainment, including old-fashioned sing-alongs around the campfire. Weekly country dancing.
Summary: Great for those who appreciate genuine country folks who love their family ranch and care about the land, their heritage, and Western traditions. Lots of heart here. Wonderful country spirit. Young, energetic, and friendly hosts—Janice was raised on the ranch. Beautiful northern Idaho scenery. Evening horse- and team-drawn buggy/wagon rides. Ask about the summer youth camps and family reunion packages. Nearby: One of the country's largest freshwater lakes and Schweitzer Mountain.

Double JJ Resort Ranch
Rothbury, Michigan

Double JJ Resort Ranch encompasses 1,200 acres and is located 20 miles north of Muskegon, in west Michigan, on Big Wildcat and Carpenter Lakes, just 10 miles east of the Great Lakes. For over 60 years the Double JJ has entertained thousands of guests in a wonderful atmosphere complete with natural wooded areas for horseback riding and the Thoroughbred Golf Club, an 18-hole championship golf course designed by noted architect Arthur Hills. Today the Double JJ is owned and operated by Bob and Joan Lipsitz who have been involved in the outdoor recreation field since the early 1970s. Since its beginning in 1937, the Double JJ has grown to accommodate a variety of guests—family reunions, singles, clubs, and corporate outings all come to enjoy golf, riding, lake activities, and more. Said to be "America's Friendliest Resort" for the young and young-at-heart, guests can participate in activities from dawn 'til dusk. Horseback riding is offered for many skill levels on miles of wooded trails and countryside. Here the beauty of native Michigan comes alive.

Address: Box 94 K, Rothbury, Michigan 49452
Telephone: 800/DOUBLEJJ (800/368-2535), 231/894-4444; fax: 231/893-5355
Email: info@doublejj.com
Internet: www.doublejj.com
Airport: Muskegon, 20 miles; Grand Rapids, 45 miles; private airstrip on ranch
Location: 20 miles north of Muskegon off U.S. 31, 189 miles east of Chicago, 200 miles west of Detroit
Memberships: Appaloosa Horse Association, West Michigan Tourist Association, American Hotel/Motel Association
Medical: Muskegon General Hospital
Conference Capacity: 300; 20,000 square feet of conference space; 1,700 for company outings and rodeos
Guest Capacity: 450
Accommodations: Double JJ Ranch has a variety of accommodations with three distinct operations—adult-exclusive bunkhouses and lodge rooms; The Back Forty Ranch—family cabins and kids-exclusive tepees, Conestoga wagons, and bunkhouses; and the Thoroughbred Golf Club-hotel and condominiums.
Rates: • $$–$$$ American Plan. May through November. Horseback riding and golf packages available. Daily, weekend, midweek, and week packages. Conference and group rates. Holiday packages.
Credit Cards: VISA, MasterCard, Discover, American Express
Season: Year-round
Activities: Summer: Resort activities include daily riding with weekly breakfast and steak rides. Individual lessons and clinics. Rides are divided into small groups by experience levels. Rides vary from one to three hours and go out five times per day. Roping, cattle penning, barrel racing, and weekly cattle drive. Private lake with fishing and boating. Outdoor heated swimming pools, water slide, rope swings, hot tubs, four tennis courts, hiking, rifle and archery ranges, baseball, mini-golf, volleyball, hayrides, campfires, evening entertainment, and more. Eighteen-hole championship golf course. Winter: Riding, sleigh rides, dogsledding, snow tubing, and cross-country skiing.
Children's Programs: Extensive children's programs. Ask about the Back Forty Ranch and full-time 24-hours a day counselors for kids over age seven. Full day care for infants to age four. Full program for ages five and older. Kids may eat together in kids' dining room.
Dining: Three meals per day. All you can eat. Weekly breakfast and steak rides. Full-service bar available.
Entertainment: All sorts of entertainment planned each day. Nightly entertainment, including live bands, DJ dances, staff shows, casinos, and staff-versus-guest volleyball. Professional rodeo each week with guest competitions and games. Hayrides, campfires, game and video room, theme weeks with costume parties.
Summary: Full-service resort ranch with adult, children, and family programs. Ranch offers a host of recreational outdoor activities with a high percentage of returning guests year after year. This ranch will keep you entertained from morning until night. Singles, couples, families, and kids will always feel a part of the Double JJ family. Thoroughbred Golf Club rated in the top 35 in the nation by *Golf Digest*. Video available. Nearby: Lake Michigan, 10 miles; Silver Lake Sand Dunes, 15 miles; antique shops.

Turkey Creek Ranch
Theodosia, Missouri

Overlooking Bull Shoals Lake in the heart of Ozark Mountain Country is the Edwards' Turkey Creek Ranch. Founded by Dick and Elda Edwards in 1959, it's run today by their oldest son and daughter-in-law, Robert and Loretta. This 700-acre working cattle ranch and lake resort offers affordable family fun with activities that appeal to all ages. Turkey Creek is a lakeside ranch resort geared to families having fun together. Some folks have been returning yearly since 1963.

Address: HC 3, Box 3180 K, Theodosia, Missouri 65761
Telephone: 417/273-4362
Internet: www.turkeycreekranch.com
Airport: Springfield/Branson Regional Airport, 85 miles
Location: 47 miles east of Branson; 47 miles northwest of Mountain Home, Arkansas
Memberships: Missouri Bull Shoals Lake Association, Branson Chamber of Commerce
Awards: Mobil 2 Star
Medical: Baxter County Hospital, Mountain Home; 47 miles
Conference Capacity: 25
Guest Capacity: 156
Accommodations: There are 24 standard or deluxe cabins and *casitas*. All cabins have kitchens complete with microwaves and full-size appliances, air-conditioning, color TV, carpeted bedrooms, the daily *Springfield News Leader* delivered to each cabin in person by son Ryan, screened porch, picnic table, and barbecue grill. Cabin sizes vary and house from 4–10 guests. Some cabins have wheelchair access.
Rates: • $–$$ Riding and boat rentals extra. Meals not included.
Credit Cards: None. Personal checks accepted.
Season: Year-round
Activities: No scheduled activities except guided trail rides, approximately one hour, going out each day. Hiking and biking trails follow the bridle paths through the forest and along the lake. Lake activities include boating, fishing, waterskiing, and scuba diving. A variety of boats available. Fishing for many types of game and pan fish (bass, crappie, walleye, trout, sunfish, etc.).

Resort activities include an indoor heated pool and whirlpool spa, outdoor pool with kiddie pool, tennis, shuffleboard, horseshoes, volleyball, basketball, and a golf putting area. Ask about the River Cliff 18-hole golf course. Ranch activities vary according to time of year and guest experience. Turkey Creek owns its riding horses and a herd of Angus crossbred beef cattle. Occasionally guests may help with ranch work. Ask about the BLM Western mustangs.
Children's Programs: No formal program. All kids welcomed by Ashley and Ryan (now teens). Children are encouraged to participate in activities with their parents. Those too young for trail rides (under age eight) may be led on rides around the resort grounds. There's also a large playground area. At times there are calves to be bottle-fed.
Dining: It is all up to you. Each cabin or *casita* has a fully equipped kitchen plus a picnic table and barbecue grill nearby. A variety of restaurants in the area. Catering for large groups with advance notice—talk to Loretta.
Entertainment: Take your pick—do a little or a lot. The 3,000-square-foot recreation building has two fireplaces, a piano and organ for sing-alongs, indoor heated pool and spa, pool tables, video games, shuffleboard, table tennis, air hockey, and much more. Turkey Creek has some of the best Ozark Mountain scenery to be found.
Summary: A family vacation ranch resort founded, owned, and run by the Edwards family. On Bull Shoals Lake in the heart of beautiful Ozark Mountain Country, the ranch has offered a wide selection of ranch and lake activities for all ages and abilities since 1959. Great for groups and family reunions. Fishermen, singles, and couples especially enjoy the spring and fall. Nearby: The famous country-music town of Branson, Missouri, with its wide variety of music shows; Silver Dollar City, Shepherd of the Hills, and White Water theme parks; Springfield, Missouri, with Bass Pro Shops Outdoor World Headquarters, Dickerson Park Zoo, and new Wonders of Wildlife Museum.

320 Guest Ranch
Big Sky, Montana

Located in the Gallatin Canyon, not far from the famous year-round resort of Big Sky, is the 320 Guest Ranch. It is situated on the Gallatin River adjacent to the U.S. 191 corridor from Bozeman to Yellowstone National Park and at the mouth of the Buffalo Horn Creek access—gateway to the million-acre Gallatin National Forest, which joins Yellowstone. The ranch first hosted guests back in 1905. Today, the ranch is owned by David Brask, who notes, "The folks who truly enjoy the 320 Guest Ranch experience appreciate our proximity to some of Montana's finest natural wonders and our flexible ranch spirit. We go out of our way to make it easy for our guests to come and go as they please, fly-fishing, hiking, riding, or traveling to Yellowstone, Bozeman, or Big Sky. The diversity of accommodations—from one-room cabins to three-bedroom log homes—no minimum-stay requirement, and its size allows the ranch to cater to a wide variety of needs from corporate groups, to weddings, to families and couples, who come to enjoy all the freedom we offer."

Address: 205 Buffalo Horn Creek, Drawer K, Gallatin Gateway, Montana 59730
Telephone: 800/243-0320, 406/995-4283; fax: 406/995-4694
Email: 320ranch@montana.net
Internet: www.320ranch.com
Airport: Bozeman, 50 miles
Location: 12 miles south of Big Sky, 36 miles north of West Yellowstone off Highway 191
Awards: AAA 3 Diamond
Medical: Bozeman Hospital, 50 miles; doctor in Big Sky
Conference Capacity: Up to 150
Guest Capacity: 200
Accommodations: Accommodations have the creature comforts that you would expect in an upscale facility. Seven three-bedroom log homes, 12 riverfront two-bedroom cabins complete with kitchenettes and fireplaces, and 38 single cabins—some with fireplaces, some with kitchens. All have telephones and cable TV. Daily maid service.
Rates: • $–$$$ American Plan. Ask about the four- and seven-night summer Western packages. No minimum stay. Arrive any day. Wedding, group, and corporate rates. Winter skiing and snowmobiling packages.
Credit Cards: VISA and MasterCard
Season: Summer: June to early October. Winter: Mid-December to mid-April.
Activities: Summer: The two main activities are horseback riding and fly-fishing. Six different rides go out each day. One-hour to all-day rides best suited for beginner to intermediate riders. Ask about the fly-fishing ride to Ramshorn Lake and the Cinnamon Mountain trail ride that offer views of the distant Tetons. The 75-by-200-foot indoor arena hosts rodeos, roping, and lessons. Anglers enjoy the on-ranch guide service by Big Sky Outfitters for novice to advanced anglers. Fully equipped fly shop. Ask about the Gallatin, Madison, and Yellowstone Rivers for fishing. Hiking, river rafting with local outfitter, and day trips to Yellowstone Park. Winter: Backcountry and downhill skiing at Big Sky; snowmobiling and sleigh rides.
Children's Programs: Children are welcome, but no formal program. Trail riding begins at age eight. Baby-sitting available.
Dining: Continental breakfast and full Western-style dinner. Sack lunches available, or you're on your own at local restaurants. Open to the public for dinner. Full bar.
Entertainment: Volleyball, hayrides, Friday night chuck wagon barbecues, horseshoes, s'mores nightly around the campfire. Winter: Nightly sleigh rides.
Summary: 320 Guest Ranch offers one of the most unique and flexible independent summer and winter programs in America. Guests savor the riverside setting and the freedom to choose from a host of outdoor activities, both on and off the ranch. A variety of upscale accommodations and summer and winter programs. Indoor riding arena, and Annual Fourth of July Big Sky 320 Ranch Rodeo. Nearby: Yellowstone National Park and Big Sky Resort.

63 Ranch
Livingston, Montana

One of the first dude ranches in the country to be chosen as a National Historic Site, the 63 Ranch, founded by Sandra's mother and father, Jinnie and Paul Christensen, is one of the oldest ranches in the business. It's still run by the same family that started it in 1930. At an altitude of 5,600 feet, you listen to the soothing sounds of Mission Creek as it tumbles down its rocky course through the ranch on its way to the Yellowstone River. The 63 offers guests an eye-opening view of what the early West was all about. Here you'll enjoy weekly cattle rides and fulfill your childhood dreams of being a cowboy or cowgirl. In July and August the 63 offers an overnight pack trip each week (limited to four guests) into the high country of the Absaroka-Beartooth Wilderness. There's also plenty of riding, fishing, hiking, and Indian lore. Sandra, Bud, and their son, Jeff, know the spirit of old-time dude ranching and welcome guests from all over the United States and many foreign countries.

Address: Box 979 K, Livingston, Montana 59047
Telephone: 406/222-0570; fax: 406/222-6363
Email: sixty3ranch@mcn.net
Internet: www.63ranch.com
Airport: Bozeman, 50 miles; or a small airstrip for private planes, six miles
Location: 12 miles southeast of Livingston
Memberships: The Dude Ranchers' Association, Montana Ranch Vacation Association, Gallatin Outfitters Association, America Outdoors
Awards: National Register of Historic Places
Medical: Livingston Hospital, 20 minutes
Conference Capacity: Off-season available only by special arrangement
Guest Capacity: 30
Accommodations: Eight comfortable one- to four-bedroom cabins with wonderful log furniture, all different and unique. All have baths and showers; some are heated with gas, others with electricity. Double and twin beds. All arriving guests find in their cabin a cotton bandanna on their pillow, fresh seasonal wildflowers, and the 63 Ranch newspaper. Daily maid service and coin-operated laundry facilities. Pay telephone and soda machine.
Rates: • $$$ American Plan. Rates vary depend-

ing on the season. Children's and pack-trip rates. One-week minimum stay, Sunday to Sunday.
Credit Cards: None. Personal and traveler's checks accepted.
Season: Mid-June to mid-September
Activities: The 63 is known for its horses and excellent high-country scenic and open-meadow riding. Sidesaddle and Western lessons available. Lessons in arena each Monday for all guests. Picnic and barbecue rides. Blue Ribbon fly-fishing (ask Sandra for her "Montana's First Best Place for Fishing" pamphlet). Ranch pond also stocked with cutthroat trout for children and fly-casting practice. Swimming in a pond (for the courageous), hiking, Sandra's history lesson, homestead ride, and evening nature walk.
Children's Programs: Best for children five and older who can participate in ranch and family activities. Each week is planned around the particular guests who are at the ranch, and children are always included. Recreation room, baby-sitter available. The ranch will teach five-year-olds to ride if they want to learn and go out on trail rides with families.
Dining: Beautiful dining room furnished with Molesworth furniture dating from the 1930s. Hearty ranch cooking. BYOB.
Entertainment: Sing-alongs, marshmallow roasts at Indian Tepee, square dancing and entertainment in the Ranch Pavilion with old-time cowboy music. Rodeo July 2–4 each year in town, or just peaceful reading and relaxing.
Summary: One of Kilgore's greatest historic ranches in North America. Wonderful, classic old-time, historic dude ranch with emphasis on riding and families. Weekly cattle rides. Some guests stay for two or three weeks. First Montana dude ranch to be listed on the National Register of Historic Places. Nearby: Historic town of Livingston, Yellowstone National Park, and world-class fly-fishing.

Averills' Ranch-Flathead Lake Lodge
Bigfork, Montana

Flathead Lake Lodge is on the shores of the largest freshwater lake in the West, encompassing 2,000 private acres that border national forest. Featured on *Good Morning America, Live with Regis and Kathie Lee*, and written up in *Better Homes & Gardens, Sunset*, and *Bon Appetit* magazines, and a Mobil 4-Star property, this full-service dude ranch features the best of two worlds. For those who like water, there are all kinds of lake activities. If you'd rather be on horseback than on water skis or in a sailboat, there are an abundance of horse and rodeo activities available. In northwestern Montana, the lodge is 35 miles from one of nature's greatest wonders—Glacier National Park. The lodge was started in 1945 by the Averills, and is operated by second generation Doug and Maureen Averill, along with their children. One of Kilgore's top ranches.

Address: Box 248 K, Bigfork, Montana 59911
Telephone: 406/837-4391; fax: 406/837-6977
Email: fll@digisys.net
Internet: www.averills.com
Airport: Kalispell
Train: Whitefish, 30 miles
Location: One mile south of Bigfork, 17 miles south of Kalispell
Memberships: The Dude Ranchers' Association, Montana Dude Ranch Association
Awards: Mobil 4 Star
Medical: Bigfork Medical Center, one mile
Conference Capacity: 90, with four meeting rooms. Conference packet and video available, computer access.
Guest Capacity: 120
Accommodations: The historic main lodge is a beauty, with a rock fireplace, dining facility, saloon, and three upper sleeping rooms. The south lodge has 15 rooms, and there are 13 two- and three-bedroom log cottages/cabins and two larger deluxe log cabins. Everything radiates warmth and charm.
Rates: • $$$$$ American Plan. Children's, teen, singles, corporate, off-season, and convention rates. One-week minimum stay summer season, Sunday to Sunday.
Credit Cards: VISA, MasterCard, American Express. Personal checks preferred.

Season: May through October
Activities: Daily horseback riding, arena horse games, and cattle penning instruction, and ranch rodeo. Breakfast, lunch, and dinner rides. Guided wilderness—ask about Jewel Basin. Heated pool right next to Flathead Lake. Four tennis courts. Extensive lake activities and private beach. Sailing on two classic 50-foot sloops, canoeing, lake cruising, and water-skiing. Tremendous lake and fly-fishing instruction available. White-water rafting and float-fishing available. Kayaking, river tubing, and mountain biking.
Children's Programs: Tremendous college staff. Ages 4–12 participate in organized children's program. Baby-sitting for younger kids available. Nature program with arts and crafts. Complete recreation room and games. Kids' overnight camp. Trail rides for kids ages six and older. Kids do everything together. Kids rodeo with parent participation at end of week. Special rides and programs for teens. Junior wrangler program and kids dining.
Dining: Social hour each evening in the private Saddle Sore Saloon. Enjoy steak barbecues, fresh seafood, even pheasant and quail. Homemade breads and desserts. Kids usually eat together but are welcome to eat with parents.
Entertainment: A huge variety of fun, competitive games. Campfires with sing-alongs, Western barn dance, guest rodeo with various horse games, team roping with local cowboys, canoe and sailboat races. Evening cruises and volleyball games.
Summary: One of Kilgore's "Best of the Best." Extensive children's program and beautiful lakeside setting. Run by old-time ranching family with a 70 percent family return rate. Fabulous location on 28-mile-long Flathead Lake with extensive lake activities. The Averills also run a large bison ranch near Glacier National Park and Elk Preserve, which is available for viewing and photography. Be sure to have a huckleberry milkshake. Nearby: Golf available at 27-hole Eagle Bend Golf Course.

Big EZ Lodge
Big Sky, Montana

The Big EZ Lodge was designed and built with luxury and breathtaking views in mind. The owners, Steve and Donna Hicks, have taken great care to assure that the design of this magnificent property not only fit into the surroundings, but also complement them. And so they did! Situated at 7,500 feet on 4,300 acres and bordered by the Gallatin National Forest, unlimited outdoor activities are available for all who visit. Created in 1999, this award-winning property consists of three distinct Western-style lodges: the Main Lodge, the Guest Inn, and the spectacular Lone Star Suite. Here, rustic elegance reigns supreme. The luxurious atmosphere of the Big EZ Lodge enables guests to relax fully so they can concentrate on the fun or business at hand. Whether riding horses, fly-fishing, playing a round of golf on the par-72 championship putting course, or enjoying the Alpine skiing and the surrounding winter wonderland, you will agree—this is one of the world's best and an exclusive member of the Kilgore Luxury Group.

Address: Box 160070 K, Big Sky, Montana 59716
Telephone: 877/244-3299, 406/995-7000; fax: 406/995-7007
Email: bigezlodge@benchmarkmanagement.com
Internet: www.bigezlodge.com
Airport: Bozeman or West Yellowstone. Transportation is included in all packages.
Location: One hour south (47 miles) of Bozeman, one hour north (43 miles) of West Yellowstone
Awards: Kilgore Luxury Group
Medical: Big Sky Clinic, 18 miles, or Bozeman Deaconess Hospital, 43 miles
Conference Capacity: 28; two state-of-the-art meeting rooms
Guest Capacity: 28
Accommodations: Luxurious rooms feature designer touches, many custom furnishings, and a collection of original art. Eleven rooms with king-size beds, one with a double queen, and the 1,800-square-foot Lone Star Suite comprise the guest accommodations. Each room has a computer laptop with high-speed T-1 Internet access, in-room voice mail, satellite TV/VCR, down comforters, oversized plush robes, and many amenities. Several rooms have fireplaces.

Rates: • $$$–$$$$$$ American Plan; all-inclusive including service charges. Ask about seasonal packages. No minimum stay.
Credit Cards: VISA, MasterCard, American Express, personal and traveler's checks
Season: Year-round; includes all holidays.
Activities: The lodge is a superb base camp for on and off-property activities. On-site activities include fishing ponds, par-72 championship golf putting course, hiking, workout facility, in-room massage therapy, and wildlife viewing. Off-site excursions include fishing Montana's fabled trout rivers, rafting, mountain biking, trail rides, hiking, dogsledding, snowmobiling, touring Yellowstone National Park, and Alpine and Nordic skiing at Big Sky Resort (19 miles away).
Children's Programs: When the entire lodge is reserved, all ages are welcome. Baby-sitting available with advance notice.
Dining: Five-star dining is provided in the lodge dining room, outside decks, or on the trail, by an outstanding team of culinary professionals featuring a relaxed approach to high-end cuisine. Wild game dishes are a specialty. House wines and spirits are included and a private reserve list is available. Room service is also available.
Entertainment: Most enjoy relaxing in the hot tub, wildlife viewing, stimulating conversation, evening strolls and music, billiards, croquet, bocci ball, or just relaxing near the fire.
Summary: Award-winning, world-class, and an exclusive member of Kilgore Luxury Group. Year-round excellence for those who appreciate the finest. Ideal for small gatherings, family reunions, honeymoons, and corporate/business meetings. Executive telecommuting facilities.

Boulder River Ranch
McLeod, Montana

THE DUDE RANCHERS'
ASSOCIATION

In a rugged mountain valley at 5,050 feet, surrounded by the Absaroka Mountains, Boulder River Ranch is a fantastic old ranch on the banks of the beautiful Boulder River. This family-owned and -operated ranch is on one of the most productive trout streams in North America. Since 1918, the Aller family has played host to families from around the world that return year after year. Now run by third and fourth generations, Steve and Jeane, together with their daughter Jordan and her husband Shane, they specialize in superb catch-and-release fly-fishing and horseback riding. Experienced and novice anglers will enjoy tremendous fishing in the cold, crystal-clear waters of the Boulder River. Hardy swimmers love the river's natural pools. Riders savor the beautiful high-country and meadow trail rides to abandoned mines, homesteads, and the Indian caves. No matter which month you choose, fisherfolk and riders alike will enjoy every moment with the Allers.

Address: 2815 Boulder Road, McLeod, Montana 59052
Telephone: 406/932-5926; fax: 406/932-6411
Email: boulderriver@mcn.net
Internet: www.boulderriverranch.com
Airport: Billings or Bozeman
Location: 110 miles southwest of Billings, 87 miles southeast of Bozeman, 28 miles south of Big Timber, off I-90 on Highway 298 South
Memberships: The Dude Ranchers' Association, Montana Ranch Vacation Association, American Quarter Horse Association, National Reining Horse Association
Medical: Certified EMT at ranch, emergency room in Big Timber
Conference Capacity: Up to 25
Guest Capacity: 30–40
Accommodations: Most of the 16 individual cabins are arranged in a semicircle around the front lawn just as they have been since 1918; each is comfortable, with fresh wildflowers, daily maid service, private bath, and woodstove or fireplace for heat. Each looks to the Absaroka Mountains across the river. Happy hour at the end of the day brings guests onto the front lawn for tale swapping. It's a nice family arrangement. Laundry facilities available.

Rates: • $$–$$$ American Plan. Children's and family rates available. Children under age three are free of charge. One-week minimum stay, Sunday to Sunday.
Credit Cards: None. Personal and traveler's checks accepted.
Season: June to mid-September
Activities: Fly-fishing, horseback riding, and relaxing are the main activities here. The ranch raises and trains its own quarter horses. Scenic half-day and all-day guided rides with walking, trotting, and some loping, depending on your level of experience. Very flexible program geared to guest desires. Catch-and-release fly-fishing. Boulder River is a haven for families who like to fish. Most fish on their own, but the Allers are always delighted to show novices the ropes. Guides are available (extra). Limited fishing gear available. Hiking. Swimming in the river.
Children's Programs: No structured children's program. Kids begin riding at age four. Kiddie wrangler, stocked pond for swimming and fishing. Baby-sitting on request with advance notice (extra).
Dining: Scrumptious family-style meals. Once-a-week breakfast rides with famous ranch "fry" bread and weekly steak barbecues. BYOB. Guests may bring their favorite bottle of wine to dinner. Advance arrangements for special diets.
Entertainment: Most guests like to retreat to the porches of their cabins and reminisce about their experiences of the day. Children love to play games on the front lawn with the crew.
Summary: A fly-fishing paradise! One of the state's oldest and most enduring family traditions. Delightful, very relaxed, very informal family-owned and -operated ranch on two miles of the Boulder River. Most come to flyfish and ride. Nearby: Yellowstone National Park, Big Timber Rodeo in June. Nine-hole golf course in Big Timber.

Circle Bar Guest Ranch
Utica, Montana

THE DUDE RANCHERS' ASSOCIATION

Montana Dude Ranch Association

The Circle Bar is located in the heart of "Charlie Russell Country" in central Montana. In operation as a cattle ranch since 1890, the Circle Bar still provides an authentic Western experience, complete with spring and fall cattle drives and routine checking and moving of herds. In 1938 the ranch began hosting guests, and today, under owner Sarah Stevenson's direction, it blends the Old West with modern conveniences. Situated in the foothills of the Little Belt Mountains and bordered on two sides by the Lewis & Clark National Forest, the terrain for horseback riding is ideal and varied, from vast rolling hills to rugged mountain trails. The horses are suited to each individual's ability and chosen for their responsiveness and temperament. The Judith River, which runs through the ranch, provides excellent fishing for brook, cutthroat, brown, and rainbow trout.

Address: HCR 81, Box 61, Utica, Montana 59452
Telephone: 888/570-0227, 406/423-5454; fax: 406/423-5686
Email: cbr@circlebarranch.com
Internet: www.circlebarranch.com
Airport: Great Falls
Location: 90 miles south of Great Falls, 13 miles southwest of Utica near Route 87
Memberships: The Dude Ranchers' Association, Montana Dude Ranchers' Association, Montana Outfitters and Guides Association, Montana Ranch Vacation Association, American Quarter Horse Association
Medical: All personnel first aid certified; Central Montana Medical Center in Lewistown, 50 miles.
Conference Capacity: 30
Guest Capacity: 35
Accommodations: The nine log cabins all have private baths and are decorated in keeping with their names, such as the Cayuse, Buffalo, or Wildlife. Most have fireplaces or wood-burning stoves, living rooms, and refrigerators. There are also four large, well-appointed suites in the main lodge. The ambiance of the main lodge is Old West, with high ceilings, large oak handmade light fixtures that reflect the spaciousness of the Big Sky Country, and a native stone fireplace separating the dining and living rooms. Daily maid service. Laundry facilities available.
Rates: • $$$ American Plan. Conference, pack trip, and special event rates available. Three-night minimum stay. Arrivals any day, but Sunday to Sunday preferred.
Credit Cards: VISA, MasterCard; personal checks accepted.
Season: May to September
Activities: Your stay can be as relaxed and unhurried or as structured and adventure-packed as you like. Flexible riding program for the accomplished rider or for those who have never ridden. Four-wheel-drive sight-seeing, Elk Refuge, wildlife viewing, and wildflower trips. Middle Fork pack trip with advance notice. Ask about Blackfoot Indian Cave, Hole-in-the-Ground, and Elk Refuge rides. Fishing on the Judith River (some equipment available). Hiking, photography, nature walks, horseshoes, outdoor heated pool, and indoor hot tub. Basketball and volleyball.
Children's Programs: Children are the responsibility of parents. All ages welcome. Unstructured children's activities. Family participation in all ranch happenings is encouraged.
Dining: Culinary-trained chef. Hearty Western breakfasts or lighter fare of yogurt, cereal, and freshly-baked cinnamon rolls start the day. Lunch could include Mexican, pastas, sandwiches, and soup. The evening meal can range from enormous rib steaks cooked over a wood fire and served outdoors, to a five-course gourmet meal featuring the chef's specialties of lemon-pepper cod, salmon, prime rib, or chicken cordon bleu. Special diets catered to with advance notice.
Entertainment: Team-drawn wagon rides, barn dances, campfire sing-alongs, pasture golf, horseshoes, basketball, volleyball, table tennis, pool table, hiking, mountain biking (BYO bike), swimming, hot tub, extensive library, solitude.
Summary: Great for families and family reunions, couples, singles, and groups. Flexible programs. Ask about the sister cattle ranch, R and S Angus, the spring and fall cattle drives in June and October, the Charlie Russell Ride, Cowboy Week, and the Lewis and Clark Adventure.

Diamond J Ranch
Ennis, Montana

THE DUDE RANCHERS'
ASSOCIATION

The Diamond J was built in the 1930s as a traditional family-style guest ranch surrounded by the Lee Metcalf Wilderness area overlooking the Madison River Valley, famous for cattle ranching and Blue Ribbon fly-fishing. In 1959 Peter and Jinny Combs were on their way to Alaska and stopped by as guests—the rest is history. Together with son Tim, the Combs family continues to carry on the Western and sporting traditions that have made this part of the country and this ranch so famous. Today, as in years gone by, the ranch attracts well-traveled families and individuals that appreciate the old-style Montana guest ranch experience. Charlie Russell, one of Montana's most famous personalities once said, "You can get in a car to see what man has made, but you have to get on a horse to see what God has made." Come to ride, flyfish, hike, wing shoot, enjoy the camaraderie around a campfire—it's all still here at the Diamond J.

Address: P.O. Box 577 K, Ennis, Montana 59729
Telephone: 877/929-4867, 406/682-4867; fax: 406/682-4106
Email: totalmgt@3rivers.net
Internet: www.diamondjranch.com
Airport: Bozeman, 60 miles; Ennis, 4,800-foot paved airstrip 12 miles away for light aircraft
Location: 14 miles east of Ennis off Highway 287, 60 miles south of Bozeman
Memberships: The Dude Ranchers' Association
Awards: Orvis-endorsed Fly-Fishing and Wing Shooting Lodge
Medical: Ennis Hospital, 12 miles
Guest Capacity: 25
Accommodations: The eight log cabins are constructed of lodgepole pine. Each has its own rock fireplace, hardwood floors, and hickory furniture and beds. Each cabin features a few Montana big-game trophies, a full bath with separate shower stall, and cast-iron tub. The bedroom-living rooms feature twin-, double-, and king-size beds; writing desks; and covered front porches, each with a different railing design. No TVs or telephones in cabins.
Rates: • $$$–$$$$$$ American Plan. Children's and seasonal rates. Guided fly-fishing and guided wing shooting packages available. Mid-June to

mid-September, one-week minimum stay, Sunday to Sunday.
Credit Cards: VISA, MasterCard, American Express
Season: Mid-June mid-September
Activities: Schedules are flexible. The ranch emphasizes a relaxed, unstructured atmosphere with riding, fly-fishing, and shooting instruction for all levels! Half-day, and all-day rides. Ask about the Yellowstone National Park ride. Hiking. Excellent fly-fishing (equipment available); the ranch is near some of the best Blue Ribbon streams in Montana: the Madison, Gallatin, Jefferson, Beaverhead, and Missouri. Ask about the scenic and white-water fly-fishing trips. Private two-acre lake with rainbow trout. Full-time guides are available. Indoor tennis, heated swimming pool, hot tub. Massage available. Wing shooting packages, 10-station sporting-clay course, skeet shooting and trapshooting with instruction.
Children's Programs: Diamond J takes pride in their kids' horses. Kiddie wrangler and riding instruction. Usually children ride and eat lunches and dinners together. Baby-sitter available on request.
Dining: Meals served family-style in three rooms. At lunch and dinner, children and adults usually eat separately (not mandatory). Special diets catered to with advance notice. Cookouts. A BYOB happy hour.
Entertainment: Square/line dancing, campfire, sing-alongs, games, and library.
Summary: Kilgore's "Best of the Best"–Fly-fishing, Wing shooting, and Family riding. Lovely, unstructured, family-owned and -operated guest, fly-fishing, and wing shooting ranch. Very flexible programs; do as much or as little as you wish. Horses for novice and experienced riders, sporting-clay, trap and skeet courses, fly-fishing, scenic and white-water float trips (see write-up in Fly-Fishing section), indoor tennis and heated swimming pool. Orvis-endorsed; smoke-free cabins and lodge. Nearby: Yellowstone National Park (70 miles), Museum of the Rockies in Bozeman, historic Virginia City.

Diamond J Ranch, Montana

Elkhorn Ranch
Gallatin Gateway, Montana

Welcome to one of Kilgore's "legends" old-time dude ranch. The Elkhorn Ranch was started in the early 1920s by Ernest and Grace Miller and is steeped in history. Located one mile from the northwest corner of Yellowstone Park, Elkhorn is at 7,000 feet in a beautiful valley surrounded by the Gallatin National Forest and the Lee Metcalf Wilderness. It is a gateway to incredible natural beauty, mountain scenery, and loads of wildlife. From ranch headquarters, rides go out in all directions. Since the early days, Elkhorn has been famous for its superb riding program and its dedication to preserving our Western heritage and to uniting families. Today, as in years gone by, the ranch combines old-fashioned Montana-style hospitality, rustic warmth, and natural beauty. At Elkhorn they still serve up the West the way it used to be.

Address: 33133 Gallatin Road, Drawer K, Gallatin Gateway, Montana 59730
Telephone: 406/995-4291; call for fax
Internet: www.elkhornranchmt.com
Airport: Bozeman and West Yellowstone
Location: 60 miles south of Bozeman off Highway 191, 30 miles north of the west entrance to Yellowstone Park
Memberships: The Dude Ranchers' Association, Montana Dude Ranch Association, American Outdoors
Medical: Bozeman Deaconess Hospital, 60 miles
Conference Capacity: 30; June and September
Guest Capacity: 40
Accommodations: 15 original log cabins radiate old-time Western charm and the early spirit of dude ranching. Most were built in the 1930s. Each is set apart from the others and varies in size, sleeping one to eight persons. Most have colorful Hudson Bay foot blankets and comforters; some even have squeaky wooden floors. All have electric heat in the bathrooms and most have woodstoves in the sitting areas. All have porches, most covered, and guests spend a good deal of time on them relaxing, reading, reflecting, and visiting. Nightly turndown. Limited laundry facilities.
Rates: • $$$ American Plan. Children's rates available. One-week minimum stay, Sunday to

Sunday, in July and August. Ask about the two-week package.
Credit Cards: None. Personal checks or traveler's checks accepted.
Season: Mid-June through September
Activities: This is a Western riding ranch. Beginners will feel just as much at home as do experienced riders. Great emphasis is placed on safety. Each morning at breakfast, guests are signed up individually for the day's riding, which starts at 10 A.M. Groups usually go out with six to eight people and two wranglers. All-day rides three times a week. Fishing rides twice a week. No riding on Sundays. Because there's such a diversity of riding, guests will seldom take the same ride twice. Fly-fishing enthusiasts will enjoy the Madison, Gallatin, and Yellowstone Rivers, all Blue Ribbon trout streams. Swimming in the ranch's spring-fed pond for the brave, and hiking. Keep an eye out: This is bear and wolf country.
Children's Program: Excellent all-day children's program. Peanut Butter Mother is with children ages 6–12 all day for dining, riding, and activities. Teenager "Jets," as they're called, ride and eat together. While kids appreciate being together, there is plenty of family time for those who wish it. Baby-sitting possible with advance notice.
Dining: Home-cooked meals served buffet-style in the main dining room of the central lodge. Children dine at their own table. Each week includes breakfast, lunch, and dinners on the trail. BYOB (no liquor in dining room). Guests often have cocktails on their porches with other guests.
Entertainment: Weekly bonfire with singing and marshmallows, square dancing.
Summary: One of the classic, old-time dude ranches with lots of authentic Old Western charm! Emphasis on horseback riding for all ages. One of the country's top children's programs. Many guests stay two to three weeks. Nearby: Excellent fly-fishing on nearby Blue Ribbon waters.

G bar M Ranch
Clyde Park, Montana

THE DUDE RANCHERS'
ASSOCIATION

Welcome to one of Montana's great old-time ranching families—and when they say the welcome mat is out and the coffeepot is on, they mean it! Sage-covered, rolling foothills of the Bridger Mountains describe Brackett Creek Valley, home to the G bar M guest ranch. The Leffingwell family has operated this 3,200-acre cattle ranch since 1900 and has welcomed guests since the early 1930s. This part of the country was made famous by one of North America's early explorers and mountain men, Jim Bridger. The Leffingwell family offers a very special, hands-on experience. At the G bar M, you can join in the daily activities that are part of this cattle/guest ranch or you can enjoy everything at your own pace. The entire ranch has been designated as a game reserve where wildlife can enjoy a safe and natural habitat. George Leffingwell points out, "We believe it is important to live in harmony with the land and to encourage eagles, elk, deer, and even hummingbirds to be a part of the ranch." While most guests come from the United States, some have come from as far away as Europe, Australia, and other parts of the world to experience great Montana hospitality and ranching.

Address: Box 29, Dept. K, Clyde Park, Montana 59018
Telephone: 406/686-4423, 406/686-4216; fax: 406/686-9108
Email: gbarm@imt.net
Internet: www.gbarm.com
Airport: Bozeman
Location: 26 miles northeast of Bozeman off State Highway 86
Memberships: The Dude Ranchers' Association
Medical: Deaconess Hospital in Bozeman, 26 miles
Guest Capacity: 17
Accommodations: Two rustic log cabins, both with full bathrooms and hot and cold running water. There are four rooms (three downstairs and one upstairs, called the Family Loft) in the ranch house, with private baths, double and twin beds, and carpeting. Ask about the new log ranch house/lodge with four rooms and private baths.
Rates: • $$$ Full American Plan. Children's rates available. Minimum stay is Sunday to Sunday.

Credit Cards: VISA. Personal checks accepted.
Season: Dude ranch: May through September; B&B remainder of year.
Activities: Ranch raises and trains most of their own horses. Steve Leffingwell heads up the riding program with an emphasis on *Natural Horsemanship* à la Ray Hunt, and horses are matched to guests' riding abilities. Guests may participate in various kinds of cattle work, mostly herding, changing pastures, checking fences, or placing salt licks for the cattle. Things are always busy as the Leffingwells not only look after their own ranch but several neighboring ranches' riding chores as well. Because this is an operating cattle ranch you're expected to fit into the varied daily program unless you wish to entertain yourself by reading, hiking, or fishing for part or all of the day. Ranch fishing for rainbow trout in Brackett Creek. Limited fishing gear available.
Children's Programs: Children are parents' responsibility and may ride with adults beginning at age four. The ranch is a wonderful learning experience and best for children ages eight and older.
Dining: Guests, ranch hands, and wranglers all eat together. Beef, pork, and vegetables are all ranch-fresh. Be sure to get copies of Mary's *Sage Brush and Snow Drifts* cookbook and *Diamonds in the Snow and Trails I Have Chosen*, an account of her life growing up in Montana. BYOB.
Entertainment: No organized entertainment. Occasional colt training, on-the-ground roping, and horseshoeing, but the best is listening to George, Mary, and Patricia tell their "kitchen-table tales" (ranch stories). Once-a-week steak fry.
Summary: Small, working, family-run cattle and horse ranch, with wonderful old-time Montana hospitality. "The coffeepot is always on here," and you're welcomed into the family. Great for families as well as singles and couples. George prefers to visit with all new guests by telephone before they make a reservation, so give him a call. Ranch-raised horses, Natural Horsemanship Program. More open riding than trail riding. Nearby: Yellowstone National Park (90 miles), Museum of the Rockies, Lewis and Clark Caverns.

Hargrave Cattle and Guest Ranch
Marion, Montana

THE DUDE RANCHERS'
ASSOCIATION

I met Leo and Ellen Hargrave in 1989 on one of the most incredible Western events of our time—the Centennial Great Montana Cattle Drive. They were my hosts and ranch outfitters and gave me one of the most wonderful experiences of my life. Our friendship has grown and continues. Today they run a wonderful cattle ranch, offering guests a rich, wholesome, and spirited experience that captures the imaginations of both the young and young-at-heart. Here the cowboy legend is alive—real cattle, real people, and a real sense of what this American way of life is all about. Come to savor the beauty of Montana and enjoy rich hospitality and friendship. Leo, Ellen, and the Hargrave Cattle Ranch are the real thing, and as Ellen says, "Here you'll live the legend."

Address: 300 Thompson River Valley, Dept. K, Marion, Montana 59925
Telephone: 406/858-2284; fax: 406/858-2444
Email: cowboys@hargraveranch.com
Internet: www.hargraveranch.com
Airport: Kalispell, 48 miles
Location: 40 miles west of Kalispell, off Highway 2 West
Memberships: The Dude Ranchers' Association, Montana Outfitters and Guides Association, National Cattlemen's Association, America Outdoors, Montana Dude Ranch Association
Medical: Kalispell Regional Hospital, 40 miles; emergency helicopter service available
Guest Capacity: 19
Accommodations: The Stable has a bedroom, loft, fireplace, kitchen, and bath, and houses two to six guests. Rooms for two to six people in the main ranch house. Ask about the Chicken House and McGregor Cabins, with down comforters on the beds and stained-glass windows. Ask about the 3,000-square-foot Pine Hill four-bedroom luxury home. Ellen likes color and usually plants red petunias and pansies in abundance. Daily maid service
Rates: • $$$–$$$$ American Plan; includes all activities and service charges. Off-season rates. Wilderness pack trips additional. Six-night minimum stay in the summer, Sunday to Saturday.
Credit Cards: VISA, MasterCard. Personal checks preferred.

Season: Year-round
Activities: This is a working ranch where you can be up with the cowboys or sleep in. Spring: Newborn calves everywhere. Horsemanship lessons and cattle herding opportunities mix with pleasure and scenic riding on 87,000 acres. The program here is flexible—do as much or as little as you wish. When not riding, guests enjoy hiking, canoeing, fly-fishing, early morning wildlife-viewing trips, roping, skeet and target shooting, or day trips to Glacier National Park. Overnight campout at Lost Lake. Ask about summer range riding and herd management. In May, Singles' and Women's Weeks. Spring cattle drives and fall roundups. Winter: Call for details.
Children's Programs: As Ellen says, "It's best for children age 10 and older who can enjoy all that we have to offer."
Dining: Western fare served family-style. Your hosts enjoy fine Western food—ranch-raised beef, local lamb and pork, fresh vegetables, and home-made desserts. Happy hours with creative hors d'oeuvres. Local microbrewery beer tasting. BYOB.
Entertainment: Relax in the horse barn/recreation center over poker or challenge the wrangler to a game of pool. Massage available. Weekly cowboy guitarist sing-alongs around the campfire.
Summary: Leo and Ellen offer one of the truly great Western experiences in America. Small, friendly, real, and lots of personality—great folks sharing a way of life they love and cherish. Hands-on program—do as much or as little as you wish. Featured ranch on VISA television commercial. Nearby: Glacier National Park, National Bison Range.

Hawley Mountain Guest Ranch
McLeod, Montana

Across from the pasture gate you'll see the saw-tooth-roofed lodge of Hawley Mountain Guest Ranch, perched on a rocky ledge and miles from nowhere. Here, surrounded by the beautiful Absaroka-Beartooth Wilderness and high above the cascading Boulder River, is a mountaintop retreat that boasts no crowds, no quick trips to town; just Old West hospitality and informal, relaxed living. Remote Hawley Mountain offers guests the opportunity to view ancient Indian pictographs, fish the Blue Ribbon waters of the upper Boulder River, explore the old ghost town of Independence by truck, or horseback ride to your heart's content. Guests who visit this wilderness hideaway appreciate the views, wildlife, and solitude. Hawley Mountain is relaxed, casual, private, and warmhearted. Be sure to ask about the locations used in the movie *A River Runs Through It.*

Address: P.O. Box 4 K, McLeod, Montana 59052
Telephone: 877/496-7848, 406/932-5791; fax: 406/932-5715 (summer only)
Email: Jarrett.Ronald@mcleodUSA.net
Internet: www.hawleymountain.com
Airport: Bozeman, 100 miles; or Billings, 120 miles. Round-trip pickup available (extra).
Location: 42 miles south of Big Timber on Highway 298, 100 miles southeast of Bozeman
Memberships: The Dude Ranchers' Association, Montana Dude Ranch Association, Rocky Mountain Elk Foundation
Medical: Pioneer Medical Clinic in Big Timber, 42 miles
Conference Capacity: 14
Guest Capacity: 20
Accommodations: Three rustic cabins and four lodge rooms. Absaroka and Beartooth cabins are set back in the pine trees for privacy with full baths, a bedroom with queen-size bed, sleeping loft, and comfortable living room with refrigerator and electric heat. In addition, the Absaroka cabin has a second-story screened-in sleeping porch accessible by ladder. All of the Eagle's Nest's A-frame lodge rooms have private baths with showers, bunk beds, queen beds, refrigerators, and balconies overlooking the spectacular Boulder River Valley where the trout pond, horse pasture, and river disappear into the wilderness.

Ask about the newer Carbonate Cabin overlooking the Boulder River with wood-burning stove and kitchenette.
Rates: • $$$ American Plan. Special June rates, Sunday to Sunday. Four-day minimum. Airport pick up available and encouraged.
Credit Cards: None. Personal or traveler's checks accepted.
Season: June through September
Activities: As Phyllis, the manager, says, "Because we take only 20 guests each week we really try to offer our guests a flexible program. Most come here to enjoy our scenic riding program, the superb fly-fishing (guide and equipment available), and our guided hiking." River rafting on the Yellowstone River and four-wheel-drive trips available too.
Children's Programs: Best for children ages six and older. Children join adults in all activities. Children six and older may ride. Baby-sitting available by advance reservation. Fishing pond is a favorite. Be sure to ask about the kids' overnight stay in one of the authentic Crow Indian tepees.
Dining: Buffet dining in the lodge provides panoramic views of the Boulder River Valley and offers hearty home-cooked meals. Weekly cookouts around the campfire with s'mores. Special diets accommodated. BYOB.
Entertainment: Volleyball, horseshoes, lively campfire discussions, and roping Norm, the ranch steer.
Summary: Hawley Mountain is a rustic and in-the-wild guest ranch, perched above the Boulder River Valley and surrounded by the wonders of nature. Great fishing, big views, and scenic trail riding. Ask about day trips to ghost town and gold mines. September is adults-only month and most come to flyfish. Smoke-free preferred. Nearby: Yellowstone National Park.

Horse Prairie Ranch
Dillon, Montana

The Horse Prairie Ranch is the oldest working cattle ranch in southwest Montana's historic Horse Prairie Valley. The ranch has 8,000 acres and 22,000 acres of public leased range and is nestled at the foot of the mountains of the Beaverhead National Forest. Owners Ken and Marie Duncan come from the business world and purchased the ranch in 1995. They, along with their five-ranch crew, continue to preserve its traditions and ranch life. The ranch shares with guests authentic ranch life and first-rate accommodations; sincere Western hospitality; and remote, beautiful scenery, including Montana's big-sky sunsets. Adventures include open-range riding, working cattle, and all the other activities typical of an authentic working cattle and guest ranch. Horse Prairie Ranch is truly a first-rate ranch in the last best place.

Address: 3300 Bachelor Mountain Road, Dept. K, Dillon, Montana 59725
Telephone: 888/RANCHLIFE (888/726-2454), 406/681-3160; fax: 406/681-3222
Email: hpr@montana.com
Internet: www.ranchlife.com
Airport: Butte, 1.5 hours (ranch shuttle service available); Idaho Falls, 2.5 hours; Bozeman, 2.5 hours
Location: 45 minutes southwest of Dillon, 2.5 hours southwest of Bozeman
Memberships: The Dude Ranchers' Association, American Angus Association, American Braunvieh Association, Montana Dude Ranch Association
Medical: Barrett Memorial Hospital, Dillon
Conference Capacity: 16; executive telecommuting services
Guest Capacity: 24
Accommodations: Accommodations are upscale enough to feel pampered without taking away the authenticity of the ranch. Five log cabins include the Lakeview with four bedrooms, two baths, large deck, and fireplace; Elkview with three bedrooms, two baths, and woodstove; Aspenview with two bedrooms, one bath, and woodstove; and the Lewis and Clark studio cabins, each with one bedroom and one bath. Cabins have fluffy down comforters and individual washers, dryers,

and refrigerators.
Rates: • $$$–$$$$ American Plan. Four- and six-night stays available. Optional overnight pack trip available. Group rates available.
Credit Cards: VISA, MasterCard
Season: June through September
Activities: There is no limit to the activities—horseback riding, cattle herding, tending the herd's medical needs, practicing roping, and arena games. The ranch hands are very personable and really enjoy teaching and helping with wrangling skills. You can participate to whatever extent you desire. Canoeing and fly-casting on the ranch's 2.5-acre lake (which is stocked with Montana's native Westslope Cutthroat trout), hiking, mountain biking, and skeet shooting. For guests whose interests extend beyond the ranch, there is guided fishing nearby on the Blue Ribbon Beaverhead River and Clark Canyon Reservoir.
Children's Programs: Older children are welcome. Best for kids age 10 and older. Kids are the full responsibility of their parents.
Dining: Dining at the Creek Side Lodge. Well-presented, hearty, Western-style meals served family-style include ranch-raised natural beef, fresh vegetables, chicken, fruit, and delicious homemade breads and desserts. Breakfast wagon rides. BYOB.
Entertainment: Informal program. Folks are usually pretty tuckered out at the end of the day and enjoy evening walks, conversation, and relaxing.
Summary: One of Kilgore's greats. Perhaps this best sums up the Horse Prairie Ranch experience: "The most beautiful, awe-inspiring, and magnificent scenery, and the most kind and hospitable people. Thanks for sharing this piece of heaven on earth." One of Montana's oldest cattle ranches is now also one of Montana's great working guest ranches. This ranch has it all—forest, sagebrush, lush meadows, mountains, cattle work, guest ranch activities, and nearby Blue Ribbon fly-fishing. Nearby: Ghost town of Bannock and Lemhi Pass. History buffs, be sure to ask about Lewis and Clark.

Klick's K Bar L Ranch
Augusta, Montana

THE DUDE RANCHERS'
ASSOCIATION

Welcome to one of Kilgore's greatest old-time ranches in North America! K Bar L is one of the only Western dude ranches that is truly "beyond all roads." To reach the ranch, you take a half-hour jet boat up Gibson Lake or ride by horse on a scenic mountain trail. If you arrive by jet boat, you may be picked up in a mule-drawn surrey for a short ride to the ranch. The ranch was founded in 1927 and hosts Dick and Nancy Klick, along with their family, welcome you. The ranch is in a magnificent setting in the confluence of the North and South Forks of the Sun River. Fly-fishing is a stone's throw from your cabin. The ranch's backyard is the 1.5-million-acre Bob Marshall Wilderness. The ranch is like "the hub of a huge wheel," with miles of mountain trails leading out in every direction. The wilderness is all scenic fish-and-game country. One of the highlights is the natural hot springs pool with a year-round temperature of 86°F—great for total relaxation with stars and fireflies twinkling overhead at night.

Address: Box 287 K, Augusta, Montana 59410
Telephone: 406/562-3551 (summer); 406/562-3589 (winter)
Airport: Great Falls, 80 miles; ranch will pick you up (extra)
Location: 80 miles west of Great Falls, 30 miles west of Augusta. If you're driving be sure to call for directions.
Memberships: The Dude Ranchers' Association, Montana Outfitters and Guides, Professional Wilderness Outfitters
Medical: Great Falls, 80 miles
Conference Capacity: 35
Guest Capacity: 35
Accommodations: The main lodge houses the kitchen, dining room, library, and Steinway piano in a comfortable fireside setting. The guest cabins are one, two, and three rooms with rustic furnishings, including Hudson Bay and Pendleton blankets and Navajo rugs, and water piped to your cabin door. A pitcher and washbasin are provided just like in the "good old days." Clean, separate cabins provide hot showers and modern toilet facilities. The ranch hydroelectric system provides basic needs so you'll enjoy "roughing it."

Rates: • $$$ American Plan. Six-day, five-night minimum stays. Most stay seven days and six nights. Three-day, two-night minimum stay in June.
Credit Cards: None. Personal and traveler's checks accepted.
Season: June to mid-September
Activities: The Klick family has a history of great horsemanship and offers each guest his or her own personal saddle horse. As founder Emil Klick used to say, "I always broke and rode a good horse." And so the tradition continues. Good fishing starts a few feet from the cabins, or you can follow the stream on foot or horseback. Miles of streams and tributaries surround the ranch, including the North and South Forks of the Sun River. Seven-day wilderness pack trips are usually planned to the Chinese Wall and the Continental Divide. Ask about two-night pack trips to Prairie Reef, the Glen Creek fish camp, and Bear Lake. Ask about the overnight hike to Arsenic Peak.
Children's Program: Children under age six not recommended.
Dining: Good, wholesome food served family-style. As Nancy Klick says, "Never had a complaint." Weekly barbecues. BYOB.
Entertainment: Your choice of horseshoes, sing-alongs, volleyball, and swimming.
Summary: A good piece of advice from Kilgore: reserve early. Others have discovered the Klicks' high-country hideaway. Dick and Nancy Klick were born into Western life and, together with their family, share this great Montana tradition. Like a step back in time, this remote ranch is accessible only by saddle horse or jet boat. Beautiful day rides to Slate Goat, Bear Lake, Pretty Prairie, and Elk Hill. Great for adventurous families, couples, or singles who love the outdoors. Saddle-horse and mule roundup in June. Three-day Castle Reef trail ride for women only. Ask about the elk, buffalo, and yak. Nearby: Glacier and Yellowstone National Parks.

Lake Upsata Guest Ranch
Ovando, Montana

What a view! Lake Upsata Guest Ranch overlooks a beautiful spring-fed mountain lake. Situated two hours south of Glacier National Park in the heart of Montana's Big Sky Country, Upsata specializes in wholesome family guest-ranch experiences. Owners and hosts Greg and Julie Gilchrist, and their two children Paige and Alan, along with Greg's father, Rod, offer a well-rounded summer and winter program for those who wish to enjoy the lakeside setting and combination of activities. Lake Upsata and the Gilchrist family bring their love of the outdoors to couples, families, and singles. As Greg says, "We have got an incredible location and we are proud to be sharing this beautiful paradise with guests of all ages."

Address: 135 Lake Upsata Road, P.O. Box 6, Ovando, Montana 59854
Telephone: 800/594-7687, 406/793-5890; fax: 406/793-5894
Email: reservations@upsata.com
Internet: www.upsata.com
Airport: Missoula, 50 miles
Location: 45 miles east of Missoula off Highway 200, north of Mile Marker 38
Memberships: Chambers of Commerce
Medical: Missoula Hospital, 45 miles
Conference Capacity: 18
Guest Capacity: 30
Accommodations: Eight comfortable log cabins with covered porches. The cabins are along the lake among the aspen and evergreen trees. Each cabin has two full-size beds, carpeting, baths, vanity, refrigerator, and coffeemaker.
Rates: • $$–$$$ American Plan. Children's, off-season, and group rates available year-round.
Credit Cards: VISA, MasterCard. Personal and traveler's checks accepted.
Season: Year-round
Activities: Summer: Scenic trail riding to Blackfoot Clear Water Game Range and Lolo National Forest, guided hiking to Holland Lake and Morrell Falls, mountain biking (30 bikes), and fly-fishing on the Blackfoot River. The ranch is located on a beautiful spring-fed lake with dock, rowboats, canoes, paddleboats, and inner tubes. The lake is also perfect for swimming. Ask about available overnight summer pack trips. Day trips to Garnet ghost town and Glacier National Park. Winter: Hot tub runs year-round. Tubing, cross-country skiing, ice fishing, snowmobiling, and sleigh rides.
Children's Programs: Half-day children's crafts and nature programs during the summer. Children's counselor on-staff full-time during the summer season. Nanny recommended for small children. Accommodations for nannies are free. Trail riding begins at age six and is dependent on ability. Kids' tree house, beach, and overnight tepees.
Dining: Hearty food served family-style in the lodge with views of Lake Upsata, Bob Marshall Wilderness, and Swan Range. Lakeside cookouts. Complimentary beer and wine with dinner.
Entertainment: Varies with seasons. Acoustic music, cowboy poetry, historical speakers from around the region. Horseshoe pits, volleyball, and pool table.
Summary: Wonderful lakeside setting! Family-oriented guest ranch with views overlooking Lake Upsata. Something for everyone, with a variety of recreational activities offered. Trips to ghost towns, bison range, and historical sites. Great for parents who wish to share outdoor experiences with their kids. Nearby: Glacier National Park, National Bison Range.

Laughing Water Ranch
Fortine, Montana

THE DUDE RANCHERS' ASSOCIATION

Montana Dude Ranch Association

If you're looking for a small, family-owned and -operated guest ranch in the forests of northwest Montana near North America's famous Glacier National Park and Canada, read on. Since 1988, the Mikitas' Laughing Water Ranch has offered singles, couples, and families a delightful personal ranch experience. You might be interested in knowing that the owner, Ted Mikita, flies internationally as pilot for Northwest Airlines and has a keen eye for service, attention to detail, and hospitality. As you drive into the 220-acre ranch you'll pass the barn and a lovely meadow and up on the rise you'll see the large main ranch house/lodge and headquarters. On the "back 40" is where you'll find the log cabins, "Fort Laramie" miniature stockade, and the "Kamp Kootenai" Indian tepee village. The ranch is bordered by the Kootenai National Forest in the Whitefish Range of the Rocky Mountains.

Address: P.O. Box 157 K, Deep Creek Road, Fortine, Montana 59918
Telephone: 800/847-5095, 406/882-4680; fax: 406/882-4880
Email: cowboy@lwranch.com
Internet: www.lwranch.com
Airport: Kalispell
Location: 50 miles north of Kalispell off Highway 93, 20 miles from the Canadian border
Memberships: The Dude Ranchers' Association, Montana Dude Ranch Association
Medical: North Valley Hospital in Whitefish, 40 miles; emergency helicopter available
Guest Capacity: 32
Accommodations: Four two-room "suites" in the family's modern, one-story, log-sided, ranch-style house. Rooms vary, with comfortable furnishings, full baths, carpeting, and baseboard heating. Family-style dining room and open-beamed living room with parquet floors. Fully equipped recreation room with fireplace. Deck and hot tub off living room. Four attractive duplex log cabins with single rooms, log furniture, private baths, and porches. Daily maid service.
Rates: • $–$$$ American Plan. Children's, family, and off-season rates available. One-week minimum stay during high season; shorter packages shoulder season.

Credit Cards: None. Personal checks accepted.
Season: May through September
Activities: Daily short and long scenic trail rides. Two-night pack trips during selected weeks in July and August. Riding instruction is tailored to individual skill level. Riding through scenic mountainous terrain. Fishing in two stocked trout ponds. Fishing gear (basic spinning equipment available), fly-casting, and off-ranch fishing can be arranged with prior notice. Weekly whitewater rafting day trips to Glacier National Park and into nearby Canada to see the historic Canadian Fort Steele.
Children's Programs: Active kid's program for ages 4–14 while parents are riding. Kamp Kootenai/Fort Laramie morning activities with Native American/Western cavalry themes. This program includes corral and pony rides, beaded crafts, nature walks, cookouts, Indian culture through sign language, and tepee campouts. At the fort, kids enjoy guard duty, rifle and pistol practice, tack and horse care and feeding, along with scouting on horseback. Parents and children enjoy the Fort Laramie powwow—a final day at the end of the week with gymkhana horse games, competitions, and dancing.
Dining: Wholesome, hearty ranch cooking. Menus include prime rib, trout fish fry, huckleberry muffins, and pies. BYOB.
Entertainment: Something is planned each evening. Hayrides, square dances, mountain-man black-powder shoot and tomahawk throw, and volleyball games. Ping-Pong, pool table, game tables, and a large video library with a selection of Westerns, musicals, and classics. Ask about PRCA rodeos.
Summary: Small, easygoing, very friendly, low-key, family-operated guest ranch 50 miles from Glacier National Park and 20 miles from the Canadian border. Kamp Kootenai/Fort Laramie for children ages four and up. Adults-only weeks. Ask about the May cattle drive/roundup. Singles week in May and September.

Logan Cattle and Guest Ranch
Clyde Park, Montana

Logan Cattle and Guest Ranch is all about the spirit and history of Montana. Here Jim and Elaine, along with their son and grandson, carry on the traditions of Montana cattle ranching. Jim's father began ranching in the 1950s, following in the footsteps of his predecessors from the turn of the century. In 1996 the Logans began a new chapter in the life of the ranch, like so many true cattle ranchers have done, and over the last seven years they have welcomed families, couples, and singles from as far away as Germany, Australia, and Capetown, South Africa. Guests come to ride in the wide-open pastures side-by-side exploring 3,000 acres in the morning and afternoon; helping with the irrigating, haying, fencing and other ranch chores; or taking a mid-day snooze to awaken refreshed and ready for the camaraderie and great ranch food when the sun goes down. While most come in the summer months, a good number visit in the fall, winter, and spring to enjoy all that nature and life here in south central Montana has to offer under the Logan stewardship.

Address: P.O. Box 86, Clyde Park, Montana 59018
Telephone: 406/686-4684 (tel./fax)
Internet: www.logansranch.com
Airport: Bozeman
Location: 50 miles northeast of Bozeman
Medical: Livingston Memorial Hospital, 25miles
Guest Capacity: 8
Accommodations: Four-bedroom, 2,000-square-foot guesthouse nestled in the trees, with carpeting, two showers and bathrooms, common living area, and kitchen.
Rates: • $$ American Plan. Children's rate, no minimum stay.
Credit Cards: None. Personal and traveler's checks accepted.
Season: Year-round
Activities: The activities and horseback riding all revolve around ranch life and vary depending on the season. Calving begins mid-February to mid-April; cattle are rounded up, sorted, and branded starting the end of April and continuing into May; cattle are driven to summer pastures in June; July and August offer haying, general riding and ranch

work, and local rodeos. September is one of Jim's favorite times of the year before the fall roundup in October. Ask about cattle shipping, ranch horses, trout fishing, and the hiking that many guest enjoy. Guided trips to Yellowstone on request.
Children's Programs: Great for kids who would enjoy ranch life and animals, and for parents who like being on vacation with their kids. Riding begins at age 12.
Dining: Hearty ranch food including fish, pasta, and ranch-raised beef. Vegetarian provided upon request. BYOB.
Entertainment: Evening strolls, roping arena where neighboring ranchers and family members practice team and calf roping, some fly- and spin-fishing in Cottonwood Creek. Weekly evening dances and singing.
Summary: Real working cattle ranch offering year-round opportunities to enjoy, explore, and experience the life of a real Montana family who loves the land and what they have been doing for 50-plus years. Nearby: Historic Western town of Livingston; Yellowstone National Park (90 miles).

Lone Mountain Ranch
Big Sky, Montana

Montana
Dude
Ranch
Association

Lone Mountain Ranch is one of the country's premier, multiseason guest ranches with a unique and very strong naturalist program. What makes this ranch so special is that it offers people from around the world the opportunity to discover nature and enjoy first-rate family guest ranching in the summer, a world-class cross-country skiing program in the winter, and fly-fishing. The ranch is in Montana's famous Gallatin Canyon, just down the road from Big Sky Ski and Summer Resort and Yellowstone National Park. Lone Mountain's naturalist program is one of the things that makes the ranch so famous. Throughout each week, naturalists lead hikes to teach visitors about the Yellowstone area's spectacular natural wonders. Activities are varied, including spotting soaring eagles, identifying wildflowers, banding birds, learning about geology or old Indian trails, taking early-morning trips to hear bugling elk, and visiting Yellowstone. Whether you're horseback riding, hiking, fishing, skiing, or just daydreaming, the Lone Mountain crew will show you Montana's best.

Address: P.O. Box 160069 K, Big Sky, Montana 59716
Telephone: 800/514-4644, 406/995-4644; fax: 406/995-4670
Email: lmr@lmranch.com
Internet: www.lmranch.com
Airport: Bozeman
Location: 40 miles south of Bozeman off Highway 191
Memberships: Greater Yellowstone Coalition, Montana Dude Ranch Association, Cross-Country Ski Area Association.
Medical: Bozeman Deaconess Hospital, 40 miles
Conference Capacity: 50
Guest Capacity: 80
Accommodations: Twenty-four well-maintained, fully insulated, one- to four-bedroom log cabins (each one sleeps two to nine) and luxury six-bedroom Ridgetop Lodge. Each features comfortable beds, electric heat, bathrooms with tub/shower, and a rock fireplace or woodstove. The cozy cabins are close to the clear mountain stream that winds through the property. All have front porches for relaxing.

Rates: • $$$–$$$$$ American Plan. Children under age two stay free (ask about nanny rates). Special package rates. Normally, minimum one-week stay, Sunday to Sunday.
Credit Cards: VISA, MasterCard, Discover
Season: Summer: Late May to mid-October; Winter: Early December to early April.
Activities: Naturalist programs, fly-fishing, horseback riding, hiking, and relaxing are the main activities. Riding instruction, with no more than eight on a ride. Exceptional Orvis-endorsed fly-fishing (see Fly-Fishing section for special fishing packages). Tennis, swimming, white-water rafting, golf, rock-climbing, and scenic tram ride nearby. In winter, the ranch offers wonderful downhill and cross-country skiing packages (see Cross-Country Skiing section). Outdoor whirlpool and massage.
Children's Programs: Extensive program for ages 4–12 and teens focusing on nature, building confidence, adventure, and fun! Experienced counselors from after-breakfast to after-dinner. Nannies encouraged for kids under age four.
Dining: Breakfast and lunch buffet-style. Dinner menu ranch favorites and nightly chef's specials. Cookouts. Special diets catered to. Restaurant open to the public on a limited basis. Full bar. No smoking policy.
Entertainment: Informative and entertaining nightly programs.
Summary: One of Kilgore's "Best of the Best." Excellent, multiseason guest ranch with world-class naturalist program and excellent children's program. Year-round Orvis-endorsed fly-fishing with guides and instruction. Great for spring and fall conferences. Superb cuisine! Video of summer and winter programs available. September and October best for adults with kids back in school.

McGinnis Meadows Cattle & Guest Ranch
Libby, Montana

Welcome to one of the country's leading Buck Brannaman-style horsemanship guest ranches. Here guests, both seasoned and novice riders, will learn excellence in horsemanship, and the art and spirit that embodies this wonderful way of life. McGinnis Meadows Cattle & Guest Ranch is operated by owners Shayne and JoAnne Jackson and general managers Dori and Randy Bock. Located in northwest Montana, the ranch was homesteaded in the 1890s by the Davis family. Cattle moved into the scene in the 1920s, and in 1998 it opened its doors as a cattle and guest ranch using the Buck Brannaman style of horsemanship, which is based on the 300-year-old Vaquero tradition. As Shayne says, "This method is both gentle and effective and creates a unique bond between horse and rider."

Address: 6600 McGinnis Meadows Road, Drawer K, Libby, Montana 59923
Telephone: 406/293-5000; fax: 406/293-5000
Email: info@mmgranch.com
Internet: www.mmgranch.com
Airport: Glacier International Airport, Kalispell; Spokane, Washington
Location: 1.5 hours west of Kalispell, 40 minutes east of Libby; 200 miles east of Spokane
Medical: St. John's Lutheran Hospital, Libby, Montana
Conference Capacity: 16–20
Guest Capacity: 16
Accommodations: Three rooms in the lodge are single and double occupancy, and five handcrafted Amish-built log cabins sleep up to four. Each has a queen-size bed with denim down comforters and Pendleton wool blankets, as well as fluffy robes, complimentary slippers, plush towels for bath and hot tub use, and water bottles for rides. Rooms in the lodge have individual private baths and are close to the coffeepot and private deck.
Rates: • $$$–$$$$ American Plan; six-night minimum Sunday to Saturday. Off-peak rates available. Three-night minimum stay in winter.
Credit Cards: VISA, MasterCard, Discover, American Express. Personal and traveler's checks accepted.
Season: January through November

Activities: Here the spirit is all about the Buck Brannaman style of horsemanship. The wranglers are trained in this style of riding and experienced in this way of life. With three guests per wrangler, quality individual attention is provided. Each day during the main season guests can choose to ride, move cattle out on 40,000 acres of summer range, practice team penning and cutting steers, further their horsemanship skills in the heated indoor arena, outdoor arenas, or out in the meadows, or ride through the open and timbered countryside. Side-by-side riding is featured. Call for the year's horsemanship and cattle working schedules. Riding and nonriding guests also enjoy hiking and mountain biking along abandoned logging trails, swimming and fishing in nearby lakes, and guided fly-fishing and white-water raft trips on the Kootenai and Flathead Rivers. Winter offers superb horsemanship activities in outdoor and heated indoor arenas, and cross-country skiing.
Children's Programs: No structured children's program. Best for kids 10 and older with an interest in horsemanship. Kids are the parents' responsibility.
Dining: Fine Western cuisine. Ask about the barbecued ribs, fresh huckleberries, and pecan pie. BYOB.
Entertainment: Most evenings are spent on the deck overlooking the meadow visiting about the day's events. Guests enjoy the hot tub, game of pool, table tennis, volleyball, horseshoes, or settling into one of the overstuffed couches to watch an old Western movie in the game room, or watch one of Buck Brannaman's instructional videos. Massage available.
Summary: Kilgore's "Best of the Best"–Horsemanship. One of the country's top Buck Brannaman-style horsemanship guest and cattle ranches, with fine custom tack, an extensive program about horses, working with cattle, and roping demonstrations.

Mountain Meadows Guest Ranch
Big Sky, Montana

Mountain Meadows Guest Ranch is Big Sky's newest and most exclusive guest ranch. Built in 1999 and opened in December of that year, Mountain Meadows is owned and operated by the Severn family. The ranch has 360-degree views and looks out to 11,000-foot Lone Mountain and Pioneer Peaks. With a guest capacity of only 26, the Severn family caters to their discerning guests who come to savor the magic and the beauty of this paradise the Severns call home.

Address: 7055 Beaver Creek Road, P.O. Box 160334 K, Big Sky, Montana 59716
Telephone: 888/644-6647, 406/995-4997; fax: 406/995-2097
Email: mmgr@mcn.net
Internet: www.mountainmeadowsranch.com
Airport: Bozeman for commercial flights and private jets
Location: Three miles south of the Big Sky turnoff on Highway 191, then seven miles up Beaver Creek Road; 50 miles south of Bozeman.
Medical: Big Sky Medical Clinic in Big Sky; Bozeman Deaconess Hospital, 55 miles
Conference Capacity: 26; year-round
Guest Capacity: 26
Accommodations: Seven guest rooms are on both levels of the 10,000-square-foot log lodge, each with private balcony and bathroom, queen- or king-size bed, one larger family room with couch/hide-a-bed but no balcony. All have fabulous views, televisions, telephones, and Internet access, and are decorated in the motif of the local wildlife. Two cabins each have two bedrooms, two bathrooms, a couch/hide-a-bed, kitchenette, television, telephone, living area, and deck. The lodge has a spacious dining room with fabulous views, the Thirsty Moose Bar, a huge rock open-pit fireplace, lounge area, large decks, sauna, and outdoor hot tub.
Rates: • $$$$$ American Plan; three-day minimum stay. Summer and winter rates.
Credit Cards: VISA, MasterCard, Discover, American Express. Personal and traveler's checks accepted.
Season: Year-round, with the exception of May and first half of November.
Activities: Year-round activities include horse-back riding, hiking, wildlife viewing, mountain biking, wildflower identification, a fly-fishing clinic, bird-watching, white-water rafting, tennis, hayrides, swimming in ponds or the pool at Big Sky, and golf at Big Sky's Arnold Palmer-designed par-72 course. Special fall activities are horseback riding and hiking to hear and see the elk bugle, and late spring activities focus on wildlife viewing. Winter and spring activities are cross-country skiing on the ranch's own 30-kilometers of groomed trails, downhill skiing at the Big Sky Ski Resort, snowshoeing, sledding and tobogganing, sleigh rides, and horseback riding. Usually two activities are scheduled per day, but guests can choose what they would like to do. Guided fly-fishing on the Blue Ribbon waters of the Gallatin River, kayaking, snowmobiling, and trips to Yellowstone National Park available at an extra charge.
Children's Programs: All children are welcome. Cribs, highchairs, roll-aways, and baby-sitting available. No formal program; family activities are the focus. Kids love the barn with the llamas, horses, goats, donkeys, sheep, and cow. Kids must be at least six years old to horseback ride and white-water raft. Playground area at lodge.
Dining: Locally famous chef prepares Western cuisine like beef tenderloin with green peppercorn sauce, baked salmon, free-range chicken, and yummy vegetarian dishes. Meals are served family-style in the beautiful dining room, out on the deck, or on a barbecue/hayride. Made to order breakfasts, lunches of soup and sandwiches, hamburgers, and stir-fry. Appetizers served in the bar every evening. Extensive wine list and full liquor license. Special dietary needs accommodated.
Entertainment: Evening activities include hayride/barbecues, cowboy poetry, s'mores at a nightly campfire, square/line dancing, singing, and classical piano music. Winter sleigh rides. Library in the lodge.
Summary: One of Montana's incredible new guest ranches. Lots of activities, fine accommodations, incredible Big Sky views, and high Western cuisine. Fabulous for honeymoons, family reunions, small group meetings—and more!

Mountain Sky Guest Ranch
Bozeman, Montana

Mountain Sky goes way back to the early days of dude ranching. Originally it was the famed Ox Yoke Ranch, run by an old Montana family. Today, managed by Shirley Arsenault and her fine staff, the ranch has guests hailing from around the globe. Together, they have succeeded in blending the excellence customarily expected in a fine hotel, with the casualness and sincerity of a Western ranch. It's in the magnificent Paradise Valley, home of the famous Yellowstone River. Just as in the early days, great emphasis is placed on the family. The staff go out of their way to ensure that both young and the young-at-heart are happy and having one of the greatest experiences of their lives. Mountain Sky offers clean fresh air, outstanding scenery, tranquility, Western accommodations, and fine dining. At this ranch, the "Sky's" the limit.

Address: Box 1128 K, Bozeman, Montana 59771
Telephone: 800/548-3392, 406/587-1244; fax: 406/587-3977
Email: mountainsky@mcn.net
Internet: www.mtnsky.com
Airport: Bozeman
Location: 60 miles southeast of Bozeman, 30 miles south of Livingston
Memberships: The Dude Ranchers' Association, Montana Dude Ranch Association
Awards: AAA 4 Diamond
Medical: Livingston Clinic, 30 miles; Bozeman Deaconess Hospital, 60 miles
Conference Capacity: 75 (off-season only), conference package available
Guest Capacity: 75
Accommodations: 27 guest cabins, some that sleep up to seven, modern baths (with bathrobes), large picture windows, and sitting rooms. The older, more rustic cabins have been preserved, keeping the Old West charm with stone fireplaces or wood-burning stoves, pine furniture, and small front decks. All of the cabins have inviting front porches with hanging flower baskets. A bowl of fresh fruit is brought to each cabin daily. Yellowstone City, the main lodge, radiates warmth and comfort with three stone fireplaces, a hand-hewn-trussed ceiling, and braided rugs. It has a lounge, cozy bar, dining room, and for those who are musically inclined, a Yamaha grand piano.

Rates: • $$$$$ American Plan; service charges included. Children's, corporate, and meeting rates. One-week minimum stay, Sunday to Sunday.
Credit Cards: VISA, MasterCard. Personal checks preferred.
Season: Mid-May to mid-October
Activities: Extensive riding program for all levels. Rides go out daily, except Sunday. Swimming in heated pool. Whirlpool and sauna. Daily guided nature hikes. Two tennis courts. Fly-fishing on the Yellowstone River with guides available. Fishing on the ranch in a stocked trout pond. Big Creek is minutes from your cabin door. Daily massage available.
Children's Programs: Exceptional children's program for infants to teens. Kiddie wrangler, kids' cookouts and meals, hiking, swimming, fishing. Children can eat evening meal together. Outstanding all-around program.
Dining: The food... wow! Gourmet, five-course dinner Tuesday and Saturday nights, featuring such favorites as poached salmon or rack of lamb, with fine wine. Hearty breakfasts; buffet-style lunch. Poolside barbecues. Children's dinners with counselor are available. Special diets catered to. Full bar.
Entertainment: Evening country and Western dancing and campfire sing-alongs. Light, relaxing music with the twice-weekly gourmet dinners. Volleyball, billiards. Monday night get-acquainted softball. Evening strolls or a moonlight soak in the hot tub.
Summary: Excellent historic old-time ranch with superb children's program and fine dining. One of Kilgore's "Best of the Best"–Historic Ranch and superb service. Excellent fly-fishing and horseback riding. River rafting on the Yellowstone River. Nearby: Yellowstone National Park (30 miles).

Nine Quarter Circle Ranch
Gallatin Gateway, Montana

One of Montana's legends! Since 1946, from early June to mid-September, the Nine Quarter Circle Ranch has been doing what it does best—welcoming families. High in the Montana Rockies, in its own secluded mountain valley, the ranch is seven miles from the northwest corner of Yellowstone National Park. There's a five-mile drive up a winding, scenic, dirt road until the ranch is visible. Taylor Fork, a fly-fishing river, runs through the ranch, and the log cabins overlook the green, grassy meadows with the striking mountain peaks in the distance. One of Montana's most famous, the ranch is run by Kim and Kelly Kelsey and their two young sons, Konnor and Kameron, and daughter, Kyleen. Kim and Kelly are the son and daughter-in-law of the founders, Howard and Martha Kelsey. As the Kelseys say, "Two things can never change or end, the goodness of nature and man's love for a friend." You'll find both here.

Address: 5000 Taylor Fork Road, Box K, Gallatin Gateway, Montana 59730
Telephone: 406/995-4276
Email: nineqtrcircle@mcn.net
Internet: www.ninequartercircle.com
Airport: Bozeman or the ranch airstrip. Contact ranch for airstrip fact sheet.
Location: 60 miles south of Bozeman
Memberships: The Dude Ranchers' Association, Montana Dude Ranch Association
Medical: Bozeman Deaconess Hospital, 60 miles; Big Sky Clinic, 30 miles
Conference Capacity: 70; off-season only
Guest Capacity: 70
Accommodations: 20 one-bedroom to four-bedroom log cabins are furnished with log forest furniture and hand-sewn quilts made at the ranch. Woodstoves and porches. Most of the cabins are named after guests, for example, Hubbards' Cupboard and Wihtol's Wickiup. All cabins have private or family baths. The main lodge has a huge rock fireplace. The Kelseys have a clever "Medallion" award board for guests who have returned year after year; it's hanging in the dining room. Some guests have medals representing over 30 years. Guest laundry facilities.
Rates: • $$$ American Plan. Children's and off-season rates available. Minimum one-week stay policy, usually Sunday to Sunday. Fall: Three-night minimum stay.
Credit Cards: None. Personal or traveler's checks accepted.
Season: Mid-June through mid-September
Activities: Riding, fly-fishing, hiking, and wildlife viewing. Plenty of horses. The ranch raises and trains over 120 Appaloosas. Four or five rides, ranging from kiddie rides to advanced rides daily, go to vistas like Inspiration Point, Sunken Forest, and Alp Basin. Two all-day rides and an overnight pack trip go out weekly, including the Kelsey Killer "for those who want a real thrill." Great fly-fishing on the Gallatin River, and on the ranch's own Taylor Fork (which runs through the ranch), with the ranch fishing guide. Individualized instruction and local fishing trips available. Stocked trout-pond for casting and kids' catch-and-release fishing. Limited loaner fly-fishing rods and retail fishing shop on ranch. A spring-fed "swimming pool" for hardy swimmers.
Children's Programs: Full program for kids ages 2–10. Kiddie wrangler. Walking-led rides for kids ages five and under around ranch pasture. Playground and playroom. Weekly kids' picnic. Child supervision is provided during the morning and afternoon rides, as well as lunch and dinner. Kids love all the bunnies!
Dining: Children and teens eat early while parents enjoy happy hour. BYOB. Meals are home-cooked and family-style. Weekly barbecues, cookouts, and a dinner ride.
Entertainment: Square dancing, hayrides, weekly Western movies, volleyball, softball, and games on horseback (a big hit with the kids).
Summary: Wonderful family-run ranch for families throughout the summer. Adults-only in the fall. Great riding and fly-fishing. Ideal for young families with kids ages 2–15, and for grandparents too. Appaloosas bred and trained on the ranch. Ask about the fall Bugle Rides! Private airstrip. Ranch store. Nearby: Yellowstone National Park, Museum of the Rockies in the Western college town of Bozeman.

Parade Rest Ranch
West Yellowstone, Montana

Parade Rest Ranch is near one of the world's most famous parks—Yellowstone National Park—and in the heart of some of North America's best fly-fishing country. With Grayling Creek literally at the back door and Blue Ribbon trout streams surrounding it, Parade Rest offers a parade of outdoor activities, natural beauty, and, for those so inclined, lots of rest. There's no timetable or regimented activity list. Your time is your own, and you may do as much or as little as you please. Life at Parade Rest is informal. The dress code is whatever's comfortable; for the most part, that means an old pair of jeans. Mornings and evenings are cool, with midday temperatures in the mid- to high 80s. Parade Rest Ranch is a small dude/fly-fishing ranch run the old-fashioned way.

Address: 7979 Grayling Creek Road, Drawer K, West Yellowstone, Montana 59758
Telephone: 800/753-5934 (summer only), 406/646-7217; fax: 406/646-7217 (summer only)
Email: resv@parade-rest-ranch.com
Internet: www.parade-rest-ranch.com
Airport: West Yellowstone, or Gallatin Field at Bozeman; also, commuter flights from Salt Lake City to West Yellowstone
Location: 10 miles northwest of Yellowstone, 90 miles south of Bozeman off Highway 191
Medical: Yellowstone Medical Clinic
Conference Capacity: 35
Guest Capacity: 60
Accommodations: 15 turn-of-the-century log cabins with 1–4 bedrooms. All are named after famous fishing rivers nearby. Ask about the Homestead Cabin and Grayling single. All have porches, wood-burning stoves, full baths, and comfortable beds; the newest is the Aspen Cabin. Several of these cabins are along Grayling Creek. Nightly turndown service. The Gallatin Lodge is a happy gathering spot for reading, visiting, playing games, and listening to music.
Rates: • $$ Full American Plan. Children's, corporate, off-season, and fly-fishing guide rates available.
Credit Cards: VISA, MasterCard
Season: Mid-May through September
Activities: Very few areas in the country offer such a diversity of fine fishing. Through the ranch flows 1.5 miles of Grayling Creek, an excellent fly-fishing stream. Nearby are the Madison, Gallatin, Firehole, and Gibbon. Full guide service is available. Just let Pam know what you'd like to do and she'll arrange it for you. Also, ask her about the three-day fly-fishing schools. Parade Rest is well known by all the local guides. Horseback riding is geared to beginner and intermediate riders. Rides are accompanied by a wrangler and vary from an hour to four-hour rides. White-water and scenic raft trips. Bicycling and hiking on many ranch trails. Six-person hot tub outside Gallatin Lodge next to Grayling Creek. Yellowstone Country Van Tours (extra charge) are a great way to see the area sights. Great for fly-fishing widows and kids. See www.yellowstone-tours.net. Guests are picked up at the ranch for full-day or half-day tours. Evening wildlife tours in Yellowstone, Jackson/Teton tours, and others.
Children's Programs: Children are welcome and are the parents' responsibility. Trail rides begin at age six with corral rides for the little ones. Various outside games for kids of all ages.
Dining: Even if you're late from your fishing excursion, dinner will be waiting for you. The warm, friendly atmosphere is matched by great, hearty ranch cooking. Western cookouts are held Monday and Friday evenings. You may ride by horseback or on a horse-drawn wagon to the cookout site overlooking Hebgen Lake. Packed lunches are available to those wishing to ride, fish, raft, or explore all day. All meals are all-you-can-eat and served buffet-style in the central dining room. BYOB.
Entertainment: Many of the die-hard anglers eat dinner, then go back out for more fishing. Evening campfires or volleyball, basketball, and horseshoes.
Summary: Since the 1920s, Parade Rest Ranch has been hosting guests who appreciate the old-time feel, easygoing pace, and horseback riding. Superb fly-fishing, scenery and close enough for tours to Yellowstone Park.

Triple Creek Ranch
Darby, Montana

Triple Creek Ranch is an exclusive mountain hideaway almost at the foot of beautiful Trapper Peak, just outside the tiny town of Darby. This "diamond in the rough" (adults-only property) was built in 1986 to create a wilderness retreat for those who yearned for nature's wildness but wanted to experience it with luxurious amenities. Wayne and Judy Kilpatrick manage Triple Creek; together with their wonderful staff, they have created a haven of rest, relaxation, and mountain splendor.

Address: 5551 West Fork Road, Darby, Montana 59829
Telephone: 406/821-4600; fax: 406/821-4666
Email: tcr@bitterroot.net
Internet: www.triplecreekranch.com
Airport: Missoula; private planes to Hamilton with 4,200-foot airstrip; helicopter pad at ranch. Airport pickup available.
Location: 12 miles south of Darby, 74 miles south of Missoula
Memberships: Relais & Chateaux
Awards: Relais & Chateaux; *Hideaway Report*, "A Romantic Gem in the Rocky Mountains"; Ranked No. 7 of 20 U.S. Resort Hideaways, *Little Gems*; *El Capitan*, "Hideout of the Year"; Kilgore Luxury Group
Medical: Marcus Daly Memorial Hospital, Hamilton; emergency helicopter service is available.
Conference Capacity: 30; booking entire ranch is generally required
Guest Capacity: 30 singles, 24 couples
Accommodations: Choose from cozy cedar to luxury log cabins. Each is tastefully furnished. Refrigerators are fully stocked with an array of beverages and there's a full complimentary supply of liquor. For those who wish, there's satellite TV/VCR. The larger luxury cabins have massive handcrafted log king-size beds, double steam showers, and a private hot tub on the deck that looks out into the forest. Telephones with data ports in each cabin. Daily housekeeping and laundry service provided.
Rates: • $$$$$$ American Plan. Single rates available. No minimum stay required.
Credit Cards: VISA, MasterCard, Discover, American Express

Season: Year-round; all holidays.
Activities: Summer: An informal program that caters to each couple or individual. Horseback riding, hiking, fly-fishing (see Fly-Fishing section), white-water river rafting, helicopter tours, swimming in the outdoor heated pool. Tennis court and putting green. Bird- and wildlife-watching and photography. Serious golfers can drive to the Hamilton 18-hole golf course. In winter (see Cross-Country Skiing section), Triple Creek comes alive with the spirit of Christmas: Hot buttered rum, sleigh rides with bells, and horseback riding in freshly fallen snow. Snowmobiling, wilderness cross-country skiing, downhill skiing (28 miles away).
Children's Programs: Children under 16 are allowed only when a family or group reserves entire ranch.
Dining: All meals are varied and designed to tempt even the most finicky diners. Complimentary wine served. Special diets not a problem. Full room service available 7 A.M.–11 P.M. Triple Creek will help you celebrate your birthday or anniversary. Open to public on very limited basis.
Entertainment: Planned evening entertainment. Lovely upstairs lounge in the main lodge with occasional live music. Many go for a stroll under the stars or enjoy a glass of fine cognac in the hot tub.
Summary: One of Kilgore's "Best of the Best"–Luxury and Telecommuting. World-class, luxurious, adults-only, mountaintop hideaway. Superb and friendly staff with personalized service second to none. Quiet, restful, intimate, romantic atmosphere (great for honeymoons), with gourmet cuisine and full room service. Individual telephone line and number in each cabin and dedicated data port. Triple Creek may be booked for family reunions and corporate retreats.

Triple Creek Ranch, Montana

Triple Creek Ranch, Montana

Hartley Guest Ranch
Roy, New Mexico

THE DUDE RANCHERS'
ASSOCIATION

Hartley Guest Ranch is located in breathtaking northeastern New Mexico; the state called "The Land of Enchantment." The ranch is a family-owned and -operated working cattle ranch that has been in the Hartley family since the 1940s. With over 25,000 acres of private land, it varies in elevation from 4,800 to 6,000 feet. There are mesas, red-rock rims and canyons, and 200 miles of trails on high open plains and through forests of juniper, oak, and ponderosa pine. Guests come to enjoy the Hartley family spirit and all the various seasonal ranch activities, which include riding, branding, looking for strays, roundups, and cattle drives. This ranch is secluded—the road ends here—and takes only 10 to 12 guests per week. Hartley Guest Ranch is all about family, ranching tradition, miles of New Mexico landscapes, and spectacular views.

Address: HCR 73, Box 55K, Roy, New Mexico 87743
Telephone: 800/OUR-DUDE (800/687-3833), 505/673-2244; fax: 505/673-2216
Email: rhart@plateautel.net
Internet: www.hartleyranch.com
Airport: Albuquerque, 220 miles
Location: 25 miles southwest of Roy, 220 miles northeast of Albuquerque (3–4 hours driving), 160 miles northeast of Santa Fe off I-25
Memberships: The Dude Ranchers' Association, New Mexico Cattle Growers Association
Medical: Health Centers of Northern New Mexico at Roy, 25 miles. Northeastern Regional Hospital at Las Vegas, New Mexico; 100 miles.
Guest Capacity: 10–12
Accommodations: Six-bedroom, 2,200-square-foot guesthouse with living and dining rooms for reading or playing board games. Most rooms have queen-size beds and private baths; one with king-size bed and Jacuzzi tub. There is a shared kitchen for snacking and morning coffee and a refrigerator full of soft drinks and juices. There are telephones in the rooms but no TVs. Laundry facility available. Smoke-free policy in buildings.
Rates: • $$$ American Plan. Five-night stays minimum, June through August. Minimum three-night stays in off-season. Children's rates.
Credit Cards: None. Personal and traveler's

checks accepted.
Season: April through mid-October
Activities: Do as much or as little as you wish. Authentic working cattle ranch with plenty of guided riding. Guests may take part in gathering and driving cattle and looking for strays. Branding weeks May through July. The guests may also flank (throw and hold down) calves, vaccinate, or tag ears, depending on abilities and interests. All-day rides to move cattle to different pastures and shorter scenic rides for those who don't want to stay in the saddle all day. Once you're qualified by a wrangler, loping rides are available. Pack trips and overnight campouts. Fishing for bass, catfish, and perch. The stocked ponds are close to the main lodge. Hiking to dinosaur tracks, ancient Indian sites, petroglyphs, and incredible geological formations. Basketball, volleyball, or relaxing in hot tub. Wildlife includes deer, roadrunners, coyotes, raccoons, turkeys, and the occasional mountain lion or bear sighting. Guided all-terrain vehicle rides for everyone ages 16 and older.
Children's Programs: Children are welcome but no formal program. Best for ages nine and older. Riding usually begins at age five.
Dining: Generous home-cooked meals served family-style in the dining room or cooked outdoors over an open fire. Homemade breads and desserts. Guests join the Hartley family for all meals. BYOB.
Entertainment: Informal. Campfires, beautiful clear bright stars at night, and storytelling with the Hartleys and other guests. Outdoor hot tub.
Summary: Spectacular country! As the Hartleys say, "Hartley Guest Ranch is for those who wish to experience the American West and fulfill the dream of being a real cowboy or cowgirl." Secluded with 25,000 acres. Featured on ESPN's *Men's Journal,* and in *Sunset* magazine's "Western Roundup of 50 Great Dude Ranches." Nearby: Santa Fe, three hours.

The Lodge at Chama
Chama, New Mexico

Welcome to The Lodge at Chama! Here, men and women come to enjoy privacy amid 36,000 acres of unspoiled mountain and forest scenery. The Lodge at Chama provides first-rate amenities and excellent service. Over the years, the lodge has hosted many business and industry leaders. Because it takes only 42 people at any one time, guests quickly feel at home. Whether it's a high-level board meeting or plain old rest and relaxation, The Lodge at Chama has what it takes for groups or families who appreciate beauty, kindness, and a host of recreational opportunities. The lodge's fine staff tailors everything to each group's preferences. Be sure to read listing in the Fly-Fishing section as well.

Address: Box 127 K, Chama, New Mexico 87520
Telephone: 505/756-2133; fax: 505/756-2519
Email: reservations@lodgeatchama.com
Internet: www.lodgeatchama.com
Airport: Albuquerque; private jets to Pagosa Springs. Call regarding ranch airstrip.
Location: 100 miles north of Santa Fe, 90 miles west of Taos, 45 miles southeast of Pagosa Springs
Awards: *Hideaway Report* 1990, "Best Sporting Retreat;" Kilgore Luxury Group
Medical: Local clinic; hospital in Española; emergency helicopter service available
Conference Capacity: 42; secretarial services, fax, speaker telephones, copy room. Ask for brochure.
Guest Capacity: 42
Accommodations: Vaulted ceilings, full animal mounts, and views of the Chama Valley beyond the well-kept lawns are the first thing you see as you enter the 27,000-square-foot main lodge. Twenty-one guest rooms, each with private bath and upscale amenities (bathrobes, hair dryers, and oversized towels), and four suites with fireplaces, TVs, and oversized baths with vanities. All rooms have telephones.
Rates: • $$$$–$$$$$$ American Plan. Special rates for full lodge rental. Winter rates available. No minimum stay required. Average stay, three nights.
Credit Cards: VISA, MasterCard, Discover. Personal and corporate checks accepted.

Season: Year-round; all holidays.
Activities: The lodge will send you a detailed brochure and video outlining the activities. During summer, guests enjoy fly-fishing (see Fly-Fishing section), hiking, drives through the ranch property to view vistas and wild game (including one of the world's largest private elk herds and bison), horseback riding, wildlife photography, and sporting clays. Be sure to ask about the historic, narrow-gauge Cumbres & Toltec Scenic Railroad, North America's longest! Limited world-class hunting is offered September to December. Winter activities November to March include cross-country skiing (gear, guides, and instruction available), snowmobiling, vehicle tours to view wildlife, snowshoeing, snow tours, and ice fishing. Fitness room and massage available.
Children's Programs: Minimum age of 12 or by special arrangement
Dining: Gourmet ranch fare. Special requests and diets accommodated. Ask about Chama's delicious northern New Mexico dishes. Bar and premium wines available.
Entertainment: Enjoy the spectacular sunsets, take an evening stroll, watch wide-screen satellite TV, relax in front of the fire or in the huge indoor whirlpool and sauna, or read yourself to sleep. Customized entertainment available on request with advance notice.
Summary: Kilgore Luxury Group. Where exclusivity, scenery, and wildlife reign supreme! One of North America's finest wildlife ranches specializing in high quality outdoor recreation for business executives, corporate groups, and sophisticated family gatherings. Personalized service, delicious cuisine, and tremendous wildlife viewing. Superb lake and stream fly-fishing, and world-class hunting. One of North America's finest wildlife ranches! One of the world's largest private elk herds; buffalo herd also.

The Lodge at Chama, New Mexico

Los Pinos Ranch
Cowles, New Mexico

"Where the road ends and the trails begin" is how Los Pinos Ranch has been described since 1912. Originally the summer residence of the Amado Chaves family, this historic guest ranch has been in operation since the 1920s. Purchased in 1965 by architect Bill McSweeney, Los Pinos continues to be run by his family. Small and private, Los Pinos is located in the heart of the Sangre de Cristo Mountains. At an elevation of 8,500 feet, the ranch perches above the wild and scenic Pecos River. Wildflowers and many birds abound in the area. Average summer temperature is 76 degrees at noon, dipping into the 40s at night. Limited to between 12 and 16 guests, Los Pinos recaptures the ambiance of an earlier, simpler time. Reading, music, or sharing tales of the day's adventures often follows candlelit dinners in the main lodge. Here the spirit of friendship and old-time Western hospitality prevail.

Address: Route 3, Box 8 K, Tererro, New Mexico 87573 (summer–September); P.O. Box 24 K, Glorieta, New Mexico 87535-0024 (winter)
Telephone: 505/757-6213
Internet: www.lospinosranch.com
Airport: Albuquerque
Location: 45 miles northeast of Santa Fe off I-25. Map sent on request.
Medical: Medical clinic in Pecos, 21 miles
Guest Capacity: 12–16
Accommodations: Guests are housed in four original 1920s and 1930s aspen-log cabins. Each cabin is equipped with front porch, private bath (some with clawfoot tubs), and wood-burning stove. Plenty of warm blankets are provided for cool nights. The 1912-vintage lodge is a gathering place for guests. Its large screened-in porch offers peaceful scenery and is a prime spot for a quiet read, games, or conversation. Inside are antique furnishings, fireplace, piano, paintings, and books.
Rates: • $$ American Plan. Riding and guided fly-fishing are offered at an additional cost. Two-night minimum stay.
Credit Cards: None. Personal checks or cash accepted.
Season: June through September
Activities: There is a really easygoing, do as much or as little as you wish, "à la carte" activities program—fly-fishing, hiking, birding, and visiting northern New Mexico's famous points of interest and colorful history. Guided half- and full-day rides wind through coniferous forest, aspen groves, and across spectacular high-mountain meadows of the Santa Fe National Forest. Beginning riders are welcome. Nearby sparkling rivers and their tributaries offer excellent fly-fishing. The "trophy" section of the Pecos begins just below the ranch. Guided fly-fishing with instruction can be arranged with local specialists. Los Pinos is a permittee of the Santa Fe National Forest and an equal opportunity service provider, with hiking trails accessed at nearby trailheads. Historic Santa Fe, with its museums, galleries, and restaurants, is an hour's drive by car. The towns of Pecos, Chimayo, and Taos, and various pueblos offer a diversity of cultures for the traveler.
Children's Programs: No children under six years of age except during family reunions when the whole ranch is booked. Children are parents' responsibility and participate in activities with their families.
Dining: Freshly-baked breads accompany most breakfasts and dinners. Lunches are packed for trail and streamside picnicking. Guests gather each evening for dinner in the lodge dining room. Cuisine offers a variety of flavorful, well-presented dishes served throughout the week. BYOB.
Entertainment: A well-stocked library of local history and nature references; fireside conversation on cool evenings. Outside, nature provides its own array of sights and sounds—hummingbirds, excellent nighttime stargazing, and a chorus of coyotes.
Summary: Lots of peace, quiet, and charm here. Rustic, cozy, and very friendly. If you like the outdoors and no planned activities, Los Pinos is terrific. Wonderful scenery, food, and fellowship. Nearby: Old Santa Fe Trail, Pecos National Historical Park, Indian pueblos, and Spanish villages.

Pinegrove Dude Ranch
Kerhonkson, New York

Pinegrove is nestled in the peaceful, gentle, rolling hills of upstate New York's Catskill Mountains, with miles of mountain trails for riding. Pinegrove is a year-round family-vacation wonderland that serves up Western hospitality. The Tarantino and O'Halloran families started Pinegrove Dude Ranch in 1971. Today it is one of the most family -oriented resort ranches in the Northeast. As David O'Halloran says, "Our family ranch caters exclusively to families and children of all ages and we've carried this tradition on for the past 30 years." At Pinegrove, all in one day, you can saddle up for a two-hour cattle drive, swim, hike, play tennis, and take an afternoon snooze before the evening entertainment begins. The ranch specializes in children's activities and the excellent full-time children's programs enable parents to enjoy themselves as well. At Pinegrove there is something to do for everyone, from toddlers to grandparents... morning, noon, and night.

Address: 30 Cherrytown Road, Drawer K, Kerhonkson, New York 12446
Telephone: 800/346-4626, 845/626-7345; fax: 800/367-3237
Email: pinegrove@ulster.net
Internet: www.pinegrove-ranch.com
Airport: JFK, Newark, or Newburgh
Train: Poughkeepsie, 25 miles
Location: 100 miles northwest of New York City, one mile west of Kerhonkson off Route 209
Memberships: American Hotel and Motel Association, Association for Horsemanship Safety Education, Camp Horsemanship Association-certified wranglers
Medical: Ellenville Hospital, six miles
Conference Capacity: Up to 300; 5,000 square feet of meeting space
Guest Capacity: 350
Accommodations: Guests sleep in comfortable, modern rooms with wall-to-wall carpeting, TVs, telephones with data ports, air-conditioning, and private baths. All 125 rooms are connected to the main lodge by air-conditioned/heated hallways. Daily maid service.
Rates: • $–$$$ American Plan. Children ages four to 16 half price. Kids under age four free. Single-parent, group, and senior discounts. Ask about family specials.
Credit Cards: VISA, MasterCard, Discover, American Express
Season: Year-round; all holidays.
Activities: Nightly riding video and lecture for all newcomers. Daily riding instruction available. Ride over acres of picturesque rolling hills. Most trails are quite wide. You can go into the forest on secluded trails that cross streams and afford distant views. Most rides have 15–20 people. Rides go out on the hour, from 10 A.M.–5 P.M. daily. Cattle-driving (call for information), bass fishing in stocked lake, boating, hiking—all on the property. Indoor and outdoor facilities; tennis, swimming pools, miniature golf, bocci ball, archery, basketball, volleyball, paddleball and handball, table tennis, and shuffleboard. Complimentary nine-hole golf nearby. Winter: Downhill skiing on two slopes, ice-skating, and nightly snow tubing. All equipment and lessons included. Ranch has its own snowmaking equipment.
Children's Program: Full day care program for kids ages 3–12. Nursery for ages three and under (extra charge). Teen program too. Ask about Junior Wrangler instruction for ages 4–7. Lots of animals and large animal farm. Winter: Great learn-to-ski program.
Dining: Three all-you-can-eat meals daily from varied menu. Sunday barbecue in season. Parents eat with their kids. Complimentary snack bar 10 A.M. to midnight.
Entertainment: Ballroom nightclub with family show. Western saloon with swinging doors, popcorn, and guitar singer. Hitching Post pool bar. Steer-roping and leather-carving demonstrations. Campfires with marshmallow roasts.
Summary: A great family-oriented, family-owned and -operated ranch resort. One of the countries best programs for children, including infants. Complete, all-inclusive packages and plenty of activities. Program for all ages. Weekly cattle drives (extra charge).

Roaring Brook Ranch and Tennis Resort
Lake George, New York

Roaring Brook Ranch and Tennis Resort is one of the country's largest destination ranch resorts. Named after the creek that "roars" through the property in the spring, Roaring Brook is in Lake George township in New York's Adirondack Mountains. A resort area for vacationers since the turn of the century, this part of the country has historic significance. In fact, when President Thomas Jefferson first saw Lake George he called it "the queen of the American lakes," suggested by its purity and picturesque setting. The ranch has been under the continuous stewardship of one family since 1946 and is run today by George Greene. This picturesque 500-acre estate specializes in family, group, and corporate activities with accommodations for 300. The high percentage of repeat guests appreciate the all-inclusive vacation packages. Although the ranch spirit prevails, tennis and poolside relaxation appeal to many. Roaring Brook has a large conference facility that can seat up to 1,000. The ranch draws most of its guests from metropolitan New York and New England.

Address: P.O. Box K, Lake George, New York 12845

Telephone: 800/882-7665 (from New York and New England only), 518/668-5767; fax: 518/668-4019

Email: mail@roaringbrookranch.com

Internet: www.roaringbrookranch.com

Airport: Albany, 60 miles

Location: Two miles south of Lake George, one mile off Interstate 87, 60 miles north of Albany, 200 miles north of New York City

Memberships: New York State Hotel/Motel Association

Awards: Mobil 3 Star, AAA 3 Diamond

Medical: Glen Falls Hospital, seven miles

Conference Capacity: 300; a total of 17,000 square feet of conference space. Full audiovisual equipment available. On-staff conference coordinator.

Guest Capacity: 300

Accommodations: There are 140 motel-style rooms in nine buildings spread out around the property. All rooms have private baths, wall-to-wall carpeting, heat and air-conditioning, color TVs, and telephones. Most have deck areas. There are 17 two-room suites.

Rates: • $–$$ Modified American Plan; includes breakfast and dinner. Children's, riding, and conference rates available. Two-day minimum stay.

Credit Cards: VISA, MasterCard

Season: Mid-May to mid-October; conference year-round.

Activities: The ranch recruits Montana wranglers to oversee the riding program. Four scheduled rides go out daily. All rides last about one hour. Groups of 25–30 go out at a time, split into experienced and inexperienced riders. New riders are encouraged, and group instruction is available. Five tennis courts, two lighted. The ranch tennis pro (who splits his tennis year between Boca Raton, Florida, and the ranch) offers all levels of tennis instruction with private lessons available. Three swimming pools (outdoor and indoor), badminton, archery, hiking, volleyball, table tennis, horseshoes, weight room.

Children's Programs: Children are parents' responsibility. Children's playground and counselor for children ages four to seven, morning and afternoons; summer season only. Pony rides, arts and crafts. Baby-sitting can be arranged.

Dining: Full-service, licensed dining room, and coffee shop; choose from varied menu. Full bar.

Entertainment: Two cocktail lounges with musical entertainment nightly in summer. Three or four family shows each week during July and August. Table tennis, billiards, movies.

Summary: Full-service destination ranch and tennis resort that appeals to families, couples, and conference groups. Singles enjoy the ranch as well, and it's also popular for family reunions. Guest referrals and repeat guests represent two-thirds of each summer's guests and families. All-inclusive packages offered. Nearby: Shoreline cruise on Lake George, Fort William Henry, National Museum of Racing, hot-air balloon festival in the fall, dinner theater in Lake George, and nearby Great Escape Amusement Park.

Rocking Horse Dude Ranch Resort
Highland, New York

Just 90 minutes north of New York City, Rocking Horse Dude Ranch Resort is one of the largest year-round resort ranches for the entire family and home to the ranch's award-winning six-horse Belgian team. Rocking Horse was started by Bucky and Toolie Turk, two brothers from Manhattan, who have created over the years their resort ranch, complete with everything from three heated pools, giant and children's waterslide system, water-skiing, and boating in the summer—to skiing, giant snow tube runs with lifts, and horse-drawn sleigh rides in the winter. Since 1958 the Turk family has operated this 500-acre ranch. Most guests come from New York, Pennsylvania, New Jersey, Massachusetts, and Connecticut. With no hidden costs, the ranch recognizes that not everyone wants to ride, so there are plenty of options. For those who love Western activity, there are square and line dancing with instruction, hayrides, horseshoes, bonfires, sing-alongs, marshmallow roasts, and lots of riding supervised by certified wranglers. Kids and parents will find a lot to do together and apart, at an affordable price.

Address: 600 Route 44-55, Highland, New York 12528
Telephone: 800/647-2624, 845/691-2927; fax: 845/691-6434
Email: ranchrhr@aol.com
Internet: www.rhranch.com
Airport: Stewart, JFK, Newark, or La Guardia
Train: Poughkeepsie
Bus: To New Paltz
Location: 75 miles north of New York City
Memberships: New York State Hotel Association
Awards: AAA 3 Diamond, Mobil Quality Rated, *Family Circle* readers voted "My Favorite Ranch Resort" three years in a row
Medical: Vassar and St. Francis Hospitals (Poughkeepsie), 6 miles
Conference Capacity: 250 in 2,800-square-foot auditorium
Guest Capacity: 400
Accommodations: 20 motel-style rooms and 100 rooms in main lodge, with two wings that sleep up to six people in each room. All rooms have TVs, telephones, air-conditioning, carpeting, double and king-size beds, private baths with showers, and daily maid service.
Rates: • $–$$ American Plan and Modified American Plan depending on season. Group rates available. Free children's specials (up to age four).
Credit Cards: VISA, MasterCard, Discover, American Express
Season: Year-round; all holidays.
Activities: Full-time activity director; over 100 horses give everyone the opportunity for plenty of rides. Riding instruction available. Safety always comes first, so guests are tested on their riding skills. Guided trail rides are divided into levels of experience. Several one-hour rides go out daily. Two heated pools with giant and children's waterslide, and one indoor heated pool with interactive water features, paddleboats, beach volleyball, tennis, softball, basketball, rifle/archery range, mini-golf, fitness program with aerobics. Winter program includes skiing and giant snow tube runs with two lifts, 100 percent snowmaking capability, horse-drawn sleigh rides, ice-skating, and year-round, horseback riding. Equipment and instruction provided at ski area.
Children's Programs: Full program with counselors. Fully coordinated day camp and nursery program. Heated children's swimming pool with interactive fountains and waterslide.
Dining: Rotating menus, all you can eat, fresh fruit and dessert assortment. Licensed bar and nightclub.
Entertainment: Dances every night with band and DJs, magic-comedy stage shows, square dancing, talent shows, movies on big-screen TV, backgammon, cards, karaoke.
Summary: Year-round destination resort ranch. Large facility with wonderful spirit and service. Excellent children's program. The Turk family and their staff do a first-rate job for families of all ages. Great for family reunions. Be sure to see the award-winning Belgian draft-horse team. Outdoor group barbecues for up to 1,000. Nearby: Oldest street in America, Kingston, Roosevelt's Hyde Park Mansion and Library, West Point Military Academy. Video available.

Cataloochee Ranch
Maggie Valley, North Carolina

In 1939 young forester Tom Alexander began the tradition and spirit of Cataloochee Ranch. A mile high in the Great Smoky Mountains of western North Carolina, Cataloochee (Cherokee for "wave upon wave") is a thousand-acre, mountaintop paradise, bordered by half a million acres of the Great Smoky Mountains National Park. Since 1939 the Alexander family has been sharing their Southern warmth and hospitality. This ranch looks out over the rolling hills of Maggie Valley, providing guests with a ringside seat for the four seasons as they unfold. Cataloochee offers an unhurried pace with the Smoky and Blue Ridge Mountains as a wonderful backdrop. Today your hosts are Alex Aumen (Tom's grandson), and his wife Ashli. For those who would rather not ride, the ranch is in the middle of western North Carolina's year-round recreational playground. In less than a day's drive, you can see everything from clogging to Appalachian folk art.

Address: 119 Ranch Drive, Maggie Valley, North Carolina 28751
Telephone: 800/868-1401, 828/926-1401; fax: 828/926-9249
Email: info@cataloochee-ranch.com
Internet: www.cataloochee-ranch.com
Airport: Asheville
Location: 35 miles west of Asheville, 150 miles northwest of Charlotte off Interstate 40 and U.S. 19, 185 miles north of Atlanta
Memberships: Friends of the Great Smoky Mountains National Park, Southeast Tourism Society, North Carolina Travel Council
Awards: Mobil 3 Star
Medical: Waynesville Hospital, 10 miles
Conference Capacity: 40
Guest Capacity: 80
Accommodations: Open fireplaces, handmade quilts, and antiques set the tone for each of the 12 cabins; some with kitchenettes. There is no air-conditioning, as the mile-high elevation brings lots of cool mountain air. Guests enjoy electric heaters, mid-morning fires, and warm summer days of about 75 degrees. Ask about the four romance cabins. Silverbell Lodge has six units, two of which have full kitchens. The main lodge is the heart of the ranch with an impressive stone fireplace and chandeliers made from ox yokes. There are a number of rooms on the second floor.
Rates: • $$–$$$ Summer: Modified American Plan; includes breakfast and dinner. Horseback riding is extra. Children's rates available. Group rates by request. Two-night minimum. Winter: Lodging only—$.
Credit Cards: VISA, MasterCard, American Express; personal checks accepted.
Season: April through November; late December to March.
Activities: Slow, easygoing, scenic mountain horseback riding. Half-day and all-day rides, usually with 8–10 guests to a ride. Ask about the Hemphill Bald and Swag rides. During May, June, and September, the ranch offers backcountry pack trips. Fishing in ranch pond. Croquet, hiking, heated swimming pool, tennis, tractor-drawn wagon rides. Float and white-water rafting trips and six golf courses nearby. Winter: Downhill ski area one mile away.
Children's Programs: Children are welcome but no formal program. Kids must be age six to horseback ride.
Dining: Summer: Weekly outdoor barbecues, fresh garden vegetables (lettuce, broccoli, cabbage, squash, and spinach), fresh homemade jams and jellies, ribs, mountain trout, fall harvest feast including regional favorites. Beer and wine available.
Entertainment: Regional mountain music, clogging, folk/ballad singer. Tractor-drawn wagon rides at ranch. Informal evening entertainment.
Summary: Spectacular Southeastern scenery. Family-owned and operated ranch with great Southern charm and beauty. Many professionals, families, and family reunions. Off-season business seminars. Nearby: Cherokee Indian Village, Biltmore Estate, Mountain Heritage Center, clogging, Blue Ridge Parkway, Great Smoky Mountain National Park.

Clear Creek Ranch
Burnsville, North Carolina

Clear Creek Ranch was born out of a longtime dream of owner Rex Frederick and his wife, Aileen, who have created their "Western guest ranch" in the beautiful mountains of North Carolina. Located in the Blue Ridge Mountains north of Asheville, the ranch was built in 1995. The Pisgah National Forest provides 80,000 acres of riding and hiking trails. Hosts Rex and Aileen offer Southern hospitality in abundance and have an enthusiastic staff. While horseback riding is the most popular activity, tubing down the South Toe River is a close second! There is also a stocked trout pond, a heated pool, hot tub, and a high-quality mountain golf course within one mile of the ranch. The warm, friendly, relaxed atmosphere is a ranch trademark and is a reflection of the hosts' own outgoing personalities and genuine friendliness. The folks at Clear Creek are doing it right! It is, indeed, one of the great family guest ranches in America with lots of Southern hospitality and fun!

Address: 100 Clear Creek Drive, Highway 80 South, Burnsville, North Carolina 28714
Telephone: 800/651-4510, 828/675-4510; fax: 828/675-5452
Email: ccrdude@prodigy.net
Internet: www.clearcreekranch.com
Airport: Asheville; pickup available at small additional charge
Location: 45 miles north of Asheville, North Carolina; three hours northeast of Knoxville, Tennessee; four hours north of Atlanta, Georgia
Memberships: North Carolina Travel & Tourism
Medical: Spruce Pine Hospital, 15 miles
Conference Capacity: 40
Guest Capacity: 50
Accommodations: Guest quarters are located in three separate buildings, all adjacent to the main lodge. There are cozy one-, two-, and three- bedroom units, all with lodgepole pine beds, air-conditioning, heating, and carpeting. Big covered porches with an ample supply of rocking chairs provide beautiful views of the mountains. The main lodge offers a big porch and huge deck, dining room, and living room with a Carolina field-stone fireplace where guests gather for cards or to tell stories about their day.

Rates: • $$–$$$ American Plan. Children's and off-season rates.
Credit Cards: VISA, MasterCard; personal checks preferred.
Season: April to December
Activities: Horseback riding is available morning and afternoon. The Buncombe Horse Trail in the Pisgah National Forest is a favorite. Wonderful rides through the spectacular, lush North Carolina forests and across the crystal clear South Toe River—WOW! Tubing down the South Toe River is popular with children. Activity trips to local crafters, gem mines, hikes to Crab Tree and Linville Waterfalls, fishing either in the pond or on the South Toe River for famous North Carolina mountain trout. Golf (five minutes away) and white-water rafting (45 minutes away) are also options.
Children's Programs: During June, July, and August, there are optional organized activities for ages 5–12 that vary day to day. This is supervised by the staff and includes a Junior Wrangler Ride and picnic lunch, nature walks, and crafts.
Dining: Three hearty meals a day. Favorites include rib and chicken cookout, lasagna, the wonderful steak cookout along the banks of the crystal clear South Toe River, and the Sunday omelet breakfast. Full bar available year-round.
Entertainment: Evening activities include Rex leading karaoke singing, line dancing, marshmallow roasts, songs around the campfire, relaxing in front of the fire in the living room. Weekend highlight is the morning "Rodeo" on Saturday with evening awards and hootenanny.
Summary: Superb hospitality and caring staff, fabulous North Carolina scenery, the crystal-clear Toe River, and a relaxed, easygoing spirit are the hallmarks of Rex and Aileen Fredericks' Clear Creek Ranch! Completely surrounded by the Pisgah National Forest. Breathtaking fall colors, superb 18-hole mountain golf course (five minutes away), and local arts and crafts famous to this part of the country. Nearby: Biltmore Estate, Grandfather Mountain, and the charming town of Blowing Rock.

Aspen Ridge Resort
Bly, Oregon

Aspen Ridge Resort offers guests a real ranch vacation. Set on the historic Fishhole Creek Ranch, which was homesteaded in the mid-1800s, the resort overlooks a high mountain meadow where cattle and sandhill cranes share the lush green expanse. Built in 1992, the resort is rustically elegant with a handcrafted log lodge and cabins. The lodge features a wonderful restaurant, large rock fireplaces in the great room and lounge, beautiful antiques, and warm hospitality. Eighteen miles off the highway, this 14,000-acre ranch is surrounded by National Forest land. This is a working cattle ranch with a resort atmosphere, running a thousand head of cattle, where guests can ride horseback with the ranch cowboys to check, doctor, or move cattle. Guests set their own pace: riding, fishing, mountain biking, playing tennis, or simply relaxing in this beautiful setting. Steve and Karen Simmons, owners and hosts at Aspen Ridge, delight in sharing the pleasures of life on a working cattle ranch.

Address: P.O. Box 2 K, Bly, Oregon 97622
Telephone: 800/393-3323 (outside Oregon), 541/884-8685; call for fax number
Email: aspenrr@starband.net
Internet: www.aspenrr.com
Airport: Klamath Falls, or Reno; Lakeview, Oregon for private aircraft; 2,200-foot dirt strip on ranch.
Location: Between Klamath Falls and Lakeview; 72 miles east of Klamath Falls; 18 miles southeast of Bly off Highway 140.
Memberships: Southern Oregon Visitors Association, Oregon Cattlemen's Association, Oregon Lodging Association
Medical: Sprague Valley Medical Clinic, Bly, 20 miles; Lake District Hospital, Lakeview, 50 miles
Conference Capacity: 40
Guest Capacity: 40
Accommodations: Five 1,200-square-foot, handcrafted, custom two-story log homes, and four hotel rooms in the lodge. Cabins are completely furnished and each has a fully equipped kitchen, living room with woodstove, two bedrooms, loft, and bathroom. Maximum occupancy is six persons. Linens, housekeeping service, and firewood are provided. Lodge rooms vary in size and sleep-

ing arrangements; all have private bathrooms. Ranch generates own power.
Rates: • $$–$$$$$ European Plan. Two-night minimum stay in cabins. Meals, riding, and fly-fishing priced separately from lodging. Guests may cook in their cabins.
Credit Cards: None. Personal checks accepted.
Season: Year-round; except March.
Activities: Horseback riding, as part of the cattle operation, is popular in late spring, summer, and fall. Horses provided or guests are welcome to bring their own horses and participate in ranch activities. Special horse events include cutting, team roping, and roping schools. Spin- and fly-fishing in nearby lakes and streams, catch-and-release fly-fishing only for trophy trout on the ranch. A tennis court, swimming lake, and miles of trails for mountain biking, jogging, and hiking are available. Seasonal wildlife viewing and wildflower gathering. Winter: Christmas and New Year's celebrations. Snowmobiling and cross-country skiing begin right at the door.
Children's Programs: No special programs. The ranch is family-oriented and encourages parents and children to participate in activities together.
Dining: The lodge restaurant serves breakfast, lunch, and dinner daily in an atmosphere of relaxed elegance. Guests order from a menu that features country breakfasts, homemade desserts, and excellent mesquite-barbecued beef, ribs, chicken, and trout. The Buffalo Saloon with full bar service is open daily. Restaurant open to the public.
Entertainment: Appearing nightly outdoors is a sky full of stars and a chorus of coyotes. Occasional cowboy poetry and live music.
Summary: One of Kilgore's "Best of the Best"–Working Ranch. A beautiful 14,000-acre cattle ranch nestled among towering pines overlooking a high-mountain meadow and run with a resort feel. Steven and Karen Simmons have been in the cattle business for years and run one of the West's most exciting year-round guest and cattle ranches with fine accommodations. Excellent riding opportunities, fly-fishing, hiking, and winter snowmobiling. Ask about the barbecued beef and Carmel connection.

Rock Springs Guest Ranch
Bend, Oregon

Just outside Bend in the foothills of the Cascade Mountains, Rock Springs Guest Ranch was founded by the late Donna Gill. A schoolteacher, Donna developed an early love for young people, their parents, and the great outdoors. Her spirit and the tradition she inspired are carried on by her nephew, John Gill, his wife, Eva, and young daughters Hannah and Marlie, along with their fine staff. "Our goal is to provide the highest quality vacation experience for each of our guests, with an emphasis on the family," says John. Rock Springs attracts guests from all over the world. With the snowcapped peaks of the Three Sisters Mountains in the distance, Rock Springs provides trappings of the West as well as modern conveniences. It is one of the best guest ranches in the West for families. The ranch is radiant with hospitality, cozy with warmth, and as for activities—you name it, they've got it. Rock Springs is also popular for business meetings and retreats during nonsummer months.

Address: 64201 Tyler Road, Drawer K, Bend, Oregon 97701
Telephone: 800/225-3833, 541/382-1957; fax: 541/382-7774
Email: info@rocksprings.com
Internet: www.rocksprings.com
Airport: Redmond/Bend, 16 miles
Location: 9 miles northwest of Bend, 180 miles southeast of Portland
Memberships: The Dude Ranchers' Association, Meeting Professionals International, America Outdoors
Medical: St. Charles Hospital, Bend, nine miles
Conference Capacity: 50; the Tamarack Conference Center with Internet access
Guest Capacity: 50
Accommodations: Individual cabins and duplex-triplex units nestled in ponderosa pines. Rooms are finished in knotty pine with private baths. All cabins have decks and most have fireplaces and refrigerators.
Rates: • $$$–$$$$ Full American Plan in summer. One-week minimum stay, Saturday to Saturday. Modified American Plan for Thanksgiving. Corporate meeting packages available. Year-round except summer.

Credit Cards: VISA, MasterCard, Discover, American Express, Diner's Club
Season: Late June through August and Thanksgiving. All other times are dedicated to corporate conferences, retreats, and seminars.
Activities: Although horseback riding is the ranch's summer specialty, central Oregon offers a host of recreational activities. Scenic trail riding with views of Cascade Mountain Range. Six usually go out per ride. Two rides daily, at 10 A.M. and 2 P.M. Weekly luncheon rides. Heated, hourglass-shaped swimming pool; two tennis courts, with tennis pro in mid-July. World-class fly-fishing in nearby Metolius and Deschutes Rivers and in lakes. Local guide service available. Guided nature walks and mountain biking. Huge free-form whirlpool overlooking the pond. Golf, canoeing, orienteering, and rafting. Billiards, table tennis, volleyball, and basketball.
Children's Programs: Terrific children's program with counselors. Adults are free to do their own thing if they wish. Children ages 3–5 and 6–12 enjoy a variety of activities and adventures. Lunch and dinner are available in a separate dining room. Counselors on duty from 9 A.M.–8:30 P.M. Children under age six ride on a lead line. Ask about kids' overnight campout and hayride.
Dining: Buffet-style meals are a highlight of the Rock Springs experience, including a wide variety of cuisine from traditional prime rib and fresh Northwest seafood to vegetarian and health-conscious choices. Special diets catered to. Fresh fruit and home-baked cookies available between meals. Local beers and Northwest wines available.
Entertainment: Scheduled nightly activities. Nature walks and a variety of games.
Summary: Kilgore's "Best of the Best"–Children's Program. One of the premier guest ranches for families with extensive children's program. Superb corporate-meeting ranch offering exclusive use of all facilities for each group. Nearby: Two-dozen championship golf courses.

Lazy Hills Guest Ranch
Ingram, Texas

TGRA Texas
Guest
Ranch
Association

Since 1959 Bob and Carol Steinruck and their family have been welcoming folks from around the world to their 750-acre guest ranch in the heart of the beautiful Texas Hill Country. Lazy Hills is family-oriented and has earned the reputation as "The Family Ranch for Folks of All Ages." The ranch is the perfect setting for family reunions, corporate, church, or school retreats, seminars, and workshops. The Roundup Room is great for meetings and will seat 150 comfortably. The mild climate and low humidity help make Lazy Hills a year-round haven for fun and relaxation. The countryside is tranquil, the pace slow. Listen to nature's peace or watch deer or an occasional armadillo. As the folks at Lazy Hills say, "Come on out and enjoy our 'brand' of fun."

Address: Box K, Ingram, Texas 78025
Telephone: 800/880-0632, 830/367-5600; fax: 830/367-5667
Email: lhills@ktc.com
Internet: www.lazyhills.com
Airport: San Antonio, 70 miles
Location: 70 miles northwest of San Antonio off Interstate 10, 105 miles southwest of Austin
Memberships: Texas Guest Ranch Association, Texas Hotel & Motel Association
Medical: Sid Peterson Memorial Hospital, Kerrville; 10 miles
Conference Capacity: 150
Guest Capacity: 100
Accommodations: Lazy Hills offers 26 guest rooms, all with electric heat, air-conditioning, private baths with showers, and pleasant porches. Some rooms also have wood-burning fireplaces. Rooms are furnished with twin or queen beds and will sleep four to six people. Daily maid service provided. Ask about the inspirational book on Praise.
Rates: • $–$$ American Plan. Group rates available. Summer, weekends, and holidays; no minimum stay.
Credit Cards: VISA, MasterCard, Discover
Season: Year-round
Activities: Year-round, guided one-hour scenic trail rides go out four times a day. More than 30 miles of wooded hiking for nature lovers. You will also find a junior-Olympic swimming pool, chil-

dren's wading pool, hot tub, volleyball, basketball, two lighted tennis courts, game room with billiards, Ping-Pong and foosball. There is also shuffleboard and horseshoes, three spring-fed stocked (bass and catfish) fishing ponds, hayrides, and cookouts.
Children's Programs: There is a great deal to keep children busy. During the summer months, scheduled children's activities in morning and afternoon. There is also a playground with a merry-go-round, sandbox, and treehouse. Babysitting is extra.
Dining: Family-style or buffet; three hearty Texas meals are served daily in spacious dining room. Guests enjoy chicken-fried steak or Mexican fiestas. Outdoor barbecues at the cookout grounds and poolside. Homemade rolls and desserts. Sack lunches always available.
Entertainment: Family-oriented entertainment is planned each night during the summer. Bonfires with s'mores, piñata parties, hay-wagon rides pulled by team of draft horses or ranch truck.
Summary: A family-owned and operated guest ranch in the Texas Hill Country. The guests who come and return year after year have high family values; the majority from Texas and surrounding states. Also ideal for small and large groups and family reunions. RV hook-ups available. Group barbecues. Off-season bed-and-breakfast. Spanish spoken. Nearby: Golf, Cowboy Artists of America Museum, Kerrville, Fredericksburg, LBJ Ranch and National Park, Fiesta Texas, Sea World, San Antonio River Walk.

Running-R Guest Ranch
Bandera, Texas

Texas Guest Ranch Association

Owned and operated by Ralph and Iris Kirchner, the Running-R Guest Ranch is located in the beautiful Texas Hill Country, just 9.5 miles southwest of Bandera. In 1992 the Running-R was converted from an early-1900s working ranch into a full-service guest ranch. It is one of the smaller ranches where guests can experience the feel of the "good old times" in authentic surroundings. The Running-R Ranch caters to beginners, as well as experienced riders and provides daily rides up to five hours long into the 5,500-plus adjoining acres of the Hill Country State Natural Area. Guests can join in the ranch activities, watch the longhorns, enjoy the swimming pool, visit the Western town of Bandera, or just relax in a rocking chair and look at the wonderful Hill Country scenery.

Address: 9059 Bandera Creek Road, Drawer K, Bandera, Texas 78003
Telephone: 830/796-3984; fax: 830/796-8189
Email: runningr@texas.net
Internet: www.rrranch.com
Airport: San Antonio, 56 miles
Location: 56 miles northwest of San Antonio, 9.5 miles southwest of Bandera
Memberships: Texas Guest Ranch Association, Texas Hotel & Motel Association, American Quarter Horse Association
Medical: Bandera Medical Clinic; Sid Peterson Hospital, Kerrville, 34 miles
Conference Capacity: 30
Guest Capacity: 50
Accommodations: 14 individual wooden cabins and duplexes with various sleeping arrangements (most have queen-size beds). Each has a sitting area, private bathroom (most with showers), air-conditioning/heating, refrigerator, and covered porch.
Rates: • $$ American Plan. Children's and weekly rates available. Two-night minimum.
Credit Cards: VISA, MasterCard, Discover. Personal and traveler's checks accepted.
Season: Year-round
Activities: Horseback riding is the biggest attraction on the ranch, with approximately 40 horses available for various levels of riders. The adjoining state park offers over 5,500 acres and 40 miles of trails for riding in the scenic and unspoiled landscape of the Hill Country. Rides are tailored to experience levels. Rates include two hours of horseback riding daily. Guests who would like to ride for more than two hours can book additional rides. A picnic lunch is provided on the trail for rides that are four hours or longer. Riding lessons are available in the large arena. Outdoor swimming pool, hiking, horseshoe pitching, pool table, table tennis, and fossil hunting are all included. Nearby activities include golfing, tubing on the Medina River in Bandera, and skeet and pistol shooting at the Bandera Gun Club.
Children's Programs: Children are always welcome, but there is no formal program. There are ranch animals to play with, roping instruction, horse care and grooming, and hayrides. A favorite activity is fossil hunting. Kids must be age six to trail ride, but the younger ones can get that little cowboy or cowgirl experience by riding in the corral while being led by their parents or a staff member.
Dining: Known for a great kitchen. Home-cooked meals are served buffet-style in the Roundup Room. Weekly Texas-style barbecues, cowboy breakfasts, and hamburger cookouts. Vegetarian fare provided cheerfully on request. BYOB.
Entertainment: Informal evening programs. Some adults enjoy a Western evening of fun in Bandera, 10 minutes away. Hayrides through the state park, outdoor barbecues, cowboy breakfasts, cowboy singing, campfires, occasional roping and cutting practice by ranch cowboys, feeding the longhorn cattle, and fossil hunting are all offered on a flexible schedule.
Summary: Authentic working ranch turned into a guest ranch without losing the charm of the "old times." Ideal for everybody who loves horses and horseback riding. Small, intimate ranch with a relaxing and friendly, international atmosphere. Owners Ralph, Iris, and Doo spend a lot of time with their guests. Warm Texas climate allows year-round operation and outdoor activities at a reasonable rate. German and French spoken. Nearby: Weekly summer rodeos, golfing, Cowboy Artists of America Museum, Fiesta Texas theme park, Sea World, San Antonio Riverwalk, and the famous Alamo.

Texas Ranch Life
Bellville, Texas

John and Taunia Elick's Texas Ranch Life program was built on a love of history, nature, ranching, and cowboy life. Both native Texans, John and Taunia, and their three daughters, have spent the past 25 years on their 450-acre Prairie Place Ranch. In 1988 they bought the 1,100-acre Lonesome Pine Ranch and in 1995 they bought 1,800-acre Eagle Roost Ranch. Today these ranches offer guests wonderful and authentic Texas Ranch Life experiences. As Taunia says, "share our beautiful Texas scenery, wildlife—some of the best Bobwhite Quail country in Texas, bass fishing in any of nine lakes, and horseback riding including cutting and roping demonstrations. Here you will sleep in beautifully restored historic Texas homes where you'll have the option to cook, or for larger groups full-service catered meals can be arranged offering native Texas cuisine." Guests can enjoy learning about the prairie chicken restoration project, watching nesting bald eagles, and riding the rolling hills of central Texas.

Address: P.O. Box 803, Bellville, Texas 77418
Telephone: 866/TEXASRL (866/839-2775, will answer "Law Office"), fax: 979/865-9461
Email: tauniae@aol.com
Internet: www.texasranchlife.com
Airport: Houston Intercontinental, one hour; Austin Bertram Airport, one hour 45 minutes
Location: One hour northwest of Houston, one hour and 45 minutes southeast of Austin
Memberships: Texas Guest Ranch Association, Historic and Hospitality Accommodations of Texas
Medical: Bellville General Hospital, eight miles; Trinity Medical Center in Brenham, 15 miles
Conference Capacity: 20–30; 700-square-foot conference room
Guest Capacity: 30
Accommodations: All accommodations are at Lonesome Pine Ranch. They include several historic Texas houses dating back to the 1840s, including two log cabins. All have been authentically restored and antique period furniture is featured in many rooms. Several homes have the original 19th-century German stenciling. Fireplaces, televisions, private baths are available, and luxurious linens and bedding are featured

throughout. Covered porches with rockers and an extensive Texas history book collection.
Rates: • $$ European Plan; breakfast and fishing included. Riding and full meal service extra. Two-day minimum stay.
Credit Cards: VISA, MasterCard, American Express. Personal and traveler's checks, and gift certificates accepted.
Season: Year-round
Activities: With over 3,300 acres of private Texas ranch land on three separate ranches, there is plenty of outdoor activities including trail rides and wagon rides. With a 22-stall barn, covered arena, and two round pens, you can bring your own horse or rent one. Bass-filled lakes offer some of the best private fishing in Texas (bring your own gear). Wing shooting is available. Cattle roundups and cattle drives in the spring and fall months. Cutting cattle available for practice. Buffalo, bird-watching, hiking, and swimming is available.
Children's Programs: No formal program, but children are welcome. Trail rides, wagon or hayrides, and there is a ranch wrangler who can provide riding lessons.
Dining: Homemade continental breakfast provided. Other meals are available upon request including chuck wagon meals, barbecue, authentic Mexican dinners. Cooking clinics and demonstrations by Houston area chefs are offered. There is a wide variety of good restaurants within a 15-mile radius and all houses have complete kitchens available for guest use.
Entertainment: Watch cutting and roping demonstrations at the ranch headquarters. The entire family holds black belts in Tae Kwon Do; ask about self-defense demonstrations. Massage available.
Summary: Three distinct and beautiful ranches serving up Texas hospitality, history, nature, and ranch life. Beautifully restored, with an independent atmosphere, offers a wide variety of activities for couples, small and large family groups, and larger corporate groups. Fishing, trail riding, cattle drives and roundups, roping and cutting demonstrations, team penning, and bird-watching. Wing hunting available year-round.

Rockin' R Ranch
Antimony (near Bryce Canyon), Utah

The Rockin' R Ranch is located in Butch Cassidy country near some of the most spectacular parks in the country—Bryce Canyon and Zion National Park. It is also close to Capitol Reef, Lake Powell, the north rim of the Grand Canyon, Arches National Monument, and Canyonlands. Many who come here to be with the Black family enjoy these incredible and important scenic wonders during, before, or after their stay. The Rockin' R lies on the edge of the small farming town of Antimony. Burns and Mona Black grew up in Utah and were raised farming and ranching. The Burns family has ranched in the same valley since the 1870s. In the 1970s the ranch was opened to guests and in 1985 the Western lodge was built. Today the ranch runs 1,000 head of cattle that summer in the mountains and winter in the valley. What makes the Rockin' R unique is its ability to attract a wide range of guests. Couples, singles, families, groups, and families all come and enjoy the friendly down-home family-style atmosphere, the wide-open country, and the proximity to some of the world's most scenic treasures. As Burns says, "We love kids and families who treasure old-fashioned values and give thanks to what God has given us."

Address: mail: 10274 Eastdell Drive, Sandy, Utah 84092; physical: 705 N. Highway 22, Antimony, Utah 84712
Telephone: 801/733-9538; fax: 801/942-2680
Email: info@rocknrranch.com
Internet: www.rocknrranch.com
Airport: Salt Lake City, Utah, and Las Vegas, Nevada; commuter flights to Cedar City and Bryce Canyon
Location: 37 miles north of Bryce Canyon on Highway 22 in the Town of Antimony; Las Vegas 4.5 hours; Salt Lake City 3.5 hours.
Medical: Richfield Hospital, one hour
Conference Capacity: 20–50 in 300-square-foot conference room; 100 in 600-square-foot meeting room.
Guest Capacity: 120
Accommodations: 37 rooms with various sleeping arrangements in the 22,000-square-foot lodge, all with telephones, and private baths with tub and/or shower. There are also common areas, including the three-story grand room with fireplace, deck, sunroom, exercise room, and hot tub. Another fourplex cabin has four rooms near the riding arena. A bunkhouse provides some additional accommodations for groups up to 200.
Rates: • $$–$$$ American Plan. Family, group, and off-season rates available.
Credit Cards: VISA, MasterCard
Season: Year-round
Activities: Guests may choose one- to two-hour trail rides in mornings or afternoons, except Sundays. Longer rides can be arranged. Hiking, swimming, or canoeing in the pond. Roping demonstrations by ranch cowboys in the arena, and guests may ride calves and barrel race if they wish. Scheduled cattle drives six times a year; high mountain overnight trail rides offered four times a year where guests camp out at a base camp in the mountains for four to six nights (extra charge). Tennis/basketball court, volleyball, stagecoach, and hay-wagon rides.
Dining: One or two entrées each night. Buffet-style meals, Dutch-oven cookouts for groups. BYOB.
Children's Programs: Kids are the responsibility of their parents. Young buckaroos enjoy pony rides and craft projects. Ask about the four-week Junior Cowboy College for ages 12–17.
Entertainment: During the summer months there is usually something planned each evening. Cowboy singing and Western line dancing, occasional cowboy poetry, and once in a while Burns and Mona will sing a few of their favorite Western songs—Burns was quite a yodeler early on.
Summary: Rockin' R Ranch offers proximity to some of America's most scenic natural wonders—Bryce Canyon and Zion National Park. Here old-fashioned values and Western hospitality reign supreme. Many come while touring the West. Great for families, couples, singles, groups, and international visitors. Ask about the summer cattle drives and 11,000-foot mountaintop excursions.

Hidden Valley Guest Ranch
Cle Elum, Washington

Hidden Valley Guest Ranch is a shining star. With charm, character, lots of personality, and hospitality, this ranch is terrific. It offers a year-round getaway in a relaxing atmosphere. The ranch is nestled at 2,500 feet in the Swauk Valley of eastern Washington (just 1.5 hours from Seattle), in the foothills of the Wenatchee Mountains. Located on 350 acres of canyon and rolling range, the ranch has been continuously operated as a guest ranch since 1947, when Hollywood cowboy and entertainer Tom Whited carved Hidden Valley from an old homestead dating to 1887. Many original buildings, including the homestead cabin, form the nucleus of the lodging facilities. Today Hidden Valley is owned and operated by second generation guest ranchers, Bruce and Kim Coe. Come to relax, visit, and enjoy the old-time charm and serenity.

Address: 3942 Hidden Valley Road, Cle Elum, Washington 98922
Telephone: 800/5-COWBOY (800/526-9269), 509/857-2344; fax: 509/857-2130
Email: info@hvranch.com
Internet: www.hvranch.com; www.ranchweb .com/hiddenvalley
Airport: Commuter flights via Seattle to Yakima; private planes use DeVere Field, six miles
Location: Eight miles northeast of Cle Elum off Highway 970, 52 miles northwest of Yakima, 85 miles east of Seattle
Awards: "Best Guest Ranch in the Northwest" by KING-TV (Seattle)
Medical: Kittitas Valley Community Hospital, 20 miles
Conference Capacity: 25
Guest Capacity: 40
Accommodations: One- and two-bedroom cabins and two fourplex cabins, each with its own personality, and names like Cedar, Aspen, Apple Tree, Spruce, or Elkhorn. The cabins are wonderful, each with its own individual Western charm! All are fully furnished with private baths, separate entries, and gas heat; some have fireplaces and private porches overlooking the scenic valley.
Rates: • $$ American Plan. Nonriding rates available. Off-season and bed-and-breakfast rates. Two-night minimum stay during summer and major holidays.
Credit Cards: VISA, MasterCard. Personal and traveler's checks accepted.
Season: Year-round; including all holidays except Christmas Day.
Activities: The activities program here is informal and flexible. The ranch offers a host of different recreational opportunities: swimming in the heated pool, hiking, fishing in Swauk Creek, picking wildflowers, great mountain biking. and birdwatching. Also available are a 10-person hot tub; a lighted sports court for paddle tennis, volleyball, and basketball; and Blue Ribbon fly-fishing and white-water rafting on the Yakima—guided trips are a favorite. The riding program offers scenic morning and afternoon rides. Lessons and special rides available. Be sure to ask about the unique "vacation with your own horse" program. In winter, cross-country skiing, sledding, and snowshoeing. Bring your own gear.
Children's Programs: Family participation in all activities is encouraged. No organized children's program. Usually children begin riding at age six. Pony rides available for younger kids.
Dining: Family-style dining served buffet-style for breakfast and lunch. Table service with choice of light entrées in evening. Ranch specialties include Midwest corn-fed prime rib, deep-fried Cajun turkey barbecue, and fiesta night. Vegetarian and special meal considerations are provided cheerfully on request. The weekly chuck wagon barbecues and breakfast rides are always favorites. BYOB.
Entertainment: Recreation lounge overlooks the pool and resembles a hunting lodge with fireplace, pool table, honky-tonk piano, and loads of atmosphere. Longtime musician Bruce Coe and his local musician friends frequently entertain in the lodge or around the campfire.
Summary: The Coes' Hidden Valley Guest Ranch is wonderful! Lots of Old West charm, warmth, and hospitality. Great setting and views. Excellent for two-day, three-day, and weeklong ranch getaways and retreats. Ask about Blue Ribbon fly-fishing and white-water rafting on the Yakima. Massage therapy available. Nearby: Seattle. (90 miles)

K-Diamond-K Cattle & Guest Ranch
Republic, Washington

As a boy and young man, Steve Konz worked at a number of guest ranches. He went on to be a teacher and married his college sweetheart, June, who went on to become a veterinarian. With a love for ranching in their blood, Steve and June came to Republic, Washington, in the early 1960s, bought their cattle ranch, and began raising their family of five children. Today, 40 years later, their grown children are overseeing the cattle and guest ranch operation. Since 1993 they have hosted guests from the United States and from around the world, including France, Germany, England, and Italy. The Colville National Forest and the Colville Indian Reservation border this 1,600-acre ranch. First time and returning guests enjoy the easygoing spirit, family hospitality, camaraderie, the various ranch activities, and the peaceful beauty and serenity.

Address: 15661 Highway 21 South, Drawer K, Republic, Washington 99166
Telephone: 888/345-5355, 509/775-3536; fax: 509/775-3520
Email: kdiamond@televar.com
Internet: www.kdiamondk.com; www.ranch web.com/kdiamondk
Airport: Spokane International, 125 miles; Seattle, 300 miles; 3,500-foot runway at Republic County Airport
Location: 125 miles northwest of Spokane; 300 miles northeast of Seattle
Medical: Ferry County Memorial Hospital, 5 miles
Conference Capacity: 12,500 square feet
Guest Capacity: 12
Accommodations: Guests are welcomed into the family's 3,500-square-foot log lodge and home. There are four large upper and lower level rooms with names like Klondike, Wrangler, Tamarack, and Cheyenne. Each room has one queen-size bed and two twin beds, with shared baths.
Rates: • $$ American Plan. Children's, group, and winter rates available. Three-night minimum.
Credit Cards: VISA, MasterCard, Discover. Personal checks accepted.
Season: Year-round

Activities: The activity program is structured in a way that enables guests to enjoy the beauty of the surrounding forests and mountains and the various ranch activities. Scheduled morning rides are through meadows, along the San Poil River, and up forested trails to fabulous view areas. Each week a number of guests enjoy helping the family with various cattle and ranch activities. Afternoons are yours—fill them with fishing for trout, swimming in nearby lakes, panning for gold, digging for fossils around the town of Republic, or reading your favorite book—you decide. Nearby there is golf and hiking. Late afternoon or early evening horseback rides are available upon request.
Children's Programs: Kids are welcomed into the family and have a ranch yard full of chickens, goats, cats, and dogs to enjoy, as well as Thunder Heart, the miniature horse, and Bubbles, the donkey. Kids usually begin trail riding around the age of eight, depending upon ability. Younger kids can always ride in the corral by lead line.
Dining: Family-style around one great big family table. Hearty ranch cuisine, offering ranch-raised beef, pasta, chicken, and fish. BYOB.
Entertainment: Campfires after dinner with guest sing-alongs. Monthly barn dance with the neighbors joining in. Ask about the local rodeos, yearly Mountain Music Festival, State Fiddle Contest, and the laser show at Grand Coulee Dam.
Summary: Family-owned guest and cattle ranch hosting only 12 guests at a time. This 1,600-acre ranch offers wonderful, friendly ranch hospitality and lots of ranch life to share. Surrounded by forests, open meadows, nearby lakes, big views, and blue skies. Nearby: Grand Coulee Dam, gold mines, and the century-old town of Republic, three miles away.

Woodside Ranch
Mauston, Wisconsin

The 1,300-acre Woodside Ranch is open year-round and offers plenty of country-style activities for families. This is one of the few guest ranches in the country with a small buffalo herd. Woodside sits in the upper Dells on a high, wooded hillside with views of the Lemonweir Valley. Woodside is a family-run guest ranch started in 1914 as a family farm by William Feldmann. Soon the Feldmanns and their half-dozen children had friends wanting to be part of their fun. Grandpa Feldmann started charging guests $10 a week and they still kept coming, so in 1926 he put an ad in the *Chicago Tribune*; the rest is history. Each year the ranch grew, until there were 21 cabins with fireplaces and a lodge. It's managed today by the Feldmanns' youngest daughter, Lucille Nichols, and their grandson, Rick Feldmann.

Address: W4015, Highway 82, Box K, Mauston, Wisconsin 53948
Telephone: 800/626-4275, 608/847-4275
Email: woodside@mwt.net
Internet: www.woodsideranch.com
Airport: Madison, 70 miles; small private airport in Mauston-New Lisbon, 11 miles
Train: Wisconsin Dells, 20 miles (free pickup)
Bus: Greyhound to Mauston, four miles (free pickup)
Location: 20 miles northwest of Wisconsin Dells, 70 miles north of Madison, 220 miles north of Chicago, 200 miles south of Minneapolis on Interstate 90/94.
Memberships: Wisconsin Innkeepers Association
Medical: Hess Memorial Hospital, six miles
Conference Capacity: 100
Guest Capacity: 150
Accommodations: Woodside offers rustic, informal accommodations. There are 21 one-, two-, and three-bedroom cabins with fireplaces, of which half are authentic log cabins. The main house has rooms with private baths that accommodate up to four people. All rooms and cabins have thermostatically controlled heat and air-conditioning. Guests bring their own towels.
Rates: • $–$$ American Plan. Three-day, six-day, and weekly rates available. Minimum three-day, two-night stay. Children's rates are available. Pets are welcome; ask about rates.

Credit Cards: VISA, MasterCard, Discover
Season: Year-round; except Thanksgiving and Christmas Eve.
Activities: Summer recreation director on staff. Eight horseback rides go out daily. Lessons available for beginners in corral. Daily breakfast rides, covered wagon, and hayrides. Two tennis courts, heated swimming and wading pool, miniature golf, volleyball, large sauna. Fishing and boating on private lake (rowboats, kayaks, and paddleboats), canoeing available nearby on Wisconsin River. Several loaner fishing poles, but you have to dig your own worms. Horseshoes and softball. Winter: Beginner Alpine skiing with rope tow, night skiing, extensive cross-country skiing with 12 miles of tracked trails (equipment and lessons included). Horseback riding, sleigh rides, ice-skating, ice fishing. Bring your own snowmobiles—Woodside is right on the club trail.
Children's Programs: Free supervised daycare 9 A.M.–noon and 1–4:30 P.M. for infants through age seven. Pony rides in ring for children of all ages.
Dining: Traditional country-style, like going to grandma's house. Barbecues, buffalo cookouts, and chicken dinners; family-style, all-you-can-eat meals with everyone assigned to a table.
Entertainment: Square dancing and line dancing, polkas, 1950s music, sing-alongs, evening hayrides, and bonfires with marshmallow roasts. Guest rodeos and professional horse shows. Trading Post Cocktail Bar with snacks, souvenirs, and game room.
Summary: Family-owned and -operated ranch resort for families that features log cabins with fireplaces, year-round horseback riding, horse-drawn wagon rides, and sleigh rides. Summer children's daycare for infants through age seven. Many repeat guests enjoy the informal atmosphere. Open seven days a week in summer, weekends the rest of the year. Winter weekend program. Small buffalo herd. Adults-only first week of June and end of August.

Absaroka Ranch
Dubois, Wyoming

THE DUDE RANCHERS'
ASSOCIATION

Wyoming
Dude
Rancher's
Association

Absaroka Ranch is at the base of the spectacular Absaroka Mountains, just 25 minutes from the town of Dubois and just one hour from the world-famous valley of Jackson Hole. The dirt road to the ranch offers exhilarating mountain views. The ranch hosts only 18 guests at a time. Budd and Emi Betts, their children Lindsay and Robert, and their staff specialize in the personal touch. At 8,000 feet, the ranch is big on outdoor space, with thousands of acres and miles of trails, mountain streams, and valleys. Wildlife abounds; it's not uncommon to see elk, moose, deer, eagles, and even occasional bear and wolves. The valley is surrounded by the Shoshone National Forest and wilderness, offering all the elements conducive to total rest and relaxation. If this catches your fancy, better get on the telephone—Budd and Emi book up quickly. Absaroka (named after the Crow Indians) is a very special place and attracts people who want a very personalized and secluded old-time guest-ranch experience. Most who travel through Budd and Emi's gates are families.

Address: P.O. Box 929-K, Dubois, Wyoming 82513
Telephone: 307/455-2275; call for fax
Email: absaroka@wyoming.com
Internet: www.dteworld.com/absaroka
Airport: Jackson or Riverton via Denver or Salt Lake City
Location: 75 miles east of Jackson Airport, 16 miles northwest of Dubois and six miles off U.S. 26/287
Memberships: The Dude Ranchers' Association; Wyoming Dude Rancher's Association
Awards: *Hideaway Report* 2000, "Family Guest Ranch of the Year".
Medical: Emergency Clinic in Dubois, 16 miles
Guest Capacity: 18
Accommodations: Four cabins (Delta Whiskey, Six Point, Five Mile, and Detimore) are snug and heated, with two bedrooms and adjoining baths, comforters, and full carpeting. One cabin has a fireplace; all have covered porches with views of the Wind River Mountains and the manicured lawn in front where kids and families gather.
Rates: • $$$ American Plan; includes fly-fishing instruction and local trips. Group, family, and children's rates available. Special rates available in June and September and for return guests.
Credit Cards: None. Personal checks accepted.
Season: Mid-June to mid-September
Activities: Activities center around guided scenic mountain horseback riding, guided hiking, and guided fly-fishing. Morning, afternoon, and weekly all-day, breakfast, and evening cookout rides. All skill levels of riding are accommodated and welcomed. Ask about Six Mile Overlook, Jackson Nob, and the beaver-pond rides. For those not inclined to ride, hikes go out as requested to the Continental Divide and to Jade Lake with picnic lunches. Anglers should talk to Budd about his all-day off-ranch fishing trips. The trout streams in this area are challenging and productive. Limited fishing gear available. Float trips in Jackson Hole can be arranged. Ask the ranch for a brochure about horse pack trips. Swimming in crystal-clear, but very chilly, streams and lakes. Many guests like to warm up in the redwood sauna at the end of the day.
Children's Programs: No organized children's program per se, but children are welcome! The Gold Pinch Palace recreation room has a foosball table, jukebox, and soda machine. Children's games, instructional horseback, and game rides. Baby-sitting can be arranged.
Dining: Creative meals served family-style. Grilled beef tenderloin and creative pasta dishes are ranch specialties. Complimentary wine with dinner. BYOB.
Entertainment: Something is usually planned every evening. Cowboy magic show, campfire sing-alongs, horseshoes, weekly history presentation, slide shows, and weekly rodeos in Jackson offered.
Summary: What a setting! Small, rustic, secluded, very personal and family-oriented dude ranch, right at the base of the Absaroka Mountains. Horse pack trips (ask for brochure), and float trips available. Spend Saturday night in the Western town of Dubois.

Bill Cody Ranch
Cody, Wyoming

Yellowstone National Park and no minimum stay—welcome to Bill Cody Ranch! Right in the middle of what Teddy Roosevelt called "the most scenic 52 miles in all of America" lies Bill Cody Ranch, just 30 minutes from the east entrance to Yellowstone National Park and the famous Western town of Cody, Wyoming. This small, friendly property gives you the freedom to plan your own guest-ranch vacation with no minimum-stay requirement and a very flexible rate structure, à la carte activities program, and lots of value. There is a ride here for everyone, as the ranch utilizes 16 trailheads, on and off the ranch, in the 2.5 million acres of the Shoshone National Forest. Due to the rugged, mountainous terrain, all the rides are done at a walk. John and Jamie are proud to share their Wyoming heritage and home with you and will create a package that is tailored to fit your family's adventure vacation.

Address: 2604 Yellowstone Highway, Dept. K, Cody, Wyoming 82414
Telephone: 800/615-2934, 307/587-6271, 307/587-2097; fax: 307/587-6272
Email: billcody@billcodyranch.com
Internet: www.billcodyranch.com
Airport: Cody or Billings
Location: 26 miles west of Cody just off U.S. Highway 14/16/20; 110 miles northwest of Billings, Montana
Awards: AAA 3 Diamond
Memberships: Cody Chamber of Commerce
Medical: West Park Hospital, Cody; 26 miles
Conference Capacity: 30
Guest Capacity: 65
Accommodations: Historic lodge built in 1925 and previously owned by the grandson of Buffalo Bill. Facilities are nestled off the Northfork Highway that leads to the park, in a valley shaded by pines and aspen. Fourteen one- and two-bedroom cabins with large private baths are log-sided with Western interiors. All are spotless and comfortable. No TVs or telephones. All cabins are smoke free. All have handmade Western furniture and covered porches.
Rates: • $$–$$$ À la carte to all-inclusive American Plan packages. Cabin-only and off-season rates.

Credit Cards: VISA, MasterCard, Discover
Season: May to September
Activities: Scheduled and unscheduled riding and guided fly-fishing are the main activities at the ranch. Rides go out morning, noon, and evenings. Rides either leave from the ranch or are trailered to points near Yellowstone National Park to provide a variety of mountain terrain. On these rides, wranglers cook your lunch over an open fire. Many of the wranglers are accomplished mountain guides who return each year. One is even an author of mountain guidebooks and Western tales. Rides go out in small groups of no more than eight per ride. Riding open to the public. Guided fishing trips, pack trips, and white-water float trips available. Basketball court, horseshoe pitching; practice roping skills on the dummy roping steers.
Children's Programs: Children ages six and older ride their own horses. Baby-sitting available for children under age six while parents ride. Children can join in most ranch activities but are their parents' responsibility.
Dining: Hearty, ranch-style breakfast served each day in the dining room. Steaks, trout, and nightly specials served with homemade breads, soup, and salad. Wednesday and Saturday night creek-side barbecues feature steaks, ribs, chicken. Licensed full-service bar and dining open to public. Sack lunches provided for excursions.
Entertainment: Weekly musical entertainment could be a Western singer or a guest with a guitar. Forest Service slide show and interpreter's program three evenings a week. Nightly trail rides. Rodeo in Cody every night, June through August (30 minutes away). Game room.
Summary: With no required minimum stays, this is one of the most flexible guest ranches in America, attracting traveling families and couples who want to experience a guest ranch and have a home base while exploring Yellowstone National Park and the West. Most come for three days, some stay for a week or longer. As Jamie says, "Our ranch is yours for a night, a week, or more—it's your vacation and we're pleased to share our home with so many interesting guests." Nearby: Yellowstone National Park.

...root Ranch
...is, Wyoming

Wyoming
Dude
Rancher's
Association

Bitterroot Ranch offers one of the premier riding experiences in North America for advanced and intermediate riders, as well as novices who are truly motivated to learn how to ride. It's bordered by the Shoshone National Forest to the north, the Wind River Indian Reservation to the east, and a 50,000-acre game habitat area to the south and west. The ranch has been owned and operated by Bayard and Mel Fox since 1971, and today, son Richard, joins them in many of the ranch activities. Bayard is a Yale graduate who lived for many years in Europe, the Middle East, and the South Pacific. Mel was brought up on a farm at the foot of Mt. Kilimanjaro and spent several years working with wildlife in one of Africa's famous game parks. Mel runs the riding program and together both of them lead rides daily. Guests are provided with at least three horses and rides are split into small groups according to ability. They have both English (for experienced riders) and Western tack, offer a jumping course for advanced riders, and give formal instruction twice per week. They raise and train their purebred Arabian horses exclusively for the use of their guests. The riding terrain is extremely varied. Sagebrush plains, grassy meadows, and colorful rocky gorges give way to forested mountains and Alpine clearings where the ranch cattle graze on a forest permit during the summer. Because of their international backgrounds and strong equestrian program, Mel and Bayard get many European guests.

Address: Box 807 K, Dubois, Wyoming 82513
Telephone: 800/545-0019 (nationwide), 307/455-2778; fax: 307/455-2354
Email: equitour@wyoming.com
Internet: www.ridingtours.com/Bitterroot
Airport: Riverton or Jackson
Location: 26 miles northeast of Dubois, 80 miles west of Riverton, 100 miles east of Jackson off Routes 287 and 26
Memberships: Wyoming Dude Rancher's Association
Medical: Clinic in Dubois; Riverton Hospital, 80 miles
Guest Capacity: 30
Accommodations: 12 cabins; many are old-time rustic log cabins with modern-day conveniences.

Most have wood-burning stoves; all have electric heat, full bathrooms. Laundry facilities.
Rates: • $$$ American Plan. Group and children's rates available. One-week minimum stay, Sunday to Sunday.
Credit Cards: VISA, Mastercard, Discover, American Express. Personal and traveler's checks accepted.
Season: Last weekend in May through last week in September.
Activities: Riders are divided by ability and optional videotaped instruction is offered. Cattle drive in July and September. Overnight pack trips offered (extra). Bayard is a keen fly-fisherman. There's good catch-and-release fly-fishing on the ranch. Two stocked trout ponds plus other excellent fishing opportunities nearby. Hiking or soaking in outdoor hot tub at the end of the day.
Children's Programs: Children are welcome and enjoy all the animals: chickens, geese, guinea fowl, peacocks, foals, sheep, cats, and dogs. Riding begins at age four and programs are tailored to a child's ability. Baby-sitting available.
Dining: Many guests are European, so the standards for the cuisine are high. Complimentary French, Italian, California, and Chilean wines with dinner. BYOL.
Entertainment: Informal cocktail hour before dinner hosted by Bayard and Mel. Piano and extensive book and video library in main lodge; pool table.
Summary: One of Kilgore's top riding ranches in America. Bitterroot is a rider's ranch offering excellent programs with both English and Western tack. Riding groups are kept small. Certified instructors. Many ranch-raised horses. Many guests are experienced riders. Great fly-fishing, occasional cattle work, and weekly team sorting. Unstructured and remote (16 miles from the highway). Its sister company, Equitour, organizes exciting riding holidays in 30 countries for riders of almost all abilities. Fluent German and French spoken.

Box R Ranch
Cora, Wyoming

THE DUDE RANCHERS'
ASSOCIATION

Since the turn of the last century, when the ranch was first homesteaded, the Lozier family has operated this backcountry working cattle ranch. As in days gone by, Sublette County is still famous for cattle ranching and its beauty, and the Box R continues to maintain many traditions of the Old West. Today the Lozier family oversees 300 head of cattle and 100 head of horses and mules. Horseback riding and cattle work are the main activities here. Bordering the Bridger Wilderness, the Loziers offer a variety of trips into the Wind River Mountains, and longer custom horseback trips for wilderness enthusiasts. If you'd like to spend a week or more with an old-time ranching family riding, getting dirty, and having fun, give the Lozier family a call today.

Address: Box 100 K, Cora, Wyoming 82925
Telephone: 800/822-8466 (inquiries and reservations), 307/367-4868 (inquiries); fax: 307/367-6260
Email: info@boxr.com
Internet: www.boxr.com
Airport: Jackson or Pinedale for private airplanes; free transportation to and from Jackson
Location: 65 miles southeast of Jackson, 20 miles north of Pinedale via State Highway 352
Memberships: The Dude Ranchers' Association, Wyoming Outfitters Association, Rocky Mountain Elk Foundation
Medical: Jackson Hospital, 65 miles; clinic in Pinedale
Guest Capacity: 20 adults, 22 family/group
Accommodations: One-, two-, and three-bedroom log cabins with private baths and daily maid "courtesy cleaning" service. Rooms range from single "Honeymoon Suite" cabins to family-style rooms that sleep five. Social and recreational rooms adjoin several of the lodge rooms.
Rates: • $$$ American Plan; Sunday to Sunday. Three- to five-day stays available. Ask about cattle drives, pack trips, spot packs, and adults-only weeks.
Credit Cards: VISA, MasterCard, and Discover for reservation deposits. Personal or traveler's checks preferred for balance.
Season: Late May to late September
Activities: Full hands-on horse work and care

during your stay. You'll be assigned your own private horse and tack for the week, and depending on your ability, you may help with the early morning wrangling of the horse "cavy." You may also lend a hand in doctoring, locating, salting, and working the ranch cattle on the open range, as well as other ranches and allotments in Sublette County. With approval, competent adult riders may have the opportunity to ride on their own. Authentic spring cattle drives and fall roundups are popular. Choose a ranch-based cattle drive or spend part of your week camping in the mountains with the cattle. Access to excellent trout fishing on the ranch's streams, 11 trout ponds, and several large nearby lakes and rivers.
Children's Programs: No program per se. The ranch is best suited for children age eight and over. Older children may ride separately or with adults. Swing set, pool table, darts, horseshoes, roping, and fishing with parental supervision.
Dining: Family-style meals specializing in ranch beef, turkey, chicken, homemade breads, pastries, soups, and full salad bar. Drinks, fruit, and cookies are available throughout the day, with evening hors d'oeuvres and social hour in BYOB bar.
Entertainment: Folks are delightfully tuckered out at the end of a long day, but some choose to go country dancing at one of the nearby saloons or sit on the porch and watch the sun go down. You're free to do as you please after dinner.
Summary: The Box R Ranch is a true working cattle/horse ranch in the heart of Wyoming's cattle ranching country, run today by fourth-generation family. Great for active, outdoor-oriented adults and older children wanting to experience a real working ranch and hands-on horse work and care. Ask about cattle drives and roundups, pack trips to Bridger Wilderness, and "spot" packs/gear drops, and ranch-based vacations. Nearby: Jackson Hole, Yellowstone, and Teton National Parks.

Breteche Creek Ranch
Cody, Wyoming

Breteche Creek is a unique, nonprofit ranch just east of Yellowstone National Park, located on the edge of the Shoshone National Forest and the 18-million-acre wilderness system that encompasses Yellowstone. The area is dramatically rugged, has a very remote feeling, and teems with wildlife, including eagles and elk. Breteche Creek combines a full family guest ranch program with specific workshop weeks during the course of the summer. Guests may choose between the day's activities of riding, hiking, fishing, or exploring on their own on the ranch's 9,000 acres. Breteche Creek is a remarkably beautiful, untrammeled area, and in keeping with its pristine nature, the ranch directs its guests' attention to the natural world around them. In creating a camp-like atmosphere, with propane lighting, flannel sheets, and gourmet meals, the Breteche Creek Ranch experience is like going to the high country with the comforts of a mountain-based, ranch-camp retreat. Here the wonders of the West and nature prevail.

Address: P.O. Box 596 K, Cody, Wyoming 82414
Telephone: 307/587-3844; fax: 307/527-7032
Email: breteche@bretechecreek.com
Internet: www.bretechecreek.com
Airport: Cody, Wyoming, or Billings, Montana; pickup service available from Cody.
Location: 18 miles west of Cody, 30 miles east of Yellowstone Park, off Yellowstone Highway 14/16/20
Medical: West Park Hospital, 18 miles
Conference Capacity: 30
Guest Capacity: 30
Accommodations: Nine delightful "tent cabins" (wooden frame buildings with canvas roofs, some heated with woodstoves) are scattered along Breteche Creek, each one tucked among aspens for privacy. Each accommodates from one person to a family of four with cozy flannel sheets, comforters, and real beds. Ask about the family yurt that sleeps six. A central lodge of native lodgepole and aspen houses the dining room and common area. Convenient guest bathhouse with eight showers. Six-person hot tub is enjoyed by all.
Rates: • $$$ American Plan. Children's and group rates available. Weekly stays Monday to Sunday.
Credit Cards: VISA, MasterCard. Personal and traveler's checks accepted.
Season: June through September
Activities: Traditional dude ranch activities: riding, hiking, fly-fishing, horsemanship, canoeing, and climbing wall. Educational programs include ecology, wildlife, photography, nature writing, and painting. Naturalist-guided day tours of Yellowstone Park. Self-guided hiking trail. Call for details.
Children's Programs: None. The ranch is better suited for kids age five and older. Families are encouraged to spend quality time together. Family reunions welcome.
Dining: Chef-prepared meals. BYOB.
Entertainment: Songs around the campfire. Famous Cody Nite Rodeo.
Summary: Breteche Creek Ranch is a 9,000-acre natural preserve and guest ranch at the edge of the Shoshone National Forest. Natural beauty, wildlife, and incredible geologic formations abound. Cozy tent cabins. Ask about the workshops offered. Nearby: Yellowstone National Park.

Brooks Lake Lodge
Dubois, Wyoming

Brooks Lake Lodge is in a world of its own. Recent guests have described the ambiance in the following terms: "Enchantment, splendor, the greatest place in North America, a spiritual place, heaven-on-earth." It's all these! When Bryant B. Brooks discovered Brooks Lake in 1889, he wrote, "Among the pines glistened a lake… what a sight! Tracks of elk and bear. Where I sat on my horse stretched a broad, peaceful valley. I stood closer that day to nature's heart than ever before." Built in 1922, the lodge was an overnight stop for bus travelers on their way to Yellowstone National Park. Today, this world-class lodge represents a unique example of the Western craftsmanship period architecture. It is listed in the National Register of Historic Places. This is a very special place and I think you will agree!

Address: 458 Brooks Lake Road, Drawer K, Dubois, Wyoming 82513
Telephone: 307/455-2121; fax: 307/455-2221
Email: brookslake@wyoming.com
Internet: www.brookslake.com
Airport: Jackson, 60 miles
Location: 60 miles northeast of Jackson off Highway 287/26, 23 miles west of Dubois off Highway 287/26
Memberships: The Dude Ranchers' Association, Wyoming Dude Rancher's Association, Association of Historic Hotels of the Rocky Mountain West
Awards: National Register of Historic Places, Kilgore Luxury Group
Medical: Jackson, 60 miles
Conference Capacity: 36
Guest Capacity: 36
Accommodations: Seven comfortable lodge rooms with a distinctive motif and exquisite handcrafted lodgepole furnishings. Eight cabins nestle in the spruce behind the lodge, with wood-burning stoves, electric heat, and private baths with bathrobes and bedding from Scandia Down. Several have wonderful old clawfoot bathtubs. The massive log lodge is furnished with wicker, antiques, and handcrafted works by Wyoming artists. The front lobby, with its large stone fireplace, serves as a gathering spot for afternoon tea and evening entertainment. Spa facilities are a welcome relief after a day of riding, hiking, or in winter, snowmobiling and cross-country skiing. Complimentary laundry service.

Rates: • $$$–$$$$$ American Plan. Children's, group, spa, and winter rates available. Three-day minimum stay in summer.
Credit Cards: VISA, MasterCard, American Express
Season: Summer: Mid-June to mid-September; Winter: Late December to mid-April.
Activities: In summer, an unstructured, informal program of daily horseback rides. The lush green meadows with abundant wildflowers lure the hiker, while Brooks Lake and other nearby lakes and streams offer enjoyable fly-fishing. Canoes, fly-fishing rods, and tackle available. Ask about the spa packages, massages, and overnight pack trips. See the Cross-Country Skiing section for winter activities.
Children's Programs: Children must be age seven or older to ride horses. Families are encouraged to vacation together. Nannies are welcome. Baby-sitting on request with advance notice.
Dining: High gourmet served on fine china with silver at breakfast and dinner; hearty regional Western cuisine and health-conscious meals. High tea is served at 4:30 P.M. in the front lobby, including English finger sandwiches, cookies, banana bread, or other baked pastries.
Entertainment: Before or after dinner, the Diamond G Saloon offers a full bar (open at 6 P.M.) with hors d'oeuvres, pool, and darts. Forest Service naturalists provide evening talks weekly.
Summary: Kilgore Luxury Group. One of the great lodges in North America. The spectacular scenery and warm hospitality leave guests with memories they treasure for years. Superb hiking and mountain trail riding. A great adventure back in time, offering rustic luxury. Listed on the National Register of Historic Places. Summer and winter programs. Be sure to ask about the overnight pack trips.

Brush Creek Ranch
Saratoga, Wyoming

THE DUDE RANCHERS'
ASSOCIATION

Wyoming
Dude
Rancher's
Association

Brush Creek Ranch serves up the best of the Old West. Nestled in dramatic granite outcroppings in the southeast portion of Wyoming, Brush Creek Ranch was home to generations of Western families like the Uihleins and, most recently, the Caldwell family, who spent the summer here. Mr. Uihlein built the main lodge in the early 1900s and consolidated several cow camps into the 6,000-acre Brush Creek Ranch as it is today. When the Caldwells took over in the mid-1950s, they used it as a private family retreat and continued the cattle operations. In 1991 they opened their ranch gates to guests from around the world. Brush Creek Ranch is managed today by family members Kinta and Gibb Blumenthal, who grew up on the ranch. For those who love to ride, fly-fish, and hike, or simply wish to rest, reflect, and enjoy the majesty of the Saratoga Platte Valley, the Brush Creek Ranch experience is old-time, real, and authentic.

Address: Star Route, Box 10, Saratoga, Wyoming 82331
Telephone: 800/RANCH-WY (800/726-2499), 307/327-5241; fax: 307/327-5384
Email: kinta@brushcreekranch.com
Internet: www.brushcreekranch.com
Airport: Denver, 195 miles; Laramie, 65 miles. Airport pickup is extra.
Location: 65 miles west of Laramie off the Snowy Range Road, Wyoming 130; 16 miles northeast of Saratoga off Wyoming 130
Memberships: The Dude Ranchers' Association, Wyoming Dude Rancher's Association, America Outdoors
Awards: Orvis-endorsed Lodge
Medical: Clinic in Saratoga Lodge, 16 miles
Conference Capacity: 26
Guest Capacity: 26
Accommodations: White-sided, green-trimmed, 1900s-style, three-story lodge or rustic cabins. A small fountain, cascading rock garden, and pine trees planted by the homesteaders front the lodge. The lodge features a native stone fireplace in the library and Western murals in the first-floor dining room. Sleeping accommodations are on the second and third floors. Each room is unique with a turn-of-the-century feel. All have private baths and entrances; some have private, screened

porches. Two cabin duplexes, located near the main lodge, were originally the icehouse and cowboy bunkhouse. Each has been completely remodeled with Western, rustic charm, private bathrooms, and queen-size beds. Daily maid service.
Rates: • $$$Full American Plan; three-day minimum stay. Children's, group, and off-season rates. Horseback riding, fly-fishing, and pack-trip packages.
Credit Cards: VISA, MasterCard. Personal checks preferred.
Season: Year-round; closed Thanksgiving and Easter.
Activities: The ranch offers superb riding and fly-fishing. This is a working cattle operation with over 1,200 head of cattle. Guests may help move cattle or enjoy magnificent, wide-open riding country with big views. Daily morning and afternoon rides. Scheduled all-day rides; sunrise and sunset rides on request. Ask about Francis Draw, Homestead Cabin and Barrett Ridge rides. The ranch is an Orvis-endorsed lodge and offers guided and nonguided fly-fishing on over three miles of Brush Creek or on the nearby North Platte and Encampment Rivers. Hiking and mountain biking. Also available in the area are golf, tennis, float trips, and a natural hot spring. Winter: Cross-country skiing, snowmobiling, and dogsledding. Enclosed hot tub.
Children's Programs: Children are the responsibility of parents. Half-day programs planned five times a week. Local baby-sitting available on request. Kids begin riding at age six.
Dining: Western-style food with a gourmet flair. BYOB.
Entertainment: Barn dances in the hayloft of the old log barn, campfire sing-alongs, horse-drawn hayrides, breakfast rides, creek-side barbecues, and pitching horseshoes. Fly-casting and fly-tying demonstrations arranged.
Summary: Kilgore's "Best of the Best"–Fly-Fishing and open riding. Wonderful ranch for those who want authentic Western charm. This is wide-open cattle country. The real down-home ranch goodness and Old West charm make Brush Creek Ranch a winner—for riding, fly-fishing, and easygoing hospitality.

CM Ranch
Dubois, Wyoming

In 1997 the Kemmerers, a family with Wyoming roots dating back 100 years, became the proud new owners of the historic and famous CM Ranch—a ranch they had visited as guests since the 1950s. The family is dedicated to carrying on its rich tradition. Life is simple on the CM Ranch, but then that's what makes ranch life so wonderful. The ranch's objective is to provide a charming and comfortable headquarters where guests can relax and enjoy informal, outdoor pleasures in the magnificent mountain country of the West. This classic ranch is listed in the National Register of Historic Places and is one of the oldest dude ranches in the United States with a fine reputation.

Address: P.O. Box 217 K, Dubois, Wyoming 82513
Telephone: 800/455-0721, 307/455-2331, fax: 307/455-3984
Email: cmranch@wyoming.com
Internet: www.cmranch.com
Airport: Jackson or Riverton; private, surfaced airstrip outside Dubois, 10 miles from ranch (large enough for small private jets)
Location: 6 miles southwest of Dubois
Awards: National Register of Historic Places
Medical: Clinic in Dubois, hospital in Jackson
Conference Capacity: 50
Guest Capacity: 50
Accommodations: Large, well-kept lawns, aspen, and cottonwoods surround 14 log cabins along Jakey's Fork, a branch of the Wind River. The green-roofed cabins have one, two, and three bedrooms; rustic wood furniture; wood-burning stoves; and comfortable porches with views of the creek, meadows, or Badlands. Three beautifully decorated log houses with full amenities sleep up to six. The CM employs a baby-sitter and offers a laundry service for guests' convenience (extra). Daily maid service for cabins and houses.
Rates: • $$$ American Plan. Reduced rate for children 12 and under. One-week minimum stay, Sunday to Sunday arrival. Nonriding rates.
Credit Cards: None. Personal or traveler's checks accepted.
Season: Mid-June to mid-September
Activities: You can ride, fish, hike, swim in the outdoor pool (children must be supervised), picnic, or relax with a book. Horses are matched to your ability. Usually six guests on each ride. Rides go out twice a day except Sunday. Weekly all-day picnic rides to Whiskey Mountain (home to the largest herd of bighorn sheep in North America). Four miles of stream run through the property, so anglers can fish privately for brook, rainbow, and brown trout. Fishing guide available for off-ranch trips (extra). Tackle shop. Fishing at nearby Torrey, Ring, and Trail Lakes. Tennis and golf in town. Ask about the two-night (or longer) pack trip to Moon Lake in the Wind River Mountains. A tent camp is set up there and offers excellent fishing and sight-seeing at nearby wilderness lakes.
Children's Programs: No set program. Children of all ages are welcome. Kids start riding at age five. Full-time kiddie wrangler and baby-sitter available on the premises. Teenage campout.
Dining: Dining room decorated with Native American treasures. Menu includes varied meals that are carefully planned, well balanced, and healthy. Picnic lunches always available for special outings. Homemade breads and vegetarian dishes. BYOB. Welcome cocktail gatherings Monday evenings.
Entertainment: The recreation building has rooms for reading and games, two pianos, table tennis, geology room, and small library. Weekly square dancing in town, music, and other entertainment. Volleyball and softball with guests and crew.
Summary: One of Kilgore's most famous old-time dude ranches in America. Tremendous warmth and personality. Second, third, and fourth generations come to the CM each summer. Great for families and large family reunions. The 7,000-foot altitude offers a predominantly dry and sunny summer climate. Four miles of private stream, 14 log cabins, and three spacious homes for large families. Ask about the Moon Lake pack trip. The extraordinary red sandstone and geological displays will fascinate rock hounds and geology buffs.

Crossed Sabres Ranch
Wapiti, Wyoming

THE DUDE RANCHERS' ASSOCIATION

Wyoming Dude Rancher's Association

Tex Holm established Crossed Sabres Ranch in 1898 as a stagecoach stop. As you walk around this historic ranch, you can imagine the old stage with a team of six stout horses chomping at the bit as they wait for passengers. Crossed Sabres exudes life and rugged character the minute you lay eyes on the place. Besides the "years gone by" ambiance, the ranch has a special feature: It's built alongside a wonderful stream that serenades all the cabins as it meanders and tumbles down the mountain. Today, the ranch is owned and operated by the second generation of the Norris family—Buck and Kerry Norris, who carry on the rich Western traditions that Buck's father and mother began and so wonderfully shared with thousands of guests from all over the world. At the end of a fun-filled day, many love to sit in the rocking chairs on the porch of the main lodge, listening, watching, and remembering. Welcome to Crossed Sabres Ranch, the real thing with the right stuff.

Address: P.O. Box K, Wapiti, Wyoming 82450
Telephone: 800/535-8944, 307/587-3750; fax: 307/587-5008
Email: bnorris@wyoming.com
Internet: www.ranchweb.com/csabres
Airport: Cody, Wyoming, or Billings, Montana
Location: 43 miles west of Cody off U.S. Highway 14/16/20
Memberships: The Dude Ranchers' Association, Wyoming Dude Rancher's Association, Wyoming Outfitters Association
Medical: Cody Hospital, 43 miles
Guest Capacity: 45
Accommodations: All 17 cabins, half of which are along Libby Creek, have names like Red Cloud, Yellow Hand, Indian Echo, and Rides on Clouds. Each is rustic but comfortable and heated, with double and single beds, log furniture, and wooden floors. Hand-hewn pine rocking chairs sit on each porch.
Rates: • $$$ American Plan; all activities included. Children's rates; children under age two free. One-week minimum stay, Sunday to Sunday. Don't arrive before 3 P.M.
Credit Cards: VISA, MasterCard. Personal or traveler's checks accepted.
Season: Early June to early September

Activities: A weekly program that gives guests a chance to relive history and to see what makes this part of Wyoming so famous. Sunday evening, after the welcome beef-and-pork barbecue dinner, Buck discusses the week's calendar of events, which includes daily horseback riding (mostly scenic riding), a day in Cody, an overnight pack trip into the Shoshone National Forest, and an all-day guided trip to Yellowstone National Park. This is really special because Fred's grandson Josh is one of the few young men alive who really knows the history of the park—in the late 1800s his great-uncle was the park's second supervisor. Also included are river rafting on the Shoshone River, fishing in nearby streams, and relaxing.
Children's Programs: No special program. Geared around families being on vacation together. Everyone rides and eats together. Younger children (under five) ride with parents.
Dining: Wholesome family meals in the beautiful authentic Old Western main lodge, built in 1898 with unique burl posts and beams. As Buck's famous father used to say, "Our food is just good. I eat it all the time. Nothing fancy, just hearty ranch cooking." BYOB in cabins only.
Entertainment: Cody rodeo, square dancing, movies, and sing-alongs. Game room.
Summary: One of the most historic dude ranches in the country. Tremendous Old West charm. Yellowstone Park tour is a must. Weekly ranch program with on- and off-ranch activities. Very family-oriented. Ask Buck about the beautiful fall pack trips. Nine miles east of the entrance to Yellowstone National Park.

Double Diamond X Ranch
Cody, Wyoming

THE DUDE RANCHERS' ASSOCIATION

Wyoming Dude Rancher's Association

The Double Diamond X Ranch makes its home along the South Fork bank of the Shoshone River, 34 miles southwest of the famous Western town of Cody, Wyoming. The ranch is surrounded by the rugged and spectacular Absaroka Mountain Range, the Washakie Wilderness, and the Shoshone National Forest. Summer months usually bring mountain breezes, cool nights, and warm daytime temperatures. The ranch was homesteaded in 1914 by the Ray Siggins family, whose descendants are still prominent in the Cody area. The guest-ranch operation began in the early 1930s and has operated continuously, first by Ray's children and grandchildren, and since 1988 by Patsy and Russ Fraser. The Double Diamond X offers a traditional Western vacation year-round, with seasonal wildlife viewing and a customized family holiday program during Christmas and Thanksgiving. Extensive travel and Western backgrounds enabled the Frasers to design a ranch program with a special emphasis on quality, personal service, and living and learning about the West. Russ's experience as Director and CEO of several major financial institutions means that groups, seminars, and retreats are at home here.

Address: 3453 Southfork Road, Dept. K, Cody, Wyoming 82414
Telephone: 800/833-7262, 307/527-6276; fax: 307/587-2708
Email: ddx@cody.wtp.net
Internet: www.ddxranch.com
Airport: Cody, 34 miles
Location: 34 miles southwest of Cody on Southfork Road
Memberships: The Dude Ranchers' Association, American Outdoors, Wyoming Outfitters, Wyoming Dude Rancher's Association
Medical: West Park Hospital in Cody, 34 miles
Conference Capacity: 38
Guest Capacity: 38
Accommodations: Five log cabins and the Trail House Lodge are arranged around the main lodge that houses the living room and dining room with fireplaces, library, gift shop, office, and original Western art. Cabins sleep from four to seven in two bedrooms, each with one or two baths. The Trail House is made up of seven units with one

suite, all with private baths. Two handicapped units. The main lodge, cabins, and Trail House all have covered porches and rockers.
Rates: • $$$$ American Plan. Children's and group rates. Six-day stays from mid-June to September. Shorter stays available other months.
Credit Cards: VISA, MasterCard, American Express
Season: Year-round; custom off-season and holiday packages. Ask about Christmas package.
Activities: Western trail riding with safety instruction weekly. Two rides daily. Weekly all-day ride and an optional overnight ride. Riding is geared wonderfully for families. Beginning, intermediate, and advanced rides available. Ask about Slide Mountain, South Fork Trail, School House River Trail, and overnight pack trips. Fly- and spin-fishing on the Shoshone River and stocked pond. Indoor heated pool and hot tub, hiking, wildlife viewing, and photography. River rafting and Yellowstone Park trips available.
Children's Programs: Extensive morning and afternoon program for children ages 1–12. The children's program is topic-oriented; topics are explored through activities including arts and crafts, music, stories, and lots of educational materials. Riding opportunities depend on child's ability. Baby-sitters and nannies welcome.
Dining: Culinary-trained chef and pastry chef serve an eclectic blend of Western and upscale regional American cuisine, as well as an extensive children's menu. A beverage and snack station is available between meals. (Birthday and anniversary cakes are available upon request.)
Entertainment: Something planned each evening. Includes sharpshooting, singing, storytelling, cookouts, and campfires. Weekly trip to Cody that includes rodeo, Old Trail Town, and Buffalo Bill Historical Center.
Summary: A year-round Western guest-ranch experience with an excellent program for kids ages 1–12. Incredible views, history, talent, and fun. Great for groups, family reunions, weddings, and business conferences. Professional entertainment, indoor heated pool, team-drawn wagon and surrey rides. Nearby: Western town of Cody, Yellowstone National Park.

Double Diamond X Ranch, Wyoming

Eatons' Ranch
Wolf, Wyoming

A legend in Kilgore's Ranch Country. Eatons' Ranch is the granddaddy of dude ranches. Started in 1879 in North Dakota by brothers Howard, Willis, and Alden, the ranch relocated to its present site 18 miles west of Sheridan in 1904 to provide "more suitable and varied riding." Run now by the fourth and fifth generations, this 7,000-acre working cattle/guest ranch has over 200 head of horses with daily rides for every type of rider. There's no end to the varied riding terrain. You can hike or ride through open rangeland and wildflower-studded trails that traverse the intricate Big Horn Mountains just west of the ranch. One guest said, "What makes the Eatons' ranch such a success is that it has just enough structure to draw a family together but enough beautiful wide-open spaces to give us our reins."

Address: P.O. Box K, Wolf, Wyoming 82844
Telephone: 800/210-1049, 307/655-9285, 307/655-9552; fax: 307/655-9269
Email: jeffway@eatonsranch.com
Internet: www.eatonsranch.com
Airport: Sheridan, 18 miles
Location: 18 miles west of Sheridan. Ask for a map if you have any questions.
Memberships: The Dude Ranchers' Association, Wyoming Dude Rancher's Association
Medical: Sheridan Memorial Hospital, 18 miles
Conference Capacity: 65 (June, late August, and September)
Guest Capacity: 125
Accommodations: One-, two-, and three-bedroom cabins suitable for large and small families, couples, and singles. Most have twin beds; all have private baths. Several have living rooms with fireplaces and real old-fashioned outdoor iceboxes, stocked and delivered the way they always have been with big blocks of ice onboard a vintage 1920s Model A pickup. Most of the original cabins were built by and named after early guests. Laundry facilities available.
Rates: • $$$ American Plan. Children's rates; children ages two and under free. Late June through early September, one-week minimum stay. You may arrive any day of the week.
Credit Cards: VISA, MasterCard, Discover. Personal checks preferred.

Season: June to October
Activities: Eatons' Ranch is one of just a handful of ranches left in the country that allow you to ride on your own (if you wish), only after the corral boss is confident that you're ready. Daily rides go out twice a day, except Sunday. Pack trips, picnics, and riding instruction available. Fishing in Wolf Creek, hiking, bird-watching, and swimming in the heated outdoor pool. Golfers will enjoy the nine-hole course at a neighboring ranch or three courses in Sheridan.
Children's Programs: Children enjoy a variety of ranch activities. Kids go to Howard Hall for crafts, games, and treasure hunts. Kids must be six years old to go on trail rides. Nannies are encouraged for younger children.
Dining: Large dining room. Hearty Western ranch cooking, barbecues, noon cookouts. At your first meal, look for your personalized wooden napkin ring marking your place. BYOB in cabins.
Entertainment: Weekly cocktail party hosted by Eaton/Ferguson families on Tuesday evenings. Team roping. Bingo, weekly country-Western dancing at Howard Hall, the ranch's recreation building. Staff-versus-guests softball games. Occasional rodeos in town. Books available in the main ranch house.
Summary: Kilgore's most famous historic dude ranches in North America! The ranch exudes history and intrigue. Many multigeneration families return the same week each summer, year after year. Wonderful ranch store and post office. Ride Museum, Little Big Horn Battlefield, Fort Phil Kearney, polo tournaments, and Bradford Brinton Museum in Big Horn, 20 miles away.

Flying A Guest Ranch
Pinedale, Wyoming

In 1965 Lowell Hansen went to Wyoming on a hunting trip and found one of the prettiest settings in America. He returned with the Flying A Guest Ranch. Today Hansen's daughter, Debbie, and her husband, Keith, offer discerning adults a distinctive Western vacation. Located just 50 miles southeast of Jackson Hole at 8,200 feet, the Flying A is near the Gros Ventre Mountains in a magnificent, wide-open meadow with 360-degree views. The drive is slow and beautiful through neighboring cattle ranches. The ranch offers an unstructured, casual Western atmosphere. You can ride through the quiet seclusion of groves of aspens and pines, fish in the abundant ponds and mountain streams, watch spectacular sunsets on the distant peaks, and enjoy the wonder of moose, deer, and elk in their natural habitat. Built in the early 1930s, the Flying A has been tastefully restored and offers exquisitely comfortable facilities. It hosts adults from across the United States and abroad.

Address: 771 Flying A Ranch Road, Drawer K, Pinedale, Wyoming 82941-9313
Telephone: 307/367-2385 (summer), call for fax; 800/678-6543 (winter). Don't be surprised if someone answers "Jack Rabbit Charters;" it's owned by the Hansen family.
Email: flyinga@wyoming.com
Internet: www.flyinga.com
Airport: Jackson, 50 miles; airport for private planes in Pinedale
Location: 50 miles southeast of Jackson off Highway 191, 27 miles north of Pinedale
Memberships: The Dude Ranchers' Association, Wyoming Dude Rancher's Association
Medical: St. John's Hospital in Jackson, medical center in Pinedale, helicopter service available
Guest Capacity: 14
Accommodations: Seven cabins named after the colorful characters that settled in the valley. All have that exquisite Ralph Lauren feel. Original hand-carved native pine furniture blends beautifully with new oak floors, tasteful art, and cozy flannel sheets and comforters. Cabins have living rooms, modern bathrooms with a shower or shower/tub combination, full-size kitchens and bedrooms. All cabins have electric heat and most

have a fireplace or wood-burning stove. Kitchens contain everything from coffeemakers to wineglasses. Each cabin also has one or two private covered porches overlooking the little stream and grassy meadow where wildlife come to graze.
Rates: • $$$ American Plan. One-week minimum stay, Sunday to Saturday.
Credit Cards: None. Personal and traveler's checks accepted.
Season: June to October
Activities: Very relaxed and unstructured. Debbie, Keith, and their staff offer a customized program. Guests are encouraged to set their own schedules around the ranch activities offered each day. Trout fishing on ranch property or mountain streams. Keith is a superb fly-fisherman and offers fly-casting instruction and guiding. Unlimited horseback riding or guided hiking to explore the high country. The riding program is very flexible for ranch guests. Ask Debbie about her favorite rides to Jack Creek, Rock Creek, and Bartlett Canyon. Mountain bikes also available. Enjoy magnificent views from the hot tub.
Children's Programs: Must be age 16 and older.
Dining: Three meals served with a casual yet gourmet flair. For that added touch, china is used at dinner. Weekly barbecues with smoked-trout appetizer. Each evening the ranch serves appetizers in the Gilded Moose Saloon, which overlooks the ranch pond and the Wind River and Gros Ventre Mountain Ranges. BYOB.
Entertainment: Visiting with other guests, lots of R&R, video library, horseshoes, and volleyball. Evening card and poker games.
Summary: One of the prettiest guest ranches in America overlooking Wind River Range and Hay Meadows! Small, adults-only. Magnificent, peaceful, remote, private setting. Take part in as many or as few of the ranch activities as you want—the choice is yours. Warm, cozy accommodations with lovely interior touches. Tremendous wildflowers in June and July; the beautiful colors of changing aspen trees and abundance of wildlife in fall.

Goosewing Ranch
Jackson Hole, Wyoming

Remote, small, magnificent views to the Tetons 45 miles away, and international cooking. Welcome to Goosewing Ranch, located deep in the Gros Ventre River Valley, the Goosewing marks the entry point to the Gros Ventre Wilderness Area in the Bridger Teton National Forest. At 7,400 feet, the ranch offers guests spectacular scenery, remoteness with cozy comforts. Proximity to Teton National Park, Yellowstone National Park, and the Snake River Valley allows guests to view abundant wild game including bison, elk, moose, mountain sheep, antelope, bear, eagles, geese, and cranes. The Gros Ventre River, home to native cutthroat trout, runs through the meadows of this historic ranch, providing fishing for children and adults. Fly-fishing instruction and guiding can be provided upon request.

Address: P.O. Box 4084, Jackson, Wyoming 83001
Telephone: 888/733-5251, 307/733-5251; fax: 307/733-1405
Email: fcorrand2@aol.com
Internet: www.goosewingranch.com
Airport: Jackson Hole, 30 miles
Location: 38 miles northeast of Jackson on Gros Ventre Road
Memberships: Jackson Hole Chamber of Commerce
Medical: St. John's Hospital, 38 miles
Conference Capacity: 25; early June and September
Guest Capacity: 25
Accommodations: The Goosewing has eight private one-bedroom, one-bath guest cabins, each with heating stoves, and covered porches. There is a large, family-style log home for large groups. With its large stone fireplace, the main lodge serves as a central gathering place for dining and relaxing. A loft bar with a pool table and television overlooks the main room.
Rates: • $$$–$$$$$ American Plan; gratuities and service charges included. Summer and winter rates.
Credit Cards: VISA, MasterCard, American Express (3 percent additional charge for payment by credit card). Personal and traveler's checks accepted.

Season: Summer: June through October; Winter: December through March.
Activities: Summer activities include horseback riding, hiking, biking, fly-fishing, and nature walks. Hands-on horse care available. Swimming in the heated pool or relaxing in the hot tub. Winter provides an incredible trip into the ranch by snowmobile. Once there, more snowmobiling, cross-country skiing, snowshoeing, and sharing the days activities with other guests while warming up in the hot tub.
Children's Programs: Most parents come to be on vacation with their kids. By request staff members will watch kids. Trailing riding begins at age six.
Dining: International cuisine. Each evening's meal offers a theme from a different country. Room service upon request, especially for honeymooners. Wine available.
Entertainment: Weekly cookouts with live entertainment, and weekly rodeo and rafting trips into Jackson during the summer. In the winter most guests enjoy the unstructured and independent atmosphere.
Summary: A slice of heaven and a piece of paradise that looks out to the distant Tetons in the magnificent Gros Ventre Wilderness. International host and cuisine. Fluent French and German spoken. Activities are offered for summer, fall and winter seasons. Be sure to ask about the incredible trip into the ranch in the winter. Nearby: The town of Jackson, the Snake River, Teton and Yellowstone National Parks.

Gros Ventre River Ranch
Moose, Wyoming

Wyoming
Dude
Rancher's
Association

At 7,000 feet, Gros Ventre River Ranch is a great place to savor the mighty Tetons, take quiet walks, fish, ride, explore, or just relax and enjoy this year-round paradise. This old ranch has been in the guest-ranching business since the early 1950s but was bought by Karl and Tina Weber in 1987. They've given the place a real face-lift without diminishing the Old West charm. In fact, the Webers and their fine staff have enhanced what was there and created a world-class guest ranch. Guests will enjoy the lodge, with views that capture the splendor of the Tetons, magnificent wilderness scenery, and the rushing Gros Ventre River. While preserving the past, the Webers and their daughter and son-in-law Tori and Sean McGough, have made it possible for people from around the world to settle in and enjoy rustic elegance and nature at its best.

Address: P.O. Box 151 K, Moose, Wyoming 83012
Telephone: 307/733-4138; fax: 307/733-4272
Email: grosventreranch@cs.com
Internet: www.ranchweb.com/grosventre
Airport: Jackson, 18 miles
Location: 18 miles northeast of Jackson. You'll be sent a map with your confirmation.
Awards: Kilgore Luxury Group
Memberships: The Dude Ranchers' Association, Wyoming Dude Rancher's Association
Medical: St. John's Hospital in Jackson, 18 miles
Conference Capacity: 34; May to June, mid-September to October
Guest Capacity: 34
Accommodations: Nine log cabins, all winterized. Four cabins have 10-foot ceilings, fireplaces, sliding glass doors that open to decks with magnificent views of the Tetons, and kitchenettes. Beds are turned down each evening. Laundry facilities available. The handsome lodge could well be on the cover of *Architectural Digest*; it features original art, two decks overlooking the Gros Ventre River with views of the distant Tetons, and a lovely dining room, living room, and bar area. On the lower level is a rec/conference room that opens out to a landscaped area overlooking the river. Winter: Cabins are on a housekeeping basis only.

Rates: • $$$$–$$$$$ American Plan. Children's and off-peak rates. Weekly minimum stay mid-June to early September; Sunday-to-Sunday arrivals.
Credit Cards: None. Personal checks, and traveler's checks accepted.
Season: May through October; December through March, cabin rentals through Christmas.
Activities: Summer: Horseback riding with slow to fast half-day, all-day, and lunch rides. Fly-fishing in the legendary Snake River, Crystal Creek, or Gros Ventre River, which runs through the ranch (fishing gear available). The stocked beaver ponds provide a sure catch for anglers and are enjoyed by all. Ranch swimming hole, canoeing in Slide Lake, hiking, mountain biking at ranch. (Bikes available.) Golf and tennis 10 miles away. Winter: Cross-country skiing (bring your own gear), snowmobiling, and Alpine skiing in Jackson.
Children's Programs: No set programs. Children age seven and older go on trail rides. Occasional baby-sitting available at an extra charge. If child care is a must, BYON (bring your own nanny).
Dining: Excellent cuisine. Rack of lamb, baked trout, barbecued chicken, ribs, and steaks grilled to order. Complimentary wine with dinner. BYOB happy hour with hors d'oeuvres.
Entertainment: Cards or quiet music. Weekly rodeos in Jackson, campfires and marshmallow roasts, weekly cookouts with country-Western singing by local entertainers. Naturalist program.
Summary: One of Kilgore's "Best of the Best"–Luxury. A world-class guest ranch with magnificent views of the Tetons and Gros Ventre River. Emphasis on horseback riding, fly-fishing, and relaxation. Excellent for families, couples, singles, and small corporate groups. Nearby: Adjacent Yellowstone National Park, National Elk Refuge, the town of Jackson, Gros Ventre Slide (largest landslide in the United States). Bordered by Grand Teton National Park.

Gros Ventre River Ranch, Wyoming

Heart Six Ranch
Moran, Wyoming

Heart Six Ranch looks out over the lush Buffalo River Valley and on to the magnificent Tetons. As an original Yellowstone stagecoach stop, the ranch has a long history of Western hospitality and over the years has entertained guests from around the world. Bordering Grand Teton National Park and offering lots of Old West charm, the ranch is owned by Brian and Millie Harris and managed by Steve and Joyce Blinkenberg, whose philosophy is to offer their guests a traditional dude ranch experience. Parents and children love the personal attention and proximity to Jackson and nearby national parks. Heart Six is a ranch where families come to catch the spirit of the West. Here children can run free, play hard, and laugh with other kids, while parents enjoy the majesty of nature, the Tetons, good food, and great company.

Address: P.O. Box 70 K, Moran, Wyoming 83013
Telephone: 888/543-2477, 307/543-2477; fax: 307/543-0918
Email: heartsix@wyoming.com
Internet: www.heartsix.com
Airport: Jackson, 28 miles
Location: 35 miles northeast of Jackson off Highway 26
Memberships: The Dude Ranchers' Association, Wyoming Dude Rancher's Association, Wyoming Professional Guide and Outfitters Association
Medical: St. John's Hospital in Jackson
Conference Capacity: 50
Guest Capacity: 50
Accommodations: Comfortable red-roofed log cabins with Western decor. Several duplexes. One, two, and three bedrooms can sleep up to 12. Many have woodstoves or fireplaces, and twin and double beds. Cozy main lodge with large fireplace and picture windows looking out over the Buffalo Fork Valley and on to the Tetons. Laundry facilities.
Rates: • $$$–$$$$ American Plan. Group, children's, and off-season rates. Six-day stay during the summer with arrivals on Monday, departures on Sunday. Spring, fall, winter, and snowmobile rates on request.
Credit Cards: VISA, MasterCard
Season: Year-round; open Christmas and New Year's.

Activities: Summer: Scenic mountain-trail horseback riding in the Bridger-Teton National Forest, from two-hour to all-day rides, morning, afternoon, and sunset ride cookout. Instruction and arena riding available. Don't miss the chance to float the Snake River through Grand Teton National Park. There's a good chance you'll see local wildlife (buffalo, moose, elk, bear, eagles). Learn about local geology and wildflowers on hikes and trail rides with a Forest Service naturalist each week. Fishing, hiking, canoeing, and mountain biking. Overnight pack trips and one-day wilderness fishing trips by reservation. Winter: Snowmobiling in Yellowstone and across the Continental Divide. One-day and overnight guided snowmobile tours offered, as well as lodging and meals.
Children's Programs: Excellent, fully supervised program with counselors for ages four and older. Kids eat together at all meals in their own adjoining dining room. Activities for all ages during the day include horseback riding, arts and crafts, organized games, hiking, swimming, fishing, and canoeing.
Dining: Ranch cuisine. Enjoy three hearty meals a day, including fresh-baked breads, cakes, and cookies. Breakfast and dinner rides. BYOB.
Entertainment: Each evening you're entertained on the ranch or in Jackson. A Monday-night welcome at the Western Dance Party with two-stepping and line dancing. Weekly Jackson Hole rodeo night, cowboy singing and poetry, and occasional Native American dancing
Summary: Great ranch for families catering to kids age four and older. Excellent children's program with lots of planned activities and separate dining with counselors. Incredible views of the valley and Grand Tetons. Horseback riding, Snake River rafting trips, sight-seeing in Yellowstone and Grand Teton National Parks. Ask about wilderness fly-fishing pack trips. Wedding parties welcome in spring and fall. Winter: Experience the beauty of Wyoming on a snowmobile. Nearby: Town of Jackson.

H F Bar Ranch
Saddlestring, Wyoming

The H F Bar Ranch, one of the great old dude ranches in America, has preserved that old-ranch feeling. Since the late 1920s, this 10,000-acre ranch has received distinguished guests from around the world. The ranch is owned and run today by Margi Schroth and her young children, Lily, Cara, Turner, and Gus. The H F Bar's horse corrals, barns, and ranch headquarters haven't changed much over the years, nor have the surrounding pastures, with native grasses rising to meet the timbered hills leading into the Big Horn Mountains. Margi has kept things as they always have been and guests keep returning. As Margi says, "I've made a tremendous effort to maintain our Old Western traditions and keep things very, very simple and family-oriented here."

Address: 1301 Rock Creek Road K, Saddlestring, Wyoming 82840
Telephone: 307/684-2487; fax: 307/684-7144
Email: HFBar@wyoming.com
Internet: www.HFBar.com
Airport: Sheridan, 35 miles; Billings, Montana, 160 miles
Location: 12 miles northwest of Buffalo, 35 miles southwest of Sheridan, 160 miles south of Billings, Montana
Medical: Family Medical Center, Buffalo
Conference Capacity: 95; audiovisual equipment available
Guest Capacity: 120
Accommodations: 28 older rustic cabins built from local timber. Each has its own charm, with names like Brookside, Meadowlark, and Round Up. Each has a living room, fireplace, one to seven bedrooms and one to two full bathrooms. Several are heated with propane or electricity. Most have that days-gone-by feeling. The ranch stream sings outside many of the cabins. Early each morning a pot of hot coffee and *New York Times* fax are delivered to your front porch. A horse-drawn wagon delivers old-fashioned blocks of ice to your cabin, as well as any items you request from town or the ranch general store—an old H F Bar tradition.
Rates: • $$$ American Plan. Children's rates; no charge for kids under five. The ranch encourages families to BYO nannies and offers a 50 percent discount for them. One-week minimum stay; no set arrival day.
Credit Cards: None. Personal or traveler's checks accepted.
Season: June to October
Activities: It's a relaxed atmosphere and guests can do as they please. Many come for the riding, fly-fishing, and hiking opportunities. With 200 horses and 10,000 acres, there's plenty of riding for beginners as well as experienced horsemen, who can ride unsupervised only after their riding ability has been checked out by the wranglers. Half-day and all-day rides, pack trips, and riding instruction available. All rides customized to families or individuals. Excellent catch-and-release fly-fishing in the North and South Forks of Rock Creek, which runs through the ranch. Ask about fishing guides and day trips to Big Horn River. Swimming in heated pool, hiking, and sporting-clay shooting. Guns available (extra).
Children's Programs: Kids of all ages welcome— very active and extensive children's programs for infants through teens. Margi says, "We are extremely child-friendly." Hayrides, craft days, hamburger cookouts. Trail riding begins at age five. Pony rides for younger kids and everyone learns about horse care.
Dining: Each family is assigned its own table. Children may eat earlier and have their own menu. Hearty country fare; everything baked and cooked from scratch. BYOB. Wine and liquor picked up with advance notice.
Entertainment: Weekly country dancing to live music; family hayrides and rodeo, softball games, storytelling, and naturalist talks. Rodeos in town.
Summary: One of Kilgore's great old-time historic ranches. A wonderful ranch for the entire family and children of all ages. Lots of family time here. Many second- and third-generation families return year after year. First-time families receive a hearty welcome. Staff of 60 college students. Fascinating geology; Indian sites on ranch. Nearby: Big Horn Equestrian Center, King's Saddlery and Museum, and Bozeman Trail site.

The Hideout at Flitner Ranch
Greybull, Wyoming

Wyoming's Flitner family ranch was founded in 1906. Today David and Paula, along with their grown children and families continue a tradition of excellence in ranching and farming. For many years they have hosted guests from all over to come and experience their Western lifestyle. In the early 1990s they built new facilities to accommodate their discerning clientele. David's college days at Dartmouth, along with Paula's European upbringing and the family's extensive travel, gave them the sensitivity and understanding to create a first-rate guest-ranch program, with rugged days in the saddle, incredible views, and grace and comfort at day's end. Here old-time ranching combines with modern-day luxuries to offer one of the country's best working-ranch experiences geared to adventurous riders.

Address: P.O. Box 206, Drawer K, Shell, Wyoming 82441
Telephone: 800/354-8637, 307/765-2080; fax: 307/765-2681
Email: info@thehideout.com
Internet: www.thehideout.com
Airport: Cody, 70 miles; Billings, 140 miles; private 6,000-foot paved airstrip nearby and helicopter service available
Location: 15 miles northeast of Greybull off Highway 14 East; 70 miles east of Cody
Memberships: The Dude Ranchers' Association, Wyoming Dude Rancher's Association
Medical: 25 miles to clinic; hospital in Cody, 70 miles.
Conference Capacity: 25
Guest Capacity: 25
Accommodations: Lower Hideout—Built in 1994, the first-class main lodge and cabins look out to the Bighorn Mountains. The 5,000-square-foot main lodge has three levels, a spacious great room with wood-burning fireplace, dining area, cozy family room with large-screen satellite TV, and a loft for small business meetings or relaxing. All rooms have private baths; two are in the main building and the others in the log cabins surrounding the lodge. Luxury suites are available with full kitchens, laundry facilities, and separate living rooms. Each cabin has its own porch with willow rocking chairs. Hot tub available. Upper

Hideout—a half-day ride away is the ranch's mountain retreat. Three log cabins and a cookhouse nestle among the trees at 8,000 feet.
Rates: • $$$–$$$$$ American Plan. June through October: five-night minimum stay. Off-season and "adults-only week" rates.
Credit Cards: VISA, MasterCard, American Express
Season: April to mid-November
Activities: Ranch and cowboy adventure programs offer all kinds of riding and cowboy opportunities. The large cattle herd requires lots of work—do as much or as little as you please. Enjoy the incredible geology of internationally known Sheep Mountain and the recently discovered dinosaur tracks. Take an airboat tour of the Bighorn River, or flyfish on four private miles of Shell Creek.
Children's Programs: Recommended age for children riding is age 10 and older, or experienced younger children.
Dining: Hearty gourmet ranch cuisine. Grilled steaks, homemade chicken and noodles, pot roasts, barbecued ribs, and ranch-family recipes. Complimentary soda, beer, and wine available. BYOL.
Entertainment: Cody Nite Rodeo, arena horseback games, cookouts, Satellite TV, and card games. Volleyball, skeet shooting, and horseshoes.
Summary: One of Kilgore's "Best of the Best"–Working Ranch and Luxury. Historic family-owned cattle ranch with beautiful first-class guest accommodations and extensive cattle and quarter horse breeding programs. Sophistication and old-time ranching go hand in hand here. Ranch work. Large cattle herd, good horses, airboat rides, and panoramic views of incredible geologic formations. Contrasting climates, with warm days and cool nights. Nearby: Many sightseeing opportunities, from active dinosaur digs to Little Big Horn Battlefield and Yellowstone National Park.

Lazy L & B Ranch
Dubois, Wyoming

The Lazy L & B has been in the guest-ranching business since the 1920s. Today it's owned and operated by Bob and Lee Naylon, a terrific couple. Together with their young daughter, Piper Alison, they've touched a lot of hearts. As the Naylons say, "After a decade of dude ranching, our pleasure comes from sharing our unspoiled part of the Old West with guests from around the world." Located in a secluded river valley of cottonwoods with contrasting red-clay cliffs, the ranch adjoins the Wind River Indian Reservation. With the 50,000-acre elk refuge, Wind River for fishing, rolling prairie, badlands, Alpine meadows, river gorges, and high mountain forests, the Lazy L & B offers incredible riding diversity and fun for all!

Address: 1072 East Fork Road, Drawer K, Dubois, Wyoming 82513
Telephone: 800/453-9488, 307/455-2839; fax: 307/455-2634
Email: lazylb@aol.com
Internet: www.ranchweb.com/lazyl&b
Airport: Jackson or Riverton; private planes may land on 5,000-foot lighted and paved airstrip in Dubois
Location: 70 miles east of Jackson, 22 miles northeast of Dubois
Memberships: The Dude Ranchers' Association, Wyoming Dude Rancher's Association
Medical: Clinic in Dubois, hospital in Lander and Jackson
Guest Capacity: 35
Accommodations: Parts of the lodge, cabins, and corrals are the original 1890s sheep-and-cattle-ranch buildings. The lodge provides a cozy fireplace, library, game tables, and a wonderful large deck that looks up to the East Fork Valley where guests can enjoy the morning sun and evening cocktails. Comfortable log cabins are arranged around a central courtyard. Two are located along the river. All have private baths or showers, electric heat, and small refrigerators. Some porches have views of the distant Absaroka and Wind River Ranges. Some have wood-burning stoves.
Rates: • $$$ American Plan. Children's, large-family, and group rates available. Minimal charge for nannies/baby-sitters.
Credit Cards: None. Personal and traveler's checks accepted.
Season: End of May through August. Adults-only in September.
Activities: Most guests come here to ride. Riding groups consist of no more than seven divided by skill level; 2.5–3.5 hour rides in the morning and afternoon. Wednesday and Thursday are optional all-day lunch rides in the high country. Although most guests wish to ride daily, other activities include hiking, rifle range, a leather-tooling and bead shop, and game room for the kids. Anglers enjoy fishing in the ranch's stocked ponds, the East Fork River, or neighboring Wiggins Fork, Bear Creek, and Wind River. Swim in the solar-heated pool or relax in the Jacuzzi by the river.
Children's Programs: Supervised riding program for children age five years and older with riding and safety instruction. Three nights a week children dine early with wranglers, one night having their own hayride barbecue. Kids enjoy feeding the horses, the "kid-size" log cabin, and the great petting zoo with Pablo, Mañuel, Ebony, Piggy Van Gogh, and friends.
Dining: Hearty ranch cooking with fresh vegetables and fruits along with ranch-baked breads and desserts daily. Family-style meals, picnic lunches and barbecues on the trail. BYOB happy hour.
Entertainment: Campfires, cowboy poetry and music. Weekly square dancing in Dubois, museum, and the National Big Horn Sheep Center.
Summary: Beautiful setting and wonderful family-oriented riding ranch with great hosts Bob, Lee, and daughter Piper. Excellent for families, singles, and adults. Surrounded by 50,000-acre Elk Refuge, Indian reservation, and national forest. Spectacular variety of riding terrain and backcountry trips. Ask about the spectacular Bear Basin wilderness trips. September, adults-only. Nearby: Grand Teton and Yellowstone National Parks.

Lost Creek
Moose, Wyoming

Lost Creek is a magnificent ranch resort. Breathtaking views of the mighty Tetons, an incredible spa, and superb cuisine make Lost Creek what it is today—a world-class showplace owned and operated by the Halpin family! Located on the eastern slope of the Jackson Hole Valley at 7,000 feet, the ranch is situated on a rise with commanding views of the entire Teton Mountain Range and the valley. This privately owned ranch and spa is bordered by Grand Teton National Park and Bridger-Teton National Forest. The beautiful lodge and cabins are furnished with high-quality decor featuring custom-made furniture and original artwork. The cabin amenities, superb service and tremendous outdoor opportunities make Lost Creek ideal for families, individuals, and corporate groups who appreciate excellence. Ride horses, float the Snake River, hike, enjoy a Dutch-oven cookout on Shadow Mountain, or relax on the expansive lodge deck and watch the sun set behind the Tetons. You can do it all at Lost Creek.

Address: P.O. Box 95 K, Moose, Wyoming 83012
Telephone: 307/733-3435; fax: 307/733-1954
Email: ranch@lostcreek.com
Internet: www.lostcreek.com
Airport: Jackson via Denver or Salt Lake City
Location: 20 miles north of Jackson
Awards: Mobil 4 Star; *Hideaway Report*; Kilgore Luxury Group
Medical: First-aid office at ranch; St. John's Hospital in Jackson, 20 miles
Conference Capacity: 20
Guest Capacity: 55
Accommodations: Luxury two-bedroom, two-bath (with tub and shower) cabins, and one-bedroom cabins, with queen and single beds in all bedrooms. All cabins have refrigerators with ice-makers, microwaves, coffee and hot chocolate, and electric heat. The living-room cabins have queen sleeper sofas, and freestanding gas log fireplaces. Beds are turned down each evening, and the "mint fairy" always leaves a surprise. Maid service twice daily. Courtesy laundry service.
Rates: • $$$$$$ Full American Plan. One-week minimum stay, Sunday to Sunday. Off-season nightly, corporate, and group rates. No charge for children age five and under.
Credit Cards: American Express. Personal checks and cash accepted.
Season: Late May through mid-October
Activities: Full riding program with instruction. Very flexible and personalized. Beginner, intermediate, and advanced rides. No more than eight to a ride. Ask about Chips Bluff, Snake River, and Cunningham's Overlook, and The Spa at Lost Creek (a luxurious full-service spa). Heated swimming pool and giant hot tub, tennis court, Snake River scenic float trips, cookouts, guided hiking. Skeet shooting on request. Many guests enjoy the Yellowstone and Grand Teton National Parks tours. Guided fishing and golf nearby (extra).
Children's Programs: Supervised kids' program (ages 6–13). Ask for details. Children under age six do not trail ride. Game room and youth cookout. Families with young children are encouraged to bring nannies.
Dining: Outstanding cuisine with two entrées served nightly. Wine list available. Optional dinner hour for children. Special diets served by prior arrangement.
Entertainment: Weekly cookouts, campfire sing-alongs, Western swing dance, weekly rodeo in Jackson, and impromptu programs.
Summary: One of Kilgore's "Best of the Best"–Luxury Resort-Spa Ranch. Superb personal service. Excellent for family vacations and corporate retreats. Ask about ranch and spa packages. Afternoon and evening children's program. Nearby: Historic Western town of Jackson (art galleries, shopping, white-water rafting, and Western events such as shoot-outs, theater groups, stagecoach rides), Yellowstone and Grand Teton National Parks, National Elk Refuge.

Moose Head Ranch
Moose, Wyoming

Wyoming
Dude
Rancher's
Association

Moose Head Ranch is a gem nestled completely within the boundaries of Grand Teton National Park. It offers guests a wonderful panoramic view of the majestic, spectacular Teton Range. Centrally located in the Jackson Hole Valley, Moose Head provides a feeling of seclusion and solitude, yet abundant activities on and off the ranch are easily accessible. While the ranch was originally homesteaded in 1923, the Mettler family has owned it since 1967. Louise Mettler Davenport and her husband, Kit, run the ranch with a personal approach. Louise sits down with every family on their first day to tell them about hikes and side trips that many guests have enjoyed. A trip to Yellowstone, white-water rafting and scenic drives fill any time you don't feel like being in the saddle. The college-age Moose Head staff is equally friendly, filled with polite manners and Southern charm—what great role models for your children! Guests leave feeling a part of the Moose Head family, usually return, and always tell their friends.

Address: P.O. Box 214 K, Moose, Wyoming 83012
Telephone: 307/733-3141, fax: 307/739-9097 (summer); 850/877-1431, fax: 850/878-7577 (winter)
Airport: Jackson, 18 miles
Location: 26 miles north of Jackson
Memberships: The Dude Ranchers' Association, Wyoming Dude Rancher's Association
Medical: St. John's Hospital in Jackson, 26 miles
Guest Capacity: 45
Accommodations: Log cabins scattered among the aspen, cottonwoods, spruce, and pines, by trout ponds, or along streams. Each of the 14 cabins offer privacy and comfort for couples and families (eight with adjoining living rooms). All have private baths with shower and tub, electric heating, coffeemakers, refrigerators, and porches. Daily maid service. Ice is brought to your cabin each day. The spacious lodge has an incredible deck with comfortable chairs, and planters overflowing with perennials—a great way to relax after a ride or before a meal. Half a dozen hummingbird feeders on the lodge deck entertain children and adults.

Rates: • $$$$ American Plan. Rates for children age six and under. Five-night minimum stay; arrivals any day.
Credit Cards: None. Personal checks accepted.
Season: Mid-June to late August
Activities: Small, supervised horseback rides twice daily, usually one family per wrangler. Weekly all-day rides. The Davenports believe in promoting family togetherness, so you ride and eat with your children. Don't come here to do a lot of fast riding, but do if you want to see lots of wildlife (elk, buffalo, mule deer, antelope, moose, coyotes). There is dry fly-fishing (catch-and-release) in several excellent, well-stocked trout ponds. Kit Davenport loves to teach the art of fly-casting, making converts and enthusiasts of all ages. Many fish off the property on the Snake River and other streams. Fishing flies and equipment available. Tennis and golf can be arranged at local clubs, as can scenic and white-water float trips on the Snake River.
Children's Programs: Children of all ages welcome. Lots of activities, but no organized children's program. Limited baby-sitting available.
Dining: Louise feels that good food is just as important as good riding. Outstanding gourmet chefs serve breakfast to order, buffet lunches, and two entrées for dinner that the whole family will enjoy. Abundant picnics provided when you need to miss a meal. Sunday night cookout. BYOB.
Entertainment: Informal, pre-dinner cocktails and hors d'oeuvres each evening where guests gather and visit. After dinner, most do their own thing. Others enjoy live weekly roping practice by colorful local talent, volleyball, table tennis, croquet, softball, horseshoes, and fly-fishing.
Summary: Kilgore's "Best of the Best." One of the great family ranches in North America with incredible views of the Tetons, family rides, a superb Southern college staff, and outstanding food. Wait until you see the 28-inch cutthroat trout in the ponds.

Paradise Guest Ranch
Buffalo, Wyoming

Wyoming
Dude
Rancher's
Association

Paradise Guest Ranch is one of the leading family guest ranches in North America offering traditional dude-ranch activities with lots of riding and fishing. As hosts and managers Clay and Leah Miller say, "We bring families together allowing them to do as much together or apart as they like." Once the prized hunting ground for the Sioux, Crow, and Cheyenne Indians, the ranch rests in a mountain valley next to French and Three Rivers Creeks, surrounded by tall forests of evergreens. The peace and tranquility are only occasionally interrupted by the calls of wildlife or the exuberant sounds of families having fun. It's little wonder that the ranch brand is "FUN." It lives up to the name "Paradise" for good reason, as it offers the rustic flavor of the Old West along with many modern conveniences.

Address: P.O. Box 790, Buffalo, Wyoming 82834
Telephone: 307/684-7876; fax: 307/684-7380
Email: FUN@paradiseranch.com
Internet: www.paradiseranch.com
Airport: Sheridan, or Buffalo for private planes or jets
Location: 46 miles south of Sheridan off Hunter Creek Road, 110 miles north of Casper, 176 miles south of Billings
Memberships: The Dude Ranchers' Association, Wyoming Dude Rancher's Association
Medical: Johnson County Memorial Hospital in Buffalo, 16 miles
Conference Capacity: 50; 2,400-square-foot meeting space off-season only
Guest Capacity: 70
Accommodations: 18 upscale one-, two-, and three-bedroom log homes, each with living room, kitchenette, fireplace, central heat, and outdoor porches with mountain meadow views. Washers/dryers in all two-bedroom or larger cabins. Each day your hot chocolate, tea, and coffee basket will be filled.
Rates: • $$–$$$ American Plan. Children's and pack-trip rates. One-week minimum stay, Sunday to Sunday, except low season.
Credit Cards: None. Personal checks accepted.
Season: Late May to October
Activities: Riding is the main activity, with one wrangler to a maximum of seven guests. An average of 9–12 separate rides each day. Guests can choose walking, trotting, or loping rides. Beginners can learn all three if they wish and are able. Adults and children may ride together or separately. Also offered are bag-lunch rides or occasionally special cooked-on-the-trail lunch rides. Mules pack all the grub, and the wranglers do all the cookin'. Ask about rides to Seven Brothers and Sherd Lakes and the cattle-ranch-country ride through spectacular Cougar, Red, and Sales Canyons. Weekly team penning. Instruction available on one of 130 horses. Extensive fly-fishing program for kids and adults with instruction. Naturalist guided hiking, heated outdoor swimming pool, and indoor whirlpool spa.
Children's Programs: Excellent children's program, activities counselor for kids, toddlers to teens. Kids' rodeo in arena with gymkhana events. Kids and parents may interact as much or as little as they like. Ask about teen social and teen overnight pack-trip campout. Special optional kids' dining and kids' rodeo.
Dining: Three hearty meals a day with a gourmet flair, served family-style. Real mule-drawn chuck wagon dinner and cookouts, home-baked breads. Extensive California wine list. Stocked saloon.
Entertainment: Square dancing, talent night, sing-alongs, and recreation center. Thursday is gourmet and country swing night for parents, while the kids go on a campout. Tuesday and Thursday feature happy hour with country music.
Summary: Paradise Ranch is one of the very best guest ranches in the business. Traditional dude ranch values with first-rate accommodations. Excellent children's program, fly-fishing, and legendary horseback riding. Lots of family reunions. Ask about kids' and adults' naturalist hiking programs. September is adults-only featuring even more riding program flexibility, as well as Ladies' Week, fly-fishing, horse training, and executive retreats and conferences. Video available.

R Lazy S Ranch
Teton Village, Wyoming

THE DUDE RANCHERS' ASSOCIATION

Wyoming Dude Rancher's Association

Magnificent Teton scenery, a friendly staff, and Western hospitality make the R Lazy S one of America's great guest ranches. At the foot of the majestic Tetons and bordering Grand Teton National Park, the R Lazy S has hosted families from all over the country since 1947. Today it is owned and run by Kelly and Nancy Stirn, and Kelly's parents, Howard and Cara, and is managed by friends and former owners, the McConaughys. While it's close to Jackson and the world-class ski resort at Teton Village, the ranch still maintains its privacy and solitude. Being so close and yet so far gives guests many options for activities and excursions. By the end of one week, you'll only have just begun. It's difficult to enjoy all of the Jackson Hole area's activities during a typical weeklong stay, which is why the ranch enjoys a high repeat clientele. Regardless of how long you stay; you'll enjoy the friendly spirit and the magnificent mountain scenery.

Address: Box 308 K, Teton Village, Wyoming 83025
Telephone: 307/733-2655
Email: info@rlazys.com
Internet: www.rlazys.com
Airport: Jackson, 13 miles
Location: 13 miles northwest of the town of Jackson, one mile north of Teton Village
Memberships: The Dude Ranchers' Association, Wyoming Dude Rancher's Association
Medical: St. John's Hospital, 13 miles
Guest Capacity: 45
Accommodations: 14 beautifully modernized one-, two-, and three-bedroom log cabins, all with electric blankets and fabulous views, scattered around the ranch property among the aspen trees. All have one or two bathrooms, depending on size; some have living or sitting rooms; all have electric heaters, fireplaces, or wood-burning stoves, and lovely hanging baskets with colorful flowers. One teen dorm (boys' or girls') with bathroom sleeps three in bunk beds. The main lodge is a favorite gathering place at day's end. Laundry facilities available.
Rates: • $$$ American Plan. Minimum one-week stay; Sunday to Sunday.
Credit Cards: None. Personal checks accepted.

Season: Mid-June through September; adults-only month of September.
Activities: The ranch has one of the most incredible locations in the world for riding, and the fly-fishing on the Snake River, which borders the ranch, is outstanding. Half-day and all-day rides with picnic lunches. Pack trips and riding instruction available. Extensive fly-fishing program. First-rate guides and fly-fishing shop three miles from the ranch. Fishing in the Snake, South Fork, Green, and North Fork Rivers, and streams, lakes, and stocked ranch pond. Weekly fishing clinic and nature walks. Hiking, swimming in ranch swimming hole, or tubing. Water-skiing or scenic boat rides once a week on Jackson Lake. River rafting, tennis, and golf can be arranged nearby.
Children's Programs: Extensive program for children seven and older. Teens and children have their own wranglers and riding program. Two or more family rides a week. Special counselor supervises nonriding activities. Children and teens eat together in their own connecting, supervised dining room—children and adults love it!
Dining: The superb cuisine is only surpassed by the incredible views of the Tetons out the dining room windows. Ranch hosts Sunday welcome happy hour. Weekly cookouts. BYOB.
Entertainment: Kids' marshmallow roasts, hayrides, and cookouts around the ranch. Jackson Rodeo, volleyball, softball, and horseshoes. Evening Western square dancing and talent night.
Summary: Kilgore's "Best of the Best." One of the greatest old-time dude ranches—incredible Teton setting, riding, fly-fishing, superb cuisine and excellent children's program for kids seven and older. September is adults-only month. Nearby: Town of Jackson, Grand Tetons and Yellowstone National Parks.

Rafter Y Ranch
Banner, Wyoming

Founded in the 1920s and in the family for over 80 years, the Goodwins' Rafter Y Ranch is famous for carrying on the traditions of old-time Western hospitality. Located in the foothills of the Big Horn Mountains, this 1,000-acre, family-run dude and cattle ranch serves up the authentic Old West and the great outdoors. As host and fourth-generation family member, Putter Goodwin, says: "It is wonderful to be able to continue the traditions of this great old ranch. Today, like before, families and family reunions are the heart and soul of the Rafter Y. Here the young and senior family members come to ride in wide-open country, fish the creeks and lakes, enjoy the camaraderie and spirit that prevails, and most of all to relax and enjoy our way of life here in Wyoming." And so it is—the Rafter Y is indeed a very special dude ranch run by a wonderful family. Putter Goodwin, together with his young daughter Annie, and his folks Wally and Nancy, make the Rafter Y one of Kilgore's great old-time ranches in America.

Address: 325 Wagon Box Road, Drawer K, Banner, Wyoming 82832
Telephone: 307/683-2258 (tel./fax)
Airport: Sheridan, Wyoming, 23 miles
Location: 23 miles south of Sheridan off Highway 87; 17 miles north of Buffalo
Memberships: Wyoming Stock Growers' Association
Medical: Sheridan Memorial Hospital, 23 miles
Guest Capacity: 22
Accommodations: Two two-bedroom and two three-bedroom old-fashioned green-roofed log cabins sleep a total of 22. Behind the cabins are huge cottonwood and willow trees and Little Piney Creek. Each has a full bath, living room, fireplace, and screened sleeping porch. Ask about the wonderful tent cabin on Little Piney Creek. Housekeeping each morning and nightly turndown service. Ice is delivered to cabins each afternoon. Laundry facilities.
Rates: • $$$ American Plan; four-day minimum.
Credit Cards: None. Personal and traveler's checks accepted.
Season: Late June through mid-September
Activities: Riding is the main activity every day except Sunday. As the Goodwins say, "Our horses are all colors, sizes, and speeds." Most guests ride each morning and early risers can help wrangle the horses. Afternoons are usually filled with other nonriding activities like playing tennis (excellent tennis court with informal guest/staff matches), swimming in the stream-fed swimming hole, fishing (some fishing gear available and guide service on request), hiking, mountain biking, playing golf nearby, or visiting the local historical sites, helping with ranch chores, reading or napping. Lots of wild game on the ranch property—photographers should bring lots of film.
Children's Programs: Kids of all ages are welcome. Families usually interact together. Children are the responsibility of their parents. Nannies welcome.
Dining: The Goodwins are very proud of their food. As they say, "We have lots of great talent in the kitchen." Buffet-style, one sitting, and second helpings are always available. Weekly barbecues at Lake De Smet are a big hit. Special diets arranged. BYOB.
Entertainment: Informal cocktails and hors d'oeuvres before dinner. Spontaneous softball, volleyball, soccer, and horseshoe games. Local rodeos.
Summary: One of America's best old-time dude ranches. Wonderful small, family-owned and operated dude/cattle ranch offering a flexible schedule and individual attention. High percentage of return families who enjoy the side-by-side riding and open country. Great for families and couples. Nearby: Sunday afternoon Big Horn polo matches held at an equestrian center. Ask for details.

Ranger Creek Guest Ranch
Big Horn Mountains, Wyoming

In the words of a recent guest, "...We stumbled into paradise and you graciously let us stay and share your bit of heaven." Since 1918, Ranger Creek Guest Ranch has been welcoming guests. Located deep within the Bighorn National Forest, the ranch started as a small cabin and tent spike camp. Today, the ranch consists of a historic mountain lodge and guest cabins. Acquired by Bill, Sue, and Brandon Comisford in 1998, the ranch has been restored and renovated to keep its Old West character and charm. Situated high in the Big Horn Mountains at an elevation of 8,300 feet, the ranch offers summer, fall, and winter activities. The ranch encompasses sparkling lakes, Blue Ribbon trout streams, historic sites, and spectacular vistas. Riding out from the ranch in any direction provides for diverse terrain and breathtaking views. Bill and Sue welcome you into their family to share in their dream and provide a place where families can come and enjoy the natural surroundings offered by this remote location.

Address: P.O. Box 47K, Shell, Wyoming 82441
Telephone: 888/817-7787, 307/751-7787 (cell phones are used because of mountain location; be patient)
Email: wildbill@rangercreekranch.net
Internet: www.rangercreekranch.net
Airport: Sheridan and Cody, Wyoming, and Billings, Montana, for commercial flights; Greybull, Wyoming for private jets and small planes.
Location: 35 miles east of Greybull, Wyoming, off U.S. Highway 14; 86 miles east of Cody; three hours south of Billings, Montana
Medical: Midway Clinic, 40 miles; Sheridan Memorial Hospital, 75 miles
Conference Capacity: 20
Guest Capacity: 28
Accommodations: The historic 1930s mountain lodge, built from logs harvested from the surrounding forest, has a special character all its own. The great room, heated by a wood-burning stove, provides a place to relax and enjoy your favorite book. The dining room, with its wall of windows, provides a picturesque view of Granite Mountain and Antelope Butte. Five individual cabins are decorated with antiques and family heirlooms, have private showers, comfortable sleeping arrangements, and covered porches.
Rates: • $$$ American Plan. Three-day minimum stay mid-June through mid-September. Group, children, and off-season rates. Winter snowmobile rates.
Credit Cards: VISA and MasterCard. Personal and traveler's checks accepted.
Season: Year-round
Activities: Summer: Scenic mountain trail riding in the Bighorn National Forest with small groups based upon skill level. Instruction, overnight rides, and pack trips available. While most guests come to ride, other activities include trout fishing in Shell Creek, hiking, horseshoes, shooting, and sight-seeing tours. The week culminates with a guest rodeo including barrel racing and other activities. Winter: snowmobiling, cross-country skiing, or snowshoeing. The ranch is located on the Big Horn Mountain/North-Central Wyoming snowmobile trail system and with over 303 miles of groomed trails the snowmobiling is terrific. Snowmobiles available.
Children's Programs: The ranch loves kids and their spirit, and the Little Pardner's Program is a mix between structured and unstructured activities with the main focus on horseback instruction and riding. Animal studies, cowboy games, leatherwork, hiking, and picnics. Optional kids' dining.
Dining: Home-cooked meals, fresh-baked breads, and Sue's famous pumpkin, cherry, and apple pies are served family-style. Breakfast cooked outdoors at Ranger Creek's Iron Skillet and lunch served along Shell Creek are weekly favorites. Children will sometimes eat with the wranglers to allow parents some time to themselves.
Entertainment: Cody Nite Rodeo. Western dancing, cowboy singers and poetry, Forest Service interpreters, and Buffalo Bill enactment.
Summary: Ranger Creek is a wonderful family-oriented ranch that loves kids, and offers year-round recreation for every member of the family. Featured in *Parents* magazine as a "great family reunion getaway." Surrounded on all four sides by 1.1 million acres of the Bighorn National Forest. Nearby: Shell Falls.

Red Rock Ranch
Kelly, Wyoming

At 7,200 feet, Red Rock Ranch is nestled in a high, secluded valley on the eastern slope of Jackson Hole's spectacular mountain country. Homesteaded in 1890, it is named for the Indian-red cliffs and rock formations you see while driving up from the little one-horse town of Kelly, some 15 miles from the ranch gates. Red Rock Ranch offers some of the best guest ranching in the business. Since 1972 it has been owned by the MacKenzie family. With a first-rate string of horses, wranglers will take you through spectacular country. Fly fishers will enjoy the stocked ranch pond and Crystal Creek, a 2.5 mile, barbless, catch-and-release fly-fishing stream that runs through the ranch. RRR is very private, very beautiful, and one of the authentic best!

Address: P.O. Box 38, Kelly, Wyoming 83011
Telephone: 307/733-6288; fax: 307/733-6287
Email: redrockranch@blissnet.com
Internet: www.theredrockranch.com
Airport: Jackson, 30 miles
Location: 30 miles northeast of Jackson
Memberships: The Dude Ranchers' Association, Wyoming Dude Rancher's Association
Medical: St. John's Hospital, Jackson, 30 miles
Conference Capacity: 30, early June and September
Guest Capacity: 25
Accommodations: Nine authentic log cabins named after Native American tribes, such as Apache, Navajo, Sioux, and Cheyenne. Built in the early 1950s, cabins are one- and two-bedrooms with private baths for each bedroom. All have twin, queen-size, or king-size beds, adjoining living rooms, electric heat, woodstoves, small refrigerators, coffeemakers, and carpeting. They're tastefully decorated in Western style. Each cabin has a small porch with chairs or a bench and an umbrella. A comfortable lodge, dining room and deck (with wonderful views), and adult pool hall/bar are available to guests. Activities room is for square dancing, Western swing, and a children's recreation room. Guest laundry and ranch gift shop.
Rates: • $$$$ American Plan; Sunday to Saturday; includes all activities except river trips and pickup at airport.

Credit Cards: None. Personal checks or cash accepted.
Season: June through September
Activities: Here you can enjoy some of the most beautiful riding in the country. Morning, afternoon, and all-day rides offered. Monday morning orientation rides (mandatory) in the arena acquaint guests with their horse for the week. Ask about the White Canyon and Grizzly Lake rides. Fly-fishing gear available along with optional weekly clinics. Swimming in a heated pool that looks out to the incredible Gros Ventre Mountain Valley, an eight-person hot tub, sauna, hiking, and plenty of relaxing. Scenic river trips can be arranged down the Snake River—a must!
Children's Programs: Children are looked after only during riding and adult dinner hour. Wranglers take kids on day rides. Minimum age for riding is six and older. Children's recreation room with pool table, foosball, board games, and library. Nannies are encouraged for young children.
Dining: Professionally trained chefs serve up a variety of Western ranch cooking. Weekly cookouts for breakfast on Wednesdays, Sunday and Friday evening barbecue; special diets catered with advance notice. Children eat evening meal before adults three nights a week. BYOB.
Entertainment: Hors d'oeuvres and drinks (BYOB) before dinner. Sing-alongs, pickle ball (mini-tennis) court, volleyball, and dancing in the Dance Hall.
Summary: One of Kilgore's best! A fun, family-oriented guest ranch with lots of camaraderie and Old West spirit and charm! Unspoiled wilderness, plenty of horseback riding. Mountain stream fishing. Return guests rarely leave the ranch once they arrive. Laid-back, relaxing atmosphere. *New York Times* fax to read each morning with your breakfast. Ask about fall fly-fishing packages.

Rimrock Ranch
Cody, Wyoming

THE DUDE RANCHERS' ASSOCIATION

Wyoming Dude Rancher's Association

Just 26 miles from Yellowstone National Park's east entrance and at the edge of the Shoshone National Forest, Rimrock Ranch is named after the rock formations that surround the property. Your hosts, Gary and Dede Fales, are continuing the great family tradition of receiving guests that was begun in 1956 by Glenn and Alice Fales. Gary grew up on the ranch and met Dede there back in 1964. This family-owned and operated ranch is located on Canyon Creek, and looks out across Wapiti Valley to the Absaroka Range of the Rocky Mountains. Today, as before, Rimrock offers its guests one of the great dude-ranching experiences. Here families, couples, and singles enjoy excellent trail riding, taking in spectacular vistas in the old-time Western spirit.

Address: 2728 Northfork Route, Dept. K, Cody, Wyoming 82414
Telephone: 800/208-7468, 307/587-3970; fax: 307/527-5014
Email: fun@rimrockranch.com
Internet: www.rimrockranch.com
Airport: Cody or Billings
Location: 26 miles west of Cody
Memberships: The Dude Ranchers' Association, Wyoming Outfitters Association
Medical: Cody Hospital, 26 miles
Guest Capacity: 32
Accommodations: Cabins are located on both sides of Canyon Creek. Comfortable, simple, and homey, each of the nine log cabins (two of which can accommodate 7–10 people) is furnished with Western decor. Some have stone fireplaces. All have private baths with hot and cold running water. Each has a porch; all but one have carpeting. Heated with gas. Laundry facilities on premises.
Rates: • $$–$$$ American Plan. Ask about sliding-scale rates for families. One-week minimum stay; Sunday to Sunday. Pack-trip rates.
Credit Cards: VISA, MasterCard. Personal checks accepted.
Season: Last week in May through September.
Activities: All-day and half-day trail rides. Gary says, "Guests can learn how to ride at three gaits: walk, trot, and canter." Terrain lends itself to spectacular views and an easygoing pace. Some loping

and challenging rides for those riders who can handle it. Ask about the Table Mountain Ride; breakfast ride to Green, Lost, and Holy City Creeks. Guests get their own horse for the week. Experienced wranglers. As many as three separate rides in different directions and at different paces go out at one time. Fishing in the ranch pond and weekly river rafting in the North Fork of the Shoshone River. Tour of Yellowstone National Park. Separate from ranch activities are horse pack trips into Yellowstone Park, Bridger-Teton, and Shoshone National Forests. Heated swimming pool.
Children's Programs: Children and parents participate in activities together. Children's fishing pond. Riding available for kids ages six and older. Very young children not advised.
Dining: Meals are served family-style, buffet, and barbecues. On or off the trail, hearty ranch cooking. Alice's famous prime rib is a specialty. BYOB.
Entertainment: Dede and Gary host an "introduction party" every Sunday evening. Cookouts and singing cowboys. Table tennis, cards, and billiards in the recreation room with lots of memorabilia. Heated swimming pool. Cody Nightly Rodeo.
Summary: Wonderful, family-oriented ranch that has hosted people from around the world since 1956. Excellent trail riding and wilderness pack trips; cabins along the river and a beautiful pool with incredible views. Ask about the famous summer trips and winter snowmobile tours into Yellowstone Park.

Savery Creek Thoroughbred Ranch
Savery, Wyoming

Joyce Saer's Savery Creek Thoroughbred Ranch is best suited for advanced/intermediate English and Western riders who can handle very good horses and are looking for rustic, down-home accommodations, with an eclectic flair. Her ranch borders the family's historic old dude ranch, the Boyer YL Ranch. Savery Creek offers unique and highly personalized riding opportunities for advanced riders. Joyce spent much of her life in Europe, particularly in Spain, and is an outstanding horsewoman. She was the first woman racehorse-trainer in Spanish history and won their *Gran Premio* in 1958. Joyce foxhunts each year in Colorado and Ireland and is a lifetime member of the USCTA. Guests stay in the ranch house. The countryside is beautiful and varied, and the ranch is in one of the last unspoiled, untouristy areas in Wyoming. The name "Wyoming," an Indian word meaning "mountains and valleys alternating," could have originated in the Savery Valley. There are deer, antelope, elk, coyotes, eagles, and other wildlife. Savery Creek Thoroughbred Ranch is for those who crave focused riding opportunities and who savor the West in low-key Western comfort.

Address: Box 24 K, Savery, Wyoming 82332
Telephone: 307/383-7840; call for fax and e-mail
Airport: Hayden, Colorado; paved landing field at Dixon, 11 miles, ranch will pick up guests at Hayden
Location: Nine miles north of Savery; 70 miles south of Rawlins; 40 miles north of Craig; 280 miles from Denver
Medical: Steamboat Hospital, two hours; clinic at Baggs, 20 miles
Guest Capacity: About four
Accommodations: The eclectic ranch house is beside Savery Creek in cottonwood trees and has three guest bedrooms. One overlooks the creek and has a private bath. The other two bedrooms are small, have queen-size beds, and share a bathroom. Most guests don't spend much time in their rooms except, as Joyce says, "to crash" at the end of a busy day. For the adventurous, there are two covered, early-day sheep wagons.
Rates: • $$$ American Plan. Three- to four-day minimum stay; most stay six days, some longer.
Credit Cards: None. Personal and traveler's checks accepted.
Season: Mid-June to October
Activities: This is a riding ranch where each guest has the opportunity to ride several different horses. The horses are exceptional, many of competition and show quality. It's possible to ride in three directions without seeing another person. Good riders may help wrangle and drive cattle out of the pastures. Savery Creek caters to experts and those wishing to improve their skills. Western and English saddles, jumping and dressage lessons available. Cross-country course in the woods and a jumping area across the creek. Fly-fishing on Savery Creek, the Little Snake, or on Hog Park Reservoir. Swimming in Savery Creek and hiking.
Children's Programs: Best for older children who are horse crazy and can ride.
Dining: Ranch specialties include garden vegetables, beef, lamb, and fruit. Dinner is usually served on the banks of Savery Creek under umbrellas, beside a blazing fire. Wine served. Guests usually bring their own spirits for cocktails and conversation before dinner. Picnics, and the Red Desert cookout over an open fire with a 360-degree view of mountains and desert is a real treat.
Entertainment: Cowboys practice team roping once a week at Dixon Arena. Bring your favorite book; most guests are pooped at the end of the day. Evening conversation and bridge; selection of books, music, *Wall Street Journal*, *The New Yorker*, and *Architectural Digest*.
Summary: Fabulous riding on quality horses in beautiful and varied countryside. The ranch is one of the few that provides both Western trail riding and English riding that includes jumping, cross-country, and dressage. Guests can also get up with the birds to wrangle the horses down from the pasture, as well as move neighboring cattle. Spanish and limited French spoken. Nearby: Towns of Saratoga and Steamboat Springs offer day trips, as does the Red Desert with its fossils, interesting formations, antelope and "real" wild horses.

Seven D Ranch
Cody, Wyoming

THE DUDE RANCHERS' ASSOCIATION

Wyoming Dude Rancher's Association

One of the old-time greats, the Seven D Ranch is a cozy haven in the midst of a magnificent wilderness. Bought in the late 1950s by Dewey and Lee Dominick, a surgeon and his wife, the family tradition continues today under their grandson Mead Dominick and longtime family friend, Ryan Selk. The ranch is in the remote and beautiful Sunlight Basin, deep within the Shoshone National Forest. Surrounded by the Absaroka Mountains, it has vast pastures where the horses are turned out each night to graze and where you'll find a small herd of registered Black Angus cattle. The Seven D appeals to all ages. For those who wish to relax, the ranch offers the peace of a mountain hideaway. The more-energetic may want to take a leisurely morning or afternoon ride, cast for trout, or hike into the Absaroka Wilderness. And folks with even more get-up-and-go may enjoy a full day of riding or fishing, or a wilderness pack trip into Yellowstone Park. Most of all, there's a wonderful atmosphere of history, camaraderie, laughter, and energetic participation. If you've ever wondered where Marlboro Country is, many of the ad photographs were taken right here at the Seven D.

Address: P.O. Box 100, Cody, Wyoming 82414
Telephone: 307/587-9885 (tel./fax)
Email: ranch7d@wyoming.com
Internet: www.7dranch.com
Airport: Cody or Billings
Location: 115 miles southwest of Billings, Montana; 50 miles northwest of Cody, Wyoming, via Chief Joseph Scenic Highway (Highway 296) and Sunlight Basin Road
Memberships: The Dude Ranchers' Association, Wyoming Dude Rancher's Association
Medical: Cody Hospital, 50 miles
Conference Capacity: 32
Guest Capacity: 32
Accommodations: A clear mountain-spring creek winds near 11 rustic log cabins that are nestled in a beautiful aspen grove and have names like Trapper, Aspen, Big Buffalo, Waldorf, and The Fireplace. Cabins vary from one to four bedrooms each, with private baths, woodstoves, and fresh wildflowers. Guests enjoy using the woodstoves during delightfully cool summer evenings.

Daily maid service. Laundry facilities available.
Rates: • $$$ American Plan; includes gratuities. Children's and off-season rates. Minimum one-week stay, Sunday to Sunday. Pack-trip rates available.
Credit Cards: VISA, MasterCard. Personal and traveler's checks accepted.
Season: Mid-June through mid-September
Activities: Rides every day except Sunday. Your choice of scenic, half-day, or all-day rides. Experienced wranglers accompany riders on beautiful and varied trails. Five to eight riders go out per ride. Ask about Big Skyline, Memorial, and the "Holy Cow" rides with views into Montana. Instruction available and encouraged. The Seven D's "world famous" 2–10 day horse pack trips into the North Absaroka Wilderness and Yellowstone Park for groups of six or less. This has been the trip of a lifetime for many. Superb fishing on and off the property. Seven D hosts a full-time fly-fishing guide and owns a private mile-long stretch of the Sunlight River. Limited fishing gear available. Many fishing opportunities for the young and the young-at-heart. Mountain biking, hiking, mountaineering, and wildflower walks, soccer, and softball. Float trips and rodeos available in Cody.
Children's Programs: Counselors for children ages 6–12 during adult daytime activities. Kids are entertained with horseback rides, arts and crafts, organized games, and hiking to the Indian caves. Pony rides for children under age five.
Dining: Excellent food! Beautiful old ranch dining room, weekly brunch rides and barbecue. Ask about Uncle Marshall's famous barbecued Chilean lamb—wow! Ranch-raised beef. Special diets catered to with advance notice. BYOB.
Entertainment: Books in the marvelous old main lodge. Recreation hall with piano, table tennis, billiards, square dancing with live caller. Gymkhanas, horseshoes. Marvelous naturalist talks.
Summary: The Seven D is one of Kilgore's old-time greats! The Dominick family members exude warmth and plenty of Western hospitality. Lots of family reunions. Excellent wilderness pack trips. Adults-only weeks in September.

T-Cross Ranch
Dubois, Wyoming

THE DUDE RANCHERS' ASSOCIATION

Wyoming Dude Rancher's Association

This is one of Kilgore's greatest dude ranches in America. When you pass through the gates of the T-Cross Ranch, the outside world is all but forgotten. This old-time authentic dude ranch has been in business since the 1920s. Today, as in years gone by, the spirit, informality, and relaxed Western atmosphere offer guests an experience of a lifetime. Located 15 miles north of the small Western town of Dubois, the ranch is situated in a private valley surrounded by the Shoshone National Forest. The ranch is owned and managed by Ken and Garey Neal. Ken has worked ranches and horses since he can remember. To his guests and friends he is the real "smoke-free" Marlboro Man! He and I go way back; in fact, we began our guest-ranching careers at the same ranch. The remote T-Cross Ranch in every way captures old-time guest ranching at its best.

Address: P.O. Box 638 K, Dubois, Wyoming 82513
Telephone: 307/455-2206; fax: 307/455-2720
Email: tcrossranch@wyoming.com
Internet: www.ranchweb.com/tcross
Airport: Jackson or Riverton. Surfaced airstrip three miles west of Dubois for private jets and planes. Free pickup from Dubois.
Location: 15 miles north of Dubois off Highway 26/287, 85 miles east of Jackson Airport
Memberships: The Dude Ranchers' Association, Wyoming Dude Rancher's Association, Dubois Outfitters Association, Wyoming Outfitters and Professional Guides Association, Nature Conservancy,
Medical: Dubois Clinic, 15 miles; Riverton Hospital and Jackson Hospital
Conference Capacity: 24 (June and September)
Guest Capacity: 24
Accommodations: Eight wonderful, cozy log cabins tucked in the pines truly capture the old spirit of the West, with Indian rugs, incredible handcrafted log furniture, down quilts, woodstoves or fireplaces, hot showers, and individual porches. The main lodge is filled with Western memorabilia and charm. Laundry facilities available.
Rates: • $$$ American Plan. Off-season, group, and nanny rates available. Sunday-to-Sunday

arrival in July and August. Four-night minimum June, September, and October.
Credit Cards: None. Personal and traveler's checks accepted.
Season: Early June to late October
Activities: The main activities are riding, hiking, fly-fishing, and relaxing. Guests are assigned a horse for the duration of their stay. Morning and afternoon rides go out daily except Sunday. All-day rides go out at least twice a week with a pack mule carrying lunch and fishing gear. Ask about rides to Five Pockets, Ramshorn Basin, Deacon Lake, and Twilight Falls. Depending on ability, guests take walking, trotting, and loping rides, or Ken's rugged ride. Fly fishers enjoy Horse Creek, which runs through the ranch. Another favorite is the Wiggins Fork of the Wind River. There are also high-mountain lakes, climbing opportunities, bird-watching, wildflowers, relaxing on the porch, or soaking in the hot tub at the end of the day. Artists should bring their art supplies along.
Children's Programs: Unstructured program. Children ages six and older ride, hike, and tube-float the river with a youth wrangler. They enjoy games, crafts, and treasure hunts. Ask about overnight tepee campouts. Friday morning gymkhanas. Nannies are encouraged for younger children.
Dining: Ranch cooking. Cook will prepare your freshly caught fish. Breakfast, lunch, and dinner cookouts. Happy hour each evening in the lodge. BYOB.
Entertainment: Weekly Western singing by local groups, square dancing in Dubois, campfires, volleyball, and horseshoes.
Summary: Kilgore's "Best of the Best"–Old-Time Authentic Guest Ranch. Here the spirit is rich in tradition and hearty in hospitality. Superb scenic horseback riding, fly-fishing, hiking, and relaxing. Perfect for family reunions. Adults-only September and October. You may bring your own horse. Featured in *National Geographic Traveler* magazine, *New York Times*, *Boston Globe*, *London Financial Times*, and *Town & Country*.

TA Guest Ranch
Buffalo, Wyoming

Wyoming
Dude
Rancher's
Association

The TA Guest Ranch is indeed a star and captures the true historic spirit of the West. Earl and Barbara Madsen realized a lifelong goal when they purchased the historic TA Ranch in 1991. After six years of exciting renovation this 1880s ranch was opened to discriminating travelers from around the world and features exquisitely restored buildings with period antiques plus all the amenities of the new century. The ranch has been featured in Bob Vila's *Restore America*, and has been written about in *Sunset* and *American Cowboy* magazines, to name just a couple. Earl and Barbara, together with their daughter Kirsten and son-in-law Rick, offer a glimpse of history and heart-warming experiences of hospitality, cuisine (great beef), and cattle ranch activities. Guests enjoy being able to ride side-by-side across the thousands of acres of open range, creek bottoms, and rolling hills of the Old West. The vistas in this part of the country are spectacular and immense. When temperatures warm up during midsummer, guests enjoy relaxing after lunch with an iced tea out on the veranda in the marvelous cottonwood groves.

Address: P.O. Box 313K, Buffalo, Wyoming 82834
Telephone: 800/368-7398, 307/684-5833; fax: 307/684-5833
Email: taranch@trib.com
Internet: www.taranch.com
Airport: Sheridan, 45 miles; Casper, 100 miles
Location: 13 miles south of Buffalo on Wyoming 196 (old Highway 87), 180 miles south of Billings, Montana
Memberships: National Cattleman's Association, Wyoming Dude Rancher's Association
Awards: National Historic Register, State of Wyoming Historic Preservation
Medical: Buffalo Medical Center, 13 miles
Conference Capacity: 32 to 75 (day)
Guest Capacity: 15; 32 for family reunions
Accommodations: Five historic beautifully renovated buildings set in a cottonwood grove on Crazy Woman Creek. The old ranch house and cookhouse are furnished with Victorian antiques, providing an elegant yet comfortable setting. The bunkhouse is cozy with hardwood floors and a

complete kitchen. The ranch house offers spacious lounging on a 65-by-12-foot covered porch in the shade of the cottonwoods. There's also a living room with wet bar and a study. Ask about The Granary, the luxury 6,000-square-foot, three-bedroom home with conference amenities.
Rates: • $$$ American Plan. Children's rates for age 15 and under. Kids age four and under free. Three-day minimum stay.
Credit Cards: VISA, MasterCard, American Express
Season: May through mid-October
Activities: The TA Guest Ranch features a riding program tailored to the skills and experience of its guests. Riding instruction is provided by the TA wranglers in a round pen, arena, and open range. Rides go out twice per day, weather permitting. Experts can ride on their own after evaluation by the TA staff. All guests are invited to participate in ranch work activities such as herding cattle, cutting pairs, and feeding. Guests can also enjoy gymkhanas in the arena, sometimes pitting the adults against the kids. Fishing is wonderful, both in the reservoir where trophy-size rainbow and brown trout can be caught and in Crazy Woman Creek. There are roping dummies and instruction, horseshoes, volleyball, reading, hiking, as well as local rodeos and other events.
Children's Programs: Children are welcome but are the complete responsibility of their parents. Minimum riding age is six.
Dining: Family-style meals feature Western menus including natural TA lean beef, homegrown trout, wild game, and some Basque cuisine. Ranch can cater to food preferences. Complimentary wine and beer served. BYOL.
Entertainment: Volleyball, horseshoes, backgammon, and cribbage. Western movie night, local living-history programs, wildlife- and bird-watching. Local rodeos.
Summary: One of Wyoming's most beautiful, historic guest and conference ranches! Authentically restored and on the National Historic Register. Incredible Western views, natural beef, and 8,000 acres of excellent riding.

Trail Creek Ranch
Wilson, Wyoming

THE DUDE RANCHERS'
ASSOCIATION

Trail Creek Ranch is very special to me—it's the ranch where my parents took me as a young child. It's here that a seed was planted, which blossomed into my love for this incredible way of life. I'm proud to say that Trail Creek Ranch is largely responsible for this guidebook. Back in the 1940s, a young Olympic skier named Elizabeth Woolsey bought a rundown ranch at the foot of Teton Pass, 10 miles from Jackson. With her tenacity and tremendous spirit, Betty transformed the ranch into one of the prettiest family-oriented ranches in the country, offering sincere Western hospitality. To the east there are lush, green hay meadows; the rest is timbered with many bridle trails and Trail Creek, which runs through the ranch. Trail Creek Ranch is a working ranch, raising hay that supports a fine string of horses. The main ranch activities are riding, swimming, and hiking, and because of the ranch's tremendous location, there is a myriad of activities that guests can choose from and enjoy. Betty touched many lives over the years. In 1997 Betty passed on and left the ranch to her longtime friend and colleague Muggs Schultz (who has worked at Trail Creek since the 1950s) and the Jackson Hole Land Trust. Today Muggs, Alex, and their staff continue to greet guests and make new friends.

Address: P.O. Box 10 K, Wilson, Wyoming 83014
Telephone: 307/733-2610 (tel./fax)
Email: TCRwilsonwy@aol.com
Airport: Jackson via Salt Lake City or Denver
Location: Two miles west of Wilson, 10 miles west of Jackson
Memberships: The Dude Ranchers' Association
Medical: St. John's Hospital, Jackson
Guest Capacity: 20 (summer); 12 (winter)
Accommodations: The Main Lodge, with the living room, library, dining rooms, and sun deck, is the heartbeat of Trail Creek. Two family cabins and multibedroom cabins with private baths comfortably house the guests. Cabins overlook the hay meadows and beyond to the Sleeping Indian, a beautiful mountain in the Gros Ventre Range.
Rates: • $$$ American Plan. Some guests stay 10 days to two weeks. Five-day minimum stay,

arrival any day. Winter rates available.
Credit Cards: None. Personal checks accepted.
Season: Summer: Mid-June to early-September; Winter: February to mid-March.
Activities: In summer, riding, swimming in the solar-heated pool, and hiking are the main activities. All rides go out in groups of 5–6 twice a day; also all-day luncheon rides to Grand Teton Park (more experienced riders). White-water rafting or scenic float trips (one of the most beautiful in America) with local outfitters. Fishing in the Snake River, nearby lakes, and ranch pond. In winter, guests enjoy cross-country skiing on the ranch and nearby downhill skiing, both in the backcountry and at Jackson Hole and Grand Targhee Ski Resorts.
Children's Programs: No formal program, but kids have the time of their lives. Kids six and older may ride together if they wish. Parents with young children are encouraged to bring their own baby-sitter or nanny.
Dining: The ranch garden supplies some of the lettuce, asparagus, and herbs for family meals of roast beef, pork chops, baked ham, roasted chicken, pasta dishes, fish, soups, and salads. BYOB. Informal cocktail hour with hors d'oeuvres daily.
Entertainment: No formal evening program. Many go to the Stagecoach Bar in Wilson for country-Western dancing or into Jackson. Jackson rodeo twice a week.
Summary: One of the all-time great small guest ranches with a lovely setting near world-famous Jackson, Wyoming. Tremendous variety of off-ranch activities. Great base camp for all kinds of outdoor enthusiasts. Be sure to buy a copy of Betty's, *Off the Beaten Track*. Nearby: The Tetons and Yellowstone National Parks, Jackson, National Elk Refuge.

Triangle C Ranch
Dubois, Wyoming

Wyoming
Dude
Rancher's
Association

The Garnicks are one of the most colorful dude ranch families in the Jackson Hole area. Over the past 30 years the family has been involved in dude ranching and entertainment. Son Cameron, who has a wonderful family himself with eight children, has 17 movies to his credit and owns the Jackson Hole Playhouse—a must to visit while you are in Jackson. If you've ever wondered what the real Marlboro Man looks like—wait until you meet him. In 1994, the Garnicks bought the Triangle C Ranch, which is located just over Togwotee Pass. The ranch has a colorful past and was nominated for the National Register of Historic Places. What attracted Cameron and his great old folks, Billie and Bill, to this ranch was a combination of big views, old-time charm, a riverside setting, and proximity to Jackson Hole and Dubois, two of Wyoming's most famous Western towns. Like the other ranches they have owned or managed before, the Garnicks have infused their magical Western spirit into the Triangle C. The Garnicks know what Western hospitality is all about and, coupled with their knowledge and love of people and children, make the Triangle C experience one of the best!

Address: 3737 Highway 26, Drawer K, Dubois, Wyoming 82513
Telephone: 800/661-4928, 307/455-2225; fax: 307/455-2031
Email: info@trianglec.com
Internet: www.trianglec.com
Airport: Jackson
Location: 50 minutes northeast of Jackson off Highway 26
Memberships: The Dude Ranchers' Association; Wyoming Dude Rancher's Association
Medical: Hospital in Jackson
Conference Capacity: 75
Guest Capacity: 60
Accommodations: The main lodge is perched on a bluff overlooking the Wind River and out across to the Absaroka Mountains. The former rustic, green-roofed, "tiehack" log cabins were built back in the 1920s; they still stand today and radiate that Old West charm. Each has its own bath with hot and cold running water. The three two-story Pinnacle Cabins, built in 1997, bring a new defi-

nition of luxury to the ranch.
Rates: • $$$$ American Plan; May to September. Six-night package (Monday through Sunday) includes a last night in Jackson with rodeo and dinner at the famous Saddle Rock Saloon. Three-night minimum, fall to spring. Children's, group, and off-season rates available.
Credit Cards: VISA, MasterCard. Personal checks preferred.
Season: Summer: May through mid-September. Winter: Mid-December through March.
Activities: As Billie says, "Do as much or as little as you like." Weekly programs with riding, hiking, and fishing. For the brave, join the Polar Bear Club and swim in the Wind River. Ask about the Pelham Lake and Shoshone Wilderness rides, Cameron's famous six-day John Coulter ride with pack mules, the sunset rides, and the "cowboy up" program. Don't miss the scenic float trip on the Snake River or a trip to Yellowstone.
Children's Programs: The Garnicks have one of the most famous children's programs in the country for ages 1–5, 6–12, and 13–19. Your youngsters are always in good company with Cameron's eight ranch-raised kids. Wonderfully fun naturalist program with awards. Kids love learning about wildlife, setting animal traps, and learning about horse care. Ask about the tepee village overnighter.
Dining: Hearty ranch fare with special diets catered to. Ranch-baked bread, prime rib, barbecued ribs, and trout almondine. The weekly steak and chicken barbecue cookout ride is a favorite, as are the breakfast rides. Tiehack Saloon happy hours.
Entertainment: Get-acquainted campfire on Monday nights. Weekly ranch rodeo and gymkhana. Jackson Hole rodeo and Cameron's theater night in Jackson. Family square dancing in Dubois.
Summary: A Kilgore's "Best of the Best" –Children's Programs. One of the greatest dude ranching families. Wonderful children's program. Old-time ranch with a great Western spirit; 85 years of storytelling and rich Western hospitality. Ask about the winter programs into Yellowstone National Park.

Triangle X Ranch
Moose, Wyoming

THE DUDE RANCHERS'
ASSOCIATION

Wyoming
Dude
Rancher's
Association

One of the greats! The Turners' Triangle X has just about everything one could ask for in old-time dude ranching, including a million-dollar view. Located in Grand Teton National Park, just outside Moose, in the world-famous Jackson Hole Valley, Triangle X has panoramic views of the awesome Teton Range and Snake River Valley. The ranch was established in 1926 by John Turner, Sr. as a cattle-and-hunting ranch. The Turner family runs a first-rate operation. Their repeat business (some guests have been returning for over 50 years) proves it. Among the ranch's unique features are its year-round summer and winter programs, its superb location, exciting wilderness pack trips, river-rafting programs, and its well-supervised Little Wrangler riding program for kids ages 5–12. The Triangle X is a wonderful family experience.

Address: 2 Triangle X Ranch Road, Moose, Wyoming 83012
Telephone: 307/733-2183; fax: 307/733-8685
Email: trianglexranch@wyoming.com
Internet: www.trianglex.com
Airport: Jackson Hole Airport, 16 miles
Location: 25 miles north of Jackson
Memberships: The Dude Ranchers' Association, Wyoming Outfitters Association, Wyoming Dude Rancher's Association, America Outdoors
Medical: St. John's Hospital in Jackson, 25 miles
Conference Capacity: 50; off-season only
Guest Capacity: 75
Accommodations: One-, two-, or three-bedroom log cabins with private baths, warm wool blankets, and covered porches. Cabins are very clean (with polished wood floors), comfortable, and ranch-cozy. Laundry facilities available. Small ranch gift shop with hats, shirts, nature books, and river-rafting reception area.
Rates: • $$$ American Plan. One-week minimum stay, Sunday to Sunday. Off-season, pack-trip, and winter rates available.
Credit Cards: None. Personal or traveler's checks.
Season: Summer: May to November; Winter: Mid-December to April.
Activities: Summer: Triangle X is predominantly a riding ranch. Riders enjoy a variety of trails to the tops of timbered mountains, through wildflower meadows, over sagebrush, and along the Snake River, always with the magnificent Teton Mountain Range as a backdrop. Breakfast rides and weekly Dutch-oven suppers. Scenic, medium, and faster trail rides. Weekly nature ride by Forest Service personnel. Ask about the famous Triangle X scenic Snake River rafting program. Trout fishing on the famous Snake River or in Yellowstone National Park for either the expert or the beginner who wants to learn. In-house fishing guides who are well versed on fly- or spin fishing. Triangle X offers the ultimate wilderness experience in the form of four-day to two-week pack trips into the Teton Wilderness and southern Yellowstone areas. Winter: Snowmobiling along the Continental Divide snowmobile trail and cross-country skiing in Grand Teton National Park adjacent to the ranch (where snowmobiling is not allowed).
Children's Programs: Children ages 5–12 have their own kiddie wrangler who supervises riding lessons, rafting, and museum trips. Children under age five don't ride. Kids are their parents' responsibility when not riding. Parents may ride with kids.
Dining: Meals are hearty and delicious, served family-style in a wonderful dining room with commanding views overlooking the Tetons. Sunday, ranch cookout; Wednesday, evening cookout ride; Friday, morning breakfast ride. Children dine separately at all meals except cookouts. Parents can eat with kids, but kids can't eat with parents. BYOB.
Entertainment: Monday evening social and square dancing. Campfires with old-fashioned sing-alongs, Western guitar music, rodeos in Jackson, weekly slide shows of local history. Forest Service nature talks.
Summary: Triangle X and the Turner family are one of Kilgore's old-time greats in the dude-ranch business. Besides its location, million-dollar views of the Tetons, and Old West dude ranch atmosphere, Triangle X is known for its riding, river rafting, and superb four-day to two-week pack trips and an exciting winter snowmobiling and cross-country program. Located in Grand Teton National Park, 32 miles from Yellowstone National Park.

UXU Ranch
Cody, Wyoming

THE DUDE RANCHERS' ASSOCIATION

Wyoming Dude Rancher's Association

Featured in *Architectural Digest*. The UXU Ranch captures the spirit of the Old West. It has an interesting history and a wonderful river that rushes by. In 1996, the ranch began a new tradition of guest ranching. Owner and host Hamilton Bryan grew up in the San Francisco Bay area. A huge part of his childhood was spent on his family's cattle ranch. Ham (as his friends call him) has traveled the world for business and pleasure and always had ranching in his heart. In 1995 he began his search for a ranch to call his own. He had three requirements: a river, proximity to a beautiful national park, and Old West charm. The UXU has all three and more! When Ham drove across the ranch bridge, he knew this was it. Today, guests come to enjoy good company, breathtaking views, delicious gourmet food, the Shoshone River, and a wide variety of outdoor activities. Just 17 miles from Yellowstone National Park.

Address: 1710 Yellowstone Highway, Wapiti, Wyoming 82450
Telephone: 800/373-9027, 307/587-2143; fax: 307/587-8307 (summer); call for winter fax
Email: uxuranch@myavista.com
Internet: www.uxuranch.com
Airport: Cody, 35 miles (served by Delta and United)
Location: 35 miles west of Cody, 17 miles east of Yellowstone National Park
Memberships: The Dude Ranchers' Association, Wyoming Dude Rancher's Association
Awards: *Mountain Living* magazine, one of five "Best Dude Ranches" for 2000 and 2001
Medical: Cody Hospital, 35 miles
Guest Capacity: 30
Accommodations: 11 one- and two-bedroom log cabins with remodeled private baths, down comforters and pillows, some with fireplaces or gas stoves, all with a sitting porch. All cabins are carpeted and include bathrobes and bathroom amenities. Ask about the Hollister and Hideout cabins overlooking the river. Hot tub by the lodge provides views of the Absaroka Mountains. Laundry available.
Rates: • $$$ American Plan. Six-night minimum stay is Sunday to Saturday. Children's and nanny

rates available. Shorter stays possible in off-season.
Credit Cards: VISA, MasterCard. Personal checks accepted.
Season: June through September
Activities: Guests come to horseback ride, flyfish, hike, white-water raft, and visit Yellowstone National Park. Favorite rides include June Ridge, Clayton Mountain, and Elks Fork all-day ride and barbecue. Mountain bikes available. Golfing and sporting clays in Cody, 35 miles away. Be sure to ask Ham about New West and the top Western furniture builder in Cody.
Children's Programs: Children six and older may trail ride and have some organized activities. The ranch creek provides hours of fun! Archery and riflery. Nannies are encouraged for younger children.
Dining: Having traveled the world, Ham appreciates fine food. Cuisine includes fine beef, excellent fish, some game, and vegetarian dishes. Over 40 California wines are featured. Children usually eat dinner together prior to adults. Special diets can be accommodated with prior notice.
Entertainment: Cocktails and hors d'oeuvres on Sunday night. Cookouts, weekly local entertainment. Cody rodeo barbecue features Ham's famous butterflied leg of lamb. Fully stocked honor bar and cigars at the main lodge. Piano and billiards.
Summary: Kilgore's "Best of the Best"–Superb Cuisine. A fabulous ranch for those who enjoy some of the finer things in life and yet are comfortable in the rugged West. Well-traveled host oversees delicious food, fine wine, and Old West charm. The UXU captures the spirit of the West and serves up a variety of outdoor adventures in a riverside setting near Yellowstone National Park. A great place for families, couples, singles, and family reunions. Featured in *Architectural Digest*, December 2000. Nearby: Yellowstone National Park and historic Western town of Cody.

Vee Bar Guest Ranch
Laramie, Wyoming

Wyoming
Dude
Rancher's
Association

Listed on the National Register of Historic Places, the Vee Bar Guest Ranch is located in the Centennial Valley. The nearby 12,000-foot Snowy Range Mountains, part of the magnificent Medicine Bow National Forest, are Wyoming's answer to the Tetons, only without the crowds. A showplace of Western charm, this old cattle ranch was once a stopover for stagecoaches traveling west on the Overland Trail. Since 1912, the ranch has had a colorful history taking in guests and running cattle and buffalo. What makes the Vee Bar special, over and above the hospitality, is the varied riding program and the Little Laramie River that traverses the ranch's 800 acres. Guests may ride in the wide-open meadows surrounding the ranch or explore the owners' other beautiful 5,000-acre cattle ranch just up the valley, bordering the national forest. The Cole family serves up one of the greatest guest-ranch experiences in the country!

Address: 2091 State Highway 130, Laramie, Wyoming 82070
Telephone: 800/483-3227, 307/745-7036; fax: 307/745-7433
Email: veebar@lariat.org
Internet: www.vee-bar.com
Airport: Laramie. Courtesy shuttle available.
Location: 20 miles west of Laramie off Highway 130
Memberships: National Register of Historic Places, The Dude Ranchers' Association, Wyoming Stock Growers' Association, Wyoming Dude Rancher's Association
Medical: Ivinson Memorial Hospital, Laramie
Conference Capacity: 30
Guest Capacity: 30
Accommodations: The lodge and cabins reflect quality and charm that characterize the Vee Bar. Guests appreciate the magnificent two- or three-bedroom cabins and duplex suites along the Little Laramie River. All have sitting areas with gas fireplaces, refrigerators, and amenities such as coffee, tea, and hot chocolate. Most of the cabins have the added convenience of built-in washers (soap provided) and dryers. Cabins have river and mountain views and all are within walking distance of the lodge. Daily housekeeping service.

Rates: • $$$–$$$$ Summer: American Plan; three-day minimum stay. Winter: Bed-and-breakfast rates. Corporate and group rates.
Credit Cards: VISA, MasterCard, Discover, American Express. Personal and traveler's check accepted.
Season: Year-round. Guest ranch early June through early September. Bed-and-breakfast, conferences, and special groups remainder of the year.
Activities: Scheduled activities program with flexibility. Varied riding and terrain for all levels and ages include wide-open meadow and mountain riding. Weekly team penning and Deerwood Ranch overnight campout. Summer cattle drives. Fishing on the Little Laramie, guided hiking into the Snowies, and river tubing for the brave. Trapshooting. Winter: Nearby cross-country and Alpine skiing and snowmobiling.
Children's Programs: No special programs. Children age six and older take part in all ranch activities. Wonderful Western environment for parents and children.
Dining: Vee Bar welcome roundup on Sunday evenings. Buffet-style dining with a gourmet touch. The ranch chef will accommodate special diets with advance notice. Wine, beer, and liquor available.
Entertainment: Live music and lots of dancing fun! Team-drawn hay-wagon rides. Old West Saloon with honor bar, pool table, and jukebox. Friday gymkhana and Awards Night.
Summary: Kilgore's "Best of the Best"–Historic Western ranch. Jim and Carla Cole are two of the very best! Wonderful service, fantastic spirit, great hospitality, and excellent wide-open riding. Tremendous environment for families, couples, singles, and corporate groups. Private fishing on the Little Laramie River. Cattle drives and overnight campouts on owners' nearby 5,000-acre cattle ranch. Adults-only weeks. Video available.

Guest and Resort Ranches
in Canada

Homeplace Guest Ranch
Priddis, Alberta, Canada

THE DUDE RANCHERS'
ASSOCIATION

The Homeplace Guest Ranch is a small, year-round, very personable ranch that is all about the horse. Located in the Canadian Rocky Mountain foothills, 30 miles southwest of Calgary, the ranch is bordered by several beautiful ranches and Kananaskis Park. Mac Makenny, his wife, Jayne, and their daughter, Jessi, offer guests a way of life for which southern Alberta is known. As Mac says, "We really enjoy folks who appreciate and respect horses and want a hands-on experience!" Guests come to share the traditions, heritage, recreation, natural beauty, and spirit of the horse. At Homeplace the staff-to-guest ratio is high, as is the horse-to-guest ratio with 50 head for 14 guests. The Makenny family welcomes you to their home and makes every effort to see that you leave with a wholesome appreciation of the outdoors and the world of horses. If you are from another country, Mac will raise your flag to welcome you.

Address: Site 2, Box 6, RR1, Dept. K, Priddis, Alberta, Canada T0L 1W0
Telephone: 877/931-3245, 403/931-3245; fax: 403/931-3245
Email: homeplace.ranch@cadvision.com
Internet: www.homeplaceranch.com
Airport: Calgary
Location: 30 miles west of Calgary off Route 22, 50 miles east of Banff off Route 22
Memberships: The Dude Ranchers' Association, Alberta Outfitters Association, Travel Alberta, Calgary Convention and Visitors Bureau
Medical: Foothills Hospital in Calgary, 30 miles
Conference Capacity: 12
Guest Capacity: 14
Accommodations: Guests are comfortable staying in the lodge's eight small private rooms. All rooms are finished in cedar. Guest bedrooms are on both levels of the two-story lodge. All have private baths, some with twin futon beds, others with four-posters. Decks off main lodge. A hot tub is outside on the back lower deck of the lodge. There's also a one-bedroom, 1912 log cabin about 200 yards away, with shower and bath in main lodge. This is a great place for couples and honeymooners.
Rates: • $$–$$$ American Plan; including service

charges. Rates vary depending on the season. Ask about the three-, four-, and seven-day packages, and particularly the Rocky Mountain Ranch Rodeo Holiday and the Calgary Stampede package.
Credit Cards: VISA. Personal checks preferred.
Season: Year-round; open all holidays.
Activities: Very hands-on horse/guest program. Guests may groom their horses. Excellent horses ranging from gentle to spirited polo ponies for really advanced riders. Wonderful all-day and half-day rides. Ask about the Hog-Back, Kananaskis, and Fish Creek Run rides. Sister ranch Homeplace Cow Camp offers magnificent pack trips. Weekly, Mac takes guests down to the neighboring Harvey Ranch to check on their cattle—some cattle-moving. Riding instruction available (many come from Calgary for daily instruction in the off-season), fishing, and hiking. Golf and tennis nearby. Winter: Cross-country skiing and sleigh rides.
Children's Programs: No planned program. Children over age seven ride. Mac usually takes the kids aside and asks them about their riding desires, and he sure does hear some exciting stuff. As Mac says, "Kids tell it like it is!" Daughter Jessi welcomes all kids.
Dining: There is lots of homemade everything here, from applesauce muffins to fresh blackberry pie and big beef barbecues. Vegetarian meals prepared on request. Beer is always in the refrigerator. BYOL.
Entertainment: Nothing formal is planned. Occasional hay-wagon rides, dances, and exhibition polo in Calgary.
Summary: Kilgore's "Best of the Best"– Horsemanship. As Mac says, "Most of our guests come here because they want to live and breathe horses and learn all about them." Ask Mac about Spruce Meadows, the Bar U Historic Ride, and the cow camp. Branding weekends end of May, Calgary Stampede early July. Polo three times a week, June to September. Rodeos throughout the summer. Nearby: Calgary.

Echo Valley Guest Ranch
Clinton, British Columbia, Canada

SUPER, NATURAL
BRITISH COLUMBIA®

Echo Valley Guest Ranch combines the wonders of the Canadian west and wilderness with the soothing and relaxing comforts of a full spa and healthy lifestyle experience. In 1995 Echo Valley began a tradition of adventure and personal service that combines both the wonders of a full guest- and adventure-ranch experience, with a world-class spa facility that offers soothing, nurturing treatments that are beneficial to body and soul. Located in a pristine area of British Columbia's Cariboo Region, the ranch is surrounded by four distinct geographic regions—mountains, deep river gorges, plateaus, and grassland. As one French guest wrote, "The landscapes are breathtaking, the international staff is so very friendly, the activities are so diverse, and there is a warm friendly atmosphere. We left enriched, rested, and with a new perspective on life." Echo Valley Guest Ranch offers a new wholesome frontier in the world of guest ranching.

Address: Echo Valley Ranch, P.O. Box 16 K, Clinton, British Columbia, Canada V0K 1K0
Telephone: 800/253-8831 (reservations), 250/459-2386 (ranch); fax: 250/459-0086
Email: evranch@uniserve.com
Internet: www.evranch.com
Airport: Private 3,612-foot paved airstrip at ranch, or Kamloops and Vancouver International for scheduled flights
Location: 270 miles north of Vancouver, 30 miles from Clinton, 100 miles from Kamloops
Memberships: British Columbia Guest Ranchers' Association, Cariboo Tourism Association, Virtuoso, ISPA
Medical: Ashcroft Hospital in Ashcroft
Conference Capacity: Up to 40; 3,000 square feet; audiovisual equipment available, satellite DSL
Guest Capacity: 26, groups up to 40
Accommodations: The Dove Lodge is of log construction with six guest bedrooms, all with private baths and spectacular views. Elegant family-style dining and sitting areas, games room, sauna, and outdoor hot tub. The Lookout Lodge has nine large bedrooms, each with private baths and spectacular views. Two cabins each have private bed-

room, bathroom, sitting area with fireplace, loft, and private deck. One log cabin with four-poster bed, fireplace, and exquisitely furnished sitting area, and private deck with its own outdoor hot tub. Be sure to ask about the Baan Thai House.
Rates: • $$–$$$ American Plan. Ask about Ranch Spa & Lifestyle Programs and "Book the Ranch" programs.
Credit Cards: VISA, MasterCard. Personal and traveler's checks accepted.
Season: April to October; December 23 to late February.
Activities: The ranch offers a great selection of activities including horseback riding, hiking, white-water rafting, overnight stays in tepees at the High Bar Indian Reserve, gold panning, bird-watching with resident naturalist featuring falcon-training, and fly-fishing with instruction available. Occasional cattle moving. Winter: Cross-country skiing, snowshoeing, sleigh rides, and ice fishing, weather permitting. Full spa services year-round with fitness and yoga instructors.
Children's Programs: Adult-oriented with a minimum age requirement of 13. Exceptions apply if you "book the ranch." Great for family reunions.
Dining: Healthy gourmet meals prepared by a professional master chef in an open kitchen; all served in a family-style setting. Special diets accommodated. Licensed to serve liquor.
Entertainment: Weekly cookout with band, full-time cowboy entertainer, satellite TV, karaoke sing-along, line dancing, billiards, shuffleboard, darts, board games, Native dancing and singing, cowboy ranch activities, and stimulating conversations. Ask about the multicultural programs.
Summary: One of Kilgore's "Best of the Best"–Guest ranch-spa and lifestyle. Echo Valley Guest Ranch combines the best of guest ranching with a full-service, year-round spa and lifestyle programs. The personal service, warm and friendly hospitality, and wide-ranging activities and ranch adventures combine to captivate and enrich the lives of guests who come from around the world.

Flying U Ranch
70 Mile House, British Columbia, Canada

The Flying U Ranch, the oldest guest ranch in Canada, is on the north shore of beautiful 15-mile Green Lake, and covers 40,000 acres. The ranch was established by rodeo personality Jack Boyd. As early as 1924, two Western movies were made here, directed by A.D. "Cowboy" Kean. Guests have come from around the world and most states and provinces of the United States and Canada. The ranch is owned and operated by John Fremlin and Paul Crepean, and their respective families. The Flying U is one of the few ranches left in North America that has preserved the spirit of the early West. Here it is authentic, rustic, and you may still ride on your own.

Address: Box 69 K, North Green Lake Road, 70 Mile House, British Columbia, Canada V0K 2K0
Telephone: 250/456-7717; fax: 250/456-7455
Email: flyingu@bcinternet.net
Internet: www.flyingu.com
Airport: Vancouver International; 3,000-foot grass airstrip on ranch. Land and sea charter flights available to ranch.
Train: British Columbia Rail from North Vancouver to Flying U Station. This is very popular.
Location: 20 miles south of 100 Mile House, five hours northeast of Vancouver by car
Memberships: Texas Longhorn Association, Wilderness Tourism Counsel, British Columbia Cattleman's Association, Caribou Tourist Association
Medical: 100 Mile House Hospital, 20 miles
Conference Capacity: 65
Guest Capacity: 100
Accommodations: Guests stay in 23 "chinker" log cabins (each sleeps 2–8), which are arranged in a "U" shape around the main lodge. Each of these rustic cabins is heated with a wood stove and features hand-hewn log furniture and a sitting porch. Separate men's and women's shower house with shower and bathroom amenities and 15-person sauna. Covered porches with rocking chairs. Ask about the tent and tepee program.
Rate: • $–$$ American Plan. Children's, group, and weekly rates. Two-day minimum low season; three-day minimum high season and long weekends.

Credit Cards: VISA, MasterCard, American Express
Season: Summer: April to November; Winter: December to March.
Activities: Upon arrival in the summer each guest is assigned a horse according to his or her ability. Guests are given a trail map and are free to ride alone or with other guests. The Flying U has 120 horses, thousands of acres, and 400 head of cattle. Riders may saddle up after breakfast each day, including Sunday. Fishing, swimming, and canoeing on Green Lake. Great hiking too. In the winter there is dogsledding, snowshoeing, cross-country skiing, snowmobiling, ice-skating, and fishing.
Children's Programs: Children participate with parents. Baby-sitting available.
Dining: The Flying U has an authentic Western saloon separate from the main lodge. Cocktails are served to the sounds of the circa 1880 nickelodeon. Mealtime at the lodge is announced with the clanging of the old ranch bell. Family and friends eat together ranch-style. Weekly outdoor lunch and dinner barbecues. Beer and a selection of wine available with meals.
Entertainment: Movies, horse-drawn hayrides, barbecues, and bonfires are topped off with an old Western whoop-de-doo dance Wednesday and Saturday nights when the Flying U Band tunes up.
Summary: Canada's oldest guest ranch, on beautiful Green Lake, hosted by a terrific family and the Flying U Band. Here the real Old West comes alive with history and authenticity. One of the few ride-on-your-own ranches left in North America. Small Flying U Western Historical Museum, general store, and authentic Western saloon. A little Japanese, German, French, and Spanish spoken.

Three Bars Cattle and Guest Ranch
Cranbrook, British Columbia, Canada

When it comes to deluxe guest ranching, the Three Bars Cattle and Guest Ranch is at the top. This magnificent ranch couples old guest- and cattle-ranch tradition with deluxe, modern-day comforts you would expect from a resort hideaway. The Old West charm has been carefully crafted with log architecture. The hospitality is under the direction of managing partners Jeff and April Beckley, a couple who grew up in the cattle- and guest-ranch business. When they say the welcome mat is out and the coffeepot is on, they mean it!

Address: 9500 Wycliffe-Perry Creek Road, Cranbrook, British Columbia, Canada V1C 7C7
Telephone: 877/426-5230, 250/426-5230; fax: 250/426-8240
Email: threebarsranch@cyberlink.bc.ca
Internet: www.threebarsranch.com
Airport: International airports in Calgary and Vancouver link regular scheduled flights to Cranbrook, or fly to Spokane, Washington, and drive four hours.
Location: Six miles north of Cranbrook off Highway 95A in southeastern British Columbia, 254 miles southwest of Calgary
Memberships: The Dude Ranchers' Association, British Columbia Guest Ranchers' Association, Tourism Rockies
Medical: Cranbrook Regional Hospital, nine miles
Conference Capacity: 40
Guest Capacity: 40
Accommodations: 10 hand-hewn log duplex cabins provide 20 units. Three of the duplexes are adjoining for families. Each unit has one queen-size or two double beds, private full bath, handmade furniture, refrigerator and coffeemaker, hardwood floor adorned with Navajo-pattern rugs, porches, and gardens all set within a landscaped yard and connected by wooden boardwalks. In the ranch's 5,000-square-foot log lodge are the dining room, fireplace lounge, library, and bar, complete with pool table and conference room.
Rate: • $$$ Full American Plan. Children's and group rates. Four-night minimum stay May to mid-June. Seven-night minimum stay July and August. No minimum stay in winter.

Credit Cards: VISA, MasterCard, bankcards
Season: May through September riding program; October through May conferences and groups.
Activities: Three Bars offers a host of summer, fall, and winter activities. Jeff is a professional reining horse trainer. Consequently there is a tremendous amount of emphasis on and opportunities for horsemanship, instruction, and personal improvement at all levels. Guests are invited to join the cattle drives or ride with the cowboys to check on the ranch's cattle herd when work is being done. This doesn't happen every day or every week; ask April about this program. Progressive trail-riding program. Morning, afternoon, and an all-day ride each week. Weekly guided hikes to Perry Waterfalls. Fly-fishing on the St. Mary's River—catch-and-release only. Guide service available on request (extra). Weekly river float trips (July and August). Tennis court, indoor heated swimming pool, outdoor spa, horseshoe pit, mountain bikes, trap and skeet shooting.
Children's Programs: Children six and older welcome. Children's riding program begins at age six. Kids are looked after only when they're horseback riding. Parents are responsible for kids when they're not riding. Children's play area and petting zoo.
Dining: Wonderful ranch cooking with weekly cookouts at the ranch and by the river. Saturday night farewell barbecue. Special diets easily accommodated.
Entertainment: Something planned each evening, including trading anecdotes on the day's riding activities in the "old-time" saloon while shooting a game of pool, or relaxing around the fireplace. Staff/guest volleyball, weekly Fort Steele Theatre, casino night, fly-casting lessons, and cowboy music.
Summary: Kilgore's "Best of the Best"—Horsemanship and accommodations. Full guest- and some cattle-ranch activities. Superb professional reining horse demonstration and horsemanship instruction, and 11,000-square-foot indoor riding arena. Beautiful lodge and indoor heated swimming pool. Historic Fort Steele 30 minutes away—a must! Delicious seasonal raspberries. Spring horsemanship clinics. Video available on request.

Fly-Fishing Ranches

Introduction

This fly-fishing chapter was designed for the novice as well as the expert angler. If you've never had a fly rod in your hands, don't worry about it. Many of the people who visit these lodges are just like you. They've dreamed about fly-fishing but for one reason or another have never taken the time to try it. Others may be intermediate-to-expert anglers. Regardless of your level of skill or aptitude, you'll have a fun and exciting time. The ranches and lodges listed here are doing what they do for one reason: they love to fish. They're running their operations for you and will do everything possible (within reason, of course) to ensure that your time with them is as pleasurable as it is exhilarating.

Fly-fishing is booming. Look at the major outdoor wear/sporting goods companies and mail-order catalogs. You'll see complete sections, sometimes entire catalogs, devoted to water, fish, and all the exciting equipment that goes with them. Fly-fishing, like golf, is a very exacting sport, and to become an expert takes skill, patience, and dedication. Those unfamiliar with the sport might wonder why anyone would put on a pair of waders that come up to your Adam's apple and stand in a cold stream whipping a long colored line through the air. But people have found that once they try it, they're hooked. Besides the thrill of hooking and landing a trophy-size (or even a small) fish, fly-fishing offers men, women, and children a chance to get out into nature and away from the pressures of daily living. I've included some of the top fly-fishing lodges in the United States where people can receive guidance, instruction, and camaraderie. While many ranches offer fly-fishing and are located on or near superb trout waters, this chapter is devoted to those that offer instruction and guide service.

In selecting a facility, you must first decide where in North America you would like to go. Read the descriptions and write or call for a brochure. As with all ranches in this guide, remember that each is unique and represents the personality of the host. Ask for references and find out if the level of instruction is sufficient to help you achieve your expectations.

The basics of fly-fishing are not difficult to master. A tremendous amount of information is available in books and videos. I strongly recommend that you contact a fly-fishing school before embarking on a fly-fishing vacation. Most leading instructors would agree that if you can master, or at least become familiar with, the techniques of fly-casting before you leave, your overall experience will be much more enjoyable. The easiest way to find out about these schools is to contact your local fly-fishing store/outfitter.

Before buying any equipment, check with the lodge to see what you'll need to bring. Many have their own shops and can take care of most of your needs. Don't be afraid to ask questions. The more you learn about this sport, the more fun you'll have.

4UR Ranch
Creede, Colorado

The 4UR, one of the oldest guest ranches in the West, was founded in 1902 by railroad tycoon General William Palmer as a personal resort for friends and dignitaries. Today, this spectacular 4000-acre ranch is owned by the Leavell family, and is known for unparalleled private fishing along seven miles of Goose Creek and the Rio Grande. Guides are available for instruction or to take you overnight to their secluded "Lost Lakes" for higher Alpine fishing. For longtime guests, this private fishing experience is what keeps them coming back year after year. Word of mouth has made this small guest ranch very popular among its loyal returning guests.

Address: P.O. Box 340K, Creede, Colorado 81130
Telephone: 719/658-2202; fax: 719/658-2308
Email: 4urranch@amigo.net
Internet: www.4urranch.com
Airport: Alamosa via Denver or Durango; 6,800-foot paved airstrip in nearby Creede
Location: 222 miles southwest of Denver, 60 miles west of Alamosa, eight miles southeast of Creede on Highway 149
Medical: Rio Grande Hospital, Del Norte, 30 miles
Conference Capacity: 50; June and September
Guest Capacity: 50
Accommodations: Guests are still housed in cabins originally built at the turn of the century. Renovated and updated, they offer comfort for today, while inspiring a dream-like quality of another time. The main lodge, with its dining and living rooms, splendid valley views, outdoor deck and fireplaces, bar and game room, is the center stage for evening socializing.
Rates: • $$$ American Plan; includes all ranch activities except massage, sporting clays, raft trips, and fly-fishing instruction. Children's rates available with kids under age five free. Ask about day care program for toddlers. Group and conference rates spring and fall. Seven-day minimum stay in July and August.
Credit Cards: VISA, MasterCard
Season: Early June through September
Activities: Fly-fishing, riding, hiking, and the hot springs are main activities. Fly-fishing instruction and guiding available by request. Each evening anglers roll the dice to select their own half-mile stretch of water for the following morning's fishing. Flies, clothing, and some equipment available at the ranch store. Horse enthusiasts of all ages and capabilities enjoy a comprehensive riding program, with breakfast, morning, afternoon, and all-day rides. In addition to its 4,000 acres, the 4UR is surrounded by Forest Service and designated wilderness lands. The ranch network of riding trails offer breathtaking views of the La Garita and San Juan Mountain Ranges, as well as the headwaters of the Rio Grande. Heated swimming pool, log bathhouse with sauna, hot sulfur baths, whirlpool. Massage available. Tennis court, hiking, and rafting, sporting clays course, and trap range available. The newly established and stunning Rio Grande Club golf course is in nearby South Fork.
Children's Programs: The "Wooly Buggers" program is a supervised activity-oriented program for children ages five and older. Weekly evening hayrides and cookouts as well. Other outdoor activities include riding, hiking, fishing, and exploring.
Dining: High-country gourmet. Rack of lamb, ahi tuna, and New York steaks. Fisherman's early continental breakfast followed by regular full-course breakfast. Weekly breakfast ride along Pierce Creek with biscuits and gravy, scrambled eggs and ham, baked apples, and cowboy coffee. Once a week the ranch features a high-noon fish fry along Goose Creek. Gourmet backcountry picnics, "Station 10" wine and cheese party, poolside barbecues. Full service bar and fine selection of wines.
Entertainment: Monday evening cocktail reception. Hayrides, children's movie classics. Evening fly-tying and the traditional candle blowing. Farewell campfires.
Summary: Wonderful guest ranch on scenic Goose Creek, famous for its fantastic family camaraderie and traditions. Excellent fly-fishing, 8.5 miles of private waters. Family-oriented during July and August; mostly adults during September. Hot sulfur pool. Special 4UR fly-fishing school. Four-seat surrey rides.

Colorado Trails Ranch
Durango, Colorado

During the summer the ranch offers an excellent family-oriented program. This enables the fishing enthusiast to enjoy his/her sport while the other members of the family enjoy participating in their favorite ranch activities. The fishing opportunities begin in June and are at their peak during the months of September and October, a glorious time to be in the Rockies. Colorado Trails Ranch boasts a wide range of fishing experiences, from stocked ponds where beginners gain confidence in casting techniques to the wide-open freestoners of the Florida and Piedra Rivers. There is something for all levels of experience. For the avid angler, the ranch even offers float and wade trips on the world-famous San Juan River. With professional guides on staff, a well-stocked tackle shop, and four miles of private water, Colorado Trails Ranch is a fly-fisher's paradise.

Address: 12161 County Road 240, Durango, Colorado 81301
Telephone: 800/323-3833, 970/247-5055; fax: 970/385-7372
Email: info@coloradotrails.com
Internet: www.coloradotrails.com
Airport: La Plata County, 18 miles from ranch
Location: 12 miles northeast of Durango on County Road 240; 200 miles north of Albuquerque; 350 miles southwest of Denver
Memberships: The Dude Ranchers' Association, Colorado Dude and Guest Ranch Association
Medical: Mercy Medical Center, Durango
Conference Capacity: 30
Guest Capacity: 65 (33 rooms)
Accommodations: Guests can stay in four types of comfortably furnished cabins. All rooms have private bathrooms, carpeting, electric baseboard heat, and porches. Complimentary laundry facilities available.
Rates: • $$$$–$$$$$ American Plan; all-inclusive. Family, off-season, and nanny rates.
Credit Cards: VISA, MasterCard, Discover, American Express, Diner's Club
Season: Early June to October; conferences: mid-May, late September, and October.
Activities: Full guest-ranch activities as highlighted in Guest and Resort Ranches chapter. Fly-fishing program includes two ponds and a mile of challenging mountain stream on the ranch. Private Florida River fishing sites are available within a four-mile radius of the ranch. Private Piedra River fishing is 30 minutes from the ranch, and the San Juan River is an hour away for world-class float and wade excursions. Colorado fishing licenses available at the ranch. Ask about special fall fly-fishing clinics.
Children's Programs: Full ranch program for kids and teens. Fly-fishing instruction available for older children who enjoy or seriously want to learn to flyfish.
Dining: The dining room overlooks scenic Shearer Creek Valley and Eagle Ridge. Hearty ranch food. A family spirit prevails, so drinking is permitted in cabins only.
Entertainment: A program every evening, hayrides, cookouts, ice-cream socials, dances; professional rodeos and melodrama in Durango.
Summary: One of the leading guest ranches in America. Outstanding programs for families, children, teens, and younger children. Caring and personable staff. Full Western riding program. Ask about adults-only weeks, family reunions, and the exciting trip to Mesa Verde Indian Cliff Dwellings. Nearby: The famous Durango-Silverton Narrow Gauge Train.

Diamond J Ranch
Ennis, Montana

THE DUDE RANCHERS'
ASSOCIATION

World-renowned for its trout fishing, Montana has incredible fly-fishing opportunities for the adventurous angler. The Madison River Valley's famous Diamond J Ranch is surrounded (within a 70-mile radius) with seven Blue Ribbon trout rivers, spring creeks, the Bear Trap Wilderness Area, and numerous high-mountain lakes. What makes the Diamond J Ranch fly-fishing experience so special is that it not only caters to experienced and novice anglers, but also provides a wonderful environment for nonanglers with a host of outdoor activities from June to October. This marvelous Orvis-endorsed ranch has been in operation since 1930 and is run today by owners Peter, Jinny, and Tim Combs.

Address: P.O. Box 577 K, Ennis, Montana 59729
Telephone: 406/682-4867; fax: 406/682-4106
Email: totalmgt@3rivers.net
Internet: www.diamondjranch.com
Airport: Bozeman
Location: 14 miles east of Ennis off Highway 287, 60 miles south of Bozeman
Memberships: The Dude Ranchers' Association
Awards: Orvis-endorsed Fly-Fishing and Wing Shooting Lodge
Medical: Ennis Hospital, 14 miles
Guest Capacity: 25
Accommodations: Eight cozy log cabins, each with hardwood floors, a rock fireplace, and hickory furniture and beds. Each has a full bath with separate shower stalls and a cast-iron tub. Cabins have writing desks and porches.
Rates: • $$$–$$$$$$ American Plan. Call for fly-fishing and wing shooting packages.
Credit Cards: VISA, MasterCard, American Express
Season: Mid-June through mid-September
Activities: The ranch is in the Madison River Valley and very close to its crown jewel, the Madison River. Many take side trips to fish the Beaverhead, Big Hole, Missouri, Jefferson, Gallatin, and Yellowstone Park waters (Firehole and Gibbon). The ranch has its own little stream (called Jackass Creek) and private, two-acre Jinny

Lake. Be sure to ask about Bear Trap Wilderness white-water trophy-trout trips. Most fishing takes place from mid-June to mid-September. Available trips include wading, floating, and belly tubes on Ennis, Quake, and Hebgen Lakes and on mountain lakes, rivers, and springs. Full guide service available. Usually one guide per two guests. Full Orvis tackle shop in Ennis. All trips are tailored individually to each guest. Nonfishing members of the family will enjoy full horseback riding programs, tennis, swimming, hot tub spa, scenic float trips, and hiking. Do as much or as little as you wish. Bird hunters: be sure to talk with the ranch about their superb wing shooting program.
Children's Programs: No set program. Kids can spin-fish or flyfish, depending on their age. Instruction available for both fly-fishing and shooting for kids generally 12 and older. Kiddie wrangler with instruction. Kids usually ride together. Baby-sitting available upon request.
Dining: Barbecue and sack lunches on shore for all those who fish. Anglers on overnight float trips get to experience the log "chalet." Back at the ranch, family-style hearty dining in three dining rooms. BYOB happy hour.
Entertainment: Informal evening programs. Campfires, sing-alongs, naturalist talks, and library.
Summary: Kilgore's "Best of the Best"–Fly-fishing and wing shooting. One of Montana's most famous old-time guest ranches run since 1959 by the Combs family. Orvis-endorsed fly-fishing, and wing shooting ranch for all levels of experience— the young and the young-at-heart. Excellent also for those who like to ride, hike, relax, and enjoy the family environment. Fishing opportunities include Blue Ribbon rivers, high-mountain lakes, and the Bear Trap Wilderness white-water trophy-trout expedition. Superb upland bird- and waterfowl- hunting on 30,000-acre ranch. See summer write-up in main section of book.

Lone Mountain Ranch
Big Sky, Montana

Lone Mountain Ranch and Orvis-endorsed fly-fishing lodge, is one of the great year-round guest ranches in North America. Besides offering wonderful summer and winter programs, the ranch also specializes in a superb fishing program for those who wish to learn the art, the science, and more about the fun of fly-fishing. As head guide Gary Lewis says, "We encourage people to have fun when fly-fishing. Our program is not about catching big fish and lots of fish, it's really showing all ages the total fly-fishing experience with a strong teaching emphasis. We encourage children 12 years and older to come along with adults and enjoy our streams and rivers, the mountains, nature, wading through swirling waters, watching eagles soar overhead, and perhaps even spotting a bear or a mountain sheep. We show folks the best possible experience with lots of hands-on teaching." Lone Mountain offers family vacations for anglers, giving them access to some of the country's best Blue Ribbon trout fishing. Nonfishing members of the family can enjoy horseback riding, naturalist activities, and full-children's program, along with the numerous other ranch activities. Lone Mountain Ranch is a winner!

Address: P.O. Box 160069 K, Big Sky, Montana 59716
Telephone: 800/514-4644, 406/995-4644; fax: 406/995-4670
Email: lmr@lmranch.com
Internet: www.lmranch.com
Airport: Bozeman
Location: 40 miles south of Bozeman off Highway 191
Memberships: Greater Yellowstone Coalition, Orvis-endorsed fly-fishing lodge, Montana Dude Ranch Association
Awards: Orvis-endorsed Guides of the Year
Medical: Bozeman Deaconess Hospital, 40 miles
Conference Capacity: 50
Guest Capacity: 80
Accommodations: 24 fully insulated one- to four-bedroom cozy log cabins that sleep two to nine; and the luxury, six-bedroom Ridgetop Lodge. Each features comfortable beds, electric heat, bathrooms with tub/shower, and a rock fireplace or woodstove. Cabins are close to the clear

mountain stream that winds through the property. All have front porches for relaxing.
Rates: • $$$–$$$$$ American Plan. Children under age two stay free (nanny rates available). Special package rates. Normally, minimum one-week stay, Sunday to Sunday.
Credit Cards: VISA, MasterCard, Discover
Season: Summer: Late May to mid-October; Winter: Early December to early April.
Activities: The fly-fishing program is best for guests ages 12 and older. In addition to the Gallatin River, a short drive from the ranch, there are numerous streams and spring creeks as well as high Alpine lakes, the Madison River, and the waters of Yellowstone Park, which offer a variety of exceptional fishing adventures. July is prime time for dry flies, with the salmon fly-hatch in full swing on most of the major rivers. Mid-September through October finds water conditions excellent and few crowds, with the scenery and wildlife viewing at their peak. Fishing in the winter is a unique experience! Ask about winter skiing vacation packages (see Cross-Country Skiing section).
Children's Programs: Extensive summer ranch program for kids ages four and older.
Dining: Ranch cooking with a gourmet flair. Special diets catered to. Restaurant open to the public on a limited basis. Full bar. No smoking.
Entertainment: Informative and entertaining nightly programs.
Summary: Kilgore's "Best of the Best"–Year-round Fly-fishing. Lone Mountain Guest Ranch offers year-round fly-fishing opportunities for adults and children over age 12. Each of the four seasons brings exciting fly-fishing coupled with full ranch activities. Winter Orvis-endorsed guided fly-fishing trips also. Great for spring and fall conferences. Fly-fishing shop, excellent restaurant, and year-round guest ranch activities for the entire family. Nearby: Big Sky Ski Resort and Yellowstone National Park.

Triple Creek Ranch
Darby, Montana

For those who wish to combine luxury, personal service (second to none), and fly-fishing in an incredible vacation package, welcome to Triple Creek Ranch and its sister ranch, the 10,000-acre CB Cattle and Guest Ranch, which together have seven miles of Bitterroot River frontage. Just one mile from the West Fork of Montana's Bitterroot River, Triple Creek is situated ideally for anglers and nonanglers alike. Fish from sunrise to sunset, relax poolside, or unwind in Montana's high country with an afternoon massage. This mountain hideaway offers superb fly-fishing guides who will take you wade- or float-fishing or in a helicopter to experience some of the best fishing in Montana. In addition, a full luxury program offers horseback riding, white-water rafting, gourmet dining, hiking, and wildlife viewing. In the world of luxury hideaways, general managers Wayne and Judy Kilpatrick and their superb staff have taken Triple Creek right to the top.

Address: 5551 West Fork Road, Darby, Montana 59829
Telephone: 406/821-4600; fax: 406/821-4666
Email: tcr@bitterroot.net
Internet: www.triplecreekranch.com
Airport: Missoula, 74 miles. Private planes to Hamilton with 4,200-foot runway. Helicopter pad at ranch. Airport pickup available.
Location: 12 miles south of Darby, 74 miles south of Missoula
Memberships: Relais & Chateaux
Awards: Relais & Chateaux; *Hideaway Report* "A Romantic Gem in the Rocky Mountains;" Ranked No. 7 of 20 U.S. Resort Hideaways, *Little Gems; El Capitan;* "Hideout of the Year;" Kilgore Luxury Group
Medical: Marcus Daly Memorial Hospital, Hamilton. Emergency medical helicopter service available.
Conference Capacity: 30; booking entire ranch is generally required
Guest Capacity: 30 singles, 24 couples
Accommodations: 19 cozy-to-luxurious cedar log cabins. All have fireplaces and refrigerators stocked with complimentary beverages and a full supply of liquor. Each cabin has satellite TV/VCR. Larger luxury cabins have handsome, handcraft-ed, king-size log beds, double steam showers, and private decks with hot tubs overlooking the forest. Telephones with data ports in each cabin. Daily housekeeping and laundry services.
Rates: $$$$$$ • American Plan. No minimum stay. Single rates. All fine wine and liquor complimentary.
Credit Cards: VISA, MasterCard, Discover, American Express
Season: Year-round; open all holidays.
Activities: A complete luxury experience, with horseback riding, hiking, and scenic drives through Montana's wild backcountry. For those who especially want to flyfish, Triple Creek offers a customized guided program. Tell the ranch what you'd like to experience (be reasonable, now), and they'll do everything possible to make your fishing dreams come true. Experienced anglers: be sure to ask about the skwala, salmon, green drakes, and caddis hatches from mid-March to October. Outdoor heated pool and hot tub.
Children's Programs: Children under age 16 allowed only when a family or group reserves entire ranch.
Dining: Excellent! Gourmet meals with menus featuring Montana beef, seafood flown in from the coast, and wild game. Special diets never a problem. Full room service available 7 A.M.–11 P.M. Extensive wine list and full bar. Open to public on very limited basis.
Entertainment: Wonderful Sunday campfire sing-along with your favorite brandy. Main lodge has book and video library and fabulous complimentary bar upstairs.
Summary: In the world of luxury and service, Triple Creek is second to none. Adults only, one of the top ranches for women in North America. Excellent fly-fishing program with guides, superb cuisine, and luxury amenities. Private and secluded. Service is the hallmark here.

The Lodge at Chama
Chama, New Mexico

The unspoiled picturesque San Juan Mountains of northern New Mexico are home to the 36,000-acre Lodge at Chama ranch. Since 1950 the ranch has maintained the highest standards of excellence in fly-fishing, wildlife management and viewing, and lodging amenities. Today, guests enjoy an atmosphere of luxury and exclusivity. Both lake and stream fly-fishing are the highlights of guest activities from June to October. Rainbow, brown, brook, and cutthroat trout thrive in this pristine environment of isolated, high-country lakes and miles of crystal-clear streams. Heavy-bodied fish from 16–25 inches will test your fishing skills. Your guide will put you where the fish are and provide you with an unforgettable fly-fishing experience of a lifetime.

Address: Box 127K, Chama, New Mexico 87520
Telephone: 505/756-2133; fax: 505/756-2519
Email: reservations@lodgeatchama.com
Internet: www.lodgeatchama.com
Airport: Albuquerque; private jets to Pagosa Springs. Call regarding ranch airstrip.
Location: 100 miles north of Santa Fe, 90 miles west of Taos
Awards: *Hideaway Report,* "Best Sporting Retreat;" Kilgore Luxury Group
Medical: Hospital in Española; emergency helicopter service available
Conference Capacity: 42, in board meeting room
Guest Capacity: 42
Accommodations: The 27,000-square-foot lodge offers panoramic views of the beautiful Chama Valley and snowcapped Colorado peaks from its 21 rooms. Two great rooms are dominated by huge rock fireplaces, original Western art, sculptures, and fish and wildlife mounts. The 21 rooms have private baths, sitting/desk areas, lofty ceilings, large closets, and upscale amenities. Four spacious suites have fireplaces, vanity baths, TVs, and lounging areas.
Rates: • $$$$–$$$$$ Full American Plan. No minimum stay. Lodge and ranch may be booked exclusively if desired.
Credit Cards: VISA, MasterCard, Discover. Personal and corporate checks accepted.
Season: May to October for fishing; mid-September to January for hunting; conferences and wildlife viewing year-round.
Activities: Private lake and stream fishing. Some waters reserved for catch-and-release only. Fishing equipment available; however, most people bring their own gear. Monthly five-day fly-fishing school package available on a limited basis in the summer. Self-guided nature trail from lodge. Hiking, picnics, wildlife tours, photography trips. Guided ranch trail rides. Nonfishing spouses enjoy off-ranch activities, including narrow-gauge train rides, shopping tours to Taos or Santa Fe, and white-water rafting. After a full day of outdoor activities, you may relax in a 10-person, indoor, hydrotherapy whirlpool or enjoy a sauna. Fitness room and massage available. Superb fall elk-hunting on limited basis.
Children's Programs: Minimum age of 12 unless by special arrangement.
Dining: Gourmet ranch cuisine. Trail lunches and fisher's special shore lunches. Excellent varied cuisine for all three daily meals. Ranch specialties include steaks, chops, buffalo, trout, and fowl as well as New Mexican specialties made with wonderful chilies grown in New Mexico. Home-baked bread, rolls, desserts, and pastries. Bar and premium wines available.
Entertainment: Wide-screen satellite TV, VCR movies. Fishing and wildlife videos.
Summary: Kilgore Luxury Group. World-class fly-fishing and wildlife viewing. One of North America's most exclusive ranch retreats. Specializing in high quality outdoor recreational experiences for business executive, corporate, and sophisticated family gatherings. Elk and deer are frequent sundown visitors to the lodge grounds. One of the world's largest private elk herds. Ranch buffalo herd too.

Brush Creek Ranch
Saratoga, Wyoming

THE DUDE RANCHERS' ASSOCIATION

Wyoming Dude Rancher's Association

At the foot of southern Wyoming's Snowy Range Mountains and in the upper North Platte Valley, Brush Creek Ranch, a 6,000-acre working cattle and guest ranch, offers fly-fishing guests the combination of a guest ranch and a superb array of fly-fishing opportunities, both on and off the ranch. Over three private miles along Brush Creek, and the 140 miles of Blue Ribbon freestone waters of the Upper North Platte and Encampment Rivers (regarded by many as some of the finest and least discovered fly-fishing opportunities in the West), offer guests wonderful fishing adventures. Whether you're fly-fishing, hiking, horseback riding, savoring the beauty of this scenic valley, or enjoying the towns of Encampment or Saratoga, Kinta and Gibb Blumenthall offer guests a rich and heartwarming adventure.

Address: Star Route, Box 10, Saratoga, Wyoming 82331

Telephone: 800/RANCH-WY (800/726-2499), 307/327-5241; fax: 307/327-5384

Email: kinta@brushcreekranch.com

Internet: www.brushcreekranch.com

Airport: Denver, 195 miles; Laramie, 65 miles. Airport pickup is extra.

Location: 65 miles west of Laramie off the Snowy Range Road, Wyoming 130; 16 miles northeast of Saratoga off Wyoming 130

Memberships: The Dude Ranchers' Association, Wyoming Dude Rancher's Association, America Outdoors

Awards: Orvis-endorsed Lodge

Medical: Clinic in Saratoga, 16 miles

Conference Capacity: 26

Guest Capacity: 26

Accommodations: Vintage 1900s-style, white-sided, green-trimmed three-story lodge or rustic cabins. The lodge features a native stone fireplace in the library and Western murals in the dining room on the first floor. Sleeping accommodations are on the second and third floors. Each room is unique. All have private baths and entrances; some have private, screened porches. These rooms have a turn-of-the-century feel. The two cabin duplexes, located near the main lodge, were originally the icehouse and cowboy bunkhouse.

Each has been completely remodeled with Western rustic charm, private bathrooms, and queen-size beds. Enclosed hot tub. Daily maid service.

Rates: • $$$ Full American Plan. Children's, group, and off-season rates. Three-day minimum stay.

Credit Cards: VISA, MasterCard. Personal checks preferred.

Season: Year-round; closed Thanksgiving and Easter.

Activities: In addition to fishing over three miles of Brush Creek on the ranch property and the trout pond, guests enjoy the Upper North Platte and Encampment Rivers, two of Wyoming's premier trout streams. These Blue Ribbon waters boast wild trout, including browns, rainbows, and cutthroats, ranging from 10–26 inches and averaging 13–17 inches. These rivers provide over 140 miles of classic Western trout waters. In addition, two tailwater sections at the "miracle mile" and gray reef on the Platte offer guests a chance to catch large browns and rainbows year-round (extra). Guests also enjoy fishing for brookies, browns, cutthroat, rainbows, splake, and golden trout in the high-mountain lakes and streams of the Snowy Range and Sierra Madre Mountains.

Children's Programs: Children are the responsibility of parents. Half-day riding and fishing programs planned five times a week for kids age six and older. Local baby-sitting available on request.

Dining: Western-style food with a gourmet flair. Breakfast rides, creekside barbecues. BYOB.

Entertainment: Barn dances in the hayloft of the historic log barn. Campfire music. Horse-drawn wagon rides, and pitching horseshoes. Fly-tying demonstrations and fly-casting lessons. Enclosed hot tub with scenic views.

Summary: Brush Creek Ranch offers families, couples, and individuals the opportunity to fish one of the least-known Blue Ribbon trout rivers in Wyoming, in addition to enjoying a full guest-ranch program. Six thousand acres of old-time Western charm. Nearby: Snowy Range Mountains and the Old West towns of Encampment and Saratoga.

Canyon Ranch
Sheridan, Wyoming

Canyon Ranch has been in the Wallop family since the late 1880s. Originally cattle and horse ranchers, the Wallops welcome executives, individual families, and very small corporate groups who come to take in the magnificent views, intimate friendly hospitality, and superb mountain fishing. Today the ranch is owned by former U.S. Senator Malcolm Wallop and run by his son, Paul. Canyon Ranch specializes in "fly-fishing the way fly-fishing used to be." This is not trophy-fish country, but what makes it special is that you won't run into lots of people and you will catch lots of fish. What Paul's guests enjoy is the total fishing experience. Paul loves the great outdoors; sharing his appreciation for wildlife, the mountains, and the old-time easygoing spirit of the West brings guests back year after year. As a British ambassador said, "I've been to a lot of places where I caught bigger fish, but this is the best fishing I've ever had."

Address: P.O. Box 11 K, Big Horn, Wyoming 82833
Telephone: 307/674-6239; fax: 307/672-2264
Email: pabs@canyonranchbighorn.com
Internet: www.canyonranchbighorn.com
Airport: Sheridan, Wyoming; Billings, Montana
Location: 13 miles south of Sheridan, 130 miles south of Billings, Montana
Medical: Sheridan County Memorial Hospital
Guest Capacity: 16
Accommodations: Two private rooms and a large loft with six beds and four full baths in the lodge, including laundry facilities, fax machine, two telephone lines, TV/VCR, and views of Lion's Head and Little Goose Canyon. Hot tub, too. The remote and private family cabin, about 20 minutes up the mountain from the main ranch, sleeps six with two bedrooms and a loft, one bath, kitchen, living/dining area, and front porch. Gas water heater, range, and refrigerator, but no electricity or telephone. Guests cook and clean for themselves, and need a four-wheel-drive vehicle to reach the cabin. All bedding is provided.
Rates: • $$$–$$$$ Weekend and weekly packages, four-night minimum stay, arrival any day.
Credit Cards: VISA, MasterCard. Personal checks preferred.

Season: Mid-June through September
Activities: Fly-fishing is the main activity. Paul and his experienced guides take you to quality, uncrowded waters throughout the Big Horn Mountains. A variety of waters are available: private streams and lakes, secluded mountain streams, and wilderness lakes. It's rare to find other fishermen around these private and public waters. All trips are walk-wade. As Paul says, "This is fishing the way it used to be." For non-fishing friends or family there are excellent opportunities for a variety of hikes, from all-day outings to evening strolls. Horseback riding available. Wildlife viewing is superb; ranch-management goal has always been to enhance wildlife habitat and diversity. Almost all of the traditional Western wildlife species inhabit the ranch. Fifteen-station sporting-clays course.
Children's Programs: Paul has developed a special instructional program for children who want to learn the art of fly-fishing. Ask Paul about the father/son and mother/daughter fishing trips.
Dining: Excellent seasonal fare and a varied menu for all three meals. Special diets catered to. Fishing lunches served streamside. Complimentary beer and wine. BYOB.
Entertainment: Paul will arrange for tickets to local events if guests wish. Videos available or just sit and watch the sunset from the front porch.
Summary: One of Kilgore's "Best of the Best"–Privacy. An exclusive, intimate, private hideaway with superb service and privacy! A 3,800-acre ranch in the Big Horn Mountains that has been in the Wallop family since the 1880s. Today it caters to families, executives, individual families, friends, or small groups. Paul Wallop works closely with guests before they arrive to insure that their expectations are met. Excellent private and public mountain-stream and lake fly-fishing, and excellent fresh food. Ask about the private bird-hunting opportunities, and Paul's "Cast and Blast" program.

Cross-Country Skiing Ranches

Introduction

Welcome to ranch country in winter! Cross-country skiing, along with snowshoeing, snowmobiling, and even dogsledding, has become a wonderful part of the winter activities at many ranches.

"Skinny-skiing" is fun for the whole family. Start with a skiing professional on machine-groomed trails, learning to travel across the flats and master descent techniques (more kinds of turns than in downhill skiing). When you can stay on the tracks, graduate to backcountry touring, lift-served slopes, hut-to-hut trips, or ski to wilderness yurts (circular, domed tents).

Author and friend Jonathan Wiesel explains, "Machine-set tracks guide skis forward so your ankles don't have the chance to splay out to the side. This transforms 'walking on skis' into gliding, helping you out-think your feet. Groomed trails open the grace and beauty of winter not just to super-athletes but to anyone at any pace, giving you the thrill of speed with confident control. Best of all, cross-country consumes enough calories that two hours on skis justifies a second dessert."

Equipment has evolved at a dizzying pace. There are track and skating skis, wider boards for breaking your own trail (bushwhacking), and metal-edged gear for telemarking. The latest innovation is the "micro ski," which is three-fourths the length of the older models. They look like toy poodles when you think you need St. Bernards, but turning and learning is a breeze and falls are reduced by 50 percent.

Each property has its own character, programs, and beauty. Here are some questions to ask.

- How many miles of machine-groomed track and skating lanes are there available?
- What is the altitude? (If it's above 6,000 feet and you're coming from sea level, plan to take it easy for at least the first day.)
- What kids' programs and facilities are available: day care, baby-sitting, narrow-track setting, snow-play area, ski equipment, or trails?
- What equipment is available: track, touring, telemarking, micro skis? Do they have modern boot-binding "systems"?
- Is instruction or guide service included in the package?
- What other recreation is available on-site? Is there a downhill ski area nearby?

Winter ranches are famous for hospitality, diverse entertainment, and culinary excellence. Regardless of whether you're a single person, couple, or family, you can visit these wonderful properties to snowshoe, ice-skate, take a sleigh ride, sit in the hot tub enjoying splendid mountain views, or relax in front of a blazing fire.

C Lazy U Ranch
Granby, Colorado

C Lazy U offers a wonderful winter riding and cross-country skiing program. The ranch invites families with children (and what a program it is for kids). The ranch caters to families who wish to savor the magic, splendor, peace, and beauty of this winter wonderland. Cross-country skiers enjoy over 25 kilometers of machine-groomed trails, in addition to hundreds of acres of wild, untracked skiing possibilities. Full instruction, guide service, and equipment are available. Imagine horseback riding all bundled up through the fresh snow. Well, you can do that too. The Christmas program brings out all the joy of the holidays with tree-trimming, caroling, filled stockings, Christmas trees for guests' rooms, turkey dinner, and, of course, Santa arriving on his sleigh all the way from the North Pole. The C Lazy U winter adventure is one you'll cherish for a lifetime.

Address: P.O. Box 379, Granby, Colorado 80446
Telephone: 970/887-3344; fax: 970/887-3917
Email: ranch@clazyu.com
Internet: www.clazyu.com
Airport: Denver
Train: Granby
Location: Six miles northwest of Granby, off Highway 125; 90 miles west of Denver
Memberships: The Dude Ranchers' Association, Colorado Dude and Guest Ranch Association, Cross-Country Ski Association
Awards: Mobil 4 Star, AAA 5 Diamond, Kilgore Luxury Group
Medical: Granby Medical Clinic, six miles
Conference Capacity: 70
Guest Capacity: 110
Accommodations: 18 fully insulated, comfortable units. Suites vary from one- to three-room family units with baths and carpeting. Some have fireplaces and Jacuzzi bathtubs. Daily fresh fruit; fireplace restocked every day. Hair dryers, nightly turndown, bathrobes, and coffeemakers with everything you need.
Rates: • $$$$ American Plan. Everything but the bar tab and trapshooting is included. Ask about the two-night winter packages and stays during Christmas and New Year's. Special children's rates

January to March.
Credit Cards: None. Personal checks accepted.
Season: Mid-December through March
Activities: 25 kilometers of groomed trails, ice-skating, sledding, inner-tubing, horse-drawn sleigh rides, and trapshooting. Fitness center with whirlpool and sauna. Downhill skiing nearby at Silver Creek and Winter Park; transportation provided. Morning and afternoon horseback riding. Here you not only ski the powder, but you can ride the powder too. Whether out on beautiful snow-covered trails or in the heated indoor riding arena, strong emphasis is placed on the winter horseback riding program, overseen by one of the nation's best horsemanship clinicians, Peter Campbell. All cross-country skiing, skating, and snowshoeing equipment provided. Off-ranch snowmobile tours can be arranged.
Children's Programs: Full children's program all winter. Ice-skating, sledding, snowmobile tubing, and horseback riding. Children eat lunch and dinner together, separate from adults.
Dining: Excellent cuisine, including homemade soups, rack of lamb, Christmas turkey dinner, and ice-cream pie. Full service bar. Extensive wine list.
Entertainment: Christmas and New Year's programs. Game room, country-Western singing, ice-skating party with bonfire and schnapps, weekly nighttime cross-country skiing along a torch-lit trail to the awaiting bonfire and goodies.
Summary: Kilgore's "Best of the Best"–Summer and Winter Activities. Kilgore Luxury Group. World-class, year-round destination ranch with wonderful winter riding and holiday programs for families. Excellent Christmas and New Year's program. Superb children's program morning, noon, and night. Full winter activities.

The Home Ranch
Clark, Colorado

THE DUDE RANCHERS' ASSOCIATION

The Home Ranch is one of the premier winter settings in North America. Host-owner Ken Jones along with a very competent and friendly staff, combine the best of two worlds—rustic elegance and winter adventure. Guests from around the world gather here to enjoy what the Home Ranch has to offer. In the beautiful Elk River Valley near the small town of Clark, not far from Steamboat Springs, this ranch provides a gracious combination of Western warmth, downhill and cross-country skiing, and snowshoeing. The ski trails that radiate from the property give skiers varied terrain, rolling valleys, and glistening forests. If that's not enough, a short drive to Steamboat will put you on downhill slopes that will challenge even the most advanced skier.

Address: P.O. Box 822 K, Clark, Colorado 80428
Telephone: 970/879-1780; fax: 970/879-1795
Email: hrclark@cmn.net
Internet: www.homeranch.com
Airport: Steamboat Springs and Hayden
Location: 18 miles north of Steamboat Springs off Highway 129
Awards: Mobil 4 Star, Kilgore Luxury Group
Memberships: The Dude Ranchers' Association, Relais & Chateaux
Medical: Routt Memorial Hospital
Conference Capacity: 30
Guest Capacity: 50
Accommodations: Eight secluded cabins and six beautiful lodge rooms, furnished with antiques, Indian rugs, original artwork, down comforters, and robes. Each cabin has its own woodstove and a private enclosed outdoor whirlpool. Large families may elect to stay in the 2,500-square-foot, hand-hewn, spacious, beautifully trimmed log cabin.
Rates: • $$$$$ American Plan. Three-night minimum stay.
Credit Cards: VISA, MasterCard, American Express
Season: Late December through March
Activities: The main focus of the winter program is the excellent downhill skiing/cross-country outdoor adventure package. The ranch offers twice daily shuttles to Steamboat Springs for downhill skiing. In addition, there are more than 50 kilometers of tracked trails throughout the valley, 20 kilometers of which are groomed for telemark skiing. The instructor-guides are qualified to teach all levels of cross-country skiing. One of the more popular excursions is lunch at the Llamasary. Guests ski, snowshoe, or take the sleigh about one mile up to the mountain cabin, have a lunch of gourmet Western fare, and return to the main lodge. Heated outdoor swimming, snowshoeing, and sauna. Equipment is available for both adults and children at Slim Boards Ski Shop.

Children's Programs: Best for kids who want to ski. During winter there are usually not many children here. Children six and older welcome.

Dining: Excellent meals with many Home Ranch specialties, such as breast of duck, fresh fish, filet mignon, European dishes, praline cheesecake. BYO wine and liquor (ranch will pick up with advance notice).

Entertainment: Well-stocked library, grand piano, recreation hall. The Ranch Hand Band performs once a week. Ask Ken about his "Family Tree Album."

Summary: One of Kilgore's "Best of the Best"–Cross-Country Skiing, Luxury, and Cuisine. One of the prettiest ranches in North America. Great for people who like to ski hard and eat well, and for those who don't like to ski—that's okay too. French and German spoken. Nearby: Famous ski town of Steamboat Springs.

Latigo Ranch
Kremmling, Colorado

Guests who keep returning to Latigo Ranch are drawn by the relaxed atmosphere, spectacular scenery, cuisine, and warm hospitality of the Yost and George families. Latigo is tucked in a corner of Arapaho and Routt National Forests, on the side of Kasdorf Mountain. With 100-mile views to the distant high mountain peaks of the Continental Divide and 250,000 acres of national forest bordering it, Latigo Ranch offers a spectacular winter wonderland of scenery, skiing, and snowshoeing. Since the ranch lies at 9,000 feet on top of Colorado's Gore Range, snow conditions are hard to beat. For most of the winter, several feet of dry powder make it just perfect for all kinds of winter activities. Hosts Kathie Yost and Lisa George have both been schoolteachers (music and English). Randy George has a degree in engineering and an MBA; Jim Yost has a Ph.D. in anthropology and has taught anthropology and linguistics at the University of Colorado. A stay at Latigo is not only a recreational heaven but can be also a stimulating intellectual experience. Above all, Latigo offers a low-key, relaxing ambiance. People leave here feeling like they've been visiting family at their private winter retreat.

Address: P.O. Box 237K, Kremmling, Colorado 80459
Telephone: 800/227-9655, 970/724-9008
Email: latigo@compuserve.com
Internet: www.latigotrails.com
Airport: Steamboat Springs or Denver
Location: 16 miles northwest of Kremmling, 55 miles southeast of Steamboat Springs, 130 miles west of Denver. Ranch will send detailed map.
Memberships: Cross-Country Ski Areas of America, The Dude Ranchers' Association, Colorado Dude and Guest Ranch Association, Colorado Cross-Country Ski Areas Association
Medical: Kremmling Memorial Hospital, 16 miles
Conference Capacity: 25, if staying overnight
Guest Capacity: 25
Accommodations: Three log duplex cabins, three bedrooms on each side with sitting room, electric heat, and wood-burning stove. A fourplex consists of four single bedrooms with two queen beds and two with double beds, all with fireplaces in the bedrooms.

Rates: • $$–$$$ American Plan; gratuities included, all inclusive except equipment rental. Group rates available.
Credit Cards: VISA, MasterCard
Season: Mid-December to early April. Open Christmas.
Activities: The ski and snowshoe trails are designed for beginners through performance enthusiasts. Latigo machine-grooms and packs over 35 miles of track for classic and skate-skiing and snowshoeing. There's also unlimited backcountry and telemark skiing for the more adventurous. Daily lessons are provided for beginning and advanced skiers on both cross-country and telemark techniques. Be sure to ask Randy or Jim about their packed telemark slope. Tubing and sledding are also enjoyed by many. Bring your own ski gear, or rentals are available at Latigo.
Children's Programs: No special program. Children's lessons available. Baby-sitting by prior arrangement. Talk to Kathie about the options for your children.
Dining: Full breakfast. You order what you want. Hot lunch (sack lunch by arrangement), family-style dinner. Can cater to special diets. BYOB.
Entertainment: Reading, card games, pool table, table tennis, and foosball. Guests enjoy lively discussions and the cozy library or relaxing hot tub.
Summary: Kilgore's "Best of the Best"–Cross-Country Skiing and Scenery. The Latigo winter experience is best for those who appreciate the majesty of the mountains and value the solitude and serenity of this remote location. Excellent private trail system. Warm, friendly family hospitality. Ask about the dogsled rides and Jim's movie on Ecuador, *Nomads of the Rain Forest*.

Skyline Guest Ranch
Telluride, Colorado

Are you looking for an incredibly fun-filled and action-packed ski week at Telluride's famous ski town and resort? Do you yearn for a classic ski lodge where you can sit around the potbellied stove, sip hot cider, and eat freshly made cookies after a fabulous day of skiing with your host, former U.S. Ski Team member and world-class skier Mike Farny and his family? You can experience both at Skyline. The beauty of the mountains will set you aglow. Skyline Guest Ranch is just five miles from Telluride Ski Resort, where you'll find incredible terrain for Alpine and Nordic skiing. The resort has 10 lifts, one of which is used for Nordic access to the mountaintop. If you want to ski at the ranch, there are backcountry trails. Ask Sheila about skiing back to the ranch from the ski area—an exciting and adventurous trip. Skyline is noted for its spectacular setting: you can see three 14,000-foot peaks from the front porch. Skyline feels secluded enough, yet it's only eight miles from the historic ski town of Telluride, 15 minutes away.

Address: 7214 Highway 145, Telluride, Colorado 81435
Telephone: 888/754-1126, 970/728-3757; fax: 970/728-6728
Email: skyline-ranch@toski.com
Internet: www.ranchweb.com/skyline
Airport: Telluride
Location: 15 minutes from Telluride
Memberships: The Dude Ranchers' Association, Colorado Dude and Guest Ranch Association
Medical: Telluride Medical Center, eight miles
Conference Capacity: 35
Guest Capacity: 35
Accommodations: Each of the 10 lodge rooms has its own comfortable log bed with down comforter and sheepskin bed cover, its own thermostat control, and a private bath. Attached to the lodge is a log addition with two apartments equipped with kitchenettes. Each of the four cabins has a kitchenette and sleeps 2–6 skiers. No smoking in any building.
Rates: • $–$$$$ European Plan; breakfast included and dinners available, or full ski package with all meals, skiing, and ski lessons. No minimum stay.

Credit Cards: VISA, MasterCard, American Express. Personal and traveler's checks accepted.
Season: Mid-December to early April. Open Christmas.
Activities: The all-inclusive Alpine ski weeks include a myriad of winter adventures for adults and children 16 and older. There are also traditional ranch activities along with snowshoeing, cross-country and Alpine skiing. Afternoon and evening horse-drawn sleigh rides. Snowshoeing and cross-country equipment available. Snowmobiling from Skyline up to old mining ghost town can be arranged (extra). Outdoor hot tub.
Children's Programs: Children are welcome but are the responsibility of parents. Baby-sitting available (extra). Excellent ski program for kids at Telluride Ski Area. Cribs and high chairs available.
Dining: The ranch serves two hearty meals each day—breakfast and dinner. Most eat at the ski area or in town for lunch. Après-ski treats and hot cider are offered in the late afternoon. Experience the magic of Skyline's horse-drawn sleigh ride to the fine dining restaurant "Spruce Lodge," which is also open to the public. Casual dining exclusively for lodging guests.
Entertainment: Cozy evening fires at the ranch and local entertainment in Telluride. Be sure to ask about moonlight cross-country skiing and boot hockey on the pond.
Summary: Kilgore's "Best of the Best"–Downhill and Cross-Country Skiing. Spectacular setting, exciting Alpine ski packages. Here you'll experience the magic of Skyline's winter wonderland. Great food, warm hospitality, and camaraderie. Located just five miles from Telluride's famous ski resort. Skyline is a marvelous base camp for winter fun in and around Telluride. Surrounded by 14,000-foot mountain peaks with lots of sunshine and mountain joy. Great for both cross-country and downhill skiing.

Vista Verde Ranch
Steamboat Springs, Colorado

With the blue Colorado sky overhead and lots of powdery snow on the ground, this secluded ranch looks like Vista Blanca. Vista Verde is a winter wonderland. The characteristics of the summer guest ranch carry over into the winter season with handsomely furnished, cozy log cabins and lodge rooms, fine dining, and a wide variety of outdoor adventures that include skiing, snowshoeing, and snowmobiling. There is also fun for all in feeding the animals, soaking in your own private hot tub, or simply reading by the fire. Holidays are traditional and special, with horse-drawn sleighs and caroling. Winter at Vista Verde is a happy, heartwarming time and brings exhilarating outdoor winter fun with great food, romance, and lots of Colorado magic.

Address: P.O. Box 465K, Steamboat Springs, Colorado 80477

Telephone: 800/526-7433, 970/879-3858; fax: 970/879-1413

Email: vistaverde@compuserve.com

Internet: www.vistaverde.com

Airport: Special winter service to Hayden via major carriers or direct service from Denver. Ranch Suburbans will pick you up.

Location: 25 miles north of Steamboat Springs, off Seed House Road

Memberships: Cross-Country Ski Areas of America, Professional Ski Instructors of America, The Dude Ranchers' Association, Colorado Dude and Guest Ranch Association

Awards: Mobil 4 Star; Kilgore Luxury Group

Medical: Yampa Valley Medical Center

Conference Capacity: 30

Guest Capacity: 40

Accommodations: Authentic log cabins are nestled among the aspens and pines overlooking the snow-covered meadows and forest. Handsomely furnished, they include woodstoves, full baths, down comforters, antiques, artwork, and private outdoor hot tubs. Spacious lodge rooms offer splendid views, convenience, and luxury.

Rates: • $$$–$$$$ American Plan. Children's post-holiday and downhill skiing packages available. Snowmobiling, dogsledding, ice climbing, and hot-air ballooning extra. Minimum stays: call for details.

Credit Cards: None. Personal checks or traveler's checks accepted.

Season: Christmas to mid-March

Activities: Variety of activities include snowshoeing, sleigh rides, horseback riding, ski-in lunches at the lodge or old homestead cabin, moonlight skiing, dogsledding, ice climbing, off-ranch snowmobiling, and even fly-fishing. Spa building with exercise equipment. Talented masseuse available. Daily transportation provided to nearby Steamboat Ski Area for downhill enthusiasts. There are about 20 miles (30 kilometers) of groomed trails with double tracks and skating lanes, telemark hills, and unlimited backcountry opportunities in the surrounding national forest; professional instruction; complimentary guided ski tours; and first-class equipment. Ski instructors meet each morning at breakfast to organize activities with guests. Many guests like to go off and ski on their own, while others enjoy being guided.

Children's Programs: Full kid's program over the holidays features fun-in-the-snow activities at the sledding hill, snow cave, and igloo; feeding the animals; and indoor games at Sweethearts Parlor.

Dining: Dining is a major part of Vista Verde's winter experience. Candlelight dinners overlooking the snow-laden meadows; lunches on the sun deck; and hearty, scrumptious breakfasts. Special diets catered to. Fine wine and beer available.

Entertainment: Each evening may include light folk music, fireside chats with local personalities, parlor games, and moonlight skiing.

Summary: A real romantic winter getaway. Kilgore's "Best of the Best"–Cross-Country Skiing. Candlelight dining, fabulous food, and lots of snow and winter activities. Perfect for honeymoons, couples, and good friends. Downhill skiing too! Holiday family and children's programs. Nearby: Steamboat Springs Ski Resort.

Teton Ridge Ranch
Tetonia, Idaho

"Teton Ridge is a gem on the other side of the Tetons." Five miles from the nearest paved road, the 4,000-acre ranch offers gracious hospitality, excellent food, elegant accommodations (hot tub, steam shower, and woodstove in each bedroom suite), and superb cross-country skiing. The delightful 10,000-square-foot log lodge and separate two-bedroom cottage accommodates only 14 guests at a time. The upper floor is largely devoted to a living room with cathedral ceiling, opening onto a deck with a stunning profile of the almost-14,000-foot Grand Tetons. The ranch is part of the largest intact ecosystem in the lower 48 states. Guests seem to acclimate quickly to the 6,800-foot altitude, which is a good thing, since 20 miles of snowcat-groomed striding and skating trails take off a dozen yards from the door. It's the only trail system in North America that ranges between two states, starting in Idaho and winding east into Wyoming. The ranch is, indeed, one of Kilgore's "Best of the Best."

Address: 200 Valley View Road, Drawer K, Tetonia, Idaho 83452
Telephone: 208/456-2650; fax: 208/456-2218
Email: info@tetonridge.com
Internet: www.ranchweb.com/teton
Airport: Jackson, 45 miles; Idaho Falls, 69 miles; small planes to Driggs Airport, 11 miles (7,200-foot paved and lighted airstrip). Extra charge for pickup at Jackson and Idaho Falls.
Location: 38 miles west of Jackson; 11 miles northeast of Driggs
Memberships: Cross-Country Ski Areas Association
Awards: *Hideaway Report*, *Travel & Leisure*, Kilgore Luxury Group
Medical: Teton Valley Hospital, 12 miles
Conference Capacity: 14 overnight, 32 for the day. Excellent for very small corporate retreats.
Guest Capacity: 14
Accommodations: The main 10,000-square-foot log lodge has a spacious living room, lower-level dining room, and five suites, each with balconies commanding views of the Teton Range, woodstoves, and large bathrooms with Jacuzzi tubs. Telephones, teleports, and computers available for all guests. Separate 2,000-square-foot cottage.

Rates: • $$$$$–$$$$$$ American Plan. Three-night minimum stay, but most come for 4–5 days. Special rate if you reserve the entire ranch.
Credit Cards: VISA, MasterCard
Season: January through March
Activities: The region is famous for its snow depth and quality (the high country receives over 40 feet of powder annually). Cross-country skiing guide and instructor on-staff. Visitors often Alpine ski at Grand Targhee or head over Teton Pass to Jackson Hole for more downhilling, shopping, and a sleigh ride in the National Elk Refuge. Other options include horse-drawn sleigh rides, dogsledding, or a snowmobile trip into Yellowstone National Park. Bring your own cross-country equipment or rent top gear in Jackson Hole or in Driggs.
Children's Programs: Winter wonderland. Parents are responsible for children. Best for older, well-behaved children.
Dining: An epicure's delight. After a wonderful day of skiing enjoy rich beet soup and freshly made bread, while you watch the sun set on the Tetons. Your entrée might be sautéed pheasant on a bed of simmered apples, cabbage and onions, with Yukon gold potatoes. Pears in puff pastry served with homemade caramel ice cream would be the only thing to make this day more perfect. Candlelight, dual fireplaces, and a good wine complete the setting to warm all your senses. Breakfast and lunch are hearty, informal, meals to fuel you for the day's outdoor activities. Don't forget the near-famous ranch cookies just a step away in the guest-friendly kitchen. Special diets always accommodated.
Entertainment: You're on your own. Most read, relax, or enjoy fireside chats and a glass of brandy. Usually "high tea" after skiing.
Summary: Kilgore's "Best of the Best"–Cross-Country Skiing, Luxury, and Cuisine. Teton Ridge is ideal for couples, families, or small groups who enjoy privacy, a pristine setting, and luxury. Massage available. Nearby: Skiing, shopping, and art galleries.

Lone Mountain Ranch
Big Sky, Montana

The magic of Lone Mountain Ranch and Montana comes alive in the winter. Here the crisp mountain air and fluffy white snow, nearby Yellowstone National Park, cozy historic cabins, a five-star dining lodge with wonderful gourmet cuisine—all nestled in a private valley of its very own—beckon to make Lone Mountain Ranch a world-class winter wonderland. Nearby Big Sky Ski Resort offers exhilarating downhill skiing and the naturalist-guided Yellowstone ski tours are a favorite. Together with a fine staff, LMR offers romantic winter vacations and adventure for individuals, couples, and families who want to commune with nature and enjoy a true shining star in the ranching world.

Address: P.O. Box 160069 K, Big Sky, Montana 59716
Telephone: 800/514-4644, 406/995-4644; fax: 406/995-4670
Email: lmr@lmranch.com
Internet: www.lmranch.com
Airport: Bozeman, 40 miles
Location: 40 miles south of Bozeman
Memberships: Greater Yellowstone Coalition, Montana Dude Ranch Association, Cross-Country Ski Area Association, Professional Ski Instructors of America (PSIA)
Awards: Various *Snow Country* magazine awards
Medical: Bozeman Deaconess Hospital
Conference Capacity: 50
Guest Capacity: 60
Accommodations: 24 fully insulated one- to four-bedroom cozy cabins with comfortable beds, electric heat, bathrooms with tub/shower, and rock fireplaces or wood-burning stoves. Six-bedroom luxury Ridgetop Lodge.
Rates: • $$$–$$$$$ American Plan. Children's rates. Normally a minimum one-week stay, Saturday to Saturday.
Credit Cards: VISA, MasterCard, Discover
Season: Early December to early April
Activities: 45 miles of cross-country trails through meadows, across ridges, and up valleys groomed for skating and diagonal striding. Miles of ungroomed trails for telemarking and packed snowshoe trails. Retail and rental cross-country shop. Lessons and naturalist-guided ski trips to Yellowstone backcountry. Shuttle service for downhill skiers to Big Sky Resort. Ask about Orvis-endorsed guided fly-fishing trips. Outdoor whirlpool.
Children's Programs: Best for children old enough to ski. Children's ski lessons available.
Dining: Tremendous log dining room with limited seating open to the public. The food consistently receives rave reviews. Old-fashioned sleigh ride to a cabin in the woods for dinner. Kerosene lanterns light the cabin, and food is cooked on a magnificent 100-year-old wood-burning cookstove. Guests enjoy a prime rib dinner and musical entertainment before their ride back to the ranch. Be sure to ask about the excellent weekly trail buffet lunch.
Entertainment: Several evening programs throughout the winter, including naturalist presentations on grizzly bears and the greater Yellowstone ecosystem. Weekly musical programs also featured.
Summary: Kilgore's "Best of the Best"–Cross-Country Skiing. Dependable snow and meticulously groomed trails. Sleigh rides and dining room open to the public. Winter: Orvis-endorsed guided fly-fishing trips. Great for spring and fall conferences. Major airline connections. Check out the interactive ski trail map with weather and ski conditions on the LMR website (see above). Video available. Nearby: Yellowstone National Park and Big Sky Ski Resort for downhill skiing.

Triple Creek Ranch
Darby, Montana

Triple Creek Ranch is one of the world's true luxury hideaways. Small, intimate, with personal service second to none, all the trappings that embrace a winter wonderland come alive here. The spirit at Triple Creek is just as magical as the surroundings. Together with an incredible staff, general managers Wayne and Judy Kilpatrick serve up the best of the best. Guests enjoy relaxing in true luxury with crackling fires and gourmet cuisine, coupled with all the outdoor winter activities, including cross-country skiing, snowmobiling, snowshoeing, horseback riding, and dogsledding, not to mention the heartwarming joys of the Christmas and New Year holidays. Winter, summer, or fall, Triple Creek is truly a slice of heaven and a piece of paradise.

Address: 5551 West Fork Road, Darby, Montana 59829
Telephone: 406/821-4600; fax: 406/821-4666
Email: tcr@bitterroot.net
Internet: www.triplecreekranch.com
Airport: Missoula, 74 miles. Private planes to Hamilton with 4,200-foot runway. Helicopter pad at ranch. Airport pickup available.
Location: 12 miles south of Darby, 74 miles south of Missoula
Memberships: Relais & Chateaux
Awards: Relais & Chateaux; *Hideaway Report*, "A Romantic Gem in the Rocky Mountains," April 2000; Ranked No. 7 of 20 U.S. Resort Hideaways, *Little Gems*, September 2000; *El Capitan*, "Hideout of the Year," December 2000
Medical: Marcus Daly Memorial Hospital, Hamilton. Emergency medical helicopter service available.
Conference Capacity: 30; booking entire ranch is generally required
Guest Capacity: 30 singles, 24 couples
Accommodations: 19 cozy-to-luxurious cedar log cabins. All have fireplaces and refrigerators stocked with an array of complimentary beverages and a full supply of liquor. Each cabin has satellite TV/VCR. Luxury cabins have handsome, handcrafted, king-size log beds; double steam showers; and private decks with hot tubs overlooking the forest. Daily housekeeping and laundry service.

Rates: • $$$$$$ 408 American Plan. No minimum stay. Single rates. All fine wine and liquor complimentary.
Credit Cards: VISA, MasterCard, Discover, American Express
Season: Year-round; all holidays.
Activities: While snowmobiling is a specialty, there's also a variety of cross-country skiing and downhill opportunities for both beginning and advanced skiers. Cross-country trails at the ranch are set with a snowmobile, or you may ski into the Bitterroot National Forest with all kinds of backcountry experiences. Downhill skiing at Lost Trail Powder Mountain (28 miles away) with shuttle service provided, or use groomed trails at Chief Joseph Pass Cross-Country Ski area. Be sure to ask about incredible all-day snowmobiling with gourmet luncheons and snacks. Snowshoeing and horseback riding too! Heated outdoor Jacuzzi.
Children's Programs: Children under age 16 allowed only when a family or group reserves entire ranch.
Dining: Gourmet meals with menus featuring Montana beef, seafood flown in from the coast, and wild game. Special diets never a problem. Full room service available. Extensive wine list and full bar. Open to the public on very limited basis.
Entertainment: Informal evening program. Occasional live music. Main lodge with library and full complimentary bar.
Summary: Kilgore's "Best of the Best"–Luxury. Adults-only, year-round luxury in Montana's wilderness. Personal service second to none! Relaxed or active winter paradise—you decide. Superb cuisine, fine wine, and amenities. Excellent for small corporate groups and family reunions. Triple Creek is tops!

Brooks Lake Lodge
Dubois, Wyoming

THE DUDE RANCHERS'
ASSOCIATION

Wyoming
Dude
Rancher's
Association

History, romance, magnificence: Brooks Lake captures the spirit and tradition of one of North America's great winter sporting lodges. It's a winter Shangri-la high in the Wyoming Rockies. The lodge is located about 63 miles northeast of Jackson, famous for Les Grand Tetons named by early French explorers. If you drive from the small towns of Dubois or Jackson, Brooks Lake staff will meet you at the trailhead just off Togwotee Pass Highway; their warm smiles are just the beginning. From this point, guests are shuttled by snowmobile five miles to the lodge. Some prefer to cross-country ski or dogsled in. Whatever you decide to do, you're in for the time of your life. Whether you're sitting by one of the blazing fires in the midst of a snowstorm or exploring the magical mountain splendor on a crisp blue-sky day, you'll never forget the Brooks Lake Lodge.

Address: 458 Brooks Lake Road, Drawer K, Dubois, Wyoming 82513
Telephone: 307/455-2121; fax: 307/455-2221
Email: brookslake@wyoming.com
Internet: www.brookslake.com
Airport: Jackson, 60 miles
Location: 60 miles northeast of Jackson off Highway 287/26, 23 miles west of Dubois off Highway 287/26
Awards: National Register of Historic Places, Kilgore Luxury Group
Memberships: The Dude Ranchers' Association, Wyoming Dude Rancher's Association, Association of Historic Hotels of the Rocky Mountain West
Medical: Jackson, 60 miles
Conference Capacity: 36 (overnight)
Guest Capacity: 36
Accommodations: Seven comfortable lodge rooms with distinctive motifs and exquisite handcrafted lodgepole furnishings. Eight cabins nestle in the spruces behind the lodge, with wood-burning stoves, electric heat, and private baths with bathrobes. Several have wonderful old clawfoot bathtubs. The massive log lodge is furnished with wicker, antiques, and handcrafted works by Wyoming artists. Spa facility available.
Rates: • $$$–$$$$$ American Plan. Snowmobiles, dogsledding, and liquor extra. No minimum stay.

Credit Cards: VISA, MasterCard, American Express. Personal and traveler's checks accepted.
Season: Late December to mid-April. Open for lodging Wednesday through Sunday.
Activities: The lodge is situated at 9,200 feet in the midst of the awesome Pinnacle formation of the Absaroka Mountains, the Brooks Mountain to the west, and the Continental Divide to the north. You may cross-country ski, snowmobile (all guided trips), snowshoe, or with prior arrangement, take a thrilling dogsled ride. Guests usually use the lodge as a base camp for a myriad of outdoor adventures. Overnight trips into Yellowstone National Park by snowmobile are available, too. Ask about Sublette Meadow, Bear Cub Pass, Austin Peak, and the bighorn sheep viewing.
Children's Programs: None, but kids are welcome. A nanny should accompany younger children if parents wish to be active outdoors.
Dining: High gourmet served on fine china with silver. Hearty regional Western cuisine and health-conscious meals. Delicious homemade soups and freshly baked breads. Lunches open to the public arriving by skis, dogsled, or snowmobile. Liquor and fine wine available.
Entertainment: The Diamond G Saloon is a gathering place before and after dinner. At 6 P.M., hors d'oeuvres are served. Occasional local entertainment.
Summary: Kilgore Luxury Group—Grand Lodge. The winter experience is magical. Snow, Old West beauty, warmth, and mountain splendor. Superb accommodations, great food, and terrific hospitality. You'll cherish your time here for the rest of your life! Lunches open to the public. Five-mile trip in winter to lodge by skis, snowmobiles, or dogsled (with prior arrangement).

Brush Creek Ranch
Saratoga, Wyoming

THE DUDE RANCHERS' ASSOCIATION

Wyoming Dude Rancher's Association

Brush Creek Ranch is one of Wyoming's old-time cattle ranches. Just outside the town of Saratoga and overlooking the Platte Valley, the ranch offers the charm and intimacy that you might expect to find on a ranch in the winter. Today, Kinta and Gibb Blumenthal offer a winter experience with very relaxed, easygoing, and independent programs for families, couples, and singles. Brush Creek offers cross-country skiing, horse-drawn sleigh rides, dogsledding, snowshoeing, and great sledding opportunities for children. You may also enjoy off-ranch snowmobile tours through Wyoming's Snowy Range Mountains, just 15 minutes away.

Address: Star Route, Box 10, Saratoga, Wyoming 82331
Telephone: 800/RANCH-WY (800/726-2499), 307/327-5241; fax: 307/327-5384
Email: kinta@brushcreekranch.com
Internet: www.brushcreekranch.com
Airport: Denver, 195 miles; Laramie, 65 miles. Airport pickup is extra.
Location: 100 miles west of Laramie. Call for details.
Memberships: Colorado Cross-Country Ski Association, The Dude Ranchers' Association, Wyoming Dude Rancher's Association, America Outdoors
Medical: Clinic in Saratoga, 16 miles
Guest Capacity: 26
Accommodations: Guests stay in either the main lodge, built in the early 1900s with a New England white-sided and green-trimmed charm, or in two historic log-cabin duplexes with private baths. The main lodge has a wonderful personality with a small, cozy library and fireplace. Wonderful enclosed hot tub with scenic views.
Rates: • $$ Full American Plan. Children's rates. Two-night minimum stay.
Credit Cards: VISA, MasterCard. Personal checks preferred.
Season: December through March
Activities: You're on your own to do as much or as little as you wish. The ranch will help you coordinate and organize both on- and off-ranch activities. Cross-country skiers enjoy over five miles of snowmobile-prepared trails and miles of untracked skiing opportunities through the cattle in the meadows, by the creek, or on thousands of acres of wonderful backcountry. Equipment available through local outfitter, or bring your own. Be sure to ask about the incredible snowmobiling in the Medicine Bow National Forest, just up the road from the ranch.
Children's Programs: Children are the responsibility of parents. Luckily, it's a kids' winter wonderland.
Dining: Western-style food with a gourmet flair. Take-along lunches for day outings. BYOB.
Entertainment: Very low-key and informal. Most relax by the fire, enjoying conversation and sharing stories. Enclosed hot tub.
Summary: A 6,000-acre winter wonderland on one of Wyoming's historic cattle ranches. Great for those who savor peace, quiet, and an unstructured program. Wonderful family atmosphere and warm, sincere hospitality. Nearby: Charming Western town of Saratoga and Wyoming's Snowy Range Mountains.

Appendix

SPECIAL RANCH CATEGORIES

Note: Subject to change without notice. Contact ranch to confirm.

Accessible Only by Boat, Horseback, Helicopter, Plane, or Train
Crystal Creek Lodge, Alaska
Grand Canyon Bar 10 Ranch, Arizona
Tall Timber, Colorado
Klick's K Bar L Ranch, Montana

Adults Only (Check with ranch on age limits and opportunities for families who book entire property)
McNamara Ranch, Colorado
Double JJ Resort Ranch, Michigan
Triple Creek Ranch, Montana
Flying A Guest Ranch, Wyoming
Echo Valley Guest Ranch, British Columbia, Canada

Adults Only (Special Weeks/Months)
Crystal Creek Lodge, Alaska
Grapevine Canyon Ranch, Arizona
Scott Valley Resort and Guest Ranch, Arkansas
Highland Ranch, California
Aspen Canyon Ranch, Colorado
Bar Lazy J Guest Ranch, Colorado
C Lazy U Ranch, Colorado
Colorado Trails Ranch, Colorado
Coulter Lake Guest Ranch, Colorado
Drowsy Water Ranch, Colorado
La Garita Creek Ranch, Colorado
Lake Mancos Ranch, Colorado
Lost Valley Ranch, Colorado
McNamara Ranch, Colorado
Peaceful Valley Ranch, Colorado
Powderhorn Guest Ranch, Colorado
Rawah Ranch, Colorado
Vista Verde Ranch, Colorado
Wilderness Trails Ranch, Colorado
Hidden Creek Ranch, Idaho
Big EZ Lodge, Montana
Boulder River Ranch, Montana
Diamond J Ranch, Montana
Hargrave Cattle and Guest Ranch, Montana
Hawley Mountain Guest Ranch, Montana
Laughing Water Ranch, Montana
Lone Mountain Ranch, Montana
Mountain Sky Guest Ranch, Montana
The Lodge at Chama, New Mexico
Pinegrove Dude Ranch, New York
Woodside Ranch, Wisconsin
Absaroka Ranch, Wyoming

Box R Ranch, Wyoming
Breteche Creek Ranch, Wyoming
Canyon Ranch, Wyoming
Gros Ventre River Ranch, Wyoming
HF Bar Ranch, Wyoming
The Hideout at Flitner Ranch, Wyoming
Lazy L & B Ranch, Wyoming
Paradise Guest Ranch, Wyoming
R Lazy S, Wyoming
Savery Creek Thoroughbred Ranch, Wyoming
Seven D Ranch, Wyoming
T-Cross Ranch, Wyoming
Triangle C Ranch, Wyoming
UXU Ranch, Wyoming
Vee Bar Guest Ranch, Wyoming
Homeplace Guest Ranch, British Columbia, Canada

Airstrip (** on or near ranch)
Crystal Creek Lodge, Alaska
Circle Z Ranch, Arizona
Flying E Ranch, Arizona
Grand Canyon Bar 10 Ranch, Arizona
Kay El Bar, Arizona
Rancho de los Caballeros, Arizona
White Stallion Ranch, Arizona
Alisal Guest Ranch, California
Coffee Creek Ranch, California
Hunewill Circle H Ranch, California
4UR Ranch, Colorado
Deer Valley Guest Ranch, Colorado
Drowsy Water Ranch, Colorado
Elk Mountain Ranch, Colorado
The Home Ranch, Colorado
La Garita Creek Ranch, Colorado
Latigo Ranch, Colorado
Skyline Guest Ranch, Colorado
Tall Timber, Colorado**
T-Lazy-7 Ranch, Colorado
Diamond D Ranch, Idaho
Teton Ridge Ranch, Idaho
Twin Peaks Ranch, Idaho
Double JJ Resort Ranch, Michigan**
63 Ranch, Montana
Averills' Ranch-Flathead Lake Lodge, Montana
Diamond J Ranch, Montana
Lake Upsata Ranch, Montana
Laughing Water Ranch, Montana
Nine Quarter Circle Ranch, Montana
Parade Rest Ranch, Montana

Hartley Guest Ranch, New Mexico
Pinegrove Dude Ranch, New York
Rocking Horse Ranch Resort, New York
Clear Creek Ranch, North Carolina
Aspen Ridge Resort, Oregon
Texas Ranch Life, Texas
Hidden Valley Guest Ranch, Washington
K Diamond K Ranch, Washington
Box R Ranch, Wyoming
Brush Creek Ranch, Wyoming
CM Ranch, Wyoming
Heart Six Ranch, Wyoming
H F Bar Ranch, Wyoming
The Hideout at Flitner Ranch, Wyoming
Lazy L & B Ranch, Wyoming
Savery Creek Thoroughbred Ranch,
    Wyoming
TA Guest Ranch, Wyoming
T-Cross Ranch, Wyoming
Triangle X Ranch, Wyoming
Vee Bar Guest Ranch, Wyoming
Echo Valley Guest Ranch, British Columbia,
    Canada
Flying U Ranch, British Columbia, Canada
Three Bars Ranch, British Columbia, Canada

ATV Tours
Grand Canyon Bar 10 Ranch, Arizona

Balloon Ranches
La Garita Creek Ranch, Colorado
Vista Verde Ranch, Colorado

Bring Your Own Horse
Flying E Ranch, Arizona
Grand Canyon Bar 10 Ranch, Arizona
Rancho de los Caballeros, Arizona
Scott Valley Resort and Guest Ranch, Arkansas
Alisal Guest Ranch, California
Circle Bar B Guest Ranch, California
Coffee Creek Ranch, California
Highland Ranch, California
Hunewill Ranch, California
Cherokee Park Ranch, Colorado
Lane Guest Ranch, Colorado
McNamara Ranch, Colorado
Bar H Bar Ranch, Idaho
Kelly Toponce Guest Ranch, Idaho
Teton Ridge Ranch, Idaho
Double JJ Resort Ranch, Michigan
Klick's K Bar L Ranch, Montana
Triple Creek Ranch, Montana
Aspen Ridge Resort, Oregon
Running-R Guest Ranch, Texas
Texas Ranch Life, Texas

Hidden Valley Guest Ranch, Washington
K Diamond K Ranch, Washington
Woodside Ranch, Wisconsin
Box R Ranch, Wyoming
Brush Creek Ranch, Wyoming
Canyon Ranch, Wyoming
Ranger Creek Guest Ranch, Wyoming
Savery Creek Thoroughbred Ranch,
    Wyoming
Seven D Ranch, Wyoming
TA Guest Ranch, Wyoming
T-Cross Ranch, Wyoming
Homeplace Guest Ranch, Alberta, Canada
Three Bars Ranch, British Columbia, Canada

Birding
The Bellota Ranch, Arizona
Elkhorn Ranch, Arizona
La Tierra Linda Guest Ranch Resort, Arizona
Rancho de los Caballeros, Arizona
Tanque Verde Ranch, Arizona
White Stallion Ranch, Arizona
Laramie River Ranch, Colorado
Tarryall River Ranch, Colorado
Boulder River Ranch, Montana
Diamond J Ranch, Montana
Los Pinos Ranch, New Mexico
Lazy Hills Guest Ranch, Texas
Running-R Guest Ranch, Texas
Texas Ranch Life, Texas
K Diamond K Ranch, Washington
Breteche Creek Ranch, Wyoming
Canyon Ranch, Wyoming
HF Bar Ranch, Wyoming
Echo Valley Guest Ranch, British Columbia,
    Canada

Bronc Riding
Triangle C Ranch, Wyoming

Buffalo Ranch (Have buffalo)
Averills' Ranch-Flathead Lake Lodge, Montana
Circle Bar Guest Ranch, Montana
Klick's K Bar L Ranch, Montana
The Lodge at Chama, New Mexico
Woodside Ranch, Wisconsin

Cattle Penning
White Stallion Ranch, Arizona
Lake Mancos Ranch, Colorado
Laramie River Ranch, Colorado
Latigo Ranch, Colorado
Wit's End Guest and Resort Ranch, Colorado
Hidden Creek Ranch, Idaho
Twin Peaks Ranch, Idaho

Double JJ Resort Ranch, Michigan
Averills' Ranch-Flathead Lake Lodge, Montana
G bar M Ranch, Montana
Hargrave Cattle & Guest Ranch, Montana
Horse Prairie Ranch, Montana
Logan Cattle & Guest Ranch, Montana
Hartley Guest Ranch, New Mexico
Texas Ranch Life, Texas
Bitterroot Ranch, Wyoming
Double Diamond X Ranch, Wyoming
TA Ranch, Wyoming
Triangle C Ranch, Wyoming
Triangle X Ranch, Wyoming

Cattle Roundups, Cattle Drives
The Bellota Ranch, Arizona
Grand Canyon Bar 10 Ranch, Arizona
Grapevine Canyon Ranch, Arizona
The Horseshoe Ranch on Bloody Basin Road,
  Arizona
Tanque Verde Ranch, Arizona
Alisal Guest Ranch, California
Hunewill Circle H Ranch, California
Cherokee Park Ranch, Colorado
La Garita Creek Ranch, Colorado
Latigo Ranch, Colorado
Lost Valley Ranch, Colorado
Vista Verde Ranch, Colorado
Wilderness Trails, Colorado
Wit's End Guest and Resort Ranch, Colorado
Bar H Bar Ranch, Idaho
Twin Peaks Ranch, Idaho
Double JJ Resort Ranch, Michigan
Circle Bar Guest Ranch, Montana
G bar M Ranch, Montana
Hargrave Cattle and Guest Ranch, Montana
Horse Prairie Ranch, Montana
Klick's K Bar L Ranch, Montana
Laughing Water Ranch, Montana
Logan Cattle & Guest Ranch, Montana
Hartley Guest Ranch, New Mexico
Pinegrove Dude Ranch, New York
Aspen Ridge Resort, Oregon
Texas Ranch Life, Texas
Grand Canyon Bar 10 Ranch, Utah
K Diamond K Ranch, Washington
Absaroka Ranch, Wyoming
Bitterroot Ranch, Wyoming
Brush Creek Ranch, Wyoming
Goosewing Ranch, Wyoming
The Hideout at Flitner Ranch, Wyoming
Lozier's Box R Ranch, Wyoming
R Lazy S Ranch, Wyoming
TA Ranch, Wyoming
Vee Bar Guest Ranch, Wyoming

Flying U Ranch, British Columbia, Canada
Three Bars Ranch, British Columbia, Canada

Cattle Work
The Bellota Ranch, Arizona
Grapevine Canyon Ranch, Arizona
White Stallion Ranch, Arizona
Hunewill Circle H Ranch, California
The Home Ranch, Colorado
Laramie River Ranch, Colorado
Latigo Ranch, Colorado
Lost Valley Ranch, Colorado
Bar H Bar Ranch, Idaho
Kelly Toponce Guest Ranch, Idaho
Turkey Creek Ranch, Missouri
63 Ranch, Montana
Averills' Ranch-Flathead Lake Lodge, Montana
Circle Bar Guest Ranch, Montana
G bar M Ranch, Montana
Hargrave Cattle and Guest Ranch, Montana
Horse Prairie Ranch, Montana
Logan Cattle & Guest Ranch, Montana
Hartley Guest Ranch, New Mexico
Aspen Ridge Resort, Oregon
Texas Ranch Life, Texas
K Diamond K Ranch, Washington
Bitterroot Ranch, Wyoming
Brush Creek Ranch, Wyoming
Box R Ranch, Wyoming
The Hideout at Flitner Ranch, Wyoming
Savery Creek Thoroughbred Ranch, Wyoming
Seven D Ranch, Wyoming
TA Guest Ranch, Wyoming
T-Cross Ranch, Wyoming
Vee Bar Guest Ranch, Wyoming
Homeplace Guest Ranch, Alberta, Canada
Echo Valley Guest Ranch, British Columbia,
  Canada
Three Bars Ranch, British Columbia, Canada

Chapel (On ranch)
The Bellota Ranch, Arizona
Tanque Verde Ranch, Arizona
Diamond D Ranch, Idaho

Children's Programs (**Infants welcome)
Rancho de los Caballeros, Arizona
Tanque Verde Ranch, Arizona
Alisal Guest Ranch, California**
Coffee Creek Ranch, California**
Rankin Ranch, California**
Aspen Canyon Ranch, Colorado
Aspen Lodge Ranch Resort, Colorado
Bar Lazy J, Colorado**
Cherokee Park Ranch, Colorado**

C Lazy U Ranch, Colorado**
Colorado Trails Ranch, Colorado**
Deer Valley Ranch, Colorado
Drowsy Water Ranch, Colorado**
Elk Mountain Ranch, Colorado**
4UR Ranch, Colorado
The Home Ranch, Colorado
La Garita Creek Ranch, Colorado
Lake Mancos Ranch, Colorado
Lane Guest Ranch, Colorado**
Laramie River Ranch, Colorado
Latigo Ranch, Colorado
Lost Valley Ranch, Colorado**
North Fork Ranch, Colorado
Peaceful Valley Ranch, Colorado**
Rainbow Trout Ranch, Colorado**
Tarryall River Ranch, Colorado**
Tumbling River Ranch, Colorado**
Vista Verde Ranch, Colorado**
Wilderness Trails Ranch, Colorado**
Wit's End Guest and Resort Ranch,
   Colorado**
Diamond D Ranch, Idaho
Hidden Creek Ranch, Idaho**
Double JJ Resort Ranch, Michigan
Averills' Ranch-Flathead Lake Lodge,
   Montana**
Elkhorn Ranch, Montana**
Lake Upsata Guest Ranch, Montana
Laughing Water Ranch, Montana
Lone Mountain Ranch, Montana**
Mountain Sky Guest Ranch, Montana**
Nine Quarter Circle Ranch, Montana
Pinegrove Dude Ranch, New York**
Rocking Horse Ranch Resort, New York
Clear Creek Ranch, North Carolina
Rock Springs Guest Ranch, Oregon
Lazy Hills Guest Ranch, Texas
Hidden Valley Guest Ranch, Washington
Woodside Ranch, Wisconsin
Brush Creek Ranch, Wyoming
Double Diamond X Ranch, Wyoming
H F Bar Ranch, Wyoming**
Heart Six Ranch, Wyoming**
Laughing Water Ranch, Wyoming
Lazy L & B Ranch, Wyoming
Lost Creek Ranch, Wyoming**
Paradise Guest Ranch, Wyoming**
R Lazy S Ranch, Wyoming**
Ranger Creek Guest Ranch, Wyoming
Seven D Ranch, Wyoming**
Triangle C Ranch, Wyoming**
Triangle X Ranch, Wyoming
UXU Ranch, Wyoming

Children's Ranch Camps
Cheley Colorado Camps, Colorado

Christian Ranches
Grand Canyon Bar 10 Ranch, Arizona
Deer Valley Ranch, Colorado
Lazy Hills Guest Ranch, Texas

Cigar-Friendly (Outdoors mostly)
Rancho de los Caballeros, Arizona
Coffee Creek Ranch, California
Bar Lazy J Guest Ranch, Colorado
Lane Guest Ranch, Colorado
Lost Valley Ranch, Colorado
Rawah Ranch, Colorado
T-Lazy-7 Ranch, Colorado
Wit's End Resort Ranch, Colorado
Diamond D Ranch, Idaho
Teton Ridge Ranch, Idaho
Double JJ Resort Ranch, Michigan
Turkey Creek Ranch, Missouri
320 Guest Ranch, Montana
Big EZ Lodge, Montana
Circle Bar Guest Ranch, Montana
Klick's K Bar L Ranch, Montana
Mountain Meadows Guest Ranch, Montana
Aspen Ridge Resort, Oregon
Rock Springs Guest Ranch, Oregon
Running-R Guest Ranch, Texas
K Diamond K Ranch, Washington
Woodside Ranch, Wisconsin
Absaroka Ranch, Wyoming
Bill Cody Ranch, Wyoming
Box R Ranch, Wyoming
Breteche Creek Ranch, Wyoming
Brooks Lake Lodge, Wyoming
Canyon Ranch, Wyoming
Double Diamond X Ranch, Wyoming
Goosewing Ranch, Wyoming
Heart Six Ranch, Wyoming
H F Bar Ranch, Wyoming
Paradise Guest Ranch, Wyoming
R Lazy S Ranch, Wyoming
TA Guest Ranch, Wyoming
T-Cross Ranch, Wyoming
UXU Ranch, Wyoming
Vee Bar Guest Ranch, Wyoming
Flying U Ranch, British Columbia, Canada

Computer/Laptop in Room
Big EZ Lodge, Montana

Concierge
Lane Guest Ranch, Colorado
Tall Timber, Colorado
Big EZ Lodge, Montana

Conference Capacity

Crystal Creek Lodge, Alaska – 24
Grand Canyon Bar 10 Ranch, Arizona – 50+
Grapevine Canyon Ranch, Arizona – 25
Rancho de los Caballeros, Arizona – 150
Tanque Verde Ranch, Arizona – 150
White Stallion Ranch, Arizona – 50
Scott Valley Resort and Guest Ranch, Arkansas – 65
Alisal Guest Ranch, California – 150
Circle Bar B Guest Ranch, California – 40
Coffee Creek Ranch, California – 50
Rankin Ranch, California – 24
Aspen Canyon Ranch, Colorado – 40
Aspen Lodge Ranch Resort, Colorado – 150
Cherokee Park Ranch, Colorado – 25
Chico Basin Ranch, Colorado – 12
C Lazy U Ranch, Colorado – 70
Colorado Trails Ranch, Colorado – 30
Coulter Lake Guest Ranch, Colorado – 20
Deer Valley Ranch, Colorado – 125
Drowsy Water Ranch, Colorado – 40
Elk Mountain Ranch, Colorado – 25
4UR Ranch, Colorado – 50
Forbes Trinchera Ranch, Colorado – 46
The Home Ranch, Colorado – 30
La Garita Creek Ranch, Colorado – 75
Lake Mancos Ranch, Colorado – 40
Laramie River Ranch, Colorado – 25
Latigo Ranch, Colorado – 38
Lost Valley Ranch, Colorado – 60
North Fork Ranch, Colorado – 20
Peaceful Valley Ranch, Colorado – 100
Powderhorn Guest Ranch, Colorado – 40
Rainbow Trout Ranch, Colorado – 60
Rawah Ranch, Colorado – 32
Skyline Guest Ranch, Colorado – 35
Tall Timber, Colorado – 24
Tarryall River Ranch, Colorado – 36
Tumbling River Ranch, Colorado – 40
Vista Verde Ranch, Colorado – 30
Wit's End Guest and Resort Ranch, Colorado – 300
Diamond D Ranch, Idaho – 35
Hidden Creek Ranch, Idaho – 40
Idaho Rocky Mountain Ranch, Idaho – 42
Teton Ridge Ranch, Idaho – 32
Twin Peaks Ranch, Idaho – 55
Western Pleasure Guest Ranch, Idaho – 34
Double JJ Resort Ranch, Michigan – 350
Turkey Creek Ranch, Missouri – 35
320 Ranch, Montana – 150
Averills' Ranch-Flathead Lake Lodge, Montana – 90
Big EZ Lodge, Montana – 28

Boulder River Ranch, Montana – 25
Circle Bar Guest Ranch, Montana – 30
Elkhorn Ranch, Montana – 30
Hargrave Cattle and Guest Ranch, Montana – 20
Hawley Mountain Guest Ranch, Montana – 14
Horse Prairie Ranch, Montana – 16
Klick's K Bar L Ranch, Montana – 35
Lake Upsata Guest Ranch, Montana – 18
McGinnis Meadows Cattle & Guest Ranch, Montana – 20
Mountain Meadows Guest Ranch, Montana – 26
Mountain Sky Guest Ranch, Montana – 75
Nine Quarter Circle Ranch, Montana – 70
Parade Rest Ranch, Montana – 35
Triple Creek Ranch, Montana – 30
The Lodge at Chama, New Mexico – 42
Pinegrove Dude Ranch, New York – 350
Roaring Brook Ranch and Tennis Resort, New York – 300
Rocking Horse Ranch, New York – 250
Cataloochee Ranch, North Carolina – 40
Clear Creek Ranch, North Carolina – 40
Aspen Ridge Resort, Oregon – 40
Rock Springs Guest Ranch, Oregon – 50
Lazy Hills Guest Ranch, Texas – 150
Running-R Guest Ranch, Texas – 30
Texas Ranch Life, Texas – 30
Rockin' R Ranch, Utah – 100
Hidden Valley Guest Ranch, Washington – 25
K-Diamond-K Cattle & Guest Ranch, Washington – 12
Woodside Ranch, Wisconsin – 100
Bill Cody Ranch, Wyoming – 30
Breteche Creek Ranch, Wyoming – 30
Brooks Lake Lodge, Wyoming – 36
Brush Creek Ranch, Wyoming – 26
Canyon Ranch, Wyoming – 12
CM Ranch, Wyoming – 50
Double Diamond X Ranch, Wyoming – 38
Eatons' Ranch, Wyoming – 65
Goosewing Ranch, Wyoming – 25
Gros Ventre River Ranch, Wyoming – 34
Heart Six Ranch, Wyoming – 50
H F Bar Ranch, Wyoming – 95
The Hideout at Flitner Ranch, Wyoming – 25
Lone Mountain Ranch, Montana – 50
Lost Creek Ranch, Wyoming – 20
Paradise Ranch, Wyoming – 50
Ranger Creek Guest Ranch, Wyoming – 20
Red Rock Ranch, Wyoming – 30
Seven D Ranch, Wyoming – 32
TA Guest Ranch, Wyoming – 75
T-Cross Ranch, Wyoming – 24

Triangle C Ranch, Wyoming – 75
Triangle X Ranch, Wyoming – 50
Vee Bar Guest Ranch, Wyoming – 30
Homeplace Guest Ranch, Alberta, Canada – 12
Echo Valley Guest Ranch, British Columbia, Canada – 40
Flying U Ranch, British Columbia, Canada – 65
Three Bars Ranch, British Columbia, Canada – 40

Cross-Country Skiing

Aspen Canyon Ranch, Colorado
Aspen Lodge Ranch Resort, Colorado
C Lazy U Ranch, Colorado
Hidden Creek Ranch, Idaho
The Home Ranch, Colorado
Latigo Ranch, Colorado
Peaceful Valley Ranch, Colorado
Skyline Guest Ranch, Colorado
Tall Timber, Colorado
Vista Verde Ranch, Colorado
Wit's End Guest and Resort Ranch, Colorado
Kelly Toponce Guest Ranch, Idaho
Teton Ridge Ranch, Idaho
Western Pleasure Guest Ranch, Idaho
Double JJ Resort Ranch, Michigan
320 Ranch, Montana
B Bar Ranch, Montana
Big EZ Lodge, Montana
Lake Upsata Guest Ranch, Montana
Lone Mountain Ranch, Montana
Mountain Meadows Guest Ranch, Montana
Triple Creek Ranch, Montana
Aspen Ridge Resort, Oregon
K Diamond K Ranch, Washington
Woodside Ranch, Wisconsin
Brooks Lake Lodge, Wyoming
Brush Creek Ranch, Wyoming
Ranger Creek Guest Ranch, Wyoming
Trail Creek Ranch, Wyoming
Triangle C Ranch, Wyoming
Triangle X Ranch, Wyoming
Flying U Ranch, British Columbia, Canada

Dinner Theater

Circle Bar B Guest Ranch, California

Downhill Skiing

Tall Timber, Colorado
The Home Ranch, Colorado
Wit's End Guest and Resort Ranch, Colorado
Western Pleasure Guest Ranch, Idaho
320 Guest Ranch, Montana
Big EZ Lodge, Montana

Lone Mountain Ranch, Montana
Mountain Meadows Guest Ranch, Montana
Vista Verde Ranch, Colorado
Rocking Horse Ranch, New York
Cataloochee Ranch, North Carolina
Woodside Ranch, Wisconsin
Trail Creek Ranch, Wyoming

English Cross-Country Jumping

Bitterroot Ranch, Wyoming
Savery Creek Thoroughbred Ranch, Wyoming

English Riding

Rancho de los Caballeros, Arizona
Tanque Verde Ranch, Arizona
White Stallion Ranch, Arizona
Highland Ranch, California
C Lazy U Ranch, Colorado
Lane Guest Ranch, Colorado
Latigo Ranch, Colorado
McNamara Ranch, Colorado
Rafter Y Ranch, Colorado
Kelly Toponce Guest Ranch, Idaho
Triple Creek, Montana
Hidden Valley Guest Ranch, Washington
Bitterroot Ranch, Wyoming
Savery Creek Thoroughbred Ranch, Wyoming
Homeplace Guest Ranch, Alberta, Canada
Echo Valley Guest Ranch, British Columbia, Canada
Flying U Ranch, British Columbia, Canada

Family Ranch Camps

Cheley Colorado Camps, Colorado

Fly-Fishing (Guided programs available; **extensive)

Crystal Creek Lodge, Alaska**
Scott Valley Resort and Guest Ranch, Arkansas
Alisal Guest Ranch, California
Coffee Creek Ranch, California
Hunewill Guest Ranch, California
4 UR Ranch, Colorado**
Bar Lazy J, Colorado
Aspen Lodge Ranch Resort, Colorado
Cherokee Park Ranch, Colorado
Colorado Trails Ranch, Colorado**
Coulter Lake Guest Ranch, Colorado
Deer Valley Ranch, Colorado
4UR Ranch, Colorado
Forbes Trinchera Ranch, Colorado
The Home Ranch, Colorado

Lane Guest Ranch, Colorado
Laramie River Ranch, Colorado
Latigo Ranch, Colorado
Lost Valley Ranch, Colorado
North Fork Ranch, Colorado
Peaceful Valley Ranch, Colorado
Powderhorn Guest Ranch, Colorado
Rafter Y Ranch, Colorado
Rainbow Trout Ranch, Colorado
Rawah Ranch, Colorado
Seven Lakes Lodge, Colorado**
Skyline Guest Ranch, Colorado
Tall Timber, Colorado**
Tarryall River Ranch, Colorado
Tumbling River Ranch, Colorado
Vista Verde Ranch, Colorado**
Wilderness Trails Ranch, Colorado
Wit's End Resort Ranch, Colorado
Diamond D Ranch, Idaho
Hidden Creek Ranch, Idaho
Kelly Toponce Guest Ranch, Idaho
Teton Ridge Ranch, Idaho
Twin Peaks Ranch, Idaho
320 Ranch, Montana
63 Ranch, Montana
Averills' Ranch-Flathead Lake Lodge,
    Montana**
Big EZ Lodge, Montana
Boulder River Ranch, Montana*
Diamond J Ranch, Montana**
Elkhorn Ranch, Montana
G bar M Ranch, Montana
Hargrave Cattle & Guest Ranch, Montana
Hawley Mountain Ranch, Montana
Horse Prairie Ranch, Montana
Klick's K Bar L Ranch, Montana
Lake Upsata Guest Ranch, Montana
Logan Cattle & Guest Ranch, Montana
Lone Mountain Ranch, Montana**
Mountain Meadows Guest Ranch, Montana**
Mountain Sky Guest Ranch, Montana**
Nine Quarter Circle Ranch, Montana
Parade Rest Ranch, Montana**
Triple Creek Ranch, Montana**
The Lodge at Chama, New Mexico
Los Pinos Ranch, New Mexico
Aspen Ridge Resort, Oregon
Texas Ranch Life, Texas
Hidden Valley Ranch, Washington
K Diamond K Ranch, Washington
Absaroka Ranch, Wyoming
Bill Cody Ranch, Wyoming
Bitterroot Ranch, Wyoming
Breteche Creek Ranch, Wyoming
Brush Creek Ranch, Wyoming**

Canyon Ranch, Wyoming**
CM Ranch, Wyoming**
Flying A Guest Ranch, Wyoming**
Goosewing Ranch, Wyoming
Heart Six Ranch, Wyoming**
H F Bar Ranch, Wyoming**
The Hideout at Flitner Ranch, Wyoming
Lazy L & B Ranch, Wyoming
Moose Head Ranch, Wyoming**
Paradise Guest Ranch, Wyoming
Ranger Creek Guest Ranch, Wyoming
R Lazy S Ranch, Wyoming
Savery Creek Thoroughbred Ranch, Wyoming
Seven D Ranch, Wyoming
TA Ranch, Wyoming
T-Cross Ranch, Wyoming
Trail Creek Ranch, Wyoming
Triangle C Ranch, Wyoming
Triangle X Ranch, Wyoming
UXU Ranch, Wyoming
Vee Bar Guest Ranch, Wyoming
Homeplace Guest Ranch, Alberta, Canada
Echo Valley Guest Ranch, British Columbia,
    Canada
Flying U Ranch, British Columbia, Canada
Three Bars Ranch, British Columbia, Canada

Foreign Language
The Bellota Ranch, Arizona—Spanish
Circle Z Ranch, Arizona—Spanish
Grand Canyon Bar 10 Ranch, Arizona—
    Spanish, German, Portuguese
Grapevine Canyon Ranch, Arizona—
    Czechoslovakian, Spanish
The Horseshoe Ranch on Bloody Basin Road,
    Arizona—Spanish, French, German
La Tierra Linda Guest Ranch Resort,
    Arizona—Spanish
Tanque Verde Ranch, Arizona—Spanish,
    French, German, Italian, Japanese
White Stallion Ranch, Arizona—Spanish,
    German, Norwegian, Swedish
Alisal Guest Ranch, California—Spanish,
    French, German, Italian, Portuguese
Circle Bar B Guest Ranch, California—
    Spanish
Coffee Creek Ranch, California—Spanish,
    Dutch, German
Highland Ranch, California—French, Italian
Hunewill Guest Ranch, California—German,
    French
Rankin Ranch, California—Spanish
Forbes Trinchera Ranch, Colorado—Spanish
The Home Ranch, Colorado—Spanish,
    French, German

Laramie River Ranch, Colorado—French
Latigo Ranch, Colorado—Spanish
Peaceful Valley Ranch, Colorado—German
Rainbow Trout Ranch, Colorado—
  Portuguese, Swahili
Seven Lakes Lodge, Colorado—Spanish
Bar H Bar Ranch, Idaho—Spanish
Hidden Creek Ranch, Idaho—German
Idaho Rocky Mountain Ranch, Idaho—
  Spanish
Double JJ Resort Ranch, Michigan—
  Multilingual
G bar M Ranch, Montana—Spanish
Horse Prairie Ranch, Montana—Spanish,
  German, Portuguese
Mountain Meadows Guest Ranch, Montana—
  Swedish
The Lodge at Chama, New Mexico—Spanish
Pinegrove Dude Ranch, New York—Spanish,
  Portuguese
Rocking Horse Ranch, New York—Spanish
Lazy Hills Guest Ranch, Texas—Spanish
Running-R Guest Ranch, Texas—French,
  German
Texas Ranch Life, Texas—Spanish
Bitterroot Ranch, Wyoming—French,
  German
Brush Creek Ranch, Wyoming—German
Double Diamond X Ranch, Wyoming—
  Spanish, German
Goosewing Ranch, Wyoming—French,
  German
Heart Six Ranch, Wyoming—French
The Hideout at Flitner Ranch, Wyoming—
  Spanish, French, German, Dutch
Savery Creek Thoroughbred Ranch,
  Wyoming—Spanish, French
TA Ranch, Wyoming—French, German
Vee Bar Guest Ranch, Wyoming—Interpreter
  available
Homeplace Guest Ranch, Alberta, Canada—
  German
Echo Valley Guest Ranch, British Columbia,
  Canada—French, German, Japanese,
  Danish, Iranian, Thai
Flying U Ranch, British Columbia, Canada—
  French, German, Japanese

Golf-on-Site

Rancho de los Caballeros, Arizona
Alisal Guest Ranch, California
Tall Timber, Colorado
Double JJ Resort Ranch, Michigan
Big EZ Lodge, Montana

Gratuities and Service Charges Included

Colorado Trails Ranch, Colorado
Lane Guest Ranch, Colorado
Latigo Ranch, Colorado
Lost Valley Ranch, Colorado
Peaceful Valley Ranch, Colorado
Rawah Ranch, Colorado
Tall Timber, Colorado
Wilderness Trails Ranch, Colorado
Hargrave Cattle & Guest Ranch, Montana
Mountain Sky Ranch, Montana
Hidden Valley Guest Ranch, Washington
Goosewing Ranch, Wyoming
Seven D Ranch, Wyoming
Homeplace Guest Ranch, Alberta, Canada

Guided Hiking

The Bellota Ranch, Arizona
Rancho de los Caballeros, Arizona
Tanque Verde Ranch, Arizona
White Stallion Ranch, Arizona
Coffee Creek Ranch, California
Aspen Canyon Ranch, Colorado
Bar Lazy J Guest Ranch, Colorado
Cherokee Park Ranch, Colorado
C Lazy U Ranch, Colorado
Colorado Trails Ranch, Colorado
The Home Ranch, Colorado
Lane Guest Ranch, Colorado
Lost Valley Ranch, Colorado
North Fork Ranch, Colorado
Peaceful Valley Ranch, Colorado
Rafter Y Ranch, Colorado
Rainbow Trout Ranch, Colorado
Rawah Ranch, Colorado
Tall Timber, Colorado
Tarryall River Ranch, Colorado
Tumbling River Ranch, Colorado
Vista Verde Ranch, Colorado
Diamond D Ranch, Idaho
Hidden Creek Ranch, Idaho
Averills' Ranch-Flathead Lake Lodge, Montana
Big EZ Lodge, Montana
Hawley Mountain Ranch, Montana
Lake Upsata Guest Ranch, Montana
Lone Mountain Ranch, Montana
Mountain Meadows Guest Ranch, Montana
Mountain Sky Guest Ranch, Montana
Triple Creek Ranch, Montana
The Lodge at Chama, New Mexico
Cataloochee Ranch, North Carolina
Absaroka Ranch, Wyoming
Bill Cody Ranch, Wyoming
Breteche Creek Ranch, Wyoming
Brush Creek Ranch, Wyoming

Canyon Ranch, Wyoming
Double Diamond X Ranch, Wyoming
Elk Mountain Ranch, Wyoming
Flying A Ranch, Wyoming
Heart Six Ranch, Wyoming
HF Bar Ranch, Wyoming
Lazy L & B Ranch, Wyoming
Seven D Ranch, Wyoming
TA Ranch, Wyoming
T-Cross Ranch, Wyoming
Triangle C Ranch, Wyoming
Echo Valley Guest Ranch, British Columbia,
    Canada
Three Bars Ranch, British Columbia, Canada

Handicapped/Wheelchair Accessible

La Tierra Linda Guest Ranch Resort, Arizona
Rancho de los Caballeros, Arizona
Tanque Verde Ranch, Arizona
White Stallion Ranch, Arizona
Alisal Guest Ranch, California
Circle Bar B Guest Ranch, California
Coffee Creek Ranch, California
4 UR Ranch, Colorado
Aspen Lodge Ranch Resort, Colorado
C Lazy U Ranch, Colorado
The Home Ranch, Colorado
Lane Guest Ranch, Colorado
Laramie River Ranch, Colorado
Latigo Ranch, Colorado
Lost Valley Ranch, Colorado
North Fork Ranch, Colorado
Peaceful Valley Ranch, Colorado
T-Lazy-7 Ranch, Colorado
Wit's End Guest and Resort Ranch, Colorado
Hidden Creek Ranch, Idaho
Diamond D Ranch, Idaho
Western Pleasure Guest Ranch, Idaho
Double JJ Resort Ranch, Michigan
Turkey Creek Ranch, Missouri
320 Guest Ranch, Montana
Big EZ Lodge, Montana
Diamond J Ranch, Montana
G bar M Ranch, Montana
Logan Cattle & Guest Ranch, Montana
Lone Mountain Ranch, Montana
Mountain Meadows Guest Ranch, Montana
Nine Quarter Circle Ranch, Montana
Pinegrove Dude Ranch, New York
Cataloochee Ranch, North Carolina
Clear Creek Ranch, North Carolina
Hidden Valley Guest Ranch, Washington
Woodside Ranch, Wisconsin
Bill Cody Ranch, Wyoming
Brooks Lake Lodge, Wyoming

Double Diamond X Ranch, Wyoming
Heart Six Ranch, Wyoming
HF Bar Ranch, Wyoming
Ranger Creek Guest Ranch, Wyoming
TA Guest Ranch, Wyoming
Triangle X Ranch, Wyoming
Vee Bar Guest Ranch, Wyoming
Flying U Ranch, British Columbia, Canada
Three Bars Ranch, British Columbia, Canada

Hands-on Horse Care (At ranch's discretion)

The Bellota Ranch, Arizona
Grapevine Canyon Ranch, Arizona
White Stallion Ranch, Arizona
Scott Valley Resort and Guest Ranch,
    Arkansas
Coffee Creek Ranch, California
Aspen Canyon Ranch, Colorado
Colorado Trails Ranch, Colorado
Elk Mountain Ranch, Colorado
The Home Ranch, Colorado
La Garita Creek Ranch, Colorado
Laramie River Ranch, Colorado
Lane Guest Ranch, Colorado
Latigo Ranch, Colorado
Lost Valley Ranch, Colorado
North Fork Ranch, Colorado
Rafter Y Ranch, Colorado
Rawah Ranch, Colorado
Skyline Guest Ranch, Colorado
Tall Timber, Colorado
Tarryall River Ranch, Colorado
Tumbling River Ranch, Colorado
Vee Bar Guest Ranch, Colorado
Vista Verde Ranch, Colorado
Wit's End Guest and Resort Ranch, Colorado
Bar H Bar Ranch, Idaho
Hidden Creek Ranch, Idaho
Kelly Toponce Guest Ranch, Idaho
Teton Ridge Ranch, Idaho
Western Pleasure Guest Ranch, Idaho
Turkey Creek Ranch, Missouri
63 Ranch, Montana
Averills' Ranch-Flathead Lake Lodge, Montana
Boulder River Ranch, Montana
Circle Bar Guest Ranch, Montana
G bar M Ranch, Montana
Elkhorn Ranch, Montana
Hargrave Cattle & Guest Ranch, Montana
Horse Prairie Ranch, Montana
Klick's K Bar L Ranch, Montana
Lake Upsata Guest Ranch, Montana
Logan Cattle & Guest Ranch, Montana
Lone Mountain Ranch, Montana
Triple Creek Ranch, Montana

Hartley Guest Ranch, New Mexico
Los Pinos Ranch, New Mexico
Running-R Guest Ranch, Texas
Texas Ranch Life, Texas
Hidden Creek Guest Ranch, Washington
K Diamond K Ranch, Washington
Absaroka Ranch, Wyoming
Box R Ranch, Wyoming
Brush Creek Ranch, Wyoming
Crossed Sabres Ranch, Wyoming
Double Diamond X Ranch, Wyoming
Flying A Ranch, Wyoming
Goosewing Ranch, Wyoming
Heart Six Ranch, Wyoming
HF Bar Ranch, Wyoming
Lazy L & B Ranch, Wyoming
Ranger Creek Guest Ranch, Wyoming
Savery Creek Thoroughbred Ranch,
  Wyoming
TA Ranch, Wyoming
T-Cross Ranch, Wyoming
Triangle C Ranch, Wyoming
UXU Ranch, Wyoming
Homeplace Guest Ranch, Alberta, Canada
Echo Valley Guest Ranch, British Columbia,
  Canada
Flying U Ranch, British Columbia, Canada

Heated Swimming Pool (**Hot tub)
La Tierra Linda, Arizona
Rancho de los Caballeros, Arizona
Tanque Verde Ranch, Arizona
Rankin Ranch, California**
C Lazy U Ranch, Colorado
Colorado Trails Ranch, Colorado
The Home Ranch, Colorado
Powderhorn Guest Ranch, Colorado**
Rainbow Trout Ranch, Colorado
Tall Timber, Colorado
Tarryall River Ranch, Colorado
Wit's End Guest and Resort Ranch, Colorado
Double JJ Resort Ranch, Michigan
Turkey Creek Ranch, Missouri
Big EZ Lodge, Montana
Diamond J Ranch, Montana
Mountain Sky Guest Ranch, Montana
Cataloochee Ranch, North Carolina
Woodside Ranch, Wisconsin
Goosewing Ranch, Wyoming**
Heart Six Ranch, Wyoming
HF Bar Ranch, Wyoming
Trail Creek Ranch, Wyoming
Echo Valley Guest Ranch, British Columbia,
  Canada

Helicopter Hiking
Tall Timber, Colorado

Historic-National Register of Historic Sites
The Bellota Ranch, Arizona
Kay El Bar, Arizona
Idaho Rocky Mountain Ranch, Idaho
63 Ranch, Montana
Texas Ranch Life, Texas
CM Ranch, Wyoming
HF Bar Ranch, Wyoming
TA Ranch, Wyoming
Vee Bar Guest Ranch, Wyoming

Horse Drives
Klick's K Bar L Ranch, Montana
Rock Springs Guest Ranch, Oregon
Box R Ranch, Wyoming
HF Bar Ranch, Wyoming

Horsemanship
Grapevine Canyon Ranch, Arizona
Hunewill Guest Ranch, California
The Home Ranch, Colorado
Western Pleasure Guest Ranch, Idaho
Averills' Ranch-Flathead Lake Lodge, Montana
G bar M Ranch, Montana
Hargrave Cattle & Guest Ranch, Montana
Mountain Sky Guest Ranch, Montana
Pinegrove Dude Ranch, New York
Homeplace Guest Ranch, Alberta, Canada

Hot Springs
4UR Ranch, Colorado
Coulter Lake Ranch, Colorado
Deer Valley Ranch, Colorado
Idaho Rocky Mountain Ranch, Idaho
Klick's K Bar L Ranch, Montana
Brush Creek Ranch, Wyoming

Indoor Riding Arena
C Lazy U Ranch, Colorado
The Home Ranch, Colorado
320 Guest Ranch, Montana
Texas Ranch Life, Texas
Breteche Creek Ranch, Wyoming
Three Bars Ranch, British Columbia, Canada

Indoor Tennis
Diamond J Ranch, Montana

Infants Program
Hunewill Guest Ranch, California
Elk Mountain Ranch, Colorado
Lane Guest Ranch, Colorado

North Fork Ranch, Colorado
Tarryall River Ranch, Colorado
Diamond J Ranch, Idaho
Double JJ Resort Ranch, Michigan
Averills' Ranch-Flathead Lake Lodge, Montana
Mountain Sky Ranch, Montana
Pinegrove Dude Ranch, New York
Woodside Ranch, Wisconsin
CM Ranch, Wyoming
HF Bar Ranch, Wyoming
Seven D Ranch, Wyoming

Kayaking
Aspen Lodge Ranch Resort, Colorado

Kids Eat Dinner Together (**Always)
Rancho de los Caballeros, Arizona
Tanque Verde Ranch, Arizona
Rankin Ranch, California
 C Lazy U Ranch, Colorado**
The Home Ranch, Colorado
Vista Verde Ranch, Colorado
Double JJ Resort Ranch, Michigan
Averills' Ranch-Flathead Lake Lodge, Montana
Diamond J Ranch, Montana
Elkhorn Ranch, Montana
Laughing Water Ranch, Montana
Mountain Sky Guest Ranch, Montana
Hidden Valley Guest Ranch, Washington
Goosewing Ranch, Wyoming
Heart Six Ranch, Wyoming
HF Bar Ranch, Wyoming
Lazy L & B Ranch, Wyoming (several days)
Ranger Creek Guest Ranch, Wyoming
Seven D Ranch, Wyoming
Trail Creek Ranch, Wyoming
Triangle X Ranch, Wyoming**
UXU Ranch, Wyoming

Kids Ride Separately
Rancho de los Caballeros, Arizona
Tanque Verde Ranch, Arizona
Rankin Ranch, California
C Lazy U Ranch, Colorado
The Home Ranch, Colorado
Double JJ Resort Ranch, Michigan
Goosewing Ranch, Wyoming (optional)
Ranger Creek Guest Ranch, Wyoming (sometimes)

Lakeside Setting
Coulter Lake Guest Ranch, Colorado
Double JJ Resort Ranch, Michigan
Averills' Ranch-Flathead Lake Lodge, Montana
Lake Upsata Guest Ranch, Montana

Texas Ranch Life, Texas
Flying U Ranch, British Columbia, Canada

Luxury
Forbes Trinchera Ranch, Colorado
The Home Ranch, Colorado
Tall Timber, Colorado
Wit's End Guest and Resort Ranch, Colorado
Teton Ridge Ranch, Idaho
Big EZ Lodge, Montana
Mountain Meadows Guest Ranch, Montana
The Lodge at Chama, New Mexico
Canyon Ranch, Wyoming
Gros Ventre River Ranch, Wyoming
Lost Creek Ranch, Wyoming
Triple Creek Ranch, Montana

Mountain Bike Friendly
The Bellota Ranch, Arizona
Circle Z Ranch, Arizona
Flying E Ranch, Arizona
Grand Canyon Bar 10 Ranch, Arizona
La Tierra Linda Guest Ranch Resort, Arizona
Rancho de los Caballeros, Arizona
Tanque Verde Ranch, Arizona
White Stallion Ranch, Arizona
Scott Valley Resort and Guest Ranch, Arkansas
Alisal Guest Ranch, California
Coffee Creek Ranch, California
Hunewill Circle H Ranch, California
Rankin Ranch, California
4UR Ranch, Colorado
Aspen Lodge Ranch Resort, Colorado (BYOB)
Aspen Canyon Ranch, Colorado
Bar Lazy J Ranch, Colorado
Cheley Colorado Camps, Colorado
Cherokee Park Ranch, Colorado
Deer Valley Ranch, Colorado
Drowsy Water Ranch, Colorado
Elk Mountain Ranch, Colorado
La Garita Creek Ranch, Colorado
Lake Mancos Ranch, Colorado
Latigo Ranch, Colorado
Peaceful Valley Ranch, Colorado
Rafter Y Ranch, Colorado
Skyline Guest Ranch, Colorado
T-Lazy-7 Ranch, Colorado
Vista Verde Ranch, Colorado
Wit's End Guest and Resort Ranch, Colorado
Diamond D Ranch, Idaho
Diamond J Ranch, Idaho
Hidden Creek Ranch, Idaho
Idaho Rocky Mountain Ranch, Idaho
Teton Ridge Ranch, Idaho
Western Pleasure Guest Ranch, Idaho

Double JJ Resort Ranch, Michigan
Turkey Creek Ranch, Missouri
320 Guest Ranch, Montana
Averills' Ranch-Flathead Lake Lodge, Montana
Big EZ Lodge, Montana
Boulder River Ranch, Montana
Circle Bar Guest Ranch, Montana
Hargrave Cattle & Guest Ranch, Montana
Lake Upsata Guest Ranch, Montana
Mountain Meadows Guest Ranch, Montana
Parade Rest Ranch, Montana
The Lodge at Chama, New Mexico
Rocking Horse Ranch, New York
Cataloochee Ranch, North Carolina
Aspen Ridge Resort, Oregon
Lazy Hills Guest Ranch, Texas
Running-R Guest Ranch, Texas
Texas Ranch Life, Texas
Hidden Valley Guest Ranch, Washington
K Diamond K Ranch, Washington
Bitterroot Ranch, Wyoming
Brooks Lake Lodge, Wyoming
Canyon Ranch, Wyoming
Flying A Guest Ranch, Wyoming
Goosewing Ranch, Wyoming
Gros Ventre River Ranch, Wyoming
Heart Six Ranch, Wyoming
The Hideout at Flitner Ranch, Wyoming
Moose Head Ranch, Wyoming
Paradise Guest Ranch, Wyoming
Ranger Creek Guest Ranch, Wyoming
Seven D Ranch, Wyoming
TA Guest Ranch, Wyoming
Trail Creek Ranch, Wyoming
Triangle C Ranch, Wyoming
UXU Ranch, Wyoming
Vee Bar Guest Ranch, Wyoming
Echo Valley Guest Ranch, British Columbia, Canada
Flying U Ranch, British Columbia, Canada
Three Bars Ranch, British Columbia, Canada

Mountain Flying and Float Plane Trips
Grand Canyon Bar 10 Ranch, Arizona
Tall Timber, Colorado
Averills' Ranch-Flathead Lake Lodge, Montana

Mule Riding (Optional)
North Fork Ranch, Colorado
Klick's K Bar L Ranch, Montana
Lazy L & B Ranch, Wyoming

Naturalist Programs & Talks
The Bellota Ranch, Arizona
Circle Z Ranch, Arizona

Grand Canyon Bar 10 Ranch, Arizona
Rancho de los Caballeros, Arizona
Tanque Verde Ranch, Arizona
White Stallion Ranch, Arizona
Alisal Guest Ranch, California
Coffee Creek Ranch, California
Deer Valley Ranch, Colorado
The Home Ranch, Colorado
Lake Mancos Ranch, Colorado
Laramie River Ranch, Colorado
Latigo Ranch, Colorado
Peaceful Valley Ranch, Colorado
Rawah Ranch, Colorado
Vista Verde Ranch, Colorado
Hidden Creek Ranch, Idaho
Double JJ Resort Ranch, Michigan
Averills' Ranch-Flathead Lake Lodge, Montana
Big EZ Lodge, Montana
Hawley Mountain Ranch, Montana
Lone Mountain Ranch, Montana
Mountain Meadows Guest Ranch, Montana
Nine Quarter Circle Ranch, Montana
Triple Creek Ranch, Montana
Cataloochee Ranch, North Carolina
Rock Springs Guest Ranch, Oregon
Texas Ranch Life, Texas
Absaroka Ranch, Wyoming
Bill Cody Ranch, Wyoming
Breteche Creek Ranch, Wyoming
Brooks Lake Lodge, Wyoming
Canyon Ranch, Wyoming
Gros Ventre River Ranch, Wyoming
Heart Six Ranch, Wyoming
HF Bar Ranch, Wyoming
Paradise Guest Ranch, Wyoming
R Lazy S Ranch, Wyoming
Seven D Ranch, Wyoming
Triangle C Ranch, Wyoming
Triangle X Ranch, Wyoming
Echo Valley Guest Ranch, British Columbia, Canada
Flying U Ranch, British Columbia, Canada

Nature Conservancy Ranch
Skyline Ranch, Colorado
Vista Verde Ranch, Colorado
Texas Ranch Life, Texas

No Minimum Stay
Tanque Verde Ranch, Arizona
Rankin Ranch, California
Double JJ Resort Ranch, Michigan
Big EZ Lodge, Montana
Logan Cattle & Guest Ranch, Montana
The Lodge at Chama, New Mexico

Aspen Ridge Resort, Oregon
Lazy Hills Guest Ranch, Texas
Bill Cody Ranch, Wyoming

Ocean Activities
Circle Bar B Guest Ranch, California

Old West Town
La Tierra Linda Guest Ranch Resort, Arizona
Double JJ Resort Ranch, Michigan

Overnight Campouts for Kids
Scott Valley Resort and Guest Ranch, Arkansas
Lane Guest Ranch, Colorado
Tarryall River Ranch, Colorado
Tumbling River Ranch, Colorado
Vista Verde Ranch, Colorado
Double JJ Resort Ranch, Michigan
Averills' Ranch-Flathead Lake Lodge, Montana
Laughing Water Ranch, Montana
CM Ranch, Wyoming (teens only)
HF Bar Ranch, Wyoming (kids)
Ranger Creek Guest Ranch, Wyoming
Triangle X Ranch, Wyoming (teens only)

Painting Instruction
Savery Creek Thoroughbred Ranch,
  Wyoming

Pets Allowed (**Returning guests only)
Scott Valley Resort and Guest Ranch,
  Arkansas
Highland Ranch, California
Lane Guest Ranch, Colorado
Tall Timber, Colorado**
Diamond J Ranch, Idaho
Teton Ridge Ranch, Idaho
Double JJ Resort Ranch, Michigan
320 Guest Ranch, Montana
Diamond J Ranch, Montana (bird dogs only)
Lake Upsata Guest Ranch, Montana
Triple Creek Ranch, Montana
Woodside Ranch, Wisconsin
Canyon Ranch, Wyoming
Flying U Ranch, British Columbia, Canada

Petting Zoo/Farm
La Tierra Linda Guest Ranch Resort, Arizona
Scott Valley Resort and Guest Ranch, Arkansas
Alisal Guest Ranch, California
Coffee Creek Ranch, California
Rankin Ranch, California
Aspen Canyon Ranch, Colorado
Cherokee Park Ranch, Colorado
Colorado Trails Ranch, Colorado

Drowsy Water Ranch, Colorado
Elk Mountain Ranch, Colorado
The Home Ranch, Colorado
Lake Mancos Ranch, Colorado
Latigo Ranch, Colorado
North Fork Ranch, Colorado
Peaceful Valley Ranch, Colorado
Tarryall River Ranch, Colorado
Tumbling River Ranch, Colorado
Vista Verde Ranch, Colorado
Hidden Creek Ranch, Idaho
Double JJ Resort Ranch, Michigan
Averills' Ranch-Flathead Lake Lodge, Montana
Circle Bar Guest Ranch, Montana
Mountain Meadows Guest Ranch, Montana
Pinegrove Dude Ranch, New York
Rocking Horse Ranch, New York
K Diamond K Ranch, Washington
Woodside Ranch, Wisconsin
Bitterroot Ranch, Wyoming
Lazy L & B Ranch, Wyoming
Seven D Ranch, Wyoming
Triangle C Ranch, Wyoming
Three Bars Ranch, British Columbia, Canada

Ranch Bed-and-Breakfast Inn (Yearly and
  seasonal)
Aspen Canyon Ranch, Colorado (winter only)
Coulter Lake Guest Ranch, Colorado (winter
  only)
La Garita Creek Ranch, Colorado
McNamara Ranch, Colorado
Peaceful Valley Ranch, Colorado
Skyline Guest Ranch, Colorado (winter only)
Bar H Bar Ranch, Idaho
G bar M Ranch, Montana
Hargrave Cattle & Guest Ranch, Montana
Lazy Hills Guest Ranch, Texas
Texas Ranch Life, Texas
Hidden Valley Guest Ranch, Washington
K Diamond K Ranch, Washington
Bill Cody Ranch, Wyoming
Brush Creek Ranch, Wyoming
Savery Creek Thoroughbred Ranch,
  Wyoming
TA Ranch, Wyoming
Vee Bar Guest Ranch, Wyoming

Ranch Camps (Children, teenagers, families)
Cheley Colorado Camps, Colorado

Ranch Resorts (Usually includes tennis and
  swimming pool)
La Tierra Linda Guest Ranch Resort, Arizona
Rancho de los Caballeros, Arizona

Tanque Verde Ranch, Arizona
White Stallion Ranch, Arizona
Alisal Guest Ranch, California
Aspen Lodge Ranch Resort, Colorado
C Lazy U Ranch, Colorado
Deer Valley Ranch, Colorado
The Home Ranch, Colorado
Lane Guest Ranch, Colorado
Lost Valley Ranch, Colorado
Peaceful Valley Ranch, Colorado
Tall Timber, Colorado
Wit's End Guest and Resort Ranch, Colorado
Double JJ Resort Ranch, Michigan
Turkey Creek Ranch, Missouri
Averills' Ranch-Flathead Lake Lodge, Montana
Diamond J Ranch, Montana
Lone Mountain Ranch, Montana
Mountain Sky Guest Ranch, Montana
The Lodge at Chama, New Mexico
Pinegrove Dude Ranch, New York
Rocking Horse Ranch, New York
Aspen Ridge Resort, Oregon
Rock Springs Guest Ranch, Oregon
Lazy Hills Guest Ranch, Texas
Woodside Ranch, Wisconsin
Lost Creek Ranch, Wyoming
The Hideout at Flitner Ranch, Wyoming
Echo Valley Guest Ranch, British Columbia, Canada
Three Bars Ranch, British Columbia, Canada

Reining Horse Training
The Home Ranch, Colorado
Three Bars Ranch, British Columbia, Canada

Ride On Your Own Without Wrangler
(At ranches' discretion; generally for experienced riders and long-time repeat guests only) **With your own horse; BYOH (bring your own horse)
Flying E Ranch, Arizona (BYOH)
Scott Valley Resort and Guest Ranch, Arkansas
Rafter Y Ranch, Colorado
Bar H Bar Ranch, Idaho
Aspen Ridge Resort, Oregon
Texas Ranch Life, Texas (BYOH)
Hidden Valley Guest Ranch, Washington (BYOH)
K Diamond K Ranch, Washington
Canyon Ranch, Wyoming**
H F Bar Ranch, Wyoming
Box R Ranch, Wyoming
Savery Creek Thoroughbred Ranch, Wyoming

TA Guest Ranch, Wyoming
T-Cross Ranch, Wyoming
Triangle X Ranch, Wyoming
Flying U Ranch, British Columbia, Canada

Rodeo Arena
Averills' Ranch-Flathead Lake Lodge, Montana
Texas Ranch Life, Texas
The Hideout at Flitner Ranch, Wyoming

Room Service (Meals)
La Tierra Linda, Arizona
Tall Timber, Colorado
Vista Verde Ranch, Colorado
Wit's End Guest and Resort Ranch, Colorado
Big EZ Lodge, Montana
Mountain Meadows Guest Ranch, Montana
Mountain Sky Guest Ranch, Montana
Triple Creek Ranch, Montana
Goosewing Ranch, Wyoming

Ropes Course
Alisal Guest Ranch, California
Aspen Lodge Ranch Resort, Colorado
Hidden Creek Ranch, Idaho
HF Bar Ranch, Wyoming

Roping Demonstrations
The Bellota Ranch, Arizona
The Home Ranch, Colorado
Hunewill Guest Ranch, California
Rainbow Trout Ranch, Colorado
Vista Verde Ranch, Colorado
Wit's End Guest and Resort Ranch, Colorado
Averills' Ranch-Flathead Lake Lodge, Montana
Logan Cattle & Guest Ranch, Montana
Aspen Ridge Resort, Oregon
Running-R Guest Ranch, Texas
Texas Ranch Life, Texas
Hidden Valley Guest Ranch, Washington
Moose Head Ranch, Wyoming

RVs
McNamara Ranch, Colorado
Double JJ Resort Ranch, Michigan
Lazy Hills Guest Ranch, Texas

Sailing
Turkey Creek Ranch, Missouri
Averills' Ranch-Flathead Lake Lodge, Montana

Side-by-Side Riding
The Bellota Ranch, Arizona
Grapevine Canyon Ranch, Arizona
Highland Ranch, California

Hunewill Guest Ranch, California
Aspen Canyon Ranch, Colorado
The Home Ranch, Colorado
La Garita Creek Ranch, Colorado
Laramie River Ranch, Colorado
McNamara Ranch, Colorado
Rafter Y Ranch, Colorado
Rawah Ranch, Colorado
Skyline Guest Ranch, Colorado
Tarryall River Ranch, Colorado
Bar H Bar Ranch, Idaho
Hidden Creek Ranch, Idaho
Kelly Toponce Guest Ranch, Idaho
Western Pleasure Guest Ranch, Idaho
63 Ranch, Montana
Averills' Ranch-Flathead Lake Lodge, Montana
Circle Bar Guest Ranch, Montana
G bar M Ranch, Montana
Hargrave Cattle & Guest Ranch, Montana
Horse Prairie Ranch, Montana
Lake Upsata Guest Ranch, Montana
Logan Cattle & Guest Ranch, Montana
Triple Creek Ranch, Montana
Hartley Guest Ranch, New Mexico
Aspen Ridge Resort, Oregon
Texas Ranch Life, Texas
K Diamond K Ranch, Washington
Absaroka Ranch, Wyoming
Box R Ranch, Wyoming
Breteche Creek Ranch, Wyoming
Brush Creek Ranch, Wyoming
Canyon Ranch, Wyoming
Flying A Ranch, Wyoming
Goosewing Ranch, Wyoming
The Hideout at Flitner Ranch, Wyoming
Lazy L & B Ranch, Wyoming
TA Ranch, Wyoming
Vee Bar Guest Ranch, Wyoming
Homeplace Guest Ranch, Alberta, Canada
Echo Valley Guest Ranch, British Columbia, Canada
Flying U Ranch, British Columbia, Canada

Snowmobiling
Aspen Canyon Ranch, Colorado
C Lazy U Ranch, Colorado
Coulter Lake Guest Ranch, Colorado
Latigo Ranch, Colorado
Peaceful Valley Ranch, Colorado
Skyline Guest Ranch, Colorado
Tall Timber, Colorado
Vista Verde Ranch, Colorado
Wit's End Guest and Resort Ranch, Colorado
Hidden Creek Ranch, Idaho
Kelly Toponce Guest Ranch, Idaho

Double JJ Resort Ranch, Michigan
320 Guest Ranch, Montana
Big EZ Lodge, Montana
Lake Upsata Guest Ranch, Montana
Mountain Meadows Guest Ranch, Montana
Triple Creek Ranch, Montana
Aspen Ridge Resort, Oregon
Hidden Valley Guest Ranch, Washington
Brooks Lake Lodge, Wyoming
Brush Creek Ranch, Wyoming
Goosewing Ranch, Wyoming
Gros Ventre River Ranch, Wyoming
Hearth Six Ranch, Wyoming
Ranger Creek Guest Ranch, Wyoming
Rimrock Ranch, Wyoming
Triangle C Ranch, Wyoming
Triangle X Ranch, Wyoming
Vee Bar Guest Ranch, Wyoming
Flying U Ranch, British Columbia, Canada

Spa/Body/Mind
Peaceful Valley Ranch, Colorado
Wit's End Guest and Resort Ranch, Colorado
Hidden Creek Ranch, Idaho
Lost Creek Ranch, Wyoming
Echo Valley Guest Ranch, British Columbia, Canada

Sporting Clays
Rancho de los Caballeros, Arizona
Highland Ranch, California
Colorado Trails Ranch, Colorado
Elk Mountain Ranch, Colorado
Hidden Creek Ranch, Idaho
Teton Ridge Ranch, Idaho
Twin Peaks Ranch, Idaho
Diamond J Ranch, Montana
Texas Ranch Life, Texas
HF Bar Ranch, Wyoming

Telephones in Rooms
La Tierra Linda Guest Ranch Resort, Arizona
Rancho de los Caballeros, Arizona
Tanque Verde Ranch, Arizona
Highland Ranch, California
Aspen Lodge Ranch Resort, Colorado
Wit's End Guest and Resort Ranch, Colorado
Double JJ Resort Ranch, Michigan
320 Guest Ranch, Montana
Big EZ Lodge, Montana
Hartley Guest Ranch, New Mexico
The Lodge at Chama, New Mexico
Texas Ranch Life, Texas

Upland Game/Bird-Hunting
Diamond J Ranch, Montana
The Lodge at Chama, New Mexico
Texas Ranch Life, Texas
Canyon Ranch, Wyoming
HF Bar Ranch, Wyoming

Water-Skiing
Colorado Trails Ranch, Colorado
Wilderness Trails Ranch, Colorado
Wit's End Guest and Resort Ranch, Colorado

Weddings (Minister on Ranch Staff)
Highland Ranch, California
Diamond D Ranch, Idaho

Wilderness Pack Trips
  ON: overnight
  **Specializes
Grapevine Canyon Ranch, Arizona
Grand Canyon Bar 10 Ranch, Arizona
Coffee Creek Ranch, California
Cheley Colorado Camps, Colorado
Coulter Lake River Ranch, Colorado
Elk Mountain Ranch, Colorado (ON)
Laramie River Ranch, Colorado
Latigo Ranch, Colorado
Skyline Guest Ranch, Colorado
Vista Verde Ranch, Colorado
Wit's End Guest and Resort Ranch, Colorado
Diamond D Ranch, Idaho
Idaho Rocky Mountain Ranch, Idaho
Teton Ridge Ranch, Idaho
Twin Peaks Ranch, Idaho
63 Ranch, Montana
Circle Bar Guest Ranch, Montana
G bar M Ranch, Montana
Klick's K Bar L Ranch, Montana**
Lake Upsata Guest Ranch, Montana
Laughing Water Ranch, Montana
Cataloochee Ranch, North Carolina
Absaroka Ranch, Wyoming**
Bitterroot Ranch, Wyoming
Box R Ranch, Wyoming
Brush Creek Ranch, Wyoming
CM Ranch, Wyoming
Crossed Sabres Ranch, Wyoming
Double Diamond X Ranch, Wyoming
Heart Six Ranch, Wyoming**
H F Bar Ranch, Wyoming**
The Hideout at Flitner Ranch, Wyoming
Lazy L & B Ranch, Wyoming**
Lost Creek Ranch, Wyoming
Paradise Guest Ranch, Wyoming
Ranger Creek Guest Ranch, Wyoming

Rimrock Ranch, Wyoming**
Seven D Ranch, Wyoming**
T-Cross Ranch, Wyoming
Triangle C Ranch, Wyoming
Triangle X Ranch, Wyoming**
Homeplace Guest Ranch, Alberta, Canada
Echo Valley Guest Ranch, British Columbia,
  Canada
Flying U Ranch, British Columbia, Canada

Winter Activities
La Tierra Linda, Arizona
Aspen Canyon Ranch, Colorado
C Lazy U Ranch, Colorado
Coulter Lake Guest Ranch, Colorado
Latigo Ranch, Colorado
The Home Ranch, Colorado
Peaceful Valley Ranch, Colorado
Skyline Guest Ranch, Colorado
Tall Timber, Colorado
Vista Verde Ranch, Colorado
Wit's End Guest and Resort Ranch, Colorado
Hidden Creek Ranch, Idaho
Kelly Toponce Guest Ranch, Idaho
Teton Ridge Ranch, Idaho
Western Pleasure Guest Ranch, Idaho
Double JJ Resort Ranch, Michigan
320 Guest Ranch, Montana
Big EZ Lodge, Montana
Lake Upsata Guest Ranch, Montana
Logan Cattle & Guest Ranch, Montana
Lone Mountain Ranch, Montana
Mountain Meadows Guest Ranch, Montana
Triple Creek Ranch, Montana
The Lodge at Chama, New Mexico
Pinegrove Dude Ranch, New York
Rocking Horse Ranch Resort, New York
Cataloochee Ranch, North Carolina
Aspen Ridge Resort, Oregon
Hidden Valley Guest Ranch, Washington
K Diamond K Ranch, Washington
Woodside Ranch, Wisconsin
Brooks Lake Lodge, Wyoming
Brush Creek Ranch, Wyoming
Canyon Ranch, Wyoming
Gros Ventre River Ranch, Wyoming
Heart Six Ranch, Wyoming
Ranger Creek Guest Ranch, Wyoming
Rimrock Ranch, Wyoming
Trail Creek Ranch, Wyoming
Triangle C Ranch, Wyoming
Triangle X Ranch, Wyoming
Vee Bar Guest Ranch, Wyoming
Homeplace Guest Ranch, Alberta, Canada
Flying U Ranch, British Columbia, Canada

Women Only (Mostly)
McNamara Ranch, Colorado
Klick's K Bar L Ranch, Montana (June ride)

Working Cattle Ranch
The Bellota Ranch, Arizona
Hunewill Guest Ranch, California
Rankin Ranch, California
Bar H Bar Ranch, Idaho
Kelly Toponce Guest Ranch, Idaho
Western Pleasure Guest Ranch, Idaho
G bar M Ranch, Montana
Hargrave Cattle & Guest Ranch, Montana
Horse Prairie Ranch, Montana
Logan Cattle & Guest Ranch, Montana
Hartley Guest Ranch, New Mexico
Aspen Ridge Resort, Oregon
Texas Ranch Life, Texas
K Diamond K Ranch, Washington
Box R Ranch, Wyoming
Brush Creek Ranch, Wyoming
The Hideout at Flitner Ranch, Wyoming
TA Ranch, Wyoming
Vee Bar Guest Ranch, Wyoming

Workshops
Grapevine Canyon Ranch, Arizona—Horse
   Clinics, Reining Clinics, History Week
Kay El Bar Ranch, Arizona—Women's Week
Tanque Verde Ranch, Arizona—Naturalist
Coffee Creek Ranch, California—
   Horsemanship
Rankin Ranch, California—Art
Bar Lazy J, Colorado—Fishing Clinic
C Lazy U Ranch, Colorado—Horsemanship,
   Cattle Clinic
Colorado Trails Ranch, Colorado—Fly-fish-
   ing, Artist, Equine Clinics
4UR Ranch, Colorado—Fishing
The Home Ranch, Colorado—Natural
   Horsemanship
La Garita Creek Ranch, Colorado—
   Photography
Laramie River Ranch, Colorado—Naturalist
Peaceful Valley Ranch, Colorado—
   Spa/Wellness, Fly-fishing, Naturalist
Rankin Ranch, Colorado—Drawing and
   Watercolor, Stamp and Sticker, Western
   Week
Diamond D Ranch, Idaho—Crafts, Weddings
Hidden Creek Ranch, Idaho—Riding, Native
   American, Survival Training, Spiritual,
   Mind, Body
Double JJ Resort Ranch, Michigan—
   Corporate Team-Building

Averills' Ranch-Flathead Lake Lodge,
   Montana—Art, Educational, Riding, Sailing,
   Cooking, Photography
Boulder River Ranch, Montana—Fly-fishing,
   Art, Working Cow Horses
Circle Bar Guest Ranch, Montana—Art,
   History, Photography
G bar M Ranch, Montana—Natural
   Horsemanship
Hargrave Cattle & Guest Ranch, Montana—
   Women's and Singles Weeks
Horse Prairie Ranch, Montana—Lewis and
   Clark Expedition
Laughing Water Ranch, Montana—Western
   Dance
Lone Mountain Ranch, Montana—Fly-fish-
   ing, Photography, Quilting, Nature, Cross-
   country Skiing
Mountain Sky Guest Ranch, Montana—
   Horse, Fly-fishing
Nine Quarter Circle Ranch, Montana—
   Quilting
Parade Rest Ranch, Montana—Fly-fishing
   Schools
63 Ranch, Montana—Photography
Rock Springs Guest Ranch, Oregon—
   Photography
Lazy Hills Guest Ranch, Texas—Rug-Hooking
Bitterroot Ranch, Wyoming—Riding, Horse-
   training
Box R Ranch, Wyoming—Horsemanship
Breteche Creek Ranch, Wyoming—
   Horsemanship, Ornithology, Writing, Artist,
   Photography
Brush Creek Ranch, Wyoming—Holistic
   Range Management
The Hideout at Flitner Ranch, Wyoming—
   Horse, Geoscience
Paradise Guest Ranch, Wyoming—Women's
   Week, Fly-fishing
Red Rock Ranch, Wyoming—Fly-fishing
Seven D Ranch, Wyoming—Photography, Art
TA Guest Ranch, Wyoming—Historic
   Preservation, Horsemanship
Triangle C Ranch, Wyoming—Photography,
   Art
Homeplace Guest Ranch, Alberta, Canada—
   Nature on Horseback, Focus on the Horse
Echo Valley Guest Ranch, British Columbia,
   Canada—Birding, Indian Culture, Spa
Flying U Ranch, British Columbia, Canada—
   Spring Ranch Work, Native Studies
Three Bars Ranch, British Columbia,
   Canada—Reining, Horsemanship

Year-Round

The Bellota Ranch, Arizona
La Tierra Linda Guest Ranch Resort, Arizona
Tanque Verde Ranch, Arizona
Alisal Guest Ranch, California
Circle Bar B Guest Ranch, California
Highland Ranch, California
Aspen Lodge Ranch Resort, Colorado
C Lazy U Ranch, Colorado
The Home Ranch, Colorado
Tall Timber, Colorado
Vista Verde Ranch, Colorado
Wit's End Guest and Resort Ranch, Colorado
Western Pleasure Guest Ranch, Idaho
Double JJ Resort Ranch, Michigan
Turkey Creek Ranch, Missouri
320 Guest Ranch, Montana
Big EZ Lodge, Montana
Lake Upsata Guest Ranch, Montana

Logan Cattle & Guest Ranch, Montana
Mountain Meadows Guest Ranch, Montana
The Lodge at Chama, New Mexico
Cataloochee Ranch, North Carolina
Aspen Ridge Resort, Oregon
Lazy Hills Guest Ranch, Texas
Running-R Guest Ranch, Texas
Texas Ranch Life, Texas
Hidden Valley Guest Ranch, Washington
K Diamond K Ranch, Washington
Canyon Ranch, Wyoming
Goosewing Ranch, Wyoming
Heart Six Ranch, Wyoming
Ranger Creek Guest Ranch, Wyoming
Trail Creek Ranch, Wyoming
Homeplace Guest Ranch, Alberta, Canada
Echo Valley Guest Ranch, British Columbia, Canada
Flying U Ranch, British Columbia, Canada

GUEST RANCH ASSOCIATIONS

Arizona Dude Ranch Association
P.O. Box 603 K
Cortaro, AZ 85652
520/297-0252
Internet: www.arizonaranches.com

Colorado Dude and Guest Ranch Association
P.O. Box 2120 K
Granby, CO 80446
970/887-3128
Internet: www.coloradoranch.com

The Dude Ranchers' Association
P.O. Box 471 K
LaPorte, CO 80535
970/223-8440
970/223-0201 Fax
Internet: www.duderanch.org
E-Mail: duderanches@compuserve.com

Montana Dude Ranch Association
300 Thompson River Road
Marion, Montana 59925
406/858-2284
406/858-2444 Fax
Internet: www.mtdra.com

Texas Guest Ranch Association
900 Congress Avenue
Suite 201, Drawer K
Austin, TX 78701
512/474-2996

Wyoming Dude Rancher's Association
P.O. Box 618
Dubois, WY 82513
307/455-2584
307/455-2634 Fax
Internet: www.wyomingdra.com

British Columbia Guest Ranchers' Association
Box 3301
Kamloops, B.C. V2C 6B9, Canada
250/374-6836
250/374-6640 Fax
Internet: www.bcguestranches.com
E-Mail: bcfroa@telus.net

BUREAUS OF TOURISM

Alabama
334/242-4169
800/252-2262
(Nationwide, Alaska and
Hawaii)
334/242/4554 Fax
www.touralabama.org

Alaska
907/465-2010
800/842-8257
907/465-2287 Fax
www.dced.state.ak.us/tourism/

Arizona
602/230-7733
800/842-8257
602/240-5475 Fax
www.arizonaguide.com
travel-info@azot.com

Arkansas
501/682-7777
800/NATURAL (628-8725)
501/682-2523 Fax
www.arkansas.com
info@arkansas.com

California
916/322-0972
800/862-2543
916/322-3402 Fax
www.gocalif.ca.gov
caltour@commerce.ca.gov

Colorado
303/892-3840
800/COLORADO (265-6723)
303/892-3848 Fax
www.colorado.com

Connecticut
860/270-8075
800/282-6863
860/270-8077 Fax
www.ctbound.org
german.rivera@po.state.ct.us

Delaware
302/672-6856
800/441-8846
302/739-5749 Fax
www.state.de.us.com

District of Columbia
Washington, D.C.
202/789-7007
202/789-7037 Fax
www.washington.org

Florida
850/488-5607
888/7-FLAUSA (735-2872)
850/414-9732 Fax
222.flausa.com

Georgia
404/656-3553
800/847-4842
404/651-9063 Fax
www.georgia.org

Hawaii
808/586-2363
808/586-2549 Fax
www.hawaii.gov/tourism

Idaho
208/334-2470
800/635-7820
208/334-2631 Fax
www.visitid.org

Illinois
313/814-4733
800/2CONNECT (226-6632)
313/814-6175 Fax
www.enjoyillinois.com
Tourism@commerce.state.il.us

Indiana
317/ 232-8864
888/ENJOY-IN (365-6946)
317/233-6887 Fax
www.indianatourism.com
webmaster@enjoyindiana.com

Iowa
515/242-4705
888/472-6035
515/242-4718 Fax
www.traveliowa.com
tourism@ided.state.ia.us

Kansas
785/296-3810
800/252-6727
785/296-6988 Fax
www.travel-kansas.com

Kentucky
502/564-4930
800/225-8747
502/564-5695 Fax
www.kentuckytourism.com

Louisiana
225/342-8115
800/334-8626
225/342-3207 Fax
www.crt.state.la.us
pjones@crt.state.la.us

Maine
207/287-5711
888-MAINE45 (624-6345)
207/287-8070 Fax
www.visitmaine.com
steve.lyons@state.me.us

Maryland
410/767-6299
800/MD IS FUN (634-7386)
410/333-6643 Fax
www.mdisfun.org

Massachusetts
617/973-8500
800/447-6277
617/973-8525 Fax
www.massvacation.com

Michigan
517/373-0670
888/784-7328

517/373-0059 Fax
www.michigan.org

Minnesota
651/296-5029
800/657-3700
651/296-7095 Fax
www.exploreminnesota.com
explore@state.mn.us

Mississippi
601/359-3297
800/WARMEST (927-6378)
601/359-5757 Fax
www.mississippi.org
tinquiry@mississippi.org

Missouri
573-751-4133
800/877-1234
573-751-5160 Fax
www.missouritourism.com
tourism@mail.state.mo.us

Montana
406/444-2654
800/847-4868
406/444-1800 Fax
www.visitmt.com

Nebraska
402/471-3791
800/228-4307
402/471-3026 Fax
www.visitnebraska.org
tourism@visitnebraska.org

Nevada
775/687-4322
800/NEVADA8 (638-2328)
775/687-6779 Fax
www.travelnevada.com
ncot@travelnevada.com

New Hampshire
603/271-2665
800/FUN IN NH (386-4664)
603/271-6784 Fax
www.visitnh.gov

New Jersey
609/292-6963
800/537-7397
609/633-7418 Fax
www.visitnj.org

New Mexico
505/827-7400
800/733-6396
502/827-7402 Fax
www.newmexico.org

New York
518-474-4116
800/CALL NYS (225-5697)
518-292-5802 Fax
www.iloveny.state.ny.us
iloveny@empire.state.ny.us

North Carolina
919/733-8372
800/VISIT NC (847-4862)
919/733-8582 Fax
www.visitnc.com
scooper@nccommerce.com

North Dakota
701/328-2525
800/HELLO ND (435-5663)
701/328-4878 Fax
www.ndtourism.com

Ohio
614/466-8844
800/BUCKEYE (282-5393)
614/466-6744 Fax
www.OhioTourism.com
AskOhioTourism@CallTech.com

Oklahoma
405/522-3932
405/521-2406
800/652-6552
405/521-3992 Fax
www.travelok.com
information@travelok.com

Oregon
503/986-0006
800/547-7842
503/986-0001 Fax

www.traveloregon.com
info@oregontourism@state.or.us

Pennsylvania
717/787-5453
800/VISIT PA (847-4872)
717/787-0687 Fax
www.state.pa.us
webmaster@experiencepa.com

Rhode Island
401/222-2601
800/556-2484
401/273-8270 Fax
www.visitrhodeisland.com
riedc@riedc.com

South Carolina
803/734-0122
800/346-3634
803/734-0138 Fax
www.travelsc.com

South Dakota
605/773-3301
800/732-5682
605/733-3256 Fax
www.travelsd.com

Tennessee
615/741-9001
800/836-6200
615/741-7225 Fax
www.tnvacation.com

Texas
512/462-9191
800/888-8839
512/936-0088 Fax
www.traveltex.com

Utah
801/538-1370
801/538-1030
800/UTAH FUN (882-4386)
801/538-1399 Fax
www.utah.com

Vermont
802/828-3649
800/837-6668

802/828-3233 Fax
www.1-800-vermont.com

Virginia
804/786-4484
800/321-3244
804/786-1919 Fax
www.virginia.org
vainfo@virginia.org

Washington
360/664-2560
800/544-1800
360/753-4470 Fax
www.tourism.wa.gov
info@tourism.wa.gov

West Virginia
304/558-2288
800/225-5982
304/558-0108 Fax
www.callwva.com
info@callwva.com

Wisconsin
608/266-2345
800/432-8747
608/266-3403 Fax
www.travelwisconsin.com
mdelaney@tourism.state.wi.us

Wyoming
307/777-2808

800/262-3425
307/777-2838 Fax
www.wyomingtourism.org
lgreen@state.wy.us

Alberta, Canada
403/427-4321
800/661-8888
403/427-0867 Fax
www.travelalberta.com

British Columbia, Canada
604/663-6000
800/663-6000
604/801-5710 Fax
www.hellobc.com

WESTERN MUSEUMS

Amon Carter Museum
3501 Camp Bowie Boulevard
Fort Worth, TX 76107
817/738-1933
800/573-1933
www.cartermuseum.org
amy.wisman@carter
  -museum.org

**Autry Museum of Western
  Heritage**
4700 Western Heritage Way
Los Angeles, CA 90027
323/667-2000
323/666-4863 Fax
www.autry-museum.org
rroom@autry-museum.org

**Buffalo Bill Historical
  Center**
720 Sheridan Avenue
Cody, WY 82414
307/587-4771
307/578-4014
www.bbhc.org
thomh@bbhc.org

Buffalo Bill Museum
720 Sheridan Avenue
Cody, WY 82414
307/587-4771
www.bbhc.org

C.M. Russell Museum
400 13th Street North
Great Falls, MT 59401
406/727-8787
406/727-2402 Fax
www.cmrussell.org
keri@cmrussell.org

Cody Firearms Museum
720 Sheridan Avenue
Cody, WY 82414
307/587-4771
307/587-5714 Fax
www.bbhc.org
bbhc@wave.park.wy.us

**Cowboy Artists of America
  Museum**
1550 Bandera Highway,
  Box 1716
Kerrville, TX 78028
830/896-2553
830/896-2556 Fax
www.caamuseum.com

**Desert Caballeros Western
  Museum**
21 North Frontier Street
Wickenburg, AZ 85390
520/684-2272
520/684-5794
www.westernmuseum.org
info@westernmuseum.org

**Eiteljorg Museum of
  American Indians and
  Western Art**
500 West Washington Street
Indianapolis, IN 46204
317/636-9378
317/264-1724 Fax
www.eiteljorg.org
museum@eiteljorg.org

**Frederic Remington Art
  Museum**
303 Washington Street
Ogdensburg, NY 13669
315/393-2425
315/393-4464 Fax
www.remington
  -museum.org

Gilcrease Museum
1400 North Gilcrease
  Museum Road
Tulsa, OK 74127
918/596-2700
www.gilcrease.org
daburke@webzone.net

The Heard Museum
2301 North Central Avenue
Phoenix, AZ 85004

602/252/8848
www.heard.org

Joslyn Art Museum
2200 Dodge Street
Omaha, NE 68102
402/342-3300
402/342-2376 Fax
www.joslyn.org
info@joslyn.org

**Lea County Cowboy Hall
  of Fame and Western
  Heritage Center**
Campus of New Mexico
  Junior College
5317 Lovington Highway
Hobbs, NM 88240
505/392-1275
505/392-5871 Fax

Montana Historical Society
225 North Roberts Street
P.O. Box 201201
Helena, MT 59620
406/444-2694
406/444-2696 Fax
www.his.state.mt.us

Museum of Fine Arts
107 West Palace Street
P.O. Box 2087
Santa Fe, NM 87504-2087
505/476-5072
505/476-5076 Fax
www.mnm.state.nm.us
Ezieselman@mnm.state
  .nm.us

**Museum of Indian Arts
  and Culture**
710 Camino Lejo
P.O. Box 2087
Santa Fe, NM 87504-2087
505/476-1250
505/476-1330 Fax
www.nmculture.org
danderson@miaclab.org

**Museum of International
  Folk Art**
706 Camino Lejo
P.O. Box 2087
Santa Fe, NM 87504-2087
505/476-1200
505/476-1300 Fax
www.state.nm.us/moifa
1may@moifa.org

**National Cowboy &
  Western Heritage
  Museum**
1700 N.E. 63rd Street
Oklahoma City, OK 73111
405/478-2250
405/478-4714 Fax
www.nationalcowboy
  -museum.org
info@nationalcowboy
  -museum.org

**National Museum of
  Wildlife Art**
P.O. Box 6825
Jackson, WY 83002
307/733-5771
800/313-9553
307/733-5787 Fax
www.wildlifeart.org
knitze@wildlifeart.org

Palace of the Governors
105 Palace Avenue
P.O. Box 2087
Santa Fe, NM 87504-2087
505/476-5100
505/476-5104 Fax
www.palaceofthe
  -governors.org

Phoenix Art Museum
1625 North Central Avenue
Phoenix, AZ 85004-1625
602/257-1880
602/253-8662 Fax
www.phxart.org
info@phxart.org

Plains Indian Museum
720 Sheridan Street
Cody, WY 82414
307/587-4771
www.bbhc.org
bbhc@wave.park.wy.us

**Pro Rodeo Hall of Fame
  and Museum of the
  American Cowboy**
101 Pro Rodeo Drive
Colorado Springs, CO
  80919-2396
719/528-4761
719/548-4876 Fax
www.prorodeo.com

**The R.W. Norton Art
  Gallery**
4747 Creswell Avenue
Shreveport, LA 71106
318/865-4201
318/869-0435
www.softdisk.com
norton@softdisk.com

The Rockwell Museum
111 Cedar Street
Corning, NY 14830
607/937-5386
607/974-4536 Fax
www.stny.com/Rockwell

Museum
info@rockwellmuseum.org

**Sid Richardson Collection
  of Western Art**
309 Main Street
Fort Worth, TX 76102
817/332-6554
817/332-8671 Fax
www.sidrmuseum.org
info@sidrmuseum.org

Stark Museum
712 Green Avenue
P.O. Box 1897
Orange, TX 77630
409/883-6661
409/883-6361 Fax
www.starkmuseumofart.org
starkart@exp.net

**Whitney Gallery of
  Western Art**
720 Sheridan Avenue
Cody, WY 82414
307/587-4771
www.bbhc.org

Woolaroc Museum
Route 3, Box 2100
P.O. Box 1647
Bartlesville, OK 74003
918/336-0307
918/336-0084 Fax
www.woolaroc.org

TOP 20 PRCA RODEOS

Professional Rodeo Cowboys Association, 101 Prorodeo Drive,
Colorado Springs, Colorado 80919, PRCA Media Dept.; 719/593-8840
Women's Professional Rodeo Association, Route 5, Box 698, Blanchard,
Oklahoma 73010; 405/485-2277

Date	City	Event
Mid-January	Denver, CO	National Western Stock Show and Rodeo
Late January	Fort Worth, TX	Southwestern Exposition and Stock Show Rodeo
Early February	San Antonio, TX	San Antonio Livestock Exposition Rodeo
Mid-February	Houston, TX	Houston Livestock Show and Rodeo
Late February	Tucson, AZ	Winter Tour Rodeo
Mid-June	Reno, NV	Reno Rodeo
Late June	Greeley, CO	Greeley Independence Stampede
	Ponoka, Alberta, Canada	Ponoka Stampede
Early July	Calgary, Alberta, Canada	Calgary Stampede
	Cody, WY	Cody Stampede
	St. Paul, OR	St. Paul Rodeo
Mid-July	Nampa, ID	Snake River Stampede
Late July	Cheyenne, WY	Cheyenne Frontier Days
	Salinas, CA	California Rodeo
Mid-August	Caldwell, ID	Summer Tour Rodeo
Early September	Ellensburg, WA	Ellensburg Rodeo
Mid-September	Pendleton, OR	Pendleton Roundup Rodeo
Early October	Phoenix, AZ	Rodeo Showdown
Mid-October	Mesquite, TX	Mesquite Championship Rodeo
Early December	Las Vegas, NV	National Finals Rodeo
Early February	El Paso, TX	Southwestern International Rodeo
Late February	Tucson, AZ	La Fiesta de los Vaqueros
Mid-March	Pocatello, ID	Dodge National Circuit Finals Rodeo
Mid-May	Cloverdale, B.C., Canada	Cloverdale Rodeo
Early July	Greeley, CO	Greeley Independence Stampede
Early August	Dodge City, KS	Dodge City Days Rodeo
Mid-August	Colorado Springs, CO	Pikes Peak or Bust Rodeo
Mid-September	Albuquerque, NM	New Mexico State Fair Rodeo
Late September	San Francisco, CA	Grand National (Cow Palace) Rodeo
Late September– Early October	Oklahoma City, OK	State Fair Championship Rodeo

ANNUAL WESTERN EVENTS
IN THE UNITED STATES AND ALBERTA
AND BRITISH COLUMBIA, CANADA

The following is a selection of annual Western events. These events and dates are subject to change. Contact the appropriate Tourism Office listed to verify dates.

Date	City	Event

UNITED STATES

ALABAMA

Date	City	Event
Late January	Town Creek	National Field Trials
Early March	Gadsden	Alabama Wagon Train
	Opp	Opp Jaycee Rattlesnake Rodeo
Late March	Montgomery	Southeastern Livestock Exposition Rodeo and Livestock Week
Mid- to Late April	Bridgeport	Indian Day
	Clayton	Little Britches Rodeo
Late April	Alexander City	Lone Eagle's Legacy
	Decatur	Annual Racking Horse Spring Celebration
Late June	Clayton	Stetson Hoedown Rodeo
Late July	Selma	Selma Jaycee's Annual Rodeo
Early August	Gadsden	Boys Club Annual Rodeo
Mid- to Late August	Alabama	Indian Powwow Festival
Mid-September	Huntsville	Ole Time Fiddling and Bluegrass Convention
Late September	Winfield	Mule Days
	Decatur	Racking Horse World Celebration
Late September to Early October	Mobile	Greater Gulf State Fair PRCA Rodeo
Early to Mid-October	Montgomery	South Alabama State Fair
	Birmingham	Alabama State Fair
	Athens	Annual Tennessee Valley Old-Time Fiddlers' Convention
Early November	Montgomery	Southern Championship Charity Horse Show
Late November	Atmore	Annual Poarch Band of Creek Indians' Thanksgiving Day Powwow

ALASKA

Date	City	Event
Early April	Juneau	Annual Alaska Folk Festival
	Valdez	World Extreme Skiing Championships
Late April	Sutton	Annual Coal Miner's Ball
	Anchorage	Native Youth Olympics
May to September	Ketchikan	Ketchikan Frontier Revue
Late May	Delta Junction	Buffalo Wallow Statewide Square Dance Festival
Early June	Palmer	Colony Days
Late June	Juneau	Gold Rush Days
Early July	Eagle River	Bear Paw Festival

Date	City	Event
Late July		World Eskimo-Indian Olympics
Early August	Fairbanks	Tanana Valley State Fair
Late August	Palmer	Alaska State Fair
	Haines	Southeast Alaska State Fair and Rodeo
Early November	Fairbanks	Athabascan Old-Time Fiddling Festival
	Haines	Alaska Bald Eagle Festival

ARIZONA

Date	City	Event
Early January	Phoenix	Arizona National Livestock Show
	Tucson	Wrangler Bull Rider's Main Event
	Scottsdale	Wild Horse & Burro Auction
	Casa Grande	Annual Arizona Old-Time Fiddlers' Jam & Country Store Bazaar & Car Show
	Scottsdale	Arizona Appaloosa Assn-Westworld
Mid-January	Bullhead City	PRCA Turquoise Circuit Finals Rodeo
	Quartzsite	Camel Races
Late January	Mesa	High Noon's Wild West Collector's Show & Auction
	Cave Creek/Carefree	County Ho Down Week
	Scottsdale	Arizona Sun Country Circuit Quarter Horse Show-Westworld
	Scottsdale	Jaycees' Parada del Sol Rodeo Parade
Early February	Tucson	American Indian Exposition
	Scottsdale	Jaycees' Parada del Sol Rodeo Week
	Scottsdale	Parada del Sol Rodeo Dance
	Buckeye	Helz-a-poppin' Senior Pro Rodeo
	Scottsdale	U.S. Team Roping Championships
	Sierra Vista	Annual Cochise Cowboy Poetry & Music Gathering
	Ajo	Fiddlers' Old-Time Contest
	Camp Verde	Saddlebag All Women Pony Express
	Safford	Old-Time Fiddlers' Contest
	Wickenburg	Gold Rush Days
	Yuma	Hospice of Yuma Roping Roundup & Barbecue
	Yuma	Yuma Jaycees Silver Spur Rodeo
	Yuma	Silver Spur Rodeo, Parade and Fiesta
	Phoenix	Annual Native American Hoop Dance Championship
Mid-February	Yuma	Cowboy Skills
	Yuma	Annual Yuma Jaycees Silver Spur Rodeo
	Scottsdale	All Arabian Horse Show and Sale
	Wickenburg	Gold Rush Days and Rodeo
	Wellton	Annual Pioneer Day Parade & Fiesta
	Benson	Territorial Days
	Buckeye	Helz-A-Poppin' Senior Pro Rodeo
	Casa Grande	O'odham Tash
	Pioneer	Pioneer Celebration Days
Late February	Goodyear	Goodyear Rodeo Days
	Scottsdale	All Arabian Horse Show

Date	City	Event
	Tucson	La Fiesta de los Vaqueros Rodeo (PRCA)
	Tucson	Tucson Rodeo Parade
	Phoenix	Annual Ranch Horse Competition and Consignment Horse Sale
	Phoenix	Pioneer Bluegrass Days
	Phoenix	Annual Colors of the Sun Consignment Horse Sale
	Quartzsite	Quartzsite Maze Days "Festival in the Desert"
March	Tucson	SAILA Open & Junior Livestock Show
Early March	Scottsdale	Annual Arizona's Touch of Class Miniature Horse Show
	Scottsdale	Equine Spectacular
	Casa Grande	Arizona State Open Chili Championship
	Winslow	Annual Baca Rough Stock Rodeo
	Scottsdale	Arizona Reining Horse Classic
Mid-March	Scottsdale	Native American Festival and Art Market
	Phoenix	Jaycees' Rodeo of Rodeos
	Scottsdale	Festival of the West
	Tucson	Annual Walk Powwow
	Tucson	Annual Wells Fargo Viva Tucson Tex-Mex Jam
	Apache Junction	Annual Dons Of Arizona Lost Dutchman Gold Mine Superstition Mountain Trek
	Scottsdale	Annual Carousel Horse Show
	Phoenix	Eight Second Thunder-American West Arena
Late March	Tombstone	Annual Territorial Days
	Duncan	Greenlee County Horse Races
	Casa Grande	Pinal County Fair
	Scottsdale	Pro Rodeo Series (PRCA)
	San Carlos	Annual Powwow
	Tombstone	Annual Territorial Days
	Duncan	Greenlee County Horse Races
	Casa Grande	Pinal County Fair
	Globe/Miami	Copper Dust Stampede Rodeo
Mid-April	Cave Creek	Fiesta Days
	Kearny	Pioneer Days
	Scottsdale	Cowboys for Kids Celebrity Rodeo & Auction
May	Eagar/Springerville	Marlen Rogers Family Fun Days
	Page	Lake Powell Rodeo
	Payson	PRCA Pro Rodeo
	Safford	AJRA Rodeo
May	Sonoita	Bull-O-Ramaz
Mid-May	Phoenix	PRCA Rodeo
Early May	Sedona	Cinco de Mayo
Early May to Mid-June	Flagstaff	Trappings of the American West
	Tucson	Arizona Boys Chorus Mother's Day Concert
Late May	Prescott	George Phippen Memorial Day Western Art Show & Sale
Late May	St. Johns	High Country Stampede Rodeo

Date	City	Event
	Tombstone	Wyatt Earp Days
June to August	Flagstaff	Hopi and Navajo Craftsman Exhibitions
June	Payson	Junior Rodeo
Early to Mid-June	Flagstaff	Trappings of the American West
Mid-June	Flagstaff	Pine Country Pro Rodeo
Mid-June to Early July	Flagstaff	Festival of Native American Arts
Late June	Prescott	PRCA Rodeo
July	Prescott	Frontier Days & World's Oldest Rodeo
	Tuba City	Youth Fair
Early July	Prescott	Prescott Rodeo Photo Workshop
	Window Rock	Fourth of July Celebration PRCA Rodeo & Powwow
	Taylor	Fourth of July Celebration
	Eagar/Springerville	Round Valley Western July Fourth Celebration
Mid-July	St. Johns	Pioneer Days
	Snowflake	Pioneer Days Celebration
August	Chinle	Central Navajo Fair
	Fredonia	Northern Arizona Fair
	Payson	Rodeo Parade and Dance
	Safford	Gila Valley Pro Rodeo
	Whiteriver	White Mountain Apache Tribal Fair & Rodeo
	Winslow	West's Best Rodeo
Mid-August	Prescott	Arizona Poets Gathering
	Payson	World's Oldest Continuous PRCA Rodeo
	Tucson	Desert Thunder Rodeo (PRCA)
Late August	Taylor	Sweet Corn Festival
	Payson	PRCA Rodeo
Late August to Early September	Sonoita	Labor Day Rodeo
	Springerville/Eagar	5K Cowboy & Indian Art Show
	Springerville/Eager	Valle Redondo Days
September	Dilcon	Southwestern Navajo Nation Fair
	Douglas	Chochise Country Fair
	Ft. Huachuca	Huachuca Mountain Open Rodeo
	Payson	State Championship Old-Time Fiddlers' Contest
	Safford/Thatcher	Gila Valley Cowboy Poet Roundup
	Scottsdale	Arizona State Firefighters Benefit Rodeo
Early September	Window Rock	Navajo Nation Fair
Mid-September	Holbrook	Navajo County Fair
Late September	Holbrook	All Indian Rodeo Cowboy Association Rodeo & Powwow
October	Benson	Butterfield Overland Stage Days
	Kingman	Andy Devine Days & PRCA Rodeo
	Marana	Founder's Day Parade & Rodeo
	Phoenix	Original Coors Rodeo Showdown
	Phoenix	Arizona State Fair
	Scottsdale	Allied Signal Cliff Garrett Memorial Rodeo & Dance

Date	City	Event
	Tuba City	Western Navajo Fair
	Tucson	John Walker Memorial Rodeo
	Vail	Rincon Valley Festival-Old Spanish Trail
Early October	Phoenix	PRCA Rodeo
	Willcox	Rex Allen Days-PRCA Rodeo
Mid-October	Tombstone	Helldorado Days
Mid-October to Late November	Phoenix	Cowboy Artists of America Show
November	San Carlos	Veteran's Memorial Fair, Pageant & Rodeo
Early November	Sells	Sells All-Indian Rodeo
Late December to Early January	Phoenix	Arizona National Livestock Show

ARKANSAS

Date	City	Event
Year-round	Toltec Mounds	Native American Events
Mid-April	Cabot	Old West Daze
Late May	Fort Smith	Old Fort Days Barrel Racing Futurity
	Crossett	Arkansas High School Rodeo Regionals
Late May to Early June	Shirley	Homecoming and Rodeo
Early June	Booneville	National Trails Day Equestrian Ride
	Huntsville	Hawgfest Pig Race, Rodeo, Music
	Newport	Riverboat Days and State Catfish Cooking Contest (Rodeo)
Mid-June	Mountain View	Western Music Weekend
	Calico Rock	IRA Championship Rodeo
	Dardanelle	PRCA Rodeo
	Siloam Springs	Rodeo and Parade
Early July	Springdale	Rodeo of the Ozarks
Mid-July	Clarksville	Roundup Club Rodeo
Late July	Fort Smith	Commissary Charity Hunter-Jumper Show
Early August	Mena	Polk County Rodeo
	Crossett	Rodeo Roundup Day
	Clinton	Bull Riding Spectacular
Late August to Early September	Clinton	National Championship Chuck Wagon Races
September	Clarksville	Roundup Club Junior Rodeo
Mid-September	Fort Smith	Arkansas/Oklahoma State Fair
	Harrison	Northwest Arkansas District Fair and PRCA Rodeo
Mid-September	Mountain View	Arkansas Old-Time Fiddlers' Association State Championship Competition
	DeQueen	Sevier County Fair and Rodeo
	Jonesboro	Northeast Arkansas District Fair Rodeo
	Marshall	Searcy County Fair and Rodeo
Late September	Pine Bluff	Southeast Arkansas Livestock Show and Rodeo
Late September to Early October	Texarkana	Four States Fair and Rodeo

Date	City	Event
Early October	Little Rock	Arkansas State Fair and Livestock Show

CALIFORNIA

Date	City	Event
Early January	Rancho Murietta	PRCA Rodeo
Late January	Red Bluff	Red Bluff Bull Sale/Ranch Rodeo
Mid-February	Kernville	Whiskey Flat Days
	Indio	Riverside County Fair and National Date Festival
Late February	Palm Springs	Mounted Police Rodeo and Parade
Mid-March	Red Bluff	Red Bluff Winter Roundup
Late March	Alturas	Livestock Market Spring Ranch Horse and Range Bull Sale
Late March to Early April	San Francisco	Junior Grand National Livestock Exposition and Rodeo
	San Jose	World's Toughest Rodeo
April	Chowchilla	Western Stampede
	King City	King City Riding Club Junior Rodeo
Early April	Oakdale	PRCA Rodeo
Mid-April	Bakersfield	Kern County Horse Show Classic on the Green
	Red Bluff	PRCA Rodeo
Late April	Auburn	Wild West Stampede (PRCA)
	Clovis	Clovis Rodeo (PRCA)
	Springville	Frontier Days
	Springville	Springville Sierra Rodeo
May	Marysville	Marysville Stampede
Early May	Borrego Springs	Cinco de Mayo Celebration
	Calexico	Cinco de Mayo Celebration
	Cottonwood	Cottonwood Rodeo Week
	Delano	Cinco de Mayo Celebration
	San Jose	Cinco de Mayo Celebration
	Santa Maria	Cinco de Mayo Celebration
	Sonoma	Cinco de Mayo Celebration
	Valley Springs	Snyder's Powwow
Mid-May	Angels Camp	Calaveras County Fair, Frog Jumping Jubilee and Rodeo
	King City	Salinas Valley Fair
	Redding	Redding Rodeo Week (PRCA)
	Sonora	Mother Lode Roundup Parade and Rodeo
Late May	Bishop	Mule Days Celebration
	Yucca Valley	Grubstake Days and PRCA Rodeo
Late May to Early June	Santa Maria	Elks Rodeo and Parade
June	Quincy	California State High School Rodeo Championships
Mid-June	Livermore	Livermore Rodeo (PRCA)
	Sonora	PRCA Rodeo
Late June	Folsom	Folsom Championship PRCA Rodeo

Date	City	Event
July	Santa Barbara	Horse and Flower Show (PRCA)
	Fortuna	Fortuna Rodeo, "Oldest, Longest, Most Westerly"
Mid-July	Merced	Merced County Fair
	Plymouth	Amador County Fair
Late July	Susanville	Doyle Days Rodeo
	Salinas	The California Rodeo
	Bridgeport	Art Festival and Rodeo
Early August	Paso Robles	California Mid-State Fair
	Santa Barbara	Old Spanish Days
	Grass Valley	Nevada County Fair
	Quincy	Plumas County Fair
Mid-August	Susanville	Lassen County Fair
	Truckee	Truckee Rodeo (PRCA)
	Inglewood	PRCA Rodeo
	San Juan Capistrano	PRCA Rodeo
Mid-August to Early September	Sacramento	California State Fair
Late August	Norco	PRCA Rodeo
	Ventura	PRCA Rodeo
Early September	Lancaster	Antelope Valley Fair, Alfalfa Festival and Rodeo
	Barstow	Calico Days Stampede Rodeo
Late September	Bishop	Tri-County Fair and Wild West Weekend
	Poway	PRCA Rodeo
	Bakersfield	Kern County Fair and PRCA Rodeo
Early October	Santa Rosa	PRCA Rodeo
Mid-October	City of Industry	Industry Hills Charity Pro Rodeo
Late October	San Francisco	Grand National Rodeo, Horse and Stock Exposition
Early November	Death Valley	Death Valley Encampment
Mid-November	Brawley	Cattle Call & PRCA Rodeo

COLORADO

Date	City	Event
Mid-January	Steamboat Springs	Cowboy Downhill
	Denver	National Western Stock Show and Rodeo (PRCA)
June to August	Durango	Durango Pro Rodeo Series
	Steamboat Springs	Cowboys' Roundup Rodeo
Mid-June	Grand Junction	Colorado Stampede
	Colorado Springs	Pikes Peak Little Britches Rodeo
Late June to Late August	Snowmass	Snowmass Stables Rodeo
Late June	Evergreen	Rodeo Weekend
	Greeley	PRCA Rodeo
July	Canon City	Royal Gorge Rodeo
Early July	Greeley	Biggest Fourth of July Rodeo
	Greeley	Independent Stampede Greeley Rodeo
	Durango	All Girls Rodeo Classic

Date	City	Event
Mid-July	Estes Park	Rooftop Rodeo
	Gunnison	Cattlemen's Days, Rodeo and Celebration
Late July	Livermore	Cheyenne Frontier Days Rodeo
	Monte Vista	Ski-Hi Stampede Rodeo
Early August	Colorado Springs	Pikes Peak or Bust Rodeo
	Loveland	Larimer County Fair and Rodeo
Mid-August	Rifle	Senior Pro Rodeo
Late August	Pueblo	Colorado State Fair, Livestock Show and Rodeo
Early September	Durango	Ghost Dancer All-Indian Rodeo
Early October	Durango	Family Ranch Rodeo

DISTRICT OF COLUMBIA

Late October	U.S. Air Arena	Washington International Horse Show

FLORIDA

January to October (Last weekend each month)	Davie	5-Star Pro Rodeo Series (PRCA)
Early to Mid-February	Kissimmee	Edition Silver Spurs Rodeo
	Tampa	Florida State Fair PRCA Rodeo
	Hollywood	Seminole Tribal Fair and Rodeo
Early February	Homestead	Frontier Days Rodeo
Mid-March	Arcadia	PRCA Rodeo
July	Kissimmee	Silver Spurs Rodeo
Early July	Arcadia	PRCA Rodeo
Early September	Ocala	PRCA Rodeo
	Okeechobee	PRCA Rodeo
Late September	Tallahassee	Native American Heritage Festival
Mid-October	Orlando	Pioneer Days
	Davies	Sunshine State Pro Rodeo Championship
Early November	Okeechobee	PRCA Rodeo

GEORGIA

Mid-April	Chatsworth	Beaulieu North American Classic
Early July	Chatsworth	Appalachian Wagon Train
Late September	Chatsworth	National Racking Horse Assocation's World Jamboree
Early October	Chatsworth	Georgia State and Red Carpet Championship Mule-Draft Horse Frolic

IDAHO

Mid-March	Pocatello	Dodge National Circuit Finals Rodeo
Late April	Lewiston	Dogwood Festival
Mid-June	Weiser	National Old-Time Fiddlers' Contest
Late June to Early July	Rupert	July 4th Celebration-IMPRA Rodeo
Early July	Grangeville	Grangeville Rodeo
Early July	Hailey	4th of July Hailey Days of the Old West
	Salmon	Salmon River Days Rodeo

Date	City	Event
Mid-July	Nampa	Snake River Stampede
Late July	Caldwell	Canyon County Fair
	Glenns Ferry	Elmore County Fair, ICA Rodeo
	Montpelier	Oregon Trail Rendezvous Pageant
	Preston	That Famous Preston Night Rodeo, PRCA Rodeo
Late July to Early August	Grace	Caribou County Fair & Rodeo, PRCA Rodeo
	Rupert	Minidoka County Fair & Rodeo
August	Caldwell	U.S. Team Roping Championships (USTRC) Northwest Finals
Early August	CascadeValley	County Fair & Rodeo
	Downey	South Bannock County Fair
	Fort Hall	Shoshone-Bannock Indian Festival
	Homedale	Owyhee County Fair
Early August	Idaho Falls	War Bonnet Roundup, PRCA Rodeo
	Jerome	Jerome County Fair & Rodeo
Early August	New Plymouth	Payette County Fair & Rodeo
	Rexburg	Madison County Fair
	Rupert	Minidoka County Fair & Rodeo
Mid-August	Burley	Cassia County Fair & PRCA Rodeo
	Caldwell	Caldwell Night Rodeo
	Emmett	Gem County Fair & Rodeo
	Gooding	Gooding County Fair & Rodeo
	Montpelier	Bear Lake County Fair
	Pocatello	North Bannock County Fair
	Preston	Franklin County Fair
	Terreton	Mud Lake Fair & IMPRA Rodeo
Mid to Late August	Boise	Western Idaho Fair & Rodeo
Late August	Coeur d'Alene	North Idaho Fair & Rodeo
	Sandpoint	Bonner County Fair
	Spalding	Nez Perce Cultural Days
	Filer/Twin Falls	County Fair & PRCA Rodeo
Late August to Early September	Blackfoot	Eastern Idaho State Fair
Early September	Ketchum	Ketchum Wagon Days Celebration
	Lewiston	Lewiston Roundup Rodeo
Mid-September	Lewiston	Nez Perce County Fair
	Orofino	Clearwater County Fair & Lumberjack Days

ILLINOIS

Early January	Peoria	World's Toughest Rodeo
Late January	Moline	World's Toughest Rodeo
	Rockford	World's Toughest Rodeo
Mid-March	Rosemont (Chicago)	World's Toughest Rodeo
Late March	Springfield	World's Toughest Rodeo
Early September	Palestine	PRCA Rodeo

INDIANA

Mid-February	Evansville	World's Toughest Rodeo

Date	City	Event
Late October	Fort Wayne	World's Toughest Rodeo

IOWA

Early February	Cedar Rapids	World's Toughest Rodeo
Late May to Early June	Cherokee	Cherokee Rodeo
Late June	Edgewood	Edgewood Rodeo Days
Early August	Sidney	Iowa Championship Rodeo
September	Audubon	Operation T-Bone
Early September	Fort Madison	Tri-State Rodeo Festival
Mid-September	Cherokee	Cherokee Rodeo

KANSAS

Early May	Hays	Spring Rodeo, FHSU
Early June	Fort Scott	Good Ol' Days Celebration
	Garden City	Beef Empire Days
Mid-July	Pretty Prairie	PRCA Rodeo
Late July	Wichita	Mid-America Inter-Tribal Indian Powwow
Late July	Manhattan	PRCA Rodeo
Early August	Dodge City	Dodge City Days (PRCA Rodeo)
	Phillipsburg	Kansas Biggest Rodeo
Mid-August	Abilene	Central Kansas Free Fair and Wild Bill Hickok Rodeo
Mid-September	Hutchinson	PRCA Rodeo
Late September	Medicine Lodge	Indian Summer Days
Early October	Medicine Lodge	Indian Peace Treaty Pageant
(Every three years; next in 2003)		

KENTUCKY

Early and Mid-February	Bowling Green	Kyana Quarter Horse Show
Early February	Bowling Green	Championship Rodeo
Mid-April	Lexington	Spring Horse Affair
	Henderson	Tri-Fest
Late April	Lexington	Rolex Kentucky CCI 3-Day Event
Early May	Louisville	The Kentucky Derby
	Lexington	Kentucky Spring Classic Horse Show I
Mid-May	Lexington	Kentucky Spring Classic Horse Show II
	Lexington	High-Hope Steeplechase
Early June	Lexington	The Egyptian Event
Early July	Lexington	Lexington Junior League Horse Show
Mid-July	Grayson County	Kentucky State Fiddlin' Festival
Late July	Lexington	Wild Horse & Burro Adoption & Exposition
Mid-August	Lexington	Kentucky Hunter/Jumper Association Annual Show
	Louisville	Kentucky State Fair, Horse Show and Rodeo
	Harrodsburg	Pioneer Days Festival
Mid-September	Lexington	Annual International Rocky Mountain Horse Show

Date	City	Event
Early November	Louisville	PRCA Rodeo

LOUISIANA

Date	City	Event
Mid-January	Lake Charles	Calcasieu Parish Junior Livestock Show
Early February	Lake Charles	Southwest District Livestock Show and Rodeo
Late February	Covington	Dixie Trail Riders
Late March	Lake Charles	Silver Spur Riders Club
Late April	Lake Charles	Silver Spur Riders Club
Mid-May	Lake Charles	Tennessee Walking and Racking Horse Show
Late May	Lake Charles	Silver Spur Riders Club
Mid-June	Lake Charles	Silver Spur Riders Club
Early July	Lake Charles	Silver Spur Riders Club
Early August	Lake Charles	Silver Spur Riders Club
Mid-September	Lake Charles	Silver Spur Riders Club
October	Angola	Angola Prison Rodeo
Mid-October	Raceland	LaFourche Parish Agriculture Fair and Livestock Show
	Lake Charles	Silver Spur Riders Club
Mid-November	Lake Charles	Silver Spur Riders Club
Mid-December	Lake Charles	Silver Spur Riders Club

MAINE

Date	City	Event
January	Kingfield	White World

MARYLAND

Date	City	Event
Early May	Crownsville	Dave Martin Championship Rodeo and Anne Arundle County Fair
Early July	McHenry	American Indian Inter-Tribal Cultural Organization Powwow
Early August	Cordova	St. Joseph Jousting Tournament and Horse Show
Early September	Easton	Tuckahoe Championship Rodeo
Mid-September	Fort Meade	Southwest Fest

MICHIGAN

Date	City	Event
Mid-January	Detroit	World's Toughest Rodeo
Mid-July	Iron River	Upper Peninsula Championship Rodeo

MINNESOTA

Date	City	Event
Early February	St. Paul	World's Toughest Rodeo
Early April	Mankato	World's Toughest Rodeo
Early May	Crookston	Great Northern Horse Extravaganza
Mid-June	Granite Falls	Western Fest Rodeo
Late June	Buffalo	Buffalo Rodeo
	Park Rapids	PRCA Rodeo
Mid-July	Detroit Lake	Little Britches Rodeo
Mid-September	Shakopee	PRCA Rodeo

Date	City	Event
MISSISSIPPI		
Early February	Jackson	Jackson Dixie National Livestock Show and Rodeo and Western Festival
Early May	Tunica	PRCA Rodeo
Late May	Natchez	Adams County Sheriff's Rodeo
Late July to Early August	Philadelphia	Neshoba County Fair
Mid-September	Natchez	Shriner's Pro Rodeo
MISSOURI		
Late June to Early July	Kansas City	Kansas City Rodeo
Early September	Independence	Santa-Cali-Gon Days
Early August	Sikeston	Jaycee Bootheel Rodeo
Mid-August	St. Joseph	Trails West!
Early November	Kansas City	American Royal Livestock, Horse Show and Rodeo
MONTANA		
Mid-January	Great Falls	PRCA Rodeo
Early February	Billings	Northern Rodeo Association Finals
Early February	Helena	Race to the Sky Sled Dog Race
Mid-February	Anaconda/Butte	Big Sky Winternational Sports Festival
Mid-March	Great Falls	C. M. Russell Auction of Original Western Art
Late March	Whitefish	North American Ski Laser Championships
Mid-May	St. Ignatius	Buffalo Feast and Powwow
	Miles City	Miles City Bucking Horse Sale
Late May	Virginia City	Spring Horseback Poker Run
	Hardin	Custer's Last Stand Re-enactment
Early June	Forsyth	Forsyth Horse Show and Rodeo
June to August	Laramie	Laramie River Rodeo
Early June to Late August	Billings	Billings Night Rodeo (nightly)
Mid-June	Bozeman	College National Finals Rodeo
Late June	Great Falls	Lewis & Clark Festival
	Hamilton	Bitterroot Festival of the American West
Early July	Red Lodge	Home of Champions Rodeo
	Butte	Butte Vigilante Rodeo Roundup
	Landers	Old-Timers' Rodeo
	Livingston	PRCA Rodeo
	Harlowton	July 4th Celebration and Rodeo
	Ennis	Fourth of July Rodeo
	Red Lodge	Home of Champions Rodeo
	Wolf Point	PRCA Rodeo
Mid-July	Bannack	Bannack Days
	Browning	North American Indian Days
	Deer Lodge	Western Heritage Days
	Libby	Libby Logger Days

Date	City	Event
	Polson	Kerr Country Rodeo
Late July	Lewistown	Central Montana Horse Show Fair and Rodeo
	Helena	Last Chance Stampede and Fair
	Red Lodge	Red Lodge Mountain Man Rendezvous
Late July to Early August	Great Falls	Montana State Fair and Rodeo
Early August	Missoula	Western Montana Fair & Rodeo
	Glendive	Dawson County Fair and Rodeo Red Lodge Festival of Nations
	Riverton	Fremont County Fair and Rodeo
	Buffalo	Johnson County Fair and Rodeo
	Pine Bluffs	Trail Days
Mid-August	Lewiston	Montana Cowboy Poetry Gathering
	Billings	Montana Fair
	Kalispell	PRCA Rodeo
	Plentywood	Sheridan County Fair and Rodeo
Late August	Dillon	Beaverhead County Fair & Jaycee Rodeo
	Plains	Sanders County Fair and Rodeo
	Roundup	Roundup Cattle Drive
	White Sulpher Springs	Labor Day Rodeo and Parade
Early September	Reedpoint	Running of the Sheep-Sheep Drive
	Dillon	PRCA Rodeo
Late September	Libby	Nordicfest
October	Billings	Northern International Livestock Exposition and Rodeo
Early October to November	West Yellowstone	Cross-Country Fall Camp
Mid-October	Billings	PRCA Rodeo

NEBRASKA

Date	City	Event
Mid-February	Lincoln	World's Toughest Rodeo
Mid-June	North Platte	Celebration and Buffalo Bill Rodeo
Late July	Burwell	Nebraska's Big Rodeo
Early July	Crawford	Crawford Rodeo
	Chadron	Fur Trade Days and Buckskin Rendezvous
Late July	Winnebago	Indian Powwow
Mid-August	Ogallala	Ogallala Roundup Rodeo
Late August	Sidney	Cheyenne County Fair
	Gordon	Sheridan County Fair and Rodeo
September	Bayard	Chimney Rock Pioneer Days
Mid-September	Ogallala	Indian Summer Rendezvous
Late September	Omaha	River City Roundup and World Championship Rodeo
Early October	Valentine	Cowboy Poetry Gathering

NEVADA

Date	City	Event
Every other weekend except in August	Mesquite	Peppermill Year-Round Roping Competition
Late January	Elko	Cowboy Poetry Gathering

Date	City	Event
	Reno	Biggest Little Cutting Horse in the World Competition
March	Dayton	Dayton Cowboy Poetry & Western Art Show
Early March	Carson City	Cowboy Jubilee & Poetry
	Reno	Reno Ranch Rodeo
Late March	Laughlin	USPA Invitational Rodeo
	Minden	Cowboy Culture Weekend
	Reno	Beefmaster and Romagnola Cattle Show/Sale
Early April	Logandale	Clark County Fair
Late April	Reno	Western National Angus Futurity
Early May	Reno	HN Spanish Rodeo
	Las Vegas	PRCA Rodeo
Mid-May	Reno	Nevada Junior Livestock State Show
	Las Vegas	Helldorado Days and Rodeo
	Wells	Buckaroo Rodeo
Late May	Mesquite	Mesquite Days
	Reno	Showcase of the West Horse Show
June	Pahrump Valley	Over the Hill Stampede Rodeo
Early June	Carson City	Kit Carson Rendezvous & Wagon Train
	Las Vegas	PRCA Rodeo
Mid-June	Reno	BLM Horse Event
	Reno	Wild Horse and Burro Show
Late June	Reno	Reno Rodeo (PRCA)
July	Ely	Lund Rodeo
	Virginia City	Way It Was Rodeo
Early July	Fallon	Silver State International Rodeo
	Fallon	International Invitational High School Rodeo
	McDermitt	Twin States Ranch Hand Rodeo
	Reno	Region III Arabian Horse Show
Mid-July	Fallon	All Indian Stampede and Pioneer Days
	Reno	Convention Rodeo and Barbecue
	Reno	Dressage in the Sierra
	Elko	Silver State Stampede Rodeo (PRCA)
Late July	Elko	Native American Festival
August	Elko	Western Folklife Roundup
	Lovelock	World Fast Draw Championship
Early August	Reno	Limousin Cattle Show
	Reno	Appahann Appaloosa Horse Show
Mid-August	Reno	Nevada and Zone II Paint Horse Show
	Ely	White Pine Country Days Fair and Pony Express Days and Horse Races
Late August	Reno	Nevada State Fair
	Yerington	Spirit of Wovoka Days Powwow
Late August to Early September	Elko	Elko County Fair and Horse Races
	Winnemucca	Buckaroo Heritage Western Art Roundup
September	Lund	Duckwater Classic Roping
	Virginia City	Virginia City Camel Races
Early September	Fallon	Nevada Cutting Horse Spectacular

Date	City	Event
(Labor Day)	Winnemucca	Nevada's Oldest Rodeo & Western Art Roundup Show and Sale and Tri-County Fair
Early September	Reno	Silver Sire Breeders Horse Show/Sale
	Reno	NSHA Horse Show
Mid-September	Pahrump Valley	Harvest Festival, Parade & Rodeo
	Reno	National Reining Cowhorse Association Snaffle Bit Futurity Competition
	Winnemucca	Pari-Mutuel Thoroughbred, Quarter Horse and Mule Racing Events
Late September	Ely	Whitepine High School Rodeo
	Reno	Bullnanza
	Elko	Spring Creek Ranch Hand Rodeo
Late October	Beatty	Great Beatty Burro Races
	Carson City	Nevada Day Celebration
	Nixon	Pyramid Lake Nevada Day Open Rodeo
	Reno	Western States Celebration
	Reno	ACTRA Team Roping
Early November	Minden	Rhymer's Rodeer Cowboy Poetry
	Reno	National Senior Pro Rodeo Finals
Early December	Las Vegas	National PRCA Finals Rodeo
	Las Vegas	NFR Bucking Horse and Bull Sale
Mid-December	Reno	Hereford Cattle Show and Sale
	Reno	American Shorthorn Cattle Show and Sale
Late December	Reno	Buck 'n' Ball New Years Eve Rodeo

NEW JERSEY

Date	City	Event
Late May to Late September	Woodstown	Cowtown Rodeo, PRCA (Weekly)
Late May to Mid-October	Netcong	Wild West City-Replica of Dodge City

NEW MEXICO

Date	City	Event
Early January	Red River	Red River Winterfest
Late February	Chama	High Country Winter Carnival
	Angel Fire	Angel Fire Winter Carnival Festival Weekend
Late March	Shakespeare	New Mexico Renegade Ride
Mid-April	Truth or Consequences	Ralph Edwards Fiesta and Rodeo
Mid-May	Deming	Fiddlers' Contest
Late May	Silver City	Endurance Horse Ride
	Cloudcroft	Mayfair Hayrides and Rodeo
Early June	Clovis	Pioneer Days Celebration and PRCA Rodeo
	Fort Sumner	Old Fort Days
	Mescalero	Apache Indian Maidens' Puberty Rites and Rodeo
	Las Vegas	Rails and Trails Days
	Farmington	Sheriff Posse Rodeo
Mid-June	Cloudcroft	Western Roundup

Date	City	Event
	Dulce	All-Indian Rodeo
	Taos	San Antonio Corn Dance
	Gallup	Lions Club Western Jubilee Week and Rodeo
Late June	Taos	Rodeo de Taos
	Tucumcari	PisRodeo de Taos Jubilee Week and Rodeo
Late June to Early July	Clayton	Rabbit Ear Roundup Rodeo
Early July	Cimarron	Cimarron Rodeo
	Eunice	Eunice Fourth of July Celebration and Junior Rodeo
	Santa Fe	Rodeo de Santa Fe
	Taos	Taos Pueblo Powwow
Mid-July	Carlsbad	Western Days and AJRA Rodeo
	Dulce	Little Beaver Roundup Rodeo
	Galisteo	Galisteo Rodeo
	Ruidoso	Billy The Kid-Pat Garrett Historical Days
Late July	Las Vegas	Fort Union's Santa Fe Trail Days
	Taos	Fiesta de Santiago y Santa Ana
August	Lovington	Lea County Fair and PRCA Rodeo
	Gallup	Inter-Tribal Indian Ceremonial and Rodeo
Early August	Los Alamos	Los Alamos County Fair and Rodeo
Mid-August	Capitan	Lincoln County Fair
	Santa Fe	Indian Market
	Albuquerque	Bernalillo County 4-H Fair and Rodeo
September	Albuquerque	New Mexico State Fair and Rodeo
	Santa Fe	Fiesta de Santa Fe
Early September	Socorro	Socorro County Fair and Rodeo
	Ruidoso Downs	All American Futurity
	Clayton	Hayden Rodeo
Late September	Lovington	Days of Old West Ranch Rodeo
	Las Cruces	Southern New Mexico State Fair and Rodeo
	Roswell	Eastern New Mexico State Fair and Rodeo
Late September	Deming	Southwestern New Mexico State Fair
	Taos	The Old Taos Trade Fair
	Taos	San Geronimo Day Trade Fair
Early October	Ruidoso	Cowboy Symposium
Mid-October	Carlsbad	Alfalfa Fest (Mule Races, Largest Parade, and Hayride)
Late October	Truth or Consequences	Old-Time Fiddlers' Contest
Mid-November	Hobbs	Llano Estacado Party and Cowboy Hall of Fame and Western Heritage Center Introduction Banquet
Late November	Albuquerque	Indian National Finals Rodeo
Late December	Taos	The Matachines Dances at Taos Pueblo

NEW YORK

Late May	Saratoga Springs	Dressage at Saratoga
Early June	Apalachin	Otsiningo Powwow and Indian Craft Fair

Date	City	Event
	Elmont	The Belmont Stakes
	Kinderhook	Columbia County Carriage Days
Late June	Lake Placid	Lake Placid Horse Show
Early July	Sandy Creek	Oswego County Fair & Horse Show
	Lake Placid	I Love New York Horse Show
Mid-July	Brookfield	Madison County Fair
	Lowville	Lewis County Fair
	Pulaski	Cowboy Roundup
Late July	Cazenovia	Horse Driving Competition
	Queen	Thunderbird American Indian Mid-Summer Powwow
Early August	Attica	Attica Rodeo
	Gerry	Rodeo
Late August	Bridgehampton	Hampton Classic Horse Show
	Howes Cave	Iroquois Indian Festival
	Rhinebeck	Dutchess County Fair
	Syracuse	The Great New York State Fair
Early September	Ballston Spa	All American Professional Rodeo
Late October	Manhattan	National Horse Show

NORTH CAROLINA

Date	City	Event
Mid-January	Raleigh	Midwinter Quarter Horse Show
Early February	Raleigh	Southern National Draft Horse Psull
Late March	Raleigh	North Carolina Quarter Horse Association Spring Show Championship Rodeo
	Pinehurst	Kiwanis Charity Horse Show
	Raleigh	Great Smokies Pro Rodeo
	Oak Ridge	Oak Ridge Easter Horse Show & Fiddlers' Convention
	Fayetteville	Shrine Club Rodeo
Early April	Blowing Rock	Opening Day Trout Fishing Derby
	Southern Pines	Moore County Pleasure Horse Drive Show
	Pembroke	Spring Racking Horse Show
	Pinehurst	Harness Horse Racing Matinee
	Raleigh	Appaloosa Horse Show
Mid-April	Raleigh	Easter Bunny Quarter Horse Circuit
Mid-April	Tryon	Tryon Thermal Belt Chamber of Commerce Horse Show
Late April	Asheville	Carolina Mountains Arabian Show
Early May	Statesville	Tarheel Classic Horse Show
	Asheville	Southern Horse Fair (PRCA)
Mid-May	Burnsville	Jaycees Championship Rodeo
	Monroe	Mid-Atlantic Championship Rodeo
	Raleigh	NC All Arabian Horse Show
	Southern Pines	Sandhills Combined Driving Event
Late May	Union Grove	Old-Time Fiddlers' and Bluegrass Festival
	Raleigh	Southern States Morgan Horse Show
	Tryon	Tryon Horse Show
Early June	Raleigh	Capitol Dressage Classic

Date	City	Event
	Wilmington	Sudan Horse Patrol Coastal Plains Horse Show
Mid-June	Love Valley	Junior Showdown
	Raleigh	Appaloosa Horse Show
Late June	Love Valley	Frontier Week Rodeo
	Andrews	Wagon Train
	Raleigh	NC Hunter Jumper Association Show
	Pembroke	Racking Horse Show
Early July	Hayesville	Clay County Rodeo
	Sparta	Lions Club Horse Show
Mid-July	Love Valley	Junior Showdown
	Raleigh	NC State 4-H Horse Show
	Waynesville	Waynesville Lions Club Horse Show
Late July	Waynesville	Trail Riders Horse Show
	Raleigh	NC All Amateur Arabian Horse Show
	Raleigh	Raleigh Summer Hunter Jumper Show
	Asheville	Carolina Mountains Summer All Arabian Horse Show
	Blowing Rock	Blowing Rock Charity Horse Show
	Tryon	Tryon Thermal Belt Chamber of Commerce Horse Show
Early August	Robbins	Farmer's Day & Wagon Train
	Waynesville	Fraternal Order of Police Horse Show
Early September	Mocksville	Lake Myers Rodeo
Mid-September	Monroe	Mid-Atlantic Championship Rodeo
	Raleigh	NC State Championship Charity Horse Show
Late September	Asheville	Carolina Mountains Fall All Arabian Horse Show
Early November	Pinehurst	Fall Horse Carriage Drive
Late November	Raleigh	Eastern Quarter Horse of NC Show & Futurity

NORTH DAKOTA

Date	City	Event
Early March	Valley City	North Dakota Winter Show and Rodeo
Mid-April	Grand Forks	Native American Days
Mid-May	Beach	Beaver Creek Ranch Roundup & Branding
Late May	Medora	Dakota Cowboy Poetry Gathering
Early June	Bottineau	Old-Time Fiddlers' Contest
Mid-June	Fessenden	Parimutuel Horse Racing
Mid-June	Williston	Fort Union Trading Post Rendezvous
Late June	Jamestown	Fort Seward Wagon Train
Early July	Dickinson	Rough Rider Days
	Mandan	Rodeo Days
Late July	Taylor	Taylor Horsefest
	Devil's Lake	Fort Totten Days
Early August	Sentinel Butte	Champions Ride Rodeo, Home on the Range for Boys
Mid-August	West Fargo	Pioneer Days
September	Bismarck	United Tribes International Powwow
Early September	Dickinson	NDRA Rodeo

Date	City	Event
Late September	Jamestown	Buffalo Days
Late October	Bismarck	Badlands Circuit Finals Rodeo

OHIO

Mid-January	Dayton	World's Toughest Rodeo
Early March	Cleveland	World's Toughest Rodeo
Mid-March	Toledo	World's Toughest Rodeo
October	Columbus	All-American Quarter Horse Congress

OKLAHOMA

January to December	Sallisaw	Parimutuel Mixed Breed Horse Racing
Mid-January	Tulsa	Longhorn World Championship Rodeo
Late January	Oklahoma City	International Finals Rodeo
February to May	Oklahoma City	Parimutuel Thoroughbred Horse Racing
Early February	Oklahoma City	Wild Horse Adoption
Early March	Guthrie	Timed Event Championship of the World
	Tulsa	Super Bull Tour
Mid-March	Oklahoma City	Western Heritage Awards
Mid-April	Guthrie	'89er Days and PRCA Rodeo
	Oklahoma City	Centennial Horse Show
Late April	Checotah	Duvall Jackpot Steer Wrestling
May to July	Oklahoma City	Parimutuel Quarter Horse Racing
Early May	Oklahoma City	Non Pro Cutting Horse Show
	Guymon	Pioneer Days and PRCA Rodeo
Mid-May	Guthrie	Ben Johnson Pro Celebrity Rodeo
Late May	Boley	Boley Rodeo and BBQ Festival
	Guthrie	OCA Range Roundup
	Henryetta	Bullchallenge
	Hugo	PRCA Rodeo
	Idabel	Oklahoma Championship Chuck Wagon Races
	Oklahoma City	Chuck Wagon Festival
June to August	Pawnee	Pawnee Bill Wild West Show
Early June	Boise City	Santa Fe Trail Daze
	Yukon	Chisholm Trail Festival
Mid-June	Claremore	Will Rogers Stampede Rodeo
	Oklahoma City	National Appalo

Date	City	Event
CANADA		
ALBERTA		
Late April	Red Deer	Silver Buckle Rodeo
Early May	Red Deer	Marching Band Festival
Late May	Alder Flats	Annual Alder Flats Rodeo & Race Meet
	Calgary	The Nationals at Spruce Meadows
Early July	Calgary	The North American: Spruce Meadows
	Calgary	Calgary Exhibition & Stampede
Late July	Red Deer	Westerner Days
	Edmonton	Edmonton Klondike Days
	Medicine Hat	Medicine Hat Exhibition & Stampede
Mid August	Jasper	Jasper Lions Indoor Professional Rodeo
Early November	Edmonton	Canadian Finals Rodeo
BRITISH COLUMBIA		
Early June	Hazelton	Kispiox Valley Rodeo
Late June	Prince Rupert	National Aboriginal Day
Mid August	Dawson Creek	Professional Stampede & Chuck Wagon Races
	Tumbler Ridge	Grizzly Valley Days

INDEX

We Want To Hear From You

Guidebooks, like children, are constantly growing and changing. One of the joys of writing this has been receiving many letters from our readers. Your thoughts and ideas are important to us. So tell us about your favorite ranch, and new ranches you've discovered that you think we should know about. We're also curious about what additional information you would like to see in future editions. We hope that you'll share your comments with us. Please write us at:

Gene Kilgore's Ranch Vacations
Worldwide Ranch Headquarters
809 Broadway, Suite 1
Sonoma, CA 95476
707/939-3801
707/939-3795 fax
www.ranchweb.com
Email: info@ranchweb.com

Thank you.

AVALON
TRAVEL
publishing

How far will our travel guides take you? As far as you want.

Discover a rhumba-fueled nightspot in Old Havana, explore prehistoric tombs in Ireland, hike beneath California's centuries-old redwoods, or embark on a classic road trip along Route 66. Our guidebooks deliver solidly researched, trip-tested information—minus any generic froth—to help globetrotters or weekend warriors create an adventure uniquely their own.

And we're not just about the printed page. Public television viewers are tuning in to Rick Steves' new travel series, *Rick Steves' Europe*. On the Web, readers can cruise the virtual black top with *Road Trip USA* author Jamie Jensen and learn travel industry secrets from Edward Hasbrouck of *The Practical Nomad*.

In print. On TV. On the Internet.

We supply the information. The rest is up to you.

Avalon Travel Publishing

Something for everyone

www.travelmatters.com

Avalon Travel Publishing guides are available at your favorite book or travel store.

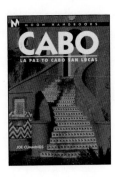

MOON HANDBOOKS

provide comprehensive coverage of a region's arts, history, land, people, and social issues in addition to detailed practical listings for accommodations, food, outdoor recreation, and entertainment. Moon Handbooks allow complete immersion in a region's culture—ideal for travelers who want to combine sightseeing with insight for an extraordinary travel experience in destinations throughout North America, Hawaii, Latin America, the Caribbean, Asia, and the Pacific.

WWW.MOON.COM

Rick Steves shows you where to travel and how to travel—all while getting the most value for your dollar. His Back Door travel philosophy is about making friends, having fun, and avoiding tourist rip-offs.

Rick has been traveling to Europe for more than 25 years and is the author of 22 guidebooks, which have sold more than a million copies. He also hosts the award-winning public television series *Rick Steves' Europe.*

WWW.RICKSTEVES.COM

ROAD TRIP USA

Getting there is half the fun, and Road Trip USA guides are your ticket to driving adventure. Taking you off the interstates and onto less-traveled, two-lane highways, each guide is filled with fascinating trivia, historical information, photographs, facts about regional writers, and details on where to sleep and eat—all contributing to your exploration of the American road.

"[Books] so full of the pleasures of the American road, you can smell the upholstery."
~BBC radio

WWW.ROADTRIPUSA.COM

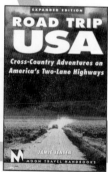

FOGHORN OUTDOORS

guides are for campers, hikers, boaters, anglers, bikers, and golfers of all levels of daring and skill. Each guide focuses on a specific U.S. region and contains site descriptions and ratings, driving directions, facilities and fees information, and easy-to-read maps that leave only the task of deciding where to go.

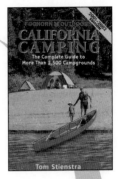

"Foghorn Outdoors has established an ecological conservation standard unmatched by any other publisher."
~Sierra Club

WWW.FOGHORN.COM

TRAVEL SMART

guidebooks are accessible, route-based driving guides focusing on regions throughout the United States and Canada. Special interest tours provide the most practical routes for family fun, outdoor activities, or regional history for a trip of anywhere from two to 22 days. Travel Smarts take the guesswork out of planning a trip by recommending only the most interesting places to eat, stay, and visit.

"One of the few travel series that rates sightseeing attractions. That's a handy feature. It helps to have some guidance so that every minute counts."
~San Diego Union-Tribune

CiTY·SMaRT™

guides are written by local authors with hometown perspectives who have personally selected the best places to eat, shop, sightsee, and simply hang out. The honest, lively, and opinionated advice is perfect for business travelers looking to relax with the locals or for longtime residents looking for something new to do Saturday night.

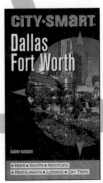